OXFORD MONOGRAPHS ON MUSIC

Music in
Renaissance Lyons

Music in Renaissance Lyons

Frank Dobbins

CLARENDON PRESS · OXFORD
1992

Oxford University Press, Walton Street, Oxford OX2 6DP
Oxford New York Toronto
Delhi Bombay Calcutta Madras Karachi
Petaling Jaya Singapore Hong Kong Tokyo
Nairobi Dar es Salaam Cape Town
Melbourne Auckland
and associated companies in
Berlin Ibadan

Oxford is a trade mark of Oxford University Press

Published in the United States
by Oxford University Press, New York

British Library Cataloguing in Publication Data
Data available

Library of Congress Cataloging in Publication Data
Music in Renaissance Lyons/Frank Dobbins.
(Oxford monographs on music)
Includes bibliographical references and index.
1. Music—France—Lyon—16th century—History and criticism.
2. Lyon (France)—Social life and customs.   I. Title.   II. Series.
ML270.8.L95D6   1992   780'.944'582309031—dc20   91-26677
ISBN 0-19-816137-9

Set by Best-set Typesetter Ltd., Hong Kong
Printed in Great Britain by
Biddles Ltd., Guildford and King's Lynn

Preface

THE key role that Lyons played in the importation of Renaissance ideas
was already acknowledged by the Parisian poet Charles Fontaine in his
Ode de l'antiquité et excellence de la Ville de Lyon of 1557:

> Lyon fait ouvrages divers
> Ouvrages premiers Italiques
> Prenans origine des vers
> Maintenant ouvrages Galliques.

Fontaine also recognized the significance here of the commercial
prosperity flowing from its banks, fairs, and trade which made Lyons
the rival of Antwerp and Venice:

> Ou est la ville ayant tel bruit
> En Change, Foires, Marchandises?
> Nulle mieux que Lyon ne bruit
> Soient les Anvers ou les Venises.

According to any interpretation of the terms 'humanism' or
'Renaissance', Lyons was clearly an important centre. Its citizens, having
rejected ecclesiastical domination while maintaining an almost republican independence from the French crown, were proud of their
ancient heritage in the former capital of Roman Gaul, and became the
first French archaeologists, eagerly excavating the Roman sites on
the Fourvière Hill to the north of their city. They readily embraced the
ideas and luxuries imported from the south by the French court, which
had made the city its base of operations during the Italian military
campaigns undertaken by Charles VIII and Louis XII and Francis I. They
also welcomed republicans fleeing from Florence after the restoration
of the Medici, swelling the ranks of enterprising merchants and industrialists. They recognized the economic and educational potential of the
new printing industry, which expanded more rapidly in Lyons than
anywhere else in France, if not in the whole of Europe. They seized
upon the liberating ideas released by the press, encouraging the spread
of Platonism and Protestantism, which attracted many of the large trading
community. The coexistence of Italianate luxury and Calvinist self-denial

left its mark on the art, literature, and music produced during the
sixteenth century.

When I began work in this field twenty-five years ago I was struck by
the dearth of information about the great wealth of fine music
published in a city whose contemporary literature was justly respected
and admired. While Lyons was recognized as an important centre of
literature during the Renaissance period, little of its music was available
in modern editions and performances were very rare. Since that time
the situation has greatly improved, with studies or editions of some of
the leading publishers and composers, particularly Moderne, Layolle,
Bourgeois, and Paladino, arriving to match the earlier attention devoted
to its distinguished writers like Dolet, Rabelais, and Scève. However,
many fine composers, such as Villiers, Lupi Second, Jambe de Fer,
Mayo, and Vecoli, are still represented today by only a few works in
anthologies, while a picture of the thriving musical life in their city
remains obscure. Yet there seemed a good deal of material available in
the city's poetry, novels, and philosophical literature, in its archives, and
in its musical publications to enhance our understanding of this music
and of the environment in which it was nurtured.

The particular situation of Lyons as a largely independent and
successful commercial centre also affords an opportunity to view
the role that music played in urban life during the period of the
Renaissance and Reformation. The close collaboration of certain poets
and musicians became the focus for my doctoral study of the songs
published in the city. Taking that study as a starting-point, the present
book has provided a chance to devote more attention to the sacred
music, composed for both the Catholic and Reformed churches, as well
as to the instrumental music which appeared there. It also allowed
some expansion upon preliminary archival searches which reflected on
the activities of the town's professional musicians, particularly the
instrumentalists, most of whose work was not copied or published for
posterity.

The picture that emerges reveals how the musical life of France's
second city reacted to prevailing social, economic, and political
circumstances, reflecting the major cultural and intellectual movements
of the time. If the philosophical musings of Champier and Rabelais
still adhere to the medieval view of music as part of the scientific
quadrivium, Dolet follows the Ancients in seeing it as more closely
related to art and literature, while the revival of the Classical lyrical
union pervades the writing of Scève and Tyard. At the same time the
musical manuscript and published collections mirror the prevailing
trends, shifting from complex Catholic polyphonic motets, masses,

chansons, and madrigals intended for princely chapels or patrician chambers to simpler monophonic or homophonic psalms, noëls, and airs designed for more modest Calvinist temples or bourgeois homes.

I would like to thank the following libraries for their kind permission to reproduce photographic illustrations: London, British Library; Lyons, Bibliothèque municipale; Munich, Bayerische Staatsbibliothek; Paris, Bibliothèque nationale; and Vienna, Österreichische National bibliothek.

I am grateful to many people for their help in preparing this book: to Frederick Sternfeld, François Lesure, and Howard Mayer Brown for providing inspiration through their enlightened and sensitive models of musical historiography, and for gently encouraging my own tentative efforts; to Laurent Guillo, Peter Christoffersen, and Pierre Pidoux for generously sharing the results of their dedicated and assiduous research; to Bonnie Blackburn and Leofranc Holford-Strevens for their invaluable suggestions and amendments to the typescript; to Professor Stanley Glasser for affording me great support in the time-consuming but fascinating peregrinations undertaken in the course of study; to the staff of the Bibliothèque nationale and other libraries too numerous to list here for providing access to their treasures; and last, but not least, to my wife Sheila for her patient labours in typing and word-processing.

Contents

Illustrations

Music Examples

1

Lyons, Metropolis of the French Renaissance

(i) *Political Liberty and Commercial Prosperity*

THE humanist philosopher and publisher Étienne Dolet, who lived in Lyons from 1534 until his execution in 1546, sketches an eloquent picture of the city:

An ancient city known by the name of Lugdunum formerly reared its head in a lofty situation; after being destroyed by fire it was rebuilt by Plancus, then in command of the Roman armies, at the foot of the mountain and looking toward the north. The sluggish waters of the Saône roll through its heart, and on one side it is girded by the Rhône; then each of the two streams flowing with a gentle current, receives the other into its bosom. Rich, populous, and adorned with splendid buildings, it opens its markets to foreigners as well as to its own citizens.[1]

The key to Lyons's commercial prosperity in the sixteenth century was its geographical situation. Standing on the south-eastern border of France at the meeting-point of important trade routes, its proximity to Italy and Switzerland and its navigable waterways ensured a profitable international mercantile activity. To the south, the Rhône was the route to the Dauphiné, Provence, Languedoc, the Mediterranean, Italy, and the Levant; to the east it provided communications with Savoy, Piedmont, Switzerland, and Germany; to the north, the Saône linked the Rhône with Paris and Flanders, while to the west, a short overland journey to Roanne made the connection with the Loire. The main roads followed these rivers and carried much of the Italian trade with France, the Low Countries, and even Germany. A post-road between Lyons and Antwerp, passing via Lons-le-Saunier, Dole, Lorraine, Luxemburg, and Brussels, was opened in 1577 and by the late sixteenth century there was a twice-weekly messenger service to Madrid.

After the Treaty of Verdun (843), the territory around Lyons was shared between France and the Empire, while the town itself was governed by an archbishop. In 1271, the French king, Philippe III, intervened as a mediator in the struggle between the governing ecclesiastical authorities and the citizens, who had organized themselves into a *commune jurée*, led by twelve consuls. Realizing the town's strategic

---

[1] R. C. Christie, *Etienne Dolet, the Martyr of the Renaissance* (London, 1880), 166.

importance as a fortress against invasion and as a gateway for commerce with Italy and the South, he offered the city the protection of the French crown. In 1320 his grandson, Philippe V, signed a charter recognizing the *commune*, giving weight to self-government by the aspiring bourgeoisie. Decline in the political influence of the church coincided with expansion in the town's industry, banking, and commerce.[2]

In 1420 the Dauphin, later Charles VII (1422–61), established at this favourable location two annual fairs, each lasting a fortnight. In 1444 he gave permission for a third fair, boosting the town's commercial expansion by allowing free trade with toll- and tax-exemptions and safe-conduct guarantees for all foreigners (except the 'traditional enemy'— the English). In March 1463, Louis XI (1461–83) sanctioned a fourth fair, and banned French merchants from attending the fairs which took place simultaneously at Geneva. The trade-fair marked an important stage in France's progress from economic stagnation, with commerce confined within the limits of local barter, to incessant economic activity, with business carried on continuously on the basis of international exchange. Lyons became the centre for trade in luxury goods, which expanded rapidly with the joint stimulus of economic prosperity, the new Renaissance fashions, and Italian influence, increased by the French military campaigns across the Alps. By the mid-sixteenth century a large proportion of imports into France passed through Lyons, where there were between five and six thousand merchants from Germany, Flanders, Spain, and Italy. The main foreign imports were furniture, silks, jewellery, faience, glass, perfumes, drugs, spices, sugar, preserves, leather, and clocks. Paris sent millinery, haberdashery, and linen, while local industry provided saffron, tapestries, pottery, plate and jewellery, paper, books, playing-cards, and musical instruments.[3]

The fair exerted a great influence in the development of banking and exchange, by establishing a system of credit and organization for international trade. In the late fifteenth century the domination of Jewish, Genoese, and Lombard usury was challenged by a new generation of German, Florentine, and Venetian financiers. A number of these, recognizing the increasing potential of Lyons and attracted by its relative political independence and municipal freedom, established branches

---

[2] The decline in the Church's political influence and the growth in the city's civic independence are outlined in C. F. Menestrier, *Éloge historique de la ville de Lyon* (Lyons, 1669), id., *Histoire civile ou consulaire de la ville de Lyon* (Lyons, 1696), and C. de Rubys, *Les priviléges, franchises et immunitez octroyées par les roys treschrestiens aux consuls, eschevins, manans et habitans de la ville de Lyon* (Lyons, 1574).

[3] The role of the fairs in Lyons's commercial expansion is described in M. Brésard, *Les Foires de Lyon aux XVe et XVIe siècles* (Paris, 1914) and R. Gascon, *Grand commerce et vie urbaine au XVIe siècle: Lyon et ses marchands* (Paris, 1971).

or centres there; the town became a natural haven for Florentine refugees, especially after the collapse of the Republic and the restoration of the Medici in 1530. By this time it had become the financial capital of Europe, although the international syndicate of German and Italian bankers continued to maintain close links with Antwerp, Bruges, Augsburg, Nuremberg, Florence, and Venice. The Fuggers still controlled the movement of capital in Germany, but the foreign bankers in Lyons held the purse-strings for the French kings during the Italian Wars (1494–1525). Whereas the Emperor Charles V raised his loans in Antwerp, Francis negotiated his in Lyons (12,500 écus in 1518, 17,187 in 1522, and 13,000 in 1545), mostly from the German immigrant banker Johann Kleberger.[4]

France's trade relations with Italy declined after 1525, when Charles V gained the ascendancy there; from being a theatre of war the peninsula became virtually a Habsburg preserve. Moreover, following new geographical discoveries the entire flow of international trade shifted; as new sea routes opened, Venice, which had hitherto been the main entrepôt for trade with the Orient, gave way to Lisbon and Antwerp.

(ii) *The Meeting-point of France and Italy*

Between 1494 and 1525 three successive French kings led their armies across the Alps in pursuit of claims to the Angevin succession in Naples and the Visconti succession in Milan. Charles VIII made Lyons his base of operations for the invasion of Naples in 1494–95, obtaining a levy of 10,000 livres from the townspeople. Louis XII concentrated his troops there for the conquest of Milan (1499–1500) and the recovery of Naples (1501). Enchanted by the city and its noble entertainments, Louis set up court there between 1499 and 1503, returning to organize an expedition against Genoa in 1507 and to avert the threat of an invasion by Swiss mercenary forces in 1511–12. Francis I's government remained in Lyons during the Marignano campaign of 1515 and asked the citizens for a loan of 300,000 écus. Francis was there again in 1522, to follow political and military developments in the peninsula more closely. His army massed in and around the town, preparing for a new offensive in August 1524; but with the volte-face of his high constable, Charles de Bourbon, threatening internal security and the Imperial army then invading Provence,

---

[4] The development of merchant banks in Lyons and the influence of the Florentine community are detailed in M. Vigne, *La Banque à Lyon du XVᵉ au XVIIᵉ siècle* (Lyons, 1903); H. A. S. de Charpin-Feugerolles, *Les Florentins à Lyon* (Lyons, 1893); A. Rouche, 'La Nation florentine de Lyon au commencement du xviᵉ siècle', *Revue d'histoire de Lyon*, 11 (1912), 22–65; R. de Roover, *The Rise and Decline of the Medici Bank* (Cambridge, Mass., 1963).

his forces did not leave France until 1525. After news of the King's defeat at Pavia reached Lyons at the end of February, his mother, Louise of Savoy, acting as regent, organized the defence of the town, commissioning the Governor, Jean d'Albon, to direct the construction of fortifications. Hostilities did not recommence until 1536, when Provence was again threatened by the army of Charles V, Holy Roman Emperor and King of Spain. With the French reoccupation of Savoy and Piedmont, Cardinal François de Tournon was sent as Viceroy to govern the south-east and to organize credit for victualling and maintaining the army. He left Lyons at the end of 1537, having earned a considerable reputation as an honest dealer and astute financier. After this the town was no longer of strategic military value: Francis I spent only four days there in 1541 and four more in 1542, while his successor, Henry II, did not revisit the town after his ceremonial entry in 1548.

The Italian military campaigns did not seem to harm the town's prosperity, which reached its height in the second quarter of the century. The sale of booty amassed by the French armies, including books and works of art, increased the propagation of Italian culture, as well as trade.

The wealthy Italian colony was of special strategic importance to the King. For its financial support, its information and advice on the conduct of affairs across the Alps, and its magnificent entertainments for the Italophile monarchs, it not only received royal franchises and rewards but benefited from the appointment of its compatriots as city governors from 1515 to 1535 and was allowed a great deal of self-government: the Florentine community was even granted the right to elect its own consul for internal matters.

In the course of the fifteenth century the Lombard and Genoese domination of French finance passed to Florentine bankers, the most notable being the Arnolfini, Capponi, Guadagni, Gondi, Medici, and Strozzi families, whose principal establishments were at Lyons.[5] The expansion of the trade-fairs and the royal war loans ensured increasing profits during the first third of the sixteenth century. At the same time Lyonese industry escaped the fiscal limitations of other French towns, with the municipality zealously guarding these privileges and offering every encouragement to foreign investors and artisans.

One example of the opportunities for private enterprise is provided by the introduction of silk manufacture from Italy. Thus Étienne

---

[5] The commercial and cultural importance of the Italians in Lyons is discussed in E. Picot, *Les Italiens en France au XVIe siècle* (Bordeaux, 1902) and id., *Les Français italianisants au XVIe siècle*, 2 vols. (Paris, 1906–7).

Turquet, a wholesale dealer in textiles and salt fish from Chieri in Piedmont, studied existing conditions in the Italian silk trade and realized the possibilities for its introduction into France. He enlisted the aid of Bartolommeo Naris, a Genoese with practical knowledge of silk-making, and in 1536 the municipality promised the partnership a five-year subvention of 500 écus per annum for the new manufacture of velvets and silk stuffs, excusing Turquet from paying dues on his other businesses.[6] In 1540 a royal decree made Lyons the sole entrepôt for foreign silks and granted special privileges in the purchase of raw materials. During the second quarter of the century Italian entrepreneurs were also responsible for the introduction of other manufacturing industries—notably linen, fustian, soap, and faience.

By 1554 the silk trade employed no less than twelve thousand citizens—nearly a fifth of the working population. Whereas there had been between thirty and thirty-five thousand inhabitants in Lyons in 1417, by 1515 the figure was around forty thousand, and by 1544 fifty thousand. The rapid population increase in the early sixteenth century reflects industrial expansion. The trend is clearly illustrated by the development of the printing industry, after movable type was introduced into Lyons by pioneers from Nuremberg, Liège, and Basle in the early 1470s.[7] Between 1510 and 1515 the number of shops increased from eighty to a hundred (a higher number than that of Paris); by 1548 the figure had grown to over four hundred. Thus by the middle of the century, although a good deal of type was still imported, the number of engravers, typesetters, correctors, binders, and publishers must have been between two and three thousand. A petition presented to Charles IX in 1572, complaining of low salaries, long working hours, and bad working conditions, actually claimed that there were more than three thousand journeymen printers active in Lyons.[8] But the number declined towards the end of the century, when less than two hundred shops were active.

The early sixteenth-century printers in Lyons also involved a number of Italians, like Benoît Bonnyn, Jean de Bergame, Jean Guido, Jacques Saçon, Jean de Savoye, Jacob de Suigo, Barthélemy Trotti, the Florentine

---

[6] See J. Godart, *L'ouvrier en soie* (Lyons and Paris, 1899).

[7] On the introduction and development of printing in Lyons see J.-B. Monfalcon, *Manuel du bibliophile et de l'archéologue lyonnais* (Paris, 1857); C. Peyrat, 'Barthélemy Buyer et les débuts de l'imprimerie à Lyon', *Humanisme et Renaissance*, 2 (1935), 103–21, 234–75, 348–75; N. Rondot, *Les Graveurs sur bois et les imprimeurs à Lyon au XVIe siècle* (Lyons, 1896); A. Claudin, *Histoire de l'imprimerie en France aux XVe et XVIe siècles*, 4 vols. (Paris, 1900–14).

[8] *Remonstrances et Memoires pour les Compagnons Imprimeurs de Paris et Lyon: Opposans. Contre les Libraires, Maistres Imprimeurs desdits lieux* (n.p., c.1572), fos. 138r–143r.

Giunti and Tinghi families, the Venetian Gabiano and Portonari families,[9] as well as Jacopo Moderno of Pinguento in Istria.

In addition to enterprising bankers, traders, and industrialists, the transalpine community included a considerable number of royal agents, diplomats, and clerics. Many of those who had suffered losses in their homeland after the French defeat at Pavia were reimbursed with secular and religious appointments or were found wealthy or noble spouses in their adopted country. The governorship of Lyons was one royal appointment which provided a suitable reward for the king's Italian supporters in the early sixteenth century: thus Cesare Borgia, the natural son of Pope Alexander VI, held the post between 1498 and 1507, when he was succeeded by Giangiacomo Trivulzio, Marquess of Vigevano, who had liberated Capua for Charles VIII and helped Louis XII in the conquest of Milan in 1499. Giangiacomo in addition served the French king as governor of Milan from 1500 until his death in 1518. His cousin Teodoro, who acted as governor of Milan after 1521, was compelled to seek refuge in France after Francis I's defeat in 1525: he was duly appointed governor of Lyons in 1529 and was buried in the Dominican church in 1532; Teodoro's nephew, Pomponio Trivulzio, held the same position until the appointment of François de Tournon in 1536. The Este of Ferrara were ardent supporters of the French cause: Duke Alfonso I fought at Ravenna and Marignano and helped finance the Pavia campaign; his eldest son, Ercole II, was given the hand of Louis XII's daughter Renée in 1528, and his younger son, Ippolito II, served as Archbishop of Lyons between 1540 and 1551.[10]

But despite the great influence of such dignitaries and prelates, the most important members of the Italian community in Lyons were the self-made businessmen, typified by the enormously wealthy Guadagni and Gondi families.[11] For as the visiting Venetian ambassador, Giovanni Corero, noted in 1569:

All the wealth in this Kingdom lies in the hands of only one of the four classes of citizens, which as you know are the clergy, impoverished by dues, the nobility, ruined by wars, the common folk, pillaged by the armies' licence, and the bourgeoisie. Only the business and professional people—presidents, counsellors, attorneys—are rich.[12]

[9] For the production of these and other Italian printers in Lyons see J. Baudrier, *Bibliographie lyonnaise*, 12 vols. (Lyons, 1895–1921).

[10] See A. Péricaud, *Notice sur Hippolyte d'Este, Cardinal-Archevêque de Lyon* (Lyons, 1865); V. Pacifici, *Ippolito II d'Este* (Tivoli, 1920).

[11] For further details on these families see L. Passerini Orsini de Rilli, *Genealogia e storia della famiglia Guadagni* (Florence, 1873); G. Yver, *De Guadagniis mercatoribus* (Paris, 1902); E. Picot, *La Mère des Gondi* (Paris, 1897).

[12] N. Tommaseo, *Relations des ambassadeurs vénitiens sur les affaires de France au XVIᵉ siècle*, 2 vols. (Paris, 1938), ii. 104.

Whereas French gentlemen spurned business affairs, and rather occupied themselves with warfare, courtly activity, and the quest for royal appointments, aristocratic Italian immigrants did not find the pursuit of wealth incompatible with nobility, good manners, and the cultivation of art and letters; in fact they introduced into Lyons the more refined aspects of their native civilization, gracious living, a love of beauty and luxury, and an intellectual stimulation and activity. They sumptuously entertained their hosts, especially the visiting monarchs, and the Florentine community adorned their chapel of Notre-Dame de Confort, in the Dominican church, with a beauty and splendour hitherto unknown in French churches. The Altoviti, Capponi, Guadagni, Gondi, Mannelli, Strozzi, and other Florentine patrician families included some notable musical patrons, as did their compatriots, the Arnolfini, Bava, Barthelemi, Buonvisi, Cenami, Grosso, Micheli from Lucca and the Este from Ferrara. The houses of the wealthier bankers and merchants, with their regular façades, vast windows, broad stairways and entrances, recall the solidity and dignity of those of their forefathers in Florence and Lucca: many still stand and may be seen today in the old quarter between Fourvière and the Saône. Thus the Italian colony set the fashion for the French Renaissance and helped to make Lyons the cultural capital of France in the second quarter of the sixteenth century.[13]

(iii) *Beneath the Brilliant Façade*

Despite royal jurisdiction, operated by the appointed governor, lieutenant-general, notaries, and lawyers of the seneschal's court, considerable administrative power was invested in the hands of the town council (the *consulat* or *commune*), which included wealthy members of the business community, as well as landowners; the Florentine, Luccan, and Genoan communities were self-governing 'nations'. The second hierarchy included the archbishop, primate of France, and the twenty-two count-canons of the cathedral of Saint-Jean, a relic of medieval suzerainty.

The splendour of Renaissance Lyons was somewhat superficial in that it concealed the dreadful poverty and atrocious working conditions of the common people. The urbanization and neglect of the surrounding countryside were reflected in the high cost of living and recurrent famines, the most serious leading to a popular uprising—*La Grande*

---

[13] See N. Rondot, *Les Artistes et les maîtres de métier étrangers à Lyon* (Lyons, 1883); id., *Les Peintres de Lyon au XVe et au XVIe siècle* (Paris, 1888); id., *Les Potiers de terre italiens à Lyon au XVIe siècle* (Lyons and Paris, 1892).

Rebeyne—in 1529, when, at the instigation of the taverners, the hungry pillaged the Abbey of the Île-Barbe in quest of corn.[14] Two years later, however, after another harvest failure which caused a sixfold increase in the price of grain, the foreign merchants donated a large sum of money to avert a similar rebellion. The Aumône générale (later known as the Hospice de la Charité), was organized by the town council at the Convent of St Bonaventure to aid the poorer citizens, as well as orphans and penniless travellers. After 1541 the Hôtel-Dieu, established fifty-five years earlier, offered free medical attention to the needy. But the guilds and corporations won few concessions for the workers during the period of great industrial expansion.

The strife of working life is reflected in the printers' strike of 1539. The principal complaints were that the masters were trying to effect economies by reducing pay—then in the form of 'pain, vin et pitance'—and by employing more apprentices than journeymen. The town council appealed to the masters to negotiate a settlement, but met with opposition; when some shops were moved to Vienne and Avignon in 1541, it appealed to King Francis I to intervene. The royal decision supported the employers and conceded that the traditional working hours of 5 a.m. to 8 p.m. were reasonable.[15] The troubles continued intermittently without achieving any improvement in working conditions. The journeymen themselves again appealed to King Charles IX in 1572, complaining that they were expected to complete 3,300 leaves per day, which required eighteen or nineteen hours' work, with meals taken in the shop and allowing no recreation. The same document laments the passing of the scholar and gentleman printers of the early sixteenth century:

... jadis il n'y avait presque sinon que gens doctes ès langues et sciences, et entre iceux on y remarquoit plusieurs gentilz hommes qui s'applicquoyent à cest estat, où il n'y ha de present gueres plus que personnes contemptibles.[16]

... in the old days they [the printers] were people well versed in languages and the arts and many of them were gentlemen ... whereas nowadays they are nearly all contemptible people.

---

[14] See S. Champier, *Cy commence ung petit livre de l'antiquité, origine et noblesse ... de Lyon: Ensemble de la rebeine et conjuration ou rebellion du populaire ... contre les conseilliers de la cité et notables marchands, à cause des bledz* (Lyons, 1529–30), fo. 26ʳ; repr. as *L'Antiquité* ... (Lyons, 1884), 41.

[15] The printers' complaints are discussed in M. Audin, 'Les Grèves dans l'imprimerie à Lyon au xviᵉ siècle', *Gutenberg-Jahrbuch* (1935), 172–89, and N. Z. Davis, 'Protestantism and the Printing Workers of Lyons: A Study in the Problem of Religion and Social Class during the Reformation' (Ph.D. diss., University of Michigan, 1959).

[16] *Remonstrances et Mémoires*, fo. 142ᵛ.

The printers' employees, many of whom hailed from Germany and Switzerland, were more educated and seditious than any other group of workers: it is hardly surprising therefore that they should have been in the forefront of the Protestant movement and that Lyons should become the centre for the publication of Huguenot psalms in France.

(iv) *The Reformation*

The growth of evangelical humanism and Protestantism also reflects the geographical and political position of Lyons. In his *Recherches de la Franco* (1560), Estienne Pasquier refers to the city as 'l'embouchure de toutes nouvelles'; new ideas, as well as consumer commodities, passed into the southern capital through its cosmopolitan community and visitors.[17] The quasi-republican government, as well as the distance and consequent freedom from the restricting influences of the Parisian Parlement and Sorbonne, gave Lyons a degree of religious liberty not found elsewhere in France. The proximity to Geneva and Ferrara and the liberal atmosphere encouraged the visits of free-thinkers and humanists like Erasmus, Rabelais, Dolet, Marot, Calvin, and Nostradamus, fleeing from bigotry and persecution.

After their long struggle against the temporal power of the archbishops, the citizens of Lyons resented ecclesiastical governments and papal control. Their initial attitude to immigrants (especially printers) from Lutheran Germany and Zwinglian Switzerland was tolerant and often sympathetic. Between 1518 and 1538 most of the regions to the east of Lyons—the Vaudois, Strasburg, Geneva, Zurich, and the Dauphiné—embraced the reformed religions. Meanwhile the chapter of Saint-Jean had become increasingly secularized and clerical discipline lax: the lack of erudite Catholic theologians meant there was no orthodox opposition to articulate humanist critics. In January 1521, the services of the royal inquisitor, Valentin Levin, were rejected by the town council, and during Lent in 1524 Aimé Meigret preached Lutheranism at Sainte-Croix. Between 1524 and 1525, the king's sister, Marguerite de Navarre, resided nearby at Saint-Just in Bourg-en-Bresse: her religious views, much influenced by neo-Platonism, were liberal, as were those of her retinue, which included Guillaume Farel and other 'zélateurs de l'Évangile'. Her protection was to save a number of evangelists and free-thinkers in the difficult times following the initial phase of the French Reformation, instigated by Lefèvre d'Étaples's

---

[17] See L. Romier, 'Lyon et le cosmopolitisme au début de la Renaissance française', *Bibliothèque d'Humanisme et Renaissance*, 11 (1949), 28–42.

vernacular translation of the Bible, which was published by C. Nourry and P. de Vingle at Lyons between 1523 and 1530. A practising Protestant community was established in the town in 1527, its early ministers including Jean Fabry, Pierre Fournelier, and Claude Monnier, and its visiting preachers Calvin, Viret, and Farel. Ten years later, Barthélemy Aneau, was appointed professor of rhetoric at the Collège de la Trinité, which had passed under municipal management a few years earlier and which remained largely free from ecclesiastical authority until the Jesuit take-over in 1567.[18] The College's earliest rectors—the surgeon Jehan Canappe, the Protestant Loys du Vergier, Jehan Rainier, and Aneau himself—were all classical humanists rather than orthodox theologians.

Before the late 1530s French Protestantism amounted to little more than the unco-ordinated, undoctrinaire ideas of free-thinking intellectuals and a few Lutherans. After Calvin's installation at Geneva in 1539 its character changed, as a rigid and disciplined framework was established. Calvinism then grew apace in Lyons, as elsewhere: by 1546 an amphitheatre large enough for three thousand people was constructed for public worship and psalm-singing in the rue Longue. Huguenots also met at a house on the corner of the Place des Cordeliers and the rue Grenette and later constructed a temple in the suburbs at Guillotière. The liberalism of the Trivulzio governors (1507–32) was not shared by Cardinal François de Tournon, who began his governorship in 1536 with a demand for a public recantation of Clément Marot's heretical views. However, between 1532 and 1550, the town's internal administration was effectively in the hands of the enlightened lieutenant-general, Jean du Peyrat, who actively supported religious liberty and used his influence to protect evangelical humanists from the Inquisition.

By the 1540s a substantial number of Lyonese printers—including Dolet, Gabiano, De Tournes, Arnoullet, Frellon, Senneton, and Vincent—embraced Protestantism. It is therefore hardly surprising that most of the prominent writers whose work flooded from the active presses of Lyons—Marot, Rabelais, Dolet, Aneau, Charles de Sainte-Marthe, Des Périers, and Scève—were far from orthodox in their religious views; their writings frequently called forth the censure of the bigoted Sorbonne, whose blighting influence, however, remained insignificant in the southern capital. Calvin sought refuge in Lyons after his flight from Paris in 1536. But most of the city's free-thinkers were in

---

[18] See L. Gerig, 'Le Collège de la Trinité à Lyon avant 1540', *Revue de la Renaissance*, 9 (1908), 73–94; 10 (1909), 137–57 and 204–15; also id., 'Barthélemy Aneau: A Study in Humanism', *Romanic Review*, 1 (1910), 181–207, 279–89, 395–410; 2 (1911), 163–85; 4 (1913), 27–57.

fact neither Calvinists nor Lutherans; their ideas merely reflect the same fermentation of humanism which led to the Reformation. As classical scholars, many of them demanded the right to free interpretation of the Scriptures, whilst their concepts were inevitably affected by the pagan culture of ancient Greece and Rome. All were united in their desire for free expression, if some showed prudence in being dissenters 'jusqu'au feu exclusivement'.

The situation for free-thinkers, however, deteriorated as France's religious troubles deepened in the 1530s. The Edicts of Coucy and Lyons, which had guaranteed religious liberty, were repealed in December 1538, while the suppression of heresy was authorized by letters patent following the stern Edict of Fontainebleau, promulgated by François de Tournon in June 1539. Although Jean du Peyrat continued his support of unobtrusive dissenters, he could not stem the reactionary tide, and the first Protestant martyrs were burnt in 1539. If Calvin and Marot, fresh from exile in Ferrara, still felt secure at Lyons in 1536, Eustorg de Beaulieu chose to retire to Geneva in 1537, as did Charles de Sainte-Marthe in 1541. New severe measures against unorthodox religious beliefs were issued in the city on 30 August 1542; and Clément Marot, being forewarned of impending arrest, fled to Geneva, where he set to work on translating the Psalms, fifty of which were printed with the approved melodies in Lyons between 1547 and 1549. Meanwhile Rabelais, under the protection of Guillaume du Bellay, Governor of Piedmont, diligently revised *Gargantua* and *Pantagruel*, expurgating heretical words and phrases and deleting satirical references to the Sorbonne. He was embarrassed therefore by Dolet's reprint of an earlier edition and bitterly criticized his former friend. Dolet was imprisoned in 1544, at the instigation of critics and enemies in the publishing business who exaggerated his heretical utterances; although he was later released after recanting, he was finally martyred at Paris in 1546, despite the delaying tactics of Peyrat. This was perhaps the inevitable outcome of the broad degree of intellectual liberty enjoyed by Lyonese writers in the past, which led to overt criticism of dogmatic assertions, going beyond contemporary Italian scepticism or mere indifference to Christian doctrine.

Within a year of Peyrat's death, the pastor Claude Monnier was burnt at the stake in Lyons. Two years later, in May 1553, five students from Lausanne were interrogated and executed as heretics in the Place des Terreaux.[19] Yet despite such persecution and in defiance of royal,

[19] See J. Crespin (ed.), *Recueil de plusieurs personnes qui ont constamment enduré la mort pour le nom de nostre Seigneur* (Geneva, 1555), fo. 375^r; (2nd edn., Geneva, 1556), fos. 434^r–438^r.

archepiscopal, and consular interdiction, the growing Protestant sect sang the new psalms as a rallying cry at their meetings. In his Chronicle Jean Guéraud wrote that in June 1551 there was an uprising in Lyons 'involving a large number of people who began to hold meetings and assemblies with two or three hundred men and women, the men carrying swords and other arms, singing, large and small together, the psalms of David translated by Clément Marot . . . to attract to their damnable sect many other people, although there were great and clear laws against singing the said psalms and holding such meetings and assemblies . . . for which a few of them were imprisoned at the King's pleasure'.[20] On 23 June 1551 the Bishop of Valence, deputizing for the absent Archbishop of Lyons, called for a ban on 'a number of Lutherans who were getting together and singing the psalms of David against the King's orders' (*plusieurs luthériens lesquelz se sont monopolez et chantent en bandes les pseaulmes David contre les inhibicions du Roy*).[21]

By September 1560, following the Conjuration d'Amboise, the Protestants felt strong enough to attempt a *coup d'état*. In the absence of promised support from Geneva and in the face of unexpected opposition and resistance, the uprising soon fizzled out. The royal governor, Antoine d'Albon, did not take violently repressive measures, although a Catholic uprising in the following June led to the murder of Barthélemy Aneau by an incensed, disorganized mob. But despite royal bans, by September 1561 Protestants were meeting publicly to worship at their new temple without hindrance. At the end of April 1562, a more serious Protestant rebellion was organized when the King's lieutenant-general, the Count of Sault, was seized. A number of churches were ransacked before royal authority was finally restored in June 1563, under a new civic administration shared between Catholics and Protestants. During the years 1562–4 numerous editions of the translated Bible and of the new Genevan psalter appeared, with tunes and harmonizations, as well as spiritual songs and biblical dramas.

Nearly a quarter of the town's population perished in a plague during 1564. The victims included Jean I de Tournes, Thomas de Straton, and probably Guillaume Guéroult, author of many *chansons spirituelles* published at Lyons in 1548. After this the Jesuits led a Catholic revival, publishing catechisms and taking over the Collège de la Trinité from Protestant domination in 1567. By the late 1560s, with the Catholics gradually gaining the upper hand, a number of reformist publishers

---

[20] J. Guéraud, *La Chronique lyonnaise de Jean Guérard, 1536–1562*, ed. J. Tricou (Lyons, 1929), 54.

[21] See F. Rolle, *Inventaire sommaire des archives communales de Lyon*, 1 (Paris, 1865), 36.

and traders moved to Geneva, ending the surge of musical activity that had accompanied the appearance of the Calvinist psalter. The full weight of the anti-Protestant reaction followed in 1572, after several years of relative calm and continuing tolerance, when hundreds of Huguenots—including the composer. Claude Goudimel—were systematically exterminated during the St Bartholomew's Day Massacre. The governor, François de Mandelot, may have been guilty of complicity in this: at all events, he proved an ardent supporter of the Catholic faction led by the Guises during the ensuing religious wars. After his death in 1588, his successor, Charles-Emmanuel of Savoy, Duke of Nemours, continued to support the Sainte Union des Catholiques. He died of poisoning early in 1594, after the town's submission to Henry of Navarre, who made his triumphal entry on 4 September 1595.

The Protestant proclivities of Lyons were thus encouraged by its close links with nearby Geneva, by its printing industry, which generally promoted liberal and humanist ideas, and by its foreign communities, which included some religious refugees as well as the predominant group of political refugees. The political ascendancy of the Huguenots was clearly reflected in the town's musical publications between 1547 and 1567, as was its subsequent decline.

2

Music in the Literature of Lyons

THIS chapter accumulates the references to music in literary works published in Lyons during the sixteenth century, relating the most significant of them to musical tradition and contemporary practice.

(i) *The Golden Age of Lyonese Literature*

The liberal atmosphere of Lyons, its active presses, and the wealth and luxury of many of its inhabitants encouraged humanists, poets, and artists. During the second third of the sixteenth century the town's intellectual life flourished to an unprecedented extent, surpassing even that of Paris, at least in literary output. Amongst the eminent humanists and writers who lived in the town for most of their lives were Symphorien Champier (*c.*1472–1539), Benoît Court (1494–1555), Jean Grolier (1499–1565), Barthélemy Aneau (d. 1561), Nicolas Bourbon (b. 1503), Pernette du Guillet (d. 1546), Louise Labé (*c.*1524–66), Claude de Taillemont (1526–after 1556), Guillaume des Autelz (1529–81), and, most important of all, Maurice Scève (*c.*1510–*c.*1564). Others residing there for shorter periods include Jean Lemaire, François Rabelais, Clément Marot, Marguerite de Navarre, Bonaventure des Périers, Luigi Alamanni, Salmon Macrin, Antoine du Saix, Jean Visagier, Étienne Dolet, Claude Roussel, Gilles Corrozet, Eustorg de Beaulieu, Gilbert Ducher, Gabriel Symeoni, Charles de Sainte-Marthe, François Habert, Jacques Peletier, Charles Fontaine, Claude Mermet, Guillaume de La Taissonnière, and Pontus de Tyard, whilst Erasmus, Budé, Calvin, Guéroult, Bèze, Héroët, La Borderie, and Jean Second paid shorter visits.

Scève and his colleagues represent the best in French literature of the generation between Clément Marot (*Adolescence clementine*, 1532) and the emergence of the Pléiade (Du Bellay's *Deffence*, 1549). Among the landmarks of the Lyonese literary scene are the following titles (preceded by date and followed by publisher):

1531 Boccaccio, Poggio, Valla, et al., *Le Parangon des nouvelles honnestes et delectables*, D. de Harsy (repr. 1532 and 1533)
1532 François Rabelais, *Pantagruel*, C. Nourry (repr. F. Juste)
1532 Luigi Alamanni, *Opere toscane*, S. Gryphe

1534–5	François Rabelais, *Gargantua*, F. Juste
1535	Juan de Flores, *La déplourable fin de Flamete*, F. Juste
1536	L. B. Alberti, *Hecatomphile*, F. Juste (repr. 1537)
1536	Maurice Scève *et al.*, *Blasons anatomiques*, F. Juste
1536–8	Étienne Dolet, *Commentarii linguae Latinae*, S. Gryphe
1537	Eustorg de Beaulieu, *Les divers rapportz*, P. de Sainte-Lucie
1538	Baldassare Castiglione, *Le Courtisan*, F. Juste
1538	Clément Marot, *Œuvres*, E. Dolet
1539	Barthélemy Aneau, *Chant natal*, S. Gryphe
1540	Étienne Dolet, *La manière de bien traduire*, E. Dolet
1540	Charles de Sainte-Marthe, *Poésie françoise*, P. de Sainte-Lucie
1541	Barthélemy Aneau, *Lyon marchant*, P. de Tours
(1542)	Antoine Héroët, *La parfaicte amye*, E. Dolet
1544	Bonaventure des Périers, *Œuvres*, J. de Tournes
1544	Maurice Scève, *Délie*, A. Constantin
1545	Pernette du Guillet, *Rymes*, J. de Tournes
1545	Charles Fontaine, *La Fontaine d'amour*, J. de Tournes
1547	Gilles Corrozet, *Le Conte du Rossignol*, J. de Tournes
1547	Mellin de Saint Gelais, *Saingelais Œuvres*, P. de Tournes
1547	Maurice Scève, *Saulsaye*, J. de Tournes
1547	François Habert, *La nouvelle Pallas, La nouvelle Juno, La nouvelle Vénus*, J. de Tournes
1547	Marguerite de Navarre, *Les Marguerites*, J. de Tournes
1548	François Rabelais, *Pantagruel, Le Quart livre*, P. de Tours
1549	Pontus de Tyard, *Erreurs amoureuses*, J. de Tournes
1550	Guillaume des Autelz, *Repos de plus grand travail*, J. de Tournes and G. Gazeau
1551	(Barthélemy Aneau), *Le Quintil Horatian*, J. Temporal
1552	Pontus de Tyard, *Solitaire premier*, J. de Tournes
1553	Guillaume des Autelz, *Les Amoureux Repos*, J. Temporal
1555	Jacques Peletier, *L'Art Poétique*, J. de Tournes and G. Gazeau
1555	Jacques Peletier, *L'Amour des Amours*, J. de Tournes and G. Gazeau
1555	Pontus de Tyard, *Solitaire second*, J. de Tournes
1555	Charles Fontaine, *Les Ruisseaux de Fontaine*, T. Payen
1555	Louise Labé, *Evvres*, J. de Tournes
1556	Claude de Taillemont, *La Tricarite*, J. Temporal
1556	Guillaume de la Taissonnière, *Les Amoureuses Occupations*, G. Roville
1557	Charles Fontaine, *Odes, énigmes et épigrammes*, J. Citoys
1557	Louis des Masures, *Œuvres poétiques*, J. de Tournes and G. Gazeau

1557   Philibert Bugnyon, *Erotasmes de Phidie et Gélasine*, J. Temporal

1558   Bonaventure des Périers, *Les nouvelles recréations et joyeux devis*, R. Granjon (repr. G. Roville, 1561)

1562   Maurice Scève, *Microcosme*, J. de Tournes

At least twenty-four anonymous verse anthologies were published in Lyons at frequent intervals through the sixteenth century, matching a similar number printed in Paris, Rouen, Geneva, and Antwerp.[1] These collections contain two principal types of poem—courtly and popular—and to a large degree draw on a repertoire already familiar in musical settings circulating and often printed a few years earlier. In some cases topical pieces are added, with novelties ('Chansons nouvelles') generally distinguished from the older poems. But an old and well-known *timbre* is frequently suggested for a new text, which always conforms to the proposed model in structure, with the same number of lines per stanza and the same number of syllables per line, often appending several extra stanzas where only one survives in musical settings.

In the attributed literature, music, both real and metaphorical, looms large. While philosophically it is the sign of nobility and harmony, in the rich array of poetry inspired by love it symbolizes the beloved's voice, her hand, her playing, the lover's consolation, the immortality of the soul, and the intermediary between the poet and his muse. The lute (the modern *lyra* or *kithara*) is not only the admired humanist symbol but the most perfect instrument for the accompaniment of song.

The foundations of this literary renaissance were firmly established during the early sixteenth century, when the Italianate town embraced the new humanist ideas. The wealthy citizens, proud of the ancient heritage of Lyons (Lugdunum) as the capital of Gaul, eagerly responded to the revival of Classical civilization and literature, proclaiming themselves as a 'second Athens' or 'a new Florence'. Jean Lemaire de Belges (*c*.1473–*c*.1514) the *rhétoriqueur* poet and author of *La Concorde des*

---

[1] Fifty-two are listed in the *Royal Musical Association Research Chronicle*, 12 (1974), 81–5. The contents of the three most significant collections published in Lyons in 1534, 1554, and 1559 are surveyed by the present author in Appendix IV of 'The Chanson at Lyons'. One more collection from Lyons has since come to light: *La Fleur de plusieurs belles Chansons nouvelles avec plusieurs aultres retirees des anciennes impressions* (Lyons, O. Arnoullet, Jan. 1542/3; In 8°, 90 × 130 mm.; 104 fos. sign. a⁸–n⁸). Arnoullet follows the texts and sequence of A. Lotrian's *S'ensuyt plusieurs belles chansons nouvelles* (Paris, 1542; repr. M. A. Percheron, Geneva, 1867) for his first 44 pieces, adding one new chanson, 'L'abesse de Maubisson' (fo. f3), before reprinting 122 poems from *S'ensuyvent plusieurs belles Chansons nouvelles* (Paris, 1535; ed. B. Jeffery, *Chanson Verse of the Early Renaissance*, ii (London, 1976), nos. 2–124).

deux langaiges,[2] an allegory on the spiritual harmony of France and Italy, extols the city's ancient heritage, privileged status, and stimulating atmosphere. The first part of *La Concorde* is an exposition of pagan hedonistic philosophy in the guise of a description of the 'Temple de Vénus', which was evidently situated in Lyons:

> Ung temple y a, plus beau ne vit oncq nulz,
> Assiz sur Roch, en lieu fort autenticque,
> Aux confluentz Darar et Rhodanus,
>   Là est le chief de la Gaule celtique,
> Reflourissant, comme ung aultre Ilion,
> Et surcroissant en sa valeur antique
>   Peuple Royal portant cueur de Lyon
> Y fait séjour dont France est decorée
> Et y voit on nymphes ung milion.[3]

> There is a temple finer than you have ever seen,
> Standing on a rock in a very authentic site,
> At the confluence of the Saône and Rhône.
> There is the capital of Celtic Gaul,
> Flowering again like another Troy,
> And abounding in its antient virtue.
> Royal people with lion hearts,
> The pride of France, stay there,
> And you can see a myriad nymphs there.

Lemaire, born and raised in Hainault, served as a choirboy in Valenciennes and continued his studies in Paris. He later spent a number of years in or around Lyons, working for the Bourbon duke Pierre II (1498–1503), and then for Margaret of Austria (who, until the death of her husband Philibert le Beau, Duke of Savoy, in September 1504, lived at Pont d'Ain, some 50 km. away). He met Guillaume Crétin at Lyons in 1498[4] and was there again in 1506;[5] his letter to Jean Perréal, painter and architect for the town's solemn entries and theatrical representations, published as a preface to the *Premiere epistre de lamant verd*,[6] is dated Lyons, 1 March, 1510 (= 1511 NS). Four months later, Lemaire was still in the town, receiving treatment for a broken arm.[7]

---

[2] J. Lemaire de Belges, *La Concorde des deux langaiges* (Paris, 1513); fac., ed. M. Françon, *La Concorde des deux langages et Les Epîtres de l'Amant Vert* (Cambridge, Mass., 1964).

[3] Ibid. fos. C2^{r-v}.

[4] G. Crétin, *Œuvres*, ed. K. Chesney (Paris, 1932), p. xii.

[5] S. Champier, *Liber de quadruplici vita* (Lyons, 1507), fo. G7^r, publishes a letter from the author to Humbert Fournier mentioning Lemaire's presence in Lyons.

[6] The letter reappears on the first page of a Parisian edition of 1512, published in facsimile by M. Françon (see above, n. 2).

[7] See J. Lemaire, *Œuvres*, ed. J. Stecher, 4 vols. (Louvain, 1888–91), iv. 382. For further on Lemaire see P. A. Becker, *Jean Lemaire, der erste humanistische Dichter Frankreichs* (Strasburg,

He explains the attractions of the city near the beginning of his description of the Temple of Venus:

> Et je qui fuz en temps de guerre et noise
> Né de Haynnau, pays enclin aux armes
> Vin de bien loing querre amour Lionnoise[8]

> And I who, in time of war and trouble, was
> Born in Hainaut, a country inclined to arms,
> Came all the way here to seek the love of Lyons

Renaissance humanism, eclecticism, and versatility are epitomized in the work of Lemaire's friend, Symphorien Champier (1472–1539), philosopher, doctor, lawyer, historian, and poet.[9] Born at Saint-Symphorien-sur-Coise, near Lyons, he studied at the best universities in Europe—Paris (1490–4), Montpellier (1496–8), and Pavia (1515–16). His philosophy followed the mystical Aristotelianism of Lefèvre d'Étaples, but was strongly influenced by the Christianized Platonism of Ficino, with occasional borrowings from Pico della Mirandola. In his first work, the *Ianua logice et phisice* (Lyons, 1498), Champier reveals his familiarity with the philosophy of the Florentine Academy, including a chapter entitled 'De mundi anima secundum Marsilium Ficinum'. Like Ficino, he maintained that the divine presence imbued the whole of creation, including man's mind, and, like Petrarch, he believed that the philosophy of antiquity could infuse a new fervour into orthodox Christianity.[10] He seems, however, to have ignored the inherent dichotomy between orthodox Christian dogma and Renaissance individualism, and his early works especially lack much of the Italians' glorification of man. Thus in *La Nef des princes* (Lyons, 1502), a didactic treatise on the physical and moral education of the prince, following the Platonist pattern, his view of man oscillates between the concept of self-willed intellect and that of the tool of a divine master.

Champier's *Liber de quadruplici vita* (Lyons, 1507) whole-heartedly endorses the philosophico-religious syncretism of Ficino, closely following the latter's *De triplici vita* (Florence, 1489), with its dual emphasis on the corporal and spiritual needs of man, progressing from Hippocrates and Galen (Part I, 'De vita sana') to Socrates and Plato (III,

---

1893); G. Doutrepont, *Jean Lemaire de Belges et la Renaissance* (Brussels, 1934); and J. Frappier, 'L'Humanisme de Jean Lemaire de Belges', *Bibliothèque d'Humanisme et Renaissance*, 25 (1963), 289–306.

[8] Lemaire, *Concorde*, fo. C1^r.

[9] P. Allut, *Étude biographique et bibliographique sur Symphorien Champier* (Lyons, 1859).

[10] M. L. Holmes, 'Renaissance Themes in Some Works of the Lyonese Doctor, Humanist and Man of Letters, Symphorien Champier', in *Cinq Études lyonnaises*, ed. H. J. Martin (Geneva, 1966), 27–54.

'De vita celi') and Jesus (IV), 'De vita supercelesti'). Printed at the end of the book is the *Tropheum Gallorum*, a brief history of France to the time of Louis XI, based on ancient inscriptions found in different parts of Lyons, showing a strong vein of nationalism, despite the constant quest for genealogical links with Greece and Rome. This Trophy of the Gauls is followed by three letters to Champier from Humbert Fournier, the first of which refers to the informal meetings of a humanist coterie in a house on the Fourvière Hill in Lyons:

Quid nunc potissime agamus in hoc olim famigerabili veneris emporio deipare virginis sacro monte scire cupis. Ecce vivimus in celibatu et ocio litterario... Imprimis sermo agitur de religione: de morte: de instituendis moribus & anime disciplinis cum socrate meo andrea victonio... Affluunt & huc hospites: qui esto rari: rara tamen virtute conspicabiles. Adest non leve curarum levamen D. Gondisalvus alter achademie nostre oculus: Idem & apollo & praxiteles: qui cum liberalium artium disciplinis candidissme sit insignitus: tum omnium ingenuorum artificum benivolentiis insinuatus: non tam studiosus amator quam sedulus imitator existit... Hinc fidibus canoris ad amplam aurium voluptatem docto pollice testudine[m] cavam orpheus discapedinat. Quibus avicule discriminantium vocularum concentibus alternatis modulis fringulciunt. Nunc girovagus flexus concave et multiforatile arundinis, fervido articulorum axe concitato levivola lingua perstrepente tinnitu argutulo museus sororius tuus auris suaviter demulcet cantu syreneo.[11]

You wish to know what now are our main activities in this once notorious Forum of Venus on the sacred hill dedicated to the Virgin. Here we are, living in celibacy and literary leisure... Mostly we discuss religion, death, the reform of morals and the disciplines of the mind with my Socrates, André Victon... To these gatherings come visitors, few in number but conspicuous in virtue. Present also, greatly to lighten our cares, is the doctor Gonsalvo [of Toledo], the other luminary of our academy. He is our Apollo and our Praxiteles, not only distinguished by his profound knowledge of the liberal arts, but also on good terms then with all artists of talent, not so much a lover of study as a sedulous imitator... Then, ravishing our ears with his melodious strings, Orpheus, with skilful thumb, plucks his lute. To this the little birds, with their consorts of clear voices, twitter with alternate [polyphonic] measures. Then Musaeus, your brother-in-law, dextrous and nimble on the hollow and many-holed flute, excites us with dazzling melismas, as his light tongue fills the instrument with high ringing sound, charming our ears with a siren song.

This letter was the basis for a claim, instigated by the Jesuit Claude Menestrier in 1704 and followed by later historians,[12] that there was a

---

[11] Champier, *Liber de quadruplici vita*, fo. G6ᵛ.

[12] C. F. Menestrier, *Bibliothèque curieuse et instructive de divers ouvrages anciens et modernes, de la littérature et des arts*, 2 vols. (Trévoux, 1704), ii. 120; P. de Colonia, *Histoire littéraire de Lyon*, 2 vols. (Lyons, 1730), ii. 466; A. Péricaud, 'Notes et documents pour servir à l'histoire de Lyon

Les lieux principaux notez, de la presente ville & Cité de Lyon.

A Saint Iean Eglise collegialle.   B Saint Paul Eglise collegialle.   C   Pierre Scife.   D .Fourruiere   E   Le Pont de Saone.
F La riuiere de Saone.   G   L'Abbaye d'Esnay.   H   Les Iacobins.   I   Saint Nisier.   K Le Pont du Rosne.   L Les
Cordeliers,   M La Platiere.   N   La coste Saint Sebastien.   O   Les Bouleurs de la porte saint Sebastien.

Pl. 1. View of sixteenth-century Lyons from the Côte Saint-Sébastien. Engraving by B. Salomon published in G. Guéroult's *Epitome de la Corographie de l'Europe* (Lyons, printed by B. Arnoullet's widow for B. Bonhomme, 1557)

flourishing 'Academy' in sixteenth-century Lyons. It suggests that a group of Champier's humanist friends met regularly for literary and philosophical discussion and musical diversion, emulating (unconsciously perhaps) the Florentine Academy.[13] The 'Forum of Venus', on the Fourvière Hill, on the northern edge of the town, may refer to the house which, according to another letter printed in the same book,[14] Fournier shared with the lawyer-theologian Victon, or to that of one of the other antiquarians who lived among the Roman ruins. Humbert's second letter also mentions the presence of Jean Lemaire, another friend, whose 'Temple of Venus' in Lyons may have inspired or been inspired by Fournier's 'Forum of Venus'. According to the first letter, Fournier himself delighted in imitating Petrarch, while others acted out the metamorphoses of Medusa and the magic transformations of Circe. Both letters imply that Champier was the group's central figure.

Although apparently lacking in rules and formalities, such a coterie may be said to constitute an academy in the Platonist or neo-Platonist sense, the subjects discussed being philosophic and encyclopaedic. Information on its subsequent history is, however, sparse, although nineteen years later a letter published in his life of the knight Bayard refers to the presence in Champier's house of the favourite court poet, Mellin de Saint-Gelais, who was renowned for his musical declamation and extolled as the French Serafino:

celle fois que tu fus en ma maison à Lyon avec plusieurs autres docteurs et lettrez, entre tous autres me pleut ton éloquence et aorné langaige.[15]

when you were in my house at Lyons with many other scholars and literary people, your eloquence and florid language pleased me more than all the others.

This letter does not, however, provide real evidence of the same academy's continued existence. Champier's house was not situated on Fourvière but near the Cordeliers' monastery (see Pl. 1). While Marguerite de Navarre and the French court were resident at Saint-Just in 1524, such meetings between Lyonese intellectuals and her neo-Platonist retinue must have been common, probably following the pattern of discussion described in Marguerite's *Heptameron*.

Fournier's name recurs in a letter by the neo-Latin poet Vulteius

(1483–1546)', *Annuaires de Lyon* (1840), 23; J.-B. Monfalcon, *Histoire monumentale de la ville de Lyon*, 9 vols. (Paris, 1866), ii. 97; Allut, *Étude biographique*, 63; E. Vial, 'La Légende de l'Académie de Fourvière', *Bibliothèque d'Humanisme et Renaissance*, 8 (1946), 253–66.

[13] See A. Della Torre, *Storia dell'Accademia Platonica di Firenze* (Florence, 1902).

[14] Champier, *Liber de quadruplici vita*, fo. G.

[15] S. Champier, *Les gestes ensemble la vie du preulx Chevalier Bayard* (Lyons, 1525), 3.

(Jean Visagier, 1510–42) dated 12 March 1537, lamenting the absence of Étienne Dolet and mentioning meetings under the auspices of the Italian writer, Girolamo Fondolo, attended also by the antiquarian Guillaume du Choul (Caulius), the lawyer-poet Benoît Court, the Protestant theologian Miguel Serveto, and the Scève cousins, Maurice and Guillaume.[16] In the late 1530s Vulteius and other neo-Latin poets refer to the fellowship of Lyonese friends (*sodalitium amicorum lugdunensium*), which also involved resident and visiting humanists like Rabelais, Marot, Scève, Champier, Aneau, Salmon Macrin, Charles Fontaine, Charles de Saint-Marthe, and Gilbert Ducher. However, despite the prominence of classical scholars, neo-Platonist philosophers, and neo-Latin poets in Lyons, the evidence suggests informal gatherings, literary salons rather than a permanent academy.

The coexistence of the medieval heritage—orthodox theology, scholasticism, and the idea of the 'summa'—with the new Florentine humanism places Champier in the third generation of Renaissance scholars. But the fourth book of his *Nef des dames vertueuses*,[18] an exposition of the Ficinian concept of love, albeit somewhat de-spiritualized and confused by the Christian ideal of marriage, bridges the gap between French scholars' first contact with the ideas of the Italian Renaissance and the introduction of these ideas into the mainstream of French literature after 1540 in the work of Des Périers, Héroët, Marguerite de Navarre, Scève, Du Guillet, Labé, and the Pléiade. Appearing in 1503, before Bembo's *Asolani*, Castiglione's *Cortegiano*, and Equicola's *Libro de natura d'Amore*, it marks the secularization of Florentine neo-Platonism and the awareness of the possibilities of Platonic love as a social force and as a literary theme.

After serving as physician to Duke Jean de Lorraine during the Italian campaigns in 1509 and 1515, Champier glorified France's chivalric heritage and military exploits in his popular biography of Bayard, first published at Lyons in 1525 and reprinted several times at Paris during the next few years.[19] Following the French defeat at Pavia, he returned to Lyons and, as a qualified doctor of law, served as an alderman between 1525 and 1529, when he published his history of the town, along with an account of the popular uprising and an outline of the town's government during the past fifty years.[20] Favouring the repressive measures of the governor, Pomponio Trivulzio, rather than

---

[16] Vial, 'La Légende', 258–9.   [17] J. Vulteius, *Epigrammaton libri IIII* (Lyons, 1537), 260.

[18] S. Champier, *Le livre de vraye amour*, ed. J. B. Wadsworth (The Hague, 1962).

[19] Champier, *Les gestes ensemble la vie du preulx Chevalier Bayard* (Lyons, G. de Villiers, 1525; repr. Paris, J. Trepperel, n.d.; Ph. Lenoir, n.d.; J. Byverd, 1525; A. Vérard, 1526; G. de Pré, 1527; J. Bonfons, n.d.; Lyons, O. Arnoullet, 1558; B. Rigaud, 1602, etc.).

[20] Champier, *Cy commence ung petit livre.*

the liberalism of the lieutenant-general, Jean du Peyrat, he saw 'artisans' (i.e. manual workers) as a necessary evil and considered their revolt in 1529 to have been instigated by the Swiss heretics. He supported the wine tax and regarded the proletariat's demand for unwatered wine as unreasonable and un-Christian, even referring to Plato to support his views.

However, Champier's name is connected with two philanthropic institutions which had an important influence on the Renaissance in Lyons: the Collège de la Trinité,[21] the municipal grammar school whose establishment he promoted, with the help of the Archbishop François de Rohan and his humanistic colleagues in the Consulate, Matthieu de Vauzelles and Claude Bellièvre (both of whom had also studied at Pavia),[22] and the Collège de Médecine, where his medical colleagues, Gonsalvo of Toledo, Jehan Canappe,[23] Pierre Tolet, and Rabelais practised and lectured. Bologna and Padua had been the most famous medical schools in the fifteenth century, but Lyons joined Montpellier in contesting this situation in the early sixteenth century. The publication of medical books in French, albeit mainly translations from Italian or Latin, reached significant proportions after 1500 and played an important role in the diffusion of Renaissance ideas.[24]

The prominent citizens of Lyons included a number of dedicated antiquarians. Pierre Sala (c.1470–c.1530),[25] author and translator of chivalric histories[26] and of 'Le Livre d'amitié'[27] (a collection of precepts and ideas on love gleaned from the Church Fathers and the ancients), bought a vineyard at Fourvière on the site of the Roman palace of Claudius, Caracalla and Germanicus, building a sumptuous house there in 1513. Diligently copying inscriptions and studying ancient writings, he recorded his observations in 'Les Antiquités de Lyon'.[28] After

---

[21] See above, Ch. 1, n. 18.

[22] E. Picot, *Les Professeurs et les étudiants de langue française à l'Université de Pavie aux XVe et au XVIe siècle* (Paris, 1916; reprinted from the *Bulletin philologique et historique* of 1915); L. de Vauzelles, 'Notice sur Matthieu de Vauzelles', *Revue du Lyonnais*, ser. 3, 9 (1870), 505–29; id., 'Poésies de Matthieu et de Jehan de Vauzelles', *Revue du Lyonnais*, ser. 4, 3 (1877), 429–42; 4 (1877), 20–30.

[23] See Baudrier, *Bibliographie lyonnaise*, v. 288–94.

[24] G. Barraud, *L'Humanisme et la médecine au XVIe siècle* (Paris, 1942); A. Cade, *Les Incunables médicaux lyonnais* (Lyons, 1942).

[25] P. Fabia, *Pierre Sala* (Lyons, 1934).

[26] P. Sala, 'Les Prouesses de plusieurs rois', Paris, Bibliothèque nationale, MS français 10420; 'Le Roman du Chevalier de Lyon', MS français 1628. Both are published in P. Sala, *Le Livre d'amytié*, ed. G. Guigue (Lyons, 1884), 34–47 and 48–9.

[27] Lyons, Bibliothèque municipale, MS 853 (dedicated to the author's brother-in-law, Claude de Laurencin, Baron de Rivirie); another copy in Paris, Bibliothèque nationale, MS français 14942 (dedicated to his friend, the painter Jean Perréal); ed. G. Guigue (Lyons, 1884).

[28] Paris, Bibliothèque nationale, MS français 5447.

travelling widely in Italy, like his fellow aldermen, Champier and Matthieu de Vauzelles, Claude Bellièvre (1487–1557) transformed the garden of his house on the Fourvière Hill into a museum modelled on the Riccardi palace in Florence and recorded his discoveries in a manuscript entitled 'Lugdunum priscum'.[29] Guillaume du Choul (Caulius), who also lived on Fourvière, was another keen archaeologist and numismatist,[30] while his son was the author of scholarly works on medicine and natural history.[31]

The liberal intellectual atmosphere which attracted humanists and free-thinkers, the early contact with the Italian Renaissance through the Florentine immigrants and the French transalpine campaigns, as well as the generous patronage of the luxury-loving Italian citizens and governors combined to make the southern capital the rival of Paris as a cultural centre in the second quarter of the sixteenth century. This would not have all been possible without the extraordinary activity of the printing industry, whose output eventually exceeded that of Paris, which suffered from the censorship of the Sorbonne and Parlement. The invention of printing from movable type reached Lyons in 1472 (a few years after Paris); the first surviving example of a vernacular book is Barthélemy Buyer's New Testament, printed for him by Guillaume le Roi under the supervision of two Augustine theologians, Julien Macho and Pierre Farget. The British Museum copy (IB 41510) is undated but the typography is the same as that used by Buyer in his *Lotharius Diaconus* of 1473. The Lyonese printers of the late fifteenth century were generally more humanistic and scholarly than their Parisian counterparts.[32] Indeed Josse Bade (1462–1535) worked in Lyons as an editor and corrector for the philosophical publications of Jean Treschel between 1491 and 1497, before setting up his own press in Paris. Meanwhile the Aldine counterfeits of Trot, Hugon, and others provided philologically sound texts of Virgil, Horace, Juvenal, Martial, Ovid, Dante, and Petrarch, stimulating an interest in classical language and literature.

The humanist advance was continued and extended in the sixteenth century by Sébastien Gryphe (c.1492–1556), a classical scholar and printer of German origin, who between 1524 and 1556 issued more than a thousand different editions in Hebrew, Greek, Latin, Italian,

---

[29] Ed. J.-B. Monfalcon (Lyons, 1846). See also C. Bellievre, *Souvenirs de voyages en Italie et en Orient*, ed. C. Perrat (Geneva, 1956).

[30] His archaeological activities are recorded in Lyons, Archives communales, CC 50, fo. 51ᵛ, and in J. Strada, *Epitome du Thrésor des Antiquitiés* (Lyons, 1553).

[31] Baudrier, *Bibliographie lyonnaise*, iv. 384.

[32] See A. Renaudet, *Préréforme et humanisme à Paris pendant les premières guerres d'Italie (1494–1517)* (Paris, 1916).

Spanish, and French (some using an italic type admired throughout Europe). Gryphe contributed more than most printers to the popularization of literature and the cause of intellectual progress. His readers and correctors included Rabelais and Dolet, the latter establishing his own press in the late 1530s. His foreman, Jean de Tournes (1504–64), also branched out on his own and established a family firm whose activity was to span more than two centuries.[33] Having assisted Gryphe in publishing Alamanni's *Opere Toscane* in 1532, De Tournes cultivated Italian literature, issuing elegant editions (of Petrarch in 1545 and 1550, Dante in 1547, Aretino in 1551, and the Florentine émigré poet Simeoni, in 1558–9), which were sold on both sides of the Alps. Guillaume Roville, whose model was the Venetian printer Giolito, also contested the Italian market with his editions of Boccaccio's *Decamerone* (1555) and Ariosto's *Orlando furioso* (1556, 1559, 1561, etc.), But both De Tournes and Roville continued to supply a large demand for the smaller and relatively cheap reprints of classical texts, and, like Claude Nourry and his successor François Juste, exploited the popular market for books in the vernacular.[34]

The popularity of books amongst the merchant class of Lyons is illustrated as early as 1495 in a warning about their potential distraction from commerce:

> Lire ystoyres et beaulx livres
> C'est ung passe temps gracieulx
> Tant ne liras que tu t'en ivres
> Plusieurs si font bi[e]n malheureux
> Trop les aymer n'est pour le mieulx
> A gens qui suyvent marchandise[35]

> Reading stories and fine books
> Is a gracious pastime.
> Read not so many that you become intoxicated.
> Many make themselves very unhappy because of them;
> Getting too attached to them is not good
> For people in business

The most renowned bibliophile of the early sixteenth century, Jean Grolier, Viscount of Aguisy (1479–1565), was a native of Lyons.[36]

---

[33] A. Cartier, *Bibliographie des éditions des de Tournes* (Paris, 1937).

[34] Most of these are catalogued in Baudrier, *Bibliographie lyonnaise*.

[35] F. Guarin, *Les complaintes et enseignemens de Françoys Guarin marchant de Lyon envoyées à son fils* (Lyons, n.d.), fo. b6ᵛ; a more corrupt edition printed in Paris in 1495 gives the poem on fo. b4ᵛ.

[36] See A. Leroux de Lincy, *Recherches sur Jean Grolier* (Paris, 1866); for a rev. edn. by R. Portalis, tr. C. Shipman, see *Researches concerning Jean Grolier* (New York, 1907); see also W. L. Andrews, *Jean Grolier de Servier ... Some Account of His Life and of His Famous Library* (New York, 1892).

Financier and statesman, he served Francis I as intendant of the army during the Italian campaigns, ambassador at Rome between 1524 and 1530, and treasurer of France from 1545. Throughout his long life he remained a keen antiquarian and a generous literary patron. His friends included Erasmus, Budé, the neo-Latin poets Nicolas Bourbon and Jean Visagier, and the Milanese musician and theorist, Franchino Gafori (1451–1522).[37]

Grolier's library contained over three thousand books, of which about ten per cent survive, including three theoretical works by Gafori, who was Francis I's 'regius musicus' in Milan during the second decade of the sixteenth century, when Grolier lived in the town:

1. *Angelicum ac divinum opus musice Franchini Gafurii Laudensis regii musici, ecclesiaeque Mediolanensis phonasci, materna lingua scriptum*, Milan, G. de Ponte, 1508. (Copies in Paris, Bibliothèque Sainte-Geneviève are inscribed 'Grolieri et amicorum').

2. *Franchini Gafuri Laudensis regii publice profitentis delubrique Mediolanensis phonasci de Harmonia musicorum instrumentorum opus*, Milan, G. de Ponte, 1518. (Copies in Paris, Bibliothèque de l'Arsenal, and Manchester, Rylands Memorial Library, and bound in brown calf with Grolier's arms in colour).

3. *Apologia Franchini Gafuri musici adversus Joannem Spatarium et complices musicos Bononienses*, Turin, A. de Vicermercato, 1520. (Copies in Paris, Bibliothèque nationale, and London, British Library).

The last two of these books were actually dedicated to the Lyonese bibliophile: the *Apologia*, an acrid reply to the criticism of Giovanni Spataro (*maestro* at San Petronio, Bologna), who questioned Gafori's calculations on intervallic proportions, calls on Grolier, described at the end of the book as 'musarum cultor', to arbitrate in the dispute, the inference being that he was well enough versed in music to be a respected judge. The dedication on the last folio indicates that Gafori enjoyed Grolier's patronage:

Quo fit: ut . . . harmonia Gafurii et Ioannes Grolierius patronus aeternum vivant

so shall the harmony of Gafori and his patron Jean Grolier live forever

Gafori's treatise on the harmony of instrumental (i.e. practical) music (Milan, 1518) is prefaced by a poem from Mauro Ugerio of Mantua, indicating that Grolier opened his house to musicians, poets, and philosophers, including perhaps Guillaume du Choul (Caulius).

---

[37] See A. Caretta, L. Cremascoli, and L. Salamina, *Franchino Gaffurio* (Lodi, 1951); C. A. Miller, 'Gaffurius's *Practica Musicae*: Origin and Contents', *Musica disciplina*, 22 (1968), 105–28.

...Grolieria tendite ad Antra
Mille sonant Cantus Dulcia Mille modos.
Vos ibi dicebant sedem posuisse Camoenae
Musica Franchini nosco sed illa fuit.
Illic fulgenti residet Grolierius Aula
Et secum Doctos continet ille viros.
Coelius inter quos facundo prominet Ore
Et nitet ut leves gemma per articulos.[38]

[Muses]...go to Grolier's house [where]
Sweetly they sound a thousand songs, a thousand tunes.
There the Camenae said you had established your seat.
But it was (I recognize) the music of Franchinus.
Grolier resides there in a resplendent palace,
And with him there he keeps learned men,
Prominent among whom is the eloquent Caulius,
Who gleams like a gem on smooth fingers...

(ii) *Jean Lemaire de Belges (c.1473–c.1524)*

Music, musicians, and musical instruments were favourite subjects for illustration and imagery in the work of the *Grands Rhétoriqueurs* like Jean Lemaire's 'précepteur et parent' Jean Molinet (1435–1507), historiographer, poet, and musician at the Burgundian court, friend of Ockeghem, Busnois, and Cornuel.[39] In Lemaire's *Temple de Venus*, which was associated with Lyons and perhaps in particular with the cathedral of Saint-Jean, where the musicians of Louis XII and Philippe le Beau performed together on 2 April 1503, the musical tradition is strongly maintained with many references both old and new:

Là est Venus, par musique enchantée
Et tout le chant prent d'amours accordance
Ou volupté, sans nulle autre est hantée
.   .   .   .

Et là seant, les oyseaux entonnerent
Ung doulx canticque, entrebrisé d'accordz.
Dont les paroys du temple resonerent
Philomena moduloit ses recordz

---

[38] F. Gafori, *De harmonia musicorum instrumentorum opus* (Milan, 1518); in his English translation C. A. Miller (Musicological Studies and Documents, 33; American Institute of Musicology, 1977), 31, interprets *Coelius* as 'More godlike'; Miller indicates that the dedication to Grolier was added later to a manuscript version (Vienna, Österreichische Nationalbibliothek, Cod. SN 12745) copied in 1507—two years before Grolier became Louis XII's treasurer and Intendant in Milan.

[39] See N. Dupire, *Jean Molinet* (Paris, 1932); M. Brenet, 'Jehan Molinet et la musique', *Revue de musicologie*, 1 (1920), 21–7; C. MacClintock, 'Molinet, Music, and Medieval Rhetoric', *Musica disciplina*, 13 (1960), 109–21.

Contretenant à progne l'arondelle
Par ung doulx bruyt, accordant sons discordz
   Merles, mauvis, de plusbelle en plusbelle
Serins, tarins, faisans proportions
Murmuroient, par tenson non rebelle
   Chardonneretz, en diminutions
Lynottes, jays, trestous, a qui mieulx mieulx
Firent ouyr leurs jubilations
   Leurs poingz d'orgues volerent aux haulx cieulx
Leurs versetz, ditz alternativement
Delecterent les oreilles des dieux
   Et quant leur hympne eut prins deffinement
Il vint avant maint nouvel Arion
Maint Orpheus, jubilant doulcement
   D'un viel Terpandre, ou d'un viel Amphion
D'un Appollo, harpant en sa quoquille
On n'a plus cure et si les deffie on
   Pour ung Lynus, chantant de voix tranquille
Ung Tamyras, Thubal ou Pictagore
Il en est cent, et pour cent en est mille
   Au nouveau chant, à la nouvelle gorre
Venus s'endort, mieulx que au chant des seraines
Ou que a menger pavotz et mandragore
   Tous vieux flaiotz, guisternes primeraines
Psalterions et anciens decacordes
Sont assourdiz par harpes souveraines
   Par le doulx son, des nouveaulx monocordes
Ont mis soubz banc les gens du Roy Clovis
Leurs viielles [sic], leurs vieux plectres et cordes
   Et maintenant frequentent a devis
Les cueurs divins, les pupitres dorez
Anges nouveaux, dont les cieulx sont serviz
   Ou fin milieu, du cueur, ouyr pourrez
Entrebriser musicque Alexandrine
Et de Josquin les verbes coulourez
   Puis d'Ockeghem l'armonie tres fine
Les termes doulx de Loyset Compere
Font melodie aux cieulx, mesme confine.
      .   .   .   .

   Musiciens de leurs voix symphonisent
Et leurs buseaux unanimes concordent
Soufflent, harpent, typanent, citharisent.[40]

---

[40] Lemaire, *La Concorde*, fos. C3–C4; J. Lemaire, *Œuvres*, ed. J. Stecher, 4 vols. (Louvain, 1882–91), iii. 110–12.

There is Venus, enchanted by music,
And the whole melody accords with love
On to which voluptuousness alone is grafted
   .   .   .   .

   And sitting there, the birds intoned
A sweet canticle, broken up with interchanging chords
With which the temple walls resounded.
   Philomena modulated her recorder,
A countertenor to Procne, the swallow,
With a sweet noise harmonizing discordant sounds,
   Blackbirds, thrushes, more and more beautiful,
Canaries, and finches, making proportions,
Twittered a *tenso* without conflict.
   Goldfinches, in diminutions,
Linnets and jays, all vying with each other,
Expressed their jubilation.
   Their pedal points flew up to the heavens,
Their versets in alternation
Delighted the ears of the gods.
   And when their hymn was over,
There appeared many a new Arion,
Many an Orpheus, sweetly jubilating.
   For old Terpander or old Amphion,
For Apollo, harping in his shell,
People care no more, and so defy them.
   For each Linus, singing with tranquil voice,
Thamyras, Tubal, or Pythagoras,
There are a hundred, and for each hundred a thousand
   To the new song in the new mode,
Venus sleeps better than to the sirens' song,
Or than after eating poppy [seed] and mandrake [root].
   All old flageolets, early gitterns,
Psalteries and ancient decachords
Are deafened by sovereign harps.
   With the sweet sound of the new monochords,
The people of King Clovis have put away
Their fiddles [hurdy-gurdies], their old plectra and strings.
   And now want to keep company with
The divine choirs [and] the golden music stands
[Of the] new angels with which the heavens are served.
   Where in the very middle of the choir you can hear
The interchanging broken phrases of Agricola
And the expressive word-setting of Josquin.
   Then the very fine harmony of Ockeghem [and]
The sweet language of Loyset Compère

Give melody to the heavens, even when heard indoors.

.   .   .   .

Musicians with their voices [join in] symphony,
And with their unanimous pipes concord,
Blowing, harping, drumming, and plucking the cithara.

The introduction of the Tuscan *terza rima* form is an innovation in French verse, but the mixture of old and new (e.g. Terpander and Compère, monochords, psalteries, and guitars, Sapphic odes and *virelais*) is familiar. The comparison of the hymn of the goldfinches and linnets—with its 'pedal-points' and 'alternating verses'—to the music of Arion, Orpheus, Terpander, and Amphion reflects the increasing intrusion of classical figures as a literary convention. Like Molinet, Lemaire praises the music of Ockeghem; but he includes that of the younger generation, singling out Agricola, Compère, and Josquin. This does not prove their presence in Lyons, although it remains probable: Agricola certainly arrived in the town, with Philippe le Beau's musical chapel, *en route* from Brussels to Madrid on 22 March 1503 while Josquin passed through on his journey from Paris to Ferrara in April 1503.

In his second Epistle to the Green Lover, written in 1505 to console Margaret of Austria on the death of her beloved parrot, Lemaire again embellishes the traditional theme of the birds' concert with reference to the modern techniques of the polyphonic motet and chanson:

Car les oiseaux de tant diverses plumes
Diversement ung motet entonnerent,
Et si tresdoulx, flajolans jargonnerent
Que impossible est noter leurs chansonnettes
Et leurs motetz tant beaux et tant honnestes.
L'une partie au bas barritonna,
Et l'autre après ung hault contre entonna;
Les cleres voix fort bien diminuerent
Et les teneurs leur train continuerent;...[41]

For the birds with such diverse feathers
Diversely intoned a motet,
And worked with such sweet fluting
That it is impossible to notate their *chansonnettes*
And their motets so fine and so gracious.
One part baritoned in the bass
And another then intoned a countertenor;
The high voices were very good at diminution [division]
And the tenors sustained their line;...

Only one text by Lemaire is known to have been set to music, 'Soubz ce tumbel qui est ung dur conclave', the final quatrain epitaph from the

---

[41] *La seconde epistre de lamant Verd*, fo. 5ᵛ; ed. J. Stecher, iii. 32.

first Epistre de Lamant Verd.[42] However, Stecher's edition of Lemaire's works includes 'Plus nulz regretz', a 'chanson nouvel' celebrating the Treaty of Calais, announced on 1 January 1508, which was set for four voices by Josquin des Prez.[43] Moreover, in 1533 Attaingnant ascribed to 'J. lemaire' the now famous four-part music later attributed to Josquin (1549) of 'Mille regretz', a quatrain whose words could well have been written by Margaret of Austria's court poet.[44]

(iii) Symphorien Champier (1472–1539)

Like Lemaire and Fournier, Champier describes his enchantment with the dawn chorus of birds in a *ballade* in the *Nef des princes*:

> Je n'ouys oncques si grande armonye
> Advis m'estoit qu'estoye en paradis
> Tant je trouvay illec de melodie
> Que tous mes sens de joye sont ravys . . .[45]

> I never heard such great harmony;
> I thought I was in Paradise,
> So much melody did I find there
> That all my senses were enraptured

More significant musically is his philosophical treatise on the 'Symphony' of the spiritual doctors, Plato and Aristotle, and the physical doctors, Hippocrates and Galen. The title-page of Josse Bade's edition (Paris, 1514) is illustrated with a woodcut of the four authorities symbolically conjoined as a string quartet, with Galen leading the group on the fiddle and the others playing viols of differing size. Champier explains 'Symphony' as follows:

Symphonia apud latinos penultima correpta consonantia & musicus concentus dicitur. Musici symphonias multas habent: que & harmonie dicuntur: sed illam clarissimam que appelatur Diatessaron: & alteram que dicitur Diapente.

---

[42] Lemaire, *La premiere epistre de Lamant Verd*, fo. 3ʳ; ed. Stecher, iii. 26. The anonymous four-voice setting in Brussels, Bibliothèque Royale, MS 228, no. 24 is published in M. Picker, *The Chanson Albums of Marguerite of Austria* (Berkeley and Los Angeles, 1965), 275–8.

[43] Lemaire, *Œuvres*, ed. Stecher, iv. 267–8. Josquin's musical setting follows 'Soubz ce tumbel' in Brussels, Bibliothèque Royale, MS 228, no. 25; cf. Picker, *Chanson Albums*, 280–5; also ed. A. Smijers, *Josquin des Prez, Werken: Wereldlijke Werken* (Amsterdam and Leipzig, 1926), no. 29.

[44] See *Werken: Wereldlijke Werken*, no. 24. The possibility of Lemaire also being the author of the text of Josquin's five-part motet-chanson 'Cueurs desolez' is discussed in M. Picker, 'Josquin and Jean Lemaire: Four Chansons Re-examined', in S. Bertelli and G. Ramakus (eds.), *Essays Presented to Myron P. Gilmore*, 2 vols. (Florence, 1978), ii. 447–56. See also F. Dobbins, 'Lemaire (de Belges), Jean', *New Grove Dictionary of Music* (London, 1980), x. 61.

[45] S. Champier, *La Nef des princes* (Lyons, 1502), fo. 12ʳ.

Harmoniam vero diapason vocant: hoc est universitatem concent[us] que ex septem tonis conficitur. Hieronymus vero ad Damasum sic habet: Symphonia non est genus organi: ut male quidam de latinis putant: cum sit chorus in laude dei concinens; & hoc vocabulo significetur. Symphonia quippe in latinum consonantia exprimitur. Symphonon consonans pactum. Symphoneo convenio: pactum facio: consentio: concino.[46]

To the Latins *Symphonia*, with a short penultimate syllable, meant consonance and musical agreement. Musicians have many *symphoniae* which are also called harmonies: but the most famous is that called Diatessaron, and the second called *Diapente*. The harmony called *Diapason* is the whole concord, made up of seven tones. Jerome, writing to Damasus, expressed it thus: Symphonia is not a kind of *organum* [instrument], as some of the Latin writers wrongly suppose: it is rather a choir singing together in praise of God; this what is meant by the word. In fact [the Greek] *Symphonia* is translated in Latin as consonance, *Symphonon* a concerted agreement, *Symphoneo* I agree, I make an agreement, I consent, I concur.

A later section of the book, entitled 'Philosophia Platonica', includes a Latin version of the *Timaeus* with two long commentaries.

Champier's last publication, a brief encyclopaedia of Platonic and Aristotelian philosophy, discussing the liberal arts (except grammar), medicine, theology, law, and politics, contains a chapter on music as part of the section dealing with mathematical speculation:

Musicae quoque operam dabimus ut ad illa eadem auditum alliciamus trahamusque, nam ut oculorum acies ad astronomiam, sic auditus ad numerum se habet sonorum. Atque astronomie vacantes à visibilibus ad invisibilem intelligibilemque illam substantiam contemplandam ducimur: Ita et vocem auribus sonoram percipientes à rebus quae auditu percipiuntur, ad ea quae mente contemplanda sunt eodem modo transimus. At si aliter, ut dictum est, hisce utuntur disciplinis, inutilis ac supervacanea nulliusque rationis digna nostra speculatio erit. Musica naturalis est et artificialis: naturalis humana et mundana: humana tribus animi partibus: intellectu, sensibus, habitu; tres efficit et rationes, diapason: diapente: diatessaron. Prima enim Ptolemæus inquit, septem continet, mentem, imaginationem, memoriam, cogitationem, opinionem, rationem, scientiam. Quo numero consonantia constat, quae vocantur ex omnibus. Secunda quatuor, visum, auditum, olfactum, tactum, nam in eo gustatus est: aequas numero partes quinariae partibus. Tertia rursum tres: actum, fastigium, decrementum: cui quaternaria respondent. Item si partes animae feceris, rationis, [i]rae, cupiditatisque sedes. In prima septem sunt: acumen, ingenium, solertia, consilium, sapientia, prudentia, [experientia]. In altera quatuor: aequanimitas, impaviditas, fortitudo, tolerantia. In tertia tres: continentia, temperantia, verecundia, quibus triplex eadem symphonia

---

[46] S. Champier, *Symphonia Platonis cum Aristotele: et Galeni cum Hippocrate* (Paris, 1514; prefatory epistle dated 27 Oct. 1513), fo. a3[r].

conflatur. Omnia autem inter se concordia iusticia nominantur. Item trinis generibus spectativae partis & activae tria illa congruunt. Enharmonion, naturali moralique: diatonicon, divino & civili: Chromaticum, mathematico & aeconomico. Productionum vero mutationes vitae morumque conversionibus respondent. Mundana musica cernitur in eo quod coelestium motus sicuti pthongus diastemate constat circularesque ambitus harmonicorum systematum referunt. Quae omnia diligentissime prosequitur Ptolemaeus. Artificialis autem harmonia aut rhytmica, aut metrica est. Harmonicae partes septem, soni, spacia, systemata, genera, toni, mutationes, modulatio. Sonorum potestates infinitae: sed et quae traditae sunt omittantur: quoniam vitamus insolentia peregrinarum vocum.[47]

We should also turn our attention to music so that we may relate hearing to those same things. For just as vision is to astronomy so is hearing to sounds in number. As when devoting our time to astronomy, we are led from the visible to contemplate the invisible and intellectual essence: so too perceiving the sound of a voice in our ears, we move in like manner from things perceived by the ear to those which must be contemplated in the mind. But if, as has been said, these disciplines are used in any other way, our speculation will be futile, meaningless and unworthy of account. Music is [of two kinds], natural and artificial: natural [music is] human and mundane: human [music] through three parts of the mind, divided into the intellect, the senses, and the character; it produces three relations, *diapason, diapente, diatessaron*. The first of these, as Ptolemy explains, contains seven [things]: mind, imagination, memory, thought, opinion, reason, and knowledge. In this number stands the consonance, that is called 'from all' [i.e. *diapason* or octave]. The second [part] has four [things]: sight, hearing, smell, touch (for this includes taste): its parts are equal in number to the parts of a *quinaria*. [i.e. *diapente* or fifth] The third [part] again has three things—rise, apex, fall—corresponding to the *quaternaria*. [i.e. *diatessaron* or fourth]. Similarly, if you consider the parts of the mind as seats of reason, temper, and desire, in the first part there are seven [things]: acumen, natural ability, shrewdness, advisedness, wisdom, prudence [and experience]. In the second [part], four: equanimity, fearlessness, fortitude, and endurance. In the third [part], three: restraint, temperance, and reserve, from which the same triple consonance results. However, all [these things] together in concord are justice. Likewise these three [genera] agree with the categories of the theoretical part and the three of the practical part: enharmonic, with the natural and moral; diatonic, with the divine and civil; chromatic, with the mathematical and the economic. The variations correspond to the revolutions of life and manners. Cosmic music may be discerned in the fact that the

[47] S. Champier, *Symphoriani Champerii philosophi ac medici ingenio eruditioneque summi viri libri VII de Dialectica, Rhethorica, Geometria, Arithmetica, Astronomia, Musica, Philosophia naturali, Medicina et Theologia: Et de legibus et repub. eaque parte philosophiae quae de moribus tractat. Atque haec omnia sunt tractata ex Aristotelis et Platonis sententia* (Basle, 1537), 23–4. Champier's list of mental qualities omits the seventh, which Ptolemy (*Harmonica* 3. 5, ed. I. Düring in Göteborgs Högskolas Årsskrift, 36/1 (1930), 97, ll. 16–20) gives as *emeiria*, translated here as *experientia*.

movement of heavenly bodies, just as musical sound consists in fixed intervals and recalls the circular revolutions of harmonic systems. Ptolemy explained all this most carefully. On the other hand, artificial [music] is rhythmic or metrical harmony. Harmony has seven parts: sounds, intervals, systems, *genera, tonoi,* mutations, [and] modulation. The powers of sounds are infinite, yet, let even those discussed by our predecessors be omitted, since we avoid the strangeness of foreign words.

This extract provides the key to the Renaissance attitude to music as expressed by the literary humanists. Their concept was fundamentally Platonist: the only music considered worthy of discussion was *naturalis* (or, to follow Boethius, *mundana*), i.e. metaphysical; to Plato and his medieval imitators it bridged the gap between the tangible and the intangible (or, in the Christianized transposition of Ficino, between the mind and the soul); to classical and medieval educationalists it stood alongside geometry, arithmetic, and astronomy in the *quadrivium* of the seven liberal arts—as outlined in the title of Champier's book. The references to Ptolemy, the third-century astronomer, mathematician, and author of the *Harmonics*, reflect the extension of Plato's interest in Pythagorean numerology. Only the *ethos* or doctrine of affects is neglected—and due apology is made for this. Melody is not mentioned independently of harmony, while practical ('artificial') music was deemed a subject fit only for 'vulgar' professionals—a view expressed in Plutarch's *Moralia* and shared by the Milanese choirmaster Gafori, who devoted most of his efforts to theoretical and speculative writing. The Platonic tradition continued by the respected philosophers— Aristotle, Aristoxenus, Cleonides, and Boethius—was reinforced by the humanists' regard for the oldest classical authorities.

(iv) *François Rabelais (1494–c.1553)*

After abandoning monastic orders to study medicine at Montpellier, François Rabelais worked as a physician in the municipal hospital at Lyons between 1532 and 1534; he assisted Sebastien Gryphe in editing Hebrew, Greek, and Latin works and wrote a number of scientific works, which he published alongside the first books of his *Gargantua* and *Pantagruel.* Also printed in Lyons was the sequel to this saga, with the Third Book (1546), the Fourth (1552); and the Fifth (1564 posthumously expanded from a rough draft).

All the books include reference to Lyons and its people, as well as to music, which is frequently used for rhetorical effect and witty charac- terization. Thus in ch. 6 of *Gargantua* (1534) the baby giant rocks himself to sleep 'strumming with his fingers and baritoning with his bum' (*monochordisant des doigtz et baritonant du cul*).[48] In ch. 21 we learn that his studies include the 'other mathematical sciences, like geometry, astronomy, and music. For while waiting for the concoction and digestion of his repast, they made myriad joyful instruments and geometric figures, and even practised astronomical canons. Afterwards they amused themselves singing music in four or five parts or improvising embellishments upon a theme. By way of musical instruments he learned to play the lute, the spinet, the harp, the flute and recorder, the viol, and the sackbut' (*aultres sciences mathematicques, comme Geometrie, Astronomie et Musicque. Car attendans la concoction et digestion de son past, ilz faisoient mille joyeulx instrumens et figures Geometriques, et de mesmes pratiquoient les canons Astronomiques. Après, s'esbaudissoient à chanter musicalement à quatre et cinq parties, ou suz un theme, à plaisir de guorge. Et au reguard des instrumens de musicque, il aprint jouer du luc, de l'espinette, de la harpe, de la fluste de Alemant et à neuf trouz, de la viole et de la sacqueboutte*). Rabelais thus continued to regard music as part of the quadrivium and felt that a well-educated giant should be able to sing polyphonic music and to play a variety of instruments, all except the sackbut being the very instruments represented in the contemporary publications of Paris and Lyons, intended for enthusiastic amateurs. Later in the same chapter he suggests that music and singing were, like dice and cards, suitable evening pastimes.

Typical of Rabelais's amusing use of technical musical terms is his comment, in the seventh chapter of *Pantagruel*, on the innate stupidity of Parisians, punning on music's naturals, sharps, and flats: (*le peuple de Paris est sot par nature, par béquarre et par bémol*). Another example is found in ch. 9 bis, where in legalistic gobbledygook Baisecul (Kissarse) and Humevesne (Smellyfart) relate that 'court gentlemen were giving the pox a *flat* order to stop going about after tinkers, . . . since the clods had already made a good start on dancing a jig at the octave' (*Messieurs de la court feissent par bémol commandement à la vérolle, de non plus alleboter après les maignans . . . car les marroufles avoient jà bon commencement à dancer l'estrindore au diapason*). In similar vein is Panurge's order to the captured King Anarch in ch. 21 to sing in the higher hexachord on G (*Chante plus hault, en g, sol, ré, ut*), or his fearful cries during a storm at sea in the nineteenth chapter of the *Quart Livre*: 'Alas! we are higher than E *la*, beyond any scale . . .

---

[48] The chapter references given are from the following editions: F. Rabelais, *Gargantua*, ed. R. Calder (Geneva, 1970); *Pantagruel*, ed. V. L. Saulnier (Geneva, 1965); *Le Tiers Livre*, ed. M. A. Screech (Geneva, 1964); *Le Quart Livre*, ed. R. Marischal (Geneva, 1947), *Le Cinquiesme Livre*, ed. J. Plattard (Paris, 1948).

[now] we are below the bottom of the gamut (*Zalas! nous sommes au dessus de E la, hors toute la gamme . . . sommes nous au dessoubs de Gamma ut*). Similarly, in ch. 38 of the *Tiers Livre* the royal jester Triboulet is described as a 'Fool on the highest scale, a fool by nature, a fool on B natural and B flat, a modal fool, a baritoning fool, an octave fool'. (*Fol de haulte gamme, Fol de nature, For de b quarre et de b mol, Fol modal, Fol barytonant, Fol en diapason*).

Rabelais's evident knowledge of music theory may in part be explained by his borrowing from Aristotle's pupil Theophrastus, as in ch. 62 of the *Quart Livre*, which reports that 'the more tuneful elder-bushes, most suited to the making of flutes, grow in places where no cocks are heard to crow, (*le suzeau croist plus canore et plus apte au jeu des flustes en pays on quel le chant des coqs ne sera ouy*); this, like the disciples of Pythagoras, he interprets allegorically to mean that 'wise and studious people should not devote themselves to trivial and vulgar music, but to the celestial, divine, angelic, and more abstruse branches of the art, which are brought from further afield' (*les gens saiges et studieux ne se doibvent adonner à la musique triviale et vulgaire, mais à la céleste, divine, angelique, plus absconse et de plus loing apportée*).

This reflection of his classical education is balanced by his interest in modern composers, fifty-eight of whom are listed in the New Prologue to the Fourth Book (1552). He divides these composers into two groups, with the first twenty-five, including Josquin, Ockeghem, Obrecht, Agricola, Brumel, de la Fage, Mouton, Compère, Févin, Conseil and other famous old masters, along with a few unfamiliar names like Camelin, Vigoris, Seguin, and Midi, singing an erotic dizain beginning with the words 'Grand Tibault se voulant coucher'. Thirty-seven years later Priapus hears another group of thirty-seven, including Willaert, Gombert, Janequin, Arcadelt, Claudin, Certon, Manchicourt, and Morales, as well as the less familiar Auxerre, Villiers, Pagnier, Millet, du Mollin, and Marault, singing a ribald quatrain beginning 'S'il est ainsi que coingnée sans manche'. Most of these composers are known through their chansons, motets, and masses published by Antico in Rome and Venice or by Moderne in Lyons, although both the chansons cited were actually set for four voices (by Janequin and Vassal respectively) in the thirteenth book of chansons published by Attaingnant in Paris in 1543: a setting of 'S'il est ainsi' by Fresneau was also published by Moderne in Lyons in 1544.

Whether or not it was written by Rabelais, the Fifth Book continues to show an intimate knowledge of musical theory and practice. Thus in ch. 20 we read how the queen Quint Essence cured every sickness merely by playing a chanson, chosen according to the nature of the illness, on a strange organ, with pipes of cassia sticks, a sounding-board of guaicum, stops of rhubarb, pedals of turbith, and a keyboard of scammany. Chapters 24 and 25 include a detailed account of the music for a ballet—*un bal joyeux en forme de tournoy*—danced upon a carpet in the pattern of a chessboard, with two bands of eight liveried musicians playing 'various fantastic instruments marvellously concordant and melodious, changing the mood by key, time, and measure' (*instrumens tous divers, de joyeuse invention, ensemble concordans et melodieux, varians en tons, en temps et mesure*). For the second tournament the music was half a beat faster (*la musique fut en mesure serrée d'un demy temps plus que le précedente*); while the third dance was even quicker than hemiola proportion, using the warlike Phrygian mode invented by Marsyas (*Et fut la musique serrée en la mesure plus que hemiole, en intonation Phrygienne et bellique, comme celle qu'inventa Marsyas*). A little later in ch. 25 is a repeat of the familiar story of the effects of music, transferred from Timotheus to Ismenias: 'we felt even more moved by the emotion and fear aroused in our hearts by the sound of the music; and I could well believe how with such modulation Ismenias excited Alexander, sitting peacefully at dinner, to rise and take up arms' (*encore plus sentions nous nos cœurs esmeus et effrayez à l'intonation de la musique; et croyais facilement que par telle modulation Ismenias excita Alexandre le Grand, estant à table, et disnant en repos, à soy lever et armes prendre*).

In ch. 27 the description of the monks on the Isle of Sandals abounds in musical terms; thus we meet the Semiquaver Friars (the *Freres Fredons*, whose name was a variation on that of their mainland counterparts, the Servites), the Minor Friars 'who are Papal bulls' semibreves' (*Freres Mineurs qui sont semibriefs de bulles*), the Minim Friars (*Freres Minimes*), and the crotchety Minim Friars (*Freres Minimes crochus*), there being no further division than the semiquaver (*que du nom plus diminuer ne pouvoit qu'en Fredons*). 'By statute and bull patent obtained from the Fifth [or Quint Essence], who was well tuned to everyone', the Semiquaver Friars were dressed as arsonists (*Par les statuts et bulle patente obtenue de la Quinte, laquelle est de tous bons accords, ils estoient tous habillez en brusleurs de maisons*). They also had an odd way of melodiously singing antiphons in their own dialect, 'through their teeth or, on closer inspection, through their ears, tuning their beautiful harmony to their bell-ringing' (*ils fredonnoient entre les dens melodieusement ne sçay quelles antiphones, car je n'entendois leur patelin: et ententivement escoutant, apperceu qu'ils ne chantoient que des aureilles. O la belle armonie et bien concordante au son de leurs cloches!*).

Incorporated as ch. 33 *bis* into the later editions of the Fifth Book from a manuscript now in the Bibliothèque nationale was a list of 175 dances performed after supper by the courtiers of Lanternland to the sound of *bouzines* (shawms). The list had already appeared in the anonymous *Disciple de Pantagruel* (Lyons, 1538) and was in turn taken from a list of 184 dances with their steps published as *S'ensuyvent plusieurs Basses dances tant Communes que Incommunes* (probably by Moderne) in Lyons between 1530 and 1538.[49]

The unusual ubiquity of references to music theory, instruments, and chansons led Nan Cooke Carpenter[50] to assume that Rabelais had been trained as a choirboy and that he pursued musical studies at Paris, Montpellier, and other universities. She also interpreted his satirical and perjorative references to liturgical plainchant and polyphony as a reaction to unpleasant experiences as choirboy and monk, attributing his more sympathetic use of Clément Marot's metrical translation of Psalm 114, 'Quand Israel hors d'Egypte sortit' in the *Quart Livre* (ch. 1) to Protestant proclivities. These proclivities, like the neo-Platonist tone of the later allusions to theoretical music, no doubt owed much to the humanist environment of Lyons in the 1530s.

(v) *Étienne Dolet (1509–1546)*

Étienne Dolet, humanist, orator, poet, philologist, and printer, held agnostic views (notably the denial of the immortality of the soul) which eventually led to his imprisonment and execution in the Place Maubert in Paris.[51] Like Champier, he must have been imbued with Platonic philosophy during his studies at Padua (1527–30); having completed the dialogues of Axiochus and Hipparchus in the *Second Enfer* (1544), he expressed the intention of translating all Plato's works. After publishing his vast philological Commentaries on the Latin language with Sébastien Gryphe, he established his own press in Lyons in 1538, printing the major works of Marot and Rabelais during the next five years.

In the second volume of his Latin Commentaries he proclaims his enthusiasm for music:

---

[49] See F. Lesure, 'Danses et chansons à danser au début du xvie siècle', in *Recueil de travaux offert à M. Clovis Brunel* (Paris, 1955), 165–84; repr. in F. Lesure, *Musique et musiciens français du XVIe siècle* (Geneva, 1976), 51–9.

[50] N. C. Carpenter, *Rabelais and Music* (Chapel Hill, NC., 1954).

[51] For further details on Dolet's life see Christie, *Étienne Dolet*, and O. Galtier, *Étienne Dolet* (Paris, 1908).

Musica inquam, & symphonia mea est una, & sola voluptas. Qua quid vel ad commovendos, vel sedandos animos accomodatius? quid ad molliendas, iras, & extinguendas, vel inflammandas aptius? quid ad oblectanda literatorum ingenia convenientius? Cibo, potu, ludo, venere facile abstinebo: vel modice certe utar. Symphonia non item: quo una omnium maxime ducor, capior, teneor, retineor, liquesco: cum vitam ipsam debeo: cui omnes meorum omnium studiorum conatus. Atque hic adeo fac tibi in mentem veniat, & sine dubitatione credas, non me tam assiduos, tam immensos, tam infinitos in his Commentariis conficiendis labores subire potuisse, nisi symphonia modo delinitum, modo acrius incensum, & ad commentationem fastidio abiectam revocatum.[52]

My only pleasures are music and harmony. What is there more suited to either exciting or soothing the mind? what more apt for allaying and extinguishing, or arousing anger? what more efficacious for delighting the talents of the learned? I can easily do without the pleasures of the table, of wine, of gaming, of love; certainly I will use them all in great moderation. But not so with harmony, which above all things guides me, captivates me, holds me, keeps me, and melts my heart: to it I owe my life itself; to it I owe all the endeavours of my studies. And I would even go so far as to suggest to you, and I believe it without doubt, that I could never have supported the incessant, immense, endless labour of compiling these Commentaries without harmony to soothe my feelings or to rouse my passion, recalling me to my commentary which I had thrown aside in disgust.

What does Dolet mean by *musica*? He recognizes Amphion as its inventor and admits a technical interpretation of the term in the vernacular sense: 'Musicam vulgo scientiam appellant, quae modum canendi demonstrat' (Music is commonly called the science that shows the method of singing). Yet, the mental and spiritual recreation he talks of above are derived from the Ancients' interpretation, signifying literature and fine arts:

Musicae vero appellatione Prisci humanitatem literarum significarunt: in qua ingenuos homines docebant ocium conterere, animumque recreare... quia Musica, velut ludus, animi a curis vexati est requies.[53]

Now by music the Ancients meant the cultivation of letters: with it they taught noble men how to spend their leisure and how to restore their spirits... because Music, just like games, is rest for the mind vexed with cares.

Dolet also recognized the encyclopaedic nature of music fourteen years before Tyard.[54]

---

[52] Dolet, *Commentarii Linguae Latinae* (Lyons, 1536–88), col. 1294.

[53] Ibid., col. 1295.

[54] This point is not mentioned in Frances Yates, 'Poetry and Music and the Encyclopedia', in *The French Academies of the Sixteenth Century* (London, 1947), 77–94.

Nam musicam veteres encylopediam dixere, in qua omnes artes sunt comprehensae.[55]

For the Ancients said that music was encyclopaedic, since it embraces all the arts.

He goes on to define various terms (*Symphonia*, *Symphoniacus*, *Canere*, *Cantor*, *Cantus*, *Cantare*, *Concentus*, *Psallere*, *Modulari*, etc.), mentioning Greek drama and Plautus, as well as numerology, voices, and modes, quoting as his authorities Damon, Aristoxenus, Cicero (*De Oratore* and *De Natura Deorum*), Quintilian, and Livy.

In 1538 Dolet collaborated with Mellin de Saint-Gelais in revising Colin's translation of Castiglione's *Il Libro del cortegiano*, a work steeped in Platonism, but with substantial reference to music, including practical as well as philosophical advice.[56]

(vi) *Luigi Alamanni (1495–1556)*

Italian neo-Platonism is also reflected in the *Opere Toscane* (Lyons, S. Gryphe, 1532) of the Florentine republican and poet, Luigi Alamanni, who visited Lyons during his exile in the 1520s, even before the restoration of the Medici in 1530 induced him to enter the service of the French king, Francis I.[57] A disciple of Ficino's pupil, Francesco da Diacceto, he had attended the humanist meetings at the Rucellai house and the Oricellari gardens. His philosophical views are less significant than his experiments in classical metre, notably his continuation of Alberti's and Tolomei's measured verse.

Alamanni has little to say about music, although he was a close friend of the Florentine composer and organist, Francesco Layolle (1492–1540), resident at Lyons from 1523. Layolle is mentioned in Alamanni's correspondence[58] and in the first eclogue, lamenting the death of Cosimo Rucellai in 1518:

> Ne men sai far che'l nostro Tosco Aiolle
> Con la voce e col suon le valli liete
> Che'l nostro Tosco Aiolle, in cui Fiorenza
> Scorge quanta armonia, quant' arte mai
> Da Terpsicore vien fra noi mortali.[59]

---

[55] Dolet, *Commentarii*, col. 1295.

[56] B. Becherini, 'Il "Cortegiano" e la musica', *La Bibliofilia*, 45 (1943), 84–96.

[57] For further on Alamanni see H. Hauvette, *Un exilé florentin à la cour de France au XVIe siècle* (Paris, 1903).

[58] See G. Guasti, *Giornale storico degli archivi toscani*, 3 (Florence, 1859), 143–5.

[59] L. Alamanni, *Opere toscane* (Lyons, 1532), 109.

You can make the valleys happy no less than our Tuscan Aiolle, with your voice and playing, than our Tuscan Aiolle, in whom Florence discovers all the harmony and art that ever comes to us mortals from Terpsichore.

Layolle was also the dedicatee of a sonnet published in the same collection:

> Aiolle mio gentil, cortese amico,
> Come spesso sent' io che'l vostro core
> Vi dice, altro non ha ch'ira e dolore
> Chi pover nacque al suo destin nemico.
>   Ma non crediate à lui, che tal mendico
> Appar d'oro e di gemme al vulgo fuore;
> Ch'è piu ricco tra' buon di vero honore
> Che di frondi e di spighe il campo aprico.
>   Vie piu d'altro thesor pregiata e chara
> Fia quell'alta virtù; che Dio vi diede
> Per mostrar l'harmonia che'n cielo ascolta.
>   Sia pur di questa ogni buon'alma avara,
> Non di richezza, ch'e d'affanni herede,
> E che fuor di ragion n'è data e tolta.[60]

> My noble Aiolle, courteous friend,
> How often do I hear your heart
> Saying to you: 'Naught but anger and pain
> Has one who is born poor, with destiny against him'.
>   But do not believe it; for what seems so wanting,
> In gold and jewels to the mob outside
> Is to good people richer in true honour
> Than the sunny field of foliage and corn.
>   Much more valued and cherished than other treasure
> Is that high virtue, given you by God,
> To reveal the harmony heard in heaven.
>   Every good soul may be greedy for this,
> But not for riches which are heir to troubles
> And which can be given or taken away without reason.

The musician returned the compliment by setting to music two of Alamanni's poems, 'Infra bianche rugiade' (*Opere toscane*, 21) and 'Lasso la bella fera' in his *Cinquanta canzoni* (Lyons, J. Moderne, *c.*1540, nos. 43 and 18), and by christening his son 'Alemanno'.

(vii) *Eustorg de Beaulieu (c.1495–1552)*

Eustorg de Beaulieu, who lived in Lyons between 1534 and 1537, would seem to personify the Pléiade's ideal union of poet and musician.

---

[60] 'Sonetto a Francesco Aiolle sia la vera ricchezza', *Opere toscane*, 190.

However, lacking Italianate interests and classical erudition, he remained somewhat outside the main literary currents of the time, a simple provincial, faithful to the forms and style of the *rhétoriqueurs* and to popular poets like Roger de Collerye, although full of admiration for Clément Marot.[61] Nevertheless, even a simple provincial could feel the reverberations of humanism, as may be seen from a marginal note to a poem written at Tulle during a famine in 1526 and published in Beaulieu's *Les Gestes des Solliciteurs* (Bordeaux, J. Guyart, 1529), fo. A2, ll. 7–19):

	Je fuz forcloz de toucher plus des mains
	Mon espinete, où souloye jouer maintz
	Petitz motetz, prins de la dulciffique
Musique inter septem	Et resonante facture de musique
artes liberales sola	Qui entre les ars (sans aucun despriser)
obtinet principatum	Est precellente et sur tous à priser
Sicut scribunt philo.	Car son organe si tresfort maintz resjoye
	Qu'ilz en contemplent la supernelle joye,
Cor meum	Et parvient l'homme par ce concordant jeu
turbatum est.	A plus songer a la gloire de dieu
Psalme xxxvii	Aussi armonye augmente la lyesse
	Des cueurs joyeux et abat la tristesse
	Des desolez, du nombre desquelz suis ...
Music, alone of	I am barred from touching any more
the seven liberal	My spinet, on which I used to play
arts, wins the prize.	Little motets, taken from the sweet
So write the philosophers.	And resonant composition of music,
	Which of the arts (without decrying any)
	Is paramount and prized above all others.
	For its organ affects many so much
	That they glimpse sublime joy.
My heart	And from this concordant playing man may
is troubled.	Think more about of God's glory.
Psalm 37	Thus harmony increases the jubilation
	Of joyful hearts and suppresses the sadness
	Of the desolate, among whom I count myself.

Another Platonist concept—the power of the musical art to ennoble man's spirit—is recorded in his letter to the Lyonese lady, Marie-Catherine de Pierrevive, wife of the Florentine Antoine de Gondi, anticipating Ronsard's preface addressed to Francis II in 1560.[62]

[61] For further details on Beaulieu's early career see E. Fage, 'E. de Beaulieu', in *Variétés limousines* (Paris, 1891), 75–174; H. Harvitt, *Eustorg de Beaulieu, a Disciple of Marot* (Lancaster, Pa., 1918).

[62] P. de Ronsard, *Œuvres complètes*, ed. P. Laumonier (Paris, 1914–19), vii. 16–20. An English translation is included in O. Strunk, *Source Readings in Music History* (New York, 1950), 60–4.

Et mesmement en l'Art qui pareil n'a
C'est la Musique, où jadis se estonna
(Ou se amusa à luy prester l'oreille)
L'esprit maulvais qui à nous tempter veille
Lors qu'il tenoit en torment trescruel
Le Roy Saul, regnant en Israel,
Fors quand David jouoit de sa Cythare.
  Par quoy, voyand que Musique separe
L'homme du Diable, & donne aux gens confort,
C'est (ce croy je) que tu l'aymes si fort.[63]

And likewise in the art which has no peer
It was music which of old
(Or which she liked to hear)
Daunted the evil spirit which is out to tempt us,
When it held in the most cruel torment
King Saul of Israel,
Except when David played his cithara.
  By which we see that music separates
Man from the Devil and gives comfort to people,
This, I think, is why you love it so much.

Similarly, the first 'Chanson' in the Lyons collection is a eulogy of the art of music, including reference to the power of the Ancients' harmony to overcome the devil enraged and to affect man's ethics:

C'est tout pour vous, dame Musique,
Vostre harmonye, au temps antique
Chassa le Diable furieux.

.   .   .   .   .   .

Le deduy repaist l'Homme ethique
De vous (aussi) Dame auctentique.
Brefvement, vostre Art dulcifique,
Vault plus que Basme precieux.[64]

Tis all for you, Lady Music.
Your harmony in ancient times
Chased away the devil enraged.

.   .   .   .   .   .

Pleasure feeds the ethical man
And you (too) true lady.
In short, your sweet art
Is worth more than precious Balm.

---

[63] E. de Beaulieu, *Les Divers Rapportz* (Lyons, 1537), fo. 82ᵛ; ed. M. A. Pegg (Geneva, 1964), 267.
[64] Ibid., fo. 63ʳ; ed. Pegg, 231.

Most of the information on Beaulieu's early life is derived from his verse.[65] Thus we learn that he was born at Beaulieu-sur-Ménoire in the Bas-Limousin, that by 1522 he was organist at the cathedral at Lectoure (Gers) and from 1524 taught music at Tulle. Entering the priesthood some time in the 1520s did not prevent him contesting a small family inheritance in a lawsuit at Bordeaux in 1529, enlisting the aid of the King's Counsellor to the Bordeaux Parlement, Bernard de Lahet, a music-lover and patron of the famous composer Janequin. The first letter published in *Les Divers Rapportz* (Lyons, 1537) refers to Lahet's fondness for Beaulieu's keyboard-playing and recounts how, along with a certain Blaise, they passed their evenings singing:

> Je pense fort si ton cueur se delecte
> (Comme j'ay veu) au jeu de l'Espinete?
> Et s'aymes tant le doulx bruyt Organique
> Comme Aultresfois, & la doulce Musique?
> Ou je t'ay veu prendre tant de plaisir
> Que bien souvent, ains que t'aller gesir
> (Pour de soucy, & peyne, estre delivre)
> Si tu trouvois de Musique aulcung Livre
> Toy, Blaise, & moy, chantions jusqu'à mynuyct
> Sçachant, que Dueil ne proffite, mais nuict.
>   Et pour plus estre à la Musique enclin,
> Tu t'acoinctoys de Clement Jennequin
> Et de aultres maintz, toutz gens d'experience
> Et où gisoit Musicalle science.[66]

> I wonder greatly whether your heart [still] delights
> (As I have seen) in playing the spinet?
> And do you still love so much the sweet sound of the organ
> As in the old days, and of sweet music?
> In which I saw you take such pleasure,
> As often before going to bed,
> (To banish trouble and care)
> You, Blaise, and I would sing until midnight
> If you found some book of music,
> Knowing that a heavy heart offers no profit, but harms.
>   And to increase your musical inclination
> You sought the friendship of Clément Jennequin
> And of many other experienced people
> Familiar with the science of music.

---

[65] See G. Colletet, *Vie d'Eustorg de Beaulieu*, ed. T. de Larroque (Paris, 1878); Harvitt, *Eustorg de Beaulieu*.

[66] Beaulieu, *Divers Rapportz*, fo. 47^r; ed. Pegg, 241.

In 1534 Beaulieu settled in Lyons, probably at the instigation of the music-loving Charles d'Estaing, one of the canons of the cathedral chapter, who introduced him to Antoine de Gondi, his wife Marie-Catherine de Pierrevive, and their daughter, Hélène, who became an enthusiastic pupil (*Les Divers Rapportz*, Rondeau 89 and Epistre 8). Beaulieu also addressed verses to other patrons in Lyons, including the town's governor, Pomponio Trivulzio, (Le troiesiesme Dixain), and the king's lieutenant-general, Jean du Peyrat (Trezain).

During his years in Lyons the poet-musician probably met Marguerite de Navarre and her secretary Antoine du Moulin (Rondeau 90 and Epistre 9). He was profoundly impressed by the former's *Miroir de l'âme pécheresse* (1531), and the evangelical ideas of her circle may have influenced his conversion to Protestantism. He left for Geneva at the end of April 1537, but soon moved on to Lausanne, where he studied the new theology. On 12 May 1540 the Berne Consistory appointed him pastor of Thierrens and Moudon.[67] This did not prevent him leading a colourful life. That summer he married Rolette, a young orphan from Geneva, who did not share his love of the countryside and who soon returned to her home city, while he was accused of homosexuality.[68] It seems that he had already set some French psalms to music, since in August 1540 he sent a letter to Pierre Giron of Freiburg, suggesting that by the winter they would hopefully be corrected and ready for Mathias Apiarius of Berne to print and bring to the Frankfurt fair.[69] This project did not apparently materialize, for on 26 May 1544 Beaulieu offered the psalms to the magistrates of Berne,[70] and on 11 March 1545 he wrote to Pierre Viret requesting Calvin's permission for the Genevan printer Jean Gérard to print the collection, which was now inflated with Pauline epistles and French chansons.[71]

These chansons finally appeared, on 12 August 1546, in an unsigned edition under the title *Chrestienne Resjouyssance*. This edition contains the texts of one hundred and sixty *chansons spirituelles* 'for the recreation of pious Christians', providing the Protestant music-lover with a repertoire of sacred songs to replace the all too popular secular ones. In the preface Beaulieu abjures his earlier worldly songs and

[67] Berne, Staatsarchiv, Ratsmanual 292, p. 7.

[68] Berne, Staatsarchiv, Chorgerichtsmanual 11, pp. 54–5: 12. p. 30.

[69] A.-L. Herminjard, *Correspondance des Réformateurs dans les pays de langue française*, 9 vols. (Geneva, 1866–97), vi. 286; P. Pidoux, *Le Psautier huguenot du XVIe siècle*, 2 vols. (Basle, 1962), ii. 5; Berne, Staatsarchiv, Ratsmanual 288, p. 250.

[70] Herminjard, *Correspondance*, ix. 248.

[71] J. Calvin, *Opera omnia* (Corpus Reformatorum 29–87; Brunswick, 1863–1900), xii, col. 44, no. 621, and col. 47, no. 623; O. Douen, *Clément Marot et le psautier huguenot*, 2 vols. (Paris, 1878), ii. 641, 742.

instrumental music (which Calvinists felt was disrespectful). However, the majority of the contents merely modify the words of well-known amorous chansons to address God rather than the beloved, and they explicitly suggest familiar *timbres*, twenty-one of them being identifiable with tunes known in polyphonic settings by Sermisy, Janequin, and other Catholic composers. Thirty-nine pieces are set apart with the following introductory note:

Je t'ay mis icy à part (amy Lecteur) trente & noeuf chansons specialles, parmy les aultres. Lesquelles j'ay ainsi sequestrées pour t'advertir expressement: que je n'ay point composé aulcun subject ou aultre partie du chant des chansons precedentes n'aussi des aultres: que tu trouveras subsequemment, apres ceulx cy. Mais, touchant ce nombre icy de ces trente & noeuf seullement: tu seras adverti, qu'après leur avoir faict la lettre: le leur ay aussi faict & composé à chascune à part: un chant, à scavoir: en note musicalement (les unes à trois & les aultres à quatre parties) selon le don que Dieu m'a administré, en ce tant noble art de Musique. Lequel chant ainsi composé, j'espère avec le temps, s'il plaict au Seigneur, (& si je trouve Imprimeur commode) communiquer publiquement: à toute l'Eglise. Ensemble encore le chant d'un nombre de mottetz latins, de ma composition, la lettre desquelz ay prinse de la saincte Escripture.[72]

Dear Reader, I have set apart here thirty-nine special songs. I have divided these off on purpose to show you that I have not composed any tune or other part of the music for the preceding songs, nor for the others that you will find subsequently, after these. But for these thirty-nine I should tell you that, after writing the text, I also made and composed for each one a tune, that is to say, music set down in notation (some for three and the rest for four parts), according to the gift which God has given me, in this most noble art of music. If it please the Lord (and if I find a suitable printer), I hope to communicate this music thus composed publicly to the whole Church, along with a number of Latin motets, of my composition, the text of which I have taken from Holy Scripture.

At the end of the book the printer confirms that the author had set these thirty-nine texts to music for three and four voices.

A similar note had preceded the twelve secular 'chansons' of *Les Divers Rapportz* in 1537:

La premiere Chanson, à la louange de l'Art de Musique, Laquelle, ensemble les aultres suyvantes, L'Aucteur a composées en note Musicallement, à trois & à quatre parties (avec d'aultres choses) en quatre Livres, à part.[73]

The first Chanson in praise of the musical art, which, together with the others

---

[72] E. de Beaulieu, *Chrestienne Resjouyssance* (n.p., 1546), 90.
[73] Fol. 62ᵛ; ed. Pegg, 231.

that follow, the author has composed in musical notation (with other things) in four separate part-books.

Three of these chansons were included complete with their music in Moderne's *Parangon des Chansons* (Lyons, 1538).[74] But no publication of the four part-books referred to in the *Divers Rapportz* is known today, and none is cited in contemporary bibliographies. Similarly, the composer does not seem to have found a printer for the Latin motets or the music of the thirty-nine 'chansons specialles' mentioned in the *Chrestienne Resjouyssance*.[75]

On 20 December 1546 Beaulieu remarried, again choosing a young bride, Madeleine Massandt, only fifteen years of age. The couple lived together for some days before the bans were posted, but a month later the husband was accused of mistreating his wife.[76] Probably as a consequence of his scandalous conduct, he was compelled to resign his post as pastor at Thierrens. He next appears at Bienne, but remained there only one year, as can be seen from his letter thanking the town council for their hospitality and letter of recommendation. He was evidently still seeking a new pastorship:

Nobles et spectables Seigneurs: pourtant qu'il me fault aller jusques a Churie, a Strasbourg (ou ailleurs la ou il plaira a Dieu) pour voir si je pourray servir à l'utilite de l'Eglise de quelque practicque chrestienne:[77]

Noble and respected Lords: I am even ready to go to Churie, Strasburg (or elsewhere if God pleases) to see if I may serve the Church with some Christian practice:

During this time Beaulieu was working on his *L'Espinglier des Filles*, a didactic collection of moral precepts for young ladies, based on the *Institutio foeminae christianae* of Juan Luis Vives. The book was published at Basle in 1548 and reprinted in 1550. Despite his advanced age, Beaulieu matriculated at the University of Basle in May 1548[78] and spent his last years in the town, enjoying the patronage of the music-

---

[74] 'Bon jour, bon an', RISM 1538[15], fo. 5, ed. N. Bridgman, 'E. de Beaulieu, Musician', *Musical Quarterly*, 37 (1951), 69–70; 'Voicy le bon temps', RISM 1538[15], fo. 9, ed. H. Albrecht, *Zwölf französische Lieder aus Jacques Moderne* (Das Chorwerk, 61; Wolfenbüttel, 1956), no. 1; 'Mondain séjour', RISM 1538[16], fo. 17.

[75] The twelve secular chansons and the thirty-nine spiritual ones from the *Chrestienne Resjouyssance* are listed in F. Dobbins, 'The Chanson at Lyons in the Sixteenth Century' (D.Phil. diss., Oxford, 1971), 1, fos. 43–8. The whole collection is analysed in J. Burdet, *La Musique dans le pays de Vaud 1536–1798* (Lausanne, 1963), 75–82.

[76] These events are documented in Berne, Staatsarchiv, Chorgerichtsmanual 17, pp. 14 and 126; Ratsmanual 300, pp. 102 and 166.

[77] Bienne, Archives communales, Lettres autographes, CXXX, fo. 7[r].

[78] W. G. Wackernagel, *Die Matrikel der Universität Basel*, 2 vols.; Basle, 1956), ii. 55.

loving Rector of the University, Boniface Amerbach (1495–1562),[79] and teaching French to his son Basil, who around this time copied a number of French chansons into manuscript.[80] An entry in the diary of the minister, Johannes Gast, notes the death of the 'studious Hector' on 8 January, 1552.[81]

The poet's most significant verses concerning music include his fifty-sixth rondeau addressed to the Florentine composer and organist, Francesco Layolle, describing the latter's garden on the banks of the Saône, where musicians gathered to join the birds in song:

> Musiciens, prenez toutz soing & cure
> De venir veoir ce Jardin, que Mercure
> Laissa jadis quand au Ciel s'en volla
> A son cher filz Francoys Layola
> Qui voz plaisirs & passetemps procure.
>   C'est luy qui veult, que sans noyse & murmure
> Gens toutz garnis d'esprit sans aultre armeure
> Viennent icy, Et par sur toutz ceulx la
>   Musiciens.
>   Venez y donq pour resjoyr nature
> Matins & soirs, Car dedans la closture
> Orrez chanter les Oyseaux ca & là
> Et decopper, Ut, Re, My, Fa, Sol, La
> En toutz endroictz qu'ont sceu metre en facture
>   Musiciens.[82]

> Musicians, take every care to ensure
> That you come and see this garden, that Mercury
> Left some time ago when he flew off to Heaven,
> To his dear son François Layola
> Who procures your pleasures and pastimes.
>   'Tis he who without any fuss or bother wants people
> Armed only with wit,
> To come here, and most of all
>   Musicians.
>   Come here then to enjoy nature
> Morning and evening; for within these walls
> You will hear the birds sing here and there,
> And divide their Ut–re–mi–fa–sol–la
> In all the places that could be composed by
>   Musicians.

---

[79] Letters by Boniface Amerbach are found in Basle, Universitätsbibliothek, MS G. II. 100–102.
[80] Basle, Universitätsbibliothek, MSS F. IX. 32–35, 59–62; F. X. 5–9, 17–20, 22–24.
[81] J. Gast, *Tagebuch*, ed. P. Burckhardt (Basle, 1945), 410.
[82] *Les Divers Rapportz*, fo. 26ᵛ; ed. Pegg, 141.

The ensuing fifty-seventh rondeau is a dialogue between Beaulieu and Layolle, in which the former outlines the orthodox Catholic view of Heaven and Hell, while the seventy-second praises Music as a Godly gift and expresses confidence that a musician will find fortune and support anywhere in the world:

> Soyez Joyeux, vrays suppostz de Musique
> Et ne craignez que Fortune vous picque
> Car par vostre art d'elle viendrez a bout
> Et si vous chasse, encor serez debout
> Et trouverez par toutz clymatz practique.
> Vostre scavoir est ung don Deifique
> Et le mestier de nature Angelique
> Pour ce vous prie où serez, tout par tout
> Soyez Joyeux.
> Soit en Europe, en Asie, ou Affrique
> Croyez de vray que vostre art dulcifique
> Vous nourrira, Car chascung y prend goust
> Mais gardez vous de mouyller soubz l'esgoust
> D'intemperence, Et sans moyen inique
> Soyez Joyeux.[83]

> Be joyful, true henchmen of music,
> And fear not that Fortune sting you,
> For by your art you will overcome her,
> And if she pursue you, you will stand up to her,
> And you will find a job anywhere.
> Your knowledge is a God-given gift
> And your profession of an angelic nature,
> And so I beg you to at all times
> Be joyful.
> Whether in Europe, Asia, or Africa
> Believe me, your dulcet art
> Will nourish you, since everyone has a taste for it.
> But make sure that you do not soak in the sewer of
> Intemperance; and without any iniquity
> Be joyful.

Beaulieu contributed six poems to the collection of *blasons*, praising various parts of the female anatomy, instigated by Clément Marot at Ferrara in 1536 and published at Paris in 1543.[84] The musician emerges

---

[83] Ibid. fo 33ʳ; ed. Pegg, 157.

[84] E. de Beaulieu *et al.*, *Sensuivent les blasons anatomiques du corps feminin, ensemble les contreblasons, de nouveau composez et aditionez, avec les figures, le tout mis par ordre. Composez par plusieurs poètes contemporains* (Paris, 1543; repr. 1550, 1554); ed. D. M. Meon (Paris, 1807); P. Lacroix (Amsterdam, 1866); J. Gay (Turin, 1866); B. Guzégan (Paris, 1931);

in the 'Blason de la voix', praising the sweet, harmonious voice that
blends with an instrument, that is artful and measured, melodious and
assured in sight-reading:

> Voix doulce, et tres armonieuse,
> Voix monstrant m'Amye joyeuse,
> Voix tu merites le vanter.
> Voix de laquelle le chanter
> A la vertu quand elle chante,
> Que tous les escoutans enchante.
> Voix consonante proprement
> Pour chanter sur ung Instrument.
> Voix argentine, haulte et clere,
> Ta bonne grace me declaire,
> Que tu ne chantes pas sans Art,
> Et que tu n'aymes le hazard
> Du chant à plaisir sans mesure,
> Comme est des Bestes la nature.
> Voix asseurée à entonner,
> Voix distincte, et qui a bon air:
> Voix de Femme, gresle, et delivre
> Chantant son party sur le Livre.
> Voix dont on dit, sans flater rien:
> C'est elle, o qu'elle chante bien.
> Voix bien remettant les parties
> Qu'aux assistans sont desparties.
> Voix ravissant le cueur, au corps
> De ceulx qui oyent tes doulx accordz.
> Voix que d'ouyr j'ay plus de cure
> Que de Orpheus, Pan, ne Mercure.
> Voix de celle qui prent tout jour
> Chanter pour honneste sejour.
> O donq Voix qu'aymes la Musique
> Je te prye n'estre si rustique
> De l'estimer à deshonneur
> Ains à vertu, grace, et bonheur.[85]

> Voice sweet and most harmonious
> Voice showing my beloved joyous,
> Voice, you deserve praise.
> Voice which endows singing
> With virtue when she sings,
> Which enchants all listeners.

J.-C. Lambert (Paris, 1967). See also R. E. Pike, 'The "Blasons" in the French Literature of the
Sixteenth Century', *Romanic Review*, 27 (1936), 233–42.

[85] *Divers Rapportz*, ed. Pegg, 297.

Voice properly consonant
To sing above an instrument.
Voice, silvery, high, and clear.
Your gracefulness declares to me
That you do not sing without art.
And that you do not like to take a chance
By singing freely without measure
As is the nature of beasts.
Voice sure in its intonation,
Voice, distinct and tuneful:
Voice of woman, high and free
Singing its part upon the book [i.e. improvising].
Voice which makes them say without any flattery
'Tis her, o how well she sings!
Voice which fits together all the parts,
That were divided up between those present.
Voice ravishing the heart in the body
Of those who hear your sweet harmony.
Voice that I want to hear
More than Orpheus, Pan, or Mercury.
Voice of the one who every day
Sings for gentle relaxation.
Therefore voice that loves music,
I beg you be not so rustic
As to consider it as dishonour
But as virtue, grace, and happiness.

In a letter written from Thierrens in May 1543, inviting Marot to leave plague-threatened Geneva and visit Beaulieu in his rural retreat, the composer claims he still has his clavichord and harp, on which he plays sacred songs and psalms translated by the great poet:

J'ay oultre encor mon jeu de Manichorde
Où les Chansons Divines par toy confictz:
Où as ouvré à mon gré mieulx qu'onq feis.
Souvent aussi je pren du croc ma harpe,
Et je la pendz à mon col en escharpe
Pour y jouer et Psalmes et Chansons
Selon que Dieu m'a instruict en leurs sons...

I still have my clavichord
On which I play the sacred songs crystallized by you:
Which in my opinion were your finest achievement.
Often too I take my harp from its hook,
And I hang it around my neck
To play Psalms and Chansons on it
To the tunes that God taught me...

But it is the influence of Calvin, whose régime proved too restricting for Marot to remain at Geneva, which predominates in the long preface to the *Chrestienne Resjouyssance*. Thus Beaulieu rejects as blasphemy the comparison of King David's psalms with the dissolute songs of his time, flattering princes and other voluptuous and worldly people, advancing the work of Satan and the pope. Christians should sing to God from the heart, modestly, without shouting, laughter, or exaggerated gestures:

Aulcuns, en se cuidans bien couvrir, disent encores que David mesmes, de son temps, chantoit bien & jouoit des instrumentz... (Or) c'est trop blasphemer contre Dieu & luy d'equiparer & comparer ses Divins Psalmes, Chansons & instrumentz aux chansons & jeux de dissolution en quoy plusieurs se delectent maintenant. Et tant s'en fault qu'il y ait quelque similitude, car tout ce que David composoit, chantoit ou jouoit sur les instrumentz de Musique tendoit toutallement à la gloire de Dieu, & ce que ces chanteurs & fleusteurs font de nostre temps en maintz lieux ne tasche aulcunement qu'à la pompe, decoration & avancement du Royaume de Satan, du Pape son vicaire general & de plusieurs Princes & aultre gens voluptueux de ce monde... Doncques, en rejettant toutes telles manieres de resjouyssances diaboliques, escoutez & incorporez en voz coeurs les tant salutaires admonitions tant de David que de S. Paul..., soyez remplis de l'esperit, parlans entre vous par Psalmes, louenges & chansons spirituelles, chantans & resonnans en vostre coeur au Seigneur, rendans tousjours graces à Dieu & pere pour toutes choses... Voyla donc la Loy divine, touchant les chansons en quoy tous chrestiens & chrestiennes se peuvent resjouyr licitement, pourveu aussi que ce soit modestment & sans hullemens, cris, ris, n'aultres gestes dissolues. Car Dieu veult qu'on chante ses chansons discretement & sagement... Quand la saincte Escripture nous incite à resjouyssance... elle dict tousjours que qui se vouldra resjouyr, que il se resjouysse au Seigneur, & qui vouldra chanter, qu'il chante aussi au Seigneur, par Psalmes & chansons spirituelles, voire non de la voix & levres seulement, ains du coeur aussi.[86]

Some, seeking to excuse themselves, still say that David himself, in his time, sang well and played instruments... (but) it is a blasphemy against God and David to compare and equate his divine psalms, chansons, and instruments with the dissolute songs and playing that many delight in today. Not by a long chalk is there any similarity; for all that David composed, sang, or played on musical instruments was entirely intended for the glory of God, and what the singers and fluters do today in many places is intended only for the pomp, decoration, and advancement of the realm of Satan, of his vicar-general the pope, and of many princes and other voluptuous people in this world... Thus, rejecting all such ways of rejoicing in the devil, listen and take to heart the very salutary admonitions of both David and St Paul... be filled with the spirit,

---

[86] E. de Beaulieu, *Chrestienne Resjouyssance*, 204.

saying amongst yourselves psalms, praises, and spiritual songs, singing and resounding in your heart to the Lord, always giving thanks to God, the father of all things... Here then is the divine Law in regard to songs in which all Christian men and women may justly rejoice, provided also that they do so modestly and without shouting, crying, laughing, or other dissolute gestures. For God wants us to sing his songs discreetly and sensibly... When the Holy Scriptures incite us to rejoicing, they always say that he who wants to rejoice should rejoice in the Lord, and he who wants to sing should also sing to the Lord, with psalms and spiritual songs, not only with the voice and lips but also with the heart.

Beaulieu continues by confessing the error of his own youthful interest in secular songs and instrumental playing, but claims now to have seen the divine light:

Or touchant à moy, freres & soeurs, je confesse publiquement avoir jadis trop souvent usé de resjouyssance mondaine et avoir par trop souvent chanté les chansons abominables dont ay faict mention cy dessus. Et mesme les ay trop curieusement estudiées & jouées sur plusieurs instrumentz de musique voir au grand deshonneur de Dieu & du dict art, tant honneste & louable. Mais quand il a pleu à Dieu de me donner à congnoistre que j'abusois trop de ses dons, j'ay soubdain tourné bride &, par l'inspiration de ce tant bon pere celeste qui m'a tiré du gouffre d'enfer par sa seule grâce, je me suis depuis quelque fois occupé à renverser & reduire à sa louange tout de chansons charnelles que m'a peu souvenir avoir jadis chanté au regne de Satan.[87]

Now as for myself, brothers and sisters, I confess publicly that in the past I all too often indulged in worldly pleasure and all too often sang the abominable songs that I mentioned above. And I even studied them with too great an interest and played them on many musical instruments, even though it greatly dishonoured God and the said art which is so honest and praiseworthy. But when it pleased God to let me see how I was misusing his gifts, I immediately turned back and, through the inspiration of the heavenly father who by his grace alone saved me from the jaws of hell, I have for some time since busied myself to turn around and adapt to his praise all the sensual songs I could remember having sung before during Satan's reign.

(viii) *Bonaventure des Périers (1498–1544)*

Born at Arnay-le-Duc in Burgundy, Bonaventure des Périers's non-conformist religious views led to his flight from Paris after the Lutheran placards affair in October 1534. In 1536 he was at Lyons, helping Dolet with the first volume of his Latin Commentaries, and later that year entered the service of Marguerite de Navarre as *valet de chambre* and

---

[87] Ibid., prelim. fos. 6ʳ–7ʳ.

secretary.[88] Perhaps under the influence of Dolet or Marguerite's circle, or perhaps as a reaction to the dogmatism of Calvin's *Institutes of the Christian Religion*, the Protestant sympathies expressed in his *Prognostication des Prognostications* (1536) soon gave way to a new free-thinking, expounded in the four dialogues of the *Cymbalum Mundi* (Lyons, 1538).[89] The scandal caused by this publication compelled the Queen of Navarre to dismiss Des Périers from her household, although she continued to pay him a salary at least until October 1541. During this time the poet probably lived in Lyons: he was certainly present at the Saint-Martin's Day festivities at the Abbey of Nôtre-Dame de L'Île-Barbe on 15 May 1539 (sponsored by the Abbot, Cardinal-Archbishop Jean de Lorraine), and he describes the journey by boat along the Saône from Lyons in a remarkable poem composed as a long series of *sizains* with freely alternating three- and seven-syllable lines. The piece, dedicated to the benevolent and liberal royal-lieutenant of Lyons, Jean du Peyrat, is notable for its musical language and references.

The verses describing how Nature's music evokes a human response may be of purely literary significance:

Oyez vous?	Can you hear
Ce bruyt tant doulx	That sound so sweet
Deliquer de la gorgette	Flowing from the little throat
Du geay mignot	Of the cute jay
Du linot	From the linnet
Et de la frisque alouette:	And from the lively lark:
Desquels nous rient	Which make us laugh
Et crient	And shout
Que chanter devons aussi?	What should we sing too?
O cures	O cares,
Vaines et dures	Vain and harsh,
Nous vous lairrons donc icy.[90]	We will leave you here
	then.

but the ensuing stanzas mention four contemporary, polyphonic chansons, the second two of which also figure in Rabelais' long list in ch. 33 *bis* of the *Cinquiesme livre* (1552):

Viens, Soulas,	Come solace,
Nous rendre las	Make us tired

[88] A. Chenevière, *Bonaventure des Périers: Sa vie et ses poésies* (Paris, 1886).

[89] B. des Périers, *Cymbalum Mundi*, ed. P. H. Nurse (Manchester, 1958). See also P. H. Nurse, 'Erasme et Des Périers', *Bibliothèque d'Humanisme et Renaissance*, 30 (1968), 53–64.

[90] B. des Périers, *Œuvres*, ed. A. du Moulin (Lyons, 1544), 58; ed. L. Lacour, *Œuvres françoises de B. des Périers*, 2 vols. (Paris, 1856), i. 59.

De Passetemps et Plaisance	Of pastimes and pleasure.
Sus, chantons tous.	Up, let us all sing.
Dirons nous	Shall we do
Le Content, ou *Jouyssance?*	*Le Content* or *Jouissance?*
Chantons en une:	Let's sing one of these:
Fortune	*Fortune*
Doulce memoire, à loysir	Or *Sweet Memory*
Et voire *Doulce memoire*	Yes even *Sweet Memory*
Avant, ou *Pour un plaisir*	Before, or *For pleasure*[91]

These last two stanzas also survive as a four-voice *fricassée* by Coste (see Music Example 1) published in the seventh book of Moderne's *Parangon des chansons* (1540[17], no. 19), which by means of melodic quotation shows that the songs referred to (in italics above) are:

1. 'Le content est riche en ce monde', set for four voices by Claudin de Sermisy[92]
2. Clément Marot's 'Jouyssance vous donneray', also set by Sermisy in a four-voice version, which was well known in various subsequent arrangements, including one for lute depicted in at least two paintings by the so-called 'maître des demi-figures'.[93]
3. 'Fortune allors que n'avois congnoissance', a setting for four voices ascribed to Pierre Clereau in the fifth book of Moderne's *Parangon des chansons* (RISM 1539[20], no. 5),[94] but to Pierre Certon in Attaingnant's sixth book (1539[15-16], no. 2).[95]
4. King Francis I's 'Doulce mémoire en plaisir consommée', whose four-voice setting by Sandrin, published by both Moderne and Attaingnant in 1538,[96] was imitated by Layolle and numerous other composers.[97]

---

[91] B. des Périers, *Œuvres*, 58–9; ed. Lacour, i. 59–60.

[92] Published in Attaingnant's *Chansons nouvelles* of 1528 and in many subsequent collections: see C. de Sermisy, *Opera omnia*, ed. G. Allaire and I. Cazeaux (Corpus Mensurabilis Musicae, 52; American Institute of Musicology, 1974), iv, no. 96. Numerous instrumental arrangements are listed in H. M. Brown, *Instrumental Music Printed before 1600: A Bibliography* (Cambridge, Mass., 1965), 529.

[93] Also printed in Attaingnant's first book of chansons and copied in several manuscripts; see C. de Sermisy, *Opera omnia*, iii, no. 85; numerous vocal imitations are listed in H. M. Brown, *Music in the French Secular Theater, 1400–1550* (Cambridge, Mass., 1963), 244–6, with instrumental arrangements in Brown, *Instrumental Music*, 527. The paintings are reproduced in J. A. Parkinson, 'A Chanson by Claudin de Sermisy', *Music and Letters*, 39 (1958), 118–22, and C. Sachs, *Our Musical Heritage* (Englewood Cliffs, NJ, 1955), pl. 13.

[94] Ed. A. Seay (Colorado College Music Press Transcriptions, 5; Colorado Springs, 1980), no. 5.

[95] P. Certon, *Chansons polyphoniques*, ed. A. Agnel, 3 vols. (Paris, 1967–8), i, no. 36.

[96] See P. Sandrin, *Opera omnia*, ed. A. Seay (Corpus Mensurabilis Musicae, 47; American Institute of Musicology, 1968), no. 4.

[97] Layolle's two-voice setting was also published by Moderne in Lyons in 1538; see *Jacques Moderne: Le Parangon des chansons: Quart livre*, ed. A. Seay (Colorado College Music Press Transcriptions, 6; Colorado Springs, Colo., 1981), no. 1. For other settings see F. Dobbins, 'Doulce

5. 'Avant l'aymer je l'ay voulu cognoistre', set for four voices by Sandrin in Attaingnant's eighteenth book (1545[12–13] no. 5).[98]
6. 'Pour ung plaisir qui si peu dure', set for four voices by Sermisy in another collection published by Attaingnant (1536[5] no. 14).[99]

Des Périers continues with a picturesque description of Nature's response to the human music:

Les Poissons	The fish
Viennent au sons	Come [up] to the sound
Des Rebecs, et Espinettes,	Of the rebecs and spinets,
Et loing du fond	And far from the bottom
De l'eau, font	Of the water
Petites gambadalettes.[100]	Leap [for joy].

The merry pilgrims included the Mantuan lutenist Alberto da Ripa (c. 1480–1551), *valet de chambre* in the service of Francis I, celebrated by Marot, Saint-Gelais, Baïf, Tyard, and Ronsard:[101]

Lá, Albert	There Albert,
Ouvrier expert	Expert worker
Du Roy en Musique haultaine	In the king's high Music,
Avecques sons	With the playing
De chansons	Of chansons
Ha sacré une Fontaine.[102]	Consecrated a
	Fountain.

In the posthumous collected edition of Des Périers's works, arranged by his friend Antoine du Moulin (who was also one of Marguerite de Navarre's secretaries), this poem was preceded by a French paraphrase of Plato's dialogue with Lysis and an exposition of the philosophy of spiritual love entitled 'Queste d'amytié',[103] which has the same irregular *sixain* form. This, like the *Prognostication* and several other shorter poems (*épigrammes, ballades, rondeaux, odes,* etc.) which follow, was

mémoire: A Study of the Parody Chanson', *Proceedings of the Royal Musical Association*, 96 (1969), 85–101, and G. Houle (ed.), *Doulce mémoire: A Study in Performance Practice* (Bloomington, Ind., 1990).

[98] See P. Sandrin, *Opera omnia*, no. 33.
[99] See C. de Sermisy, *Opera omnia*, iv, no. 126.
[100] B. des Periers, *Œuvres*, 59; ed. Lacour, i. 60.
[101] See J. G. Prodhomme, 'G. Morlaye, éditeur d'A. de Rippe', *Revue de musicologie*, 9 (1925), 157–65; J. M. Vaccaro (ed.), *Œuvres d'Albert de Rippe*, 3 vols. (Paris, 1972–5).
[102] Des Périers, *Œuvres*, 67–8; ed. Lacour, i. 67–8.
[103] P. H. Nurse, 'Christian Platonism in the Poetry of Bonaventure des Périers', *Bibliothèque d'Humanisme et Renaissance*, 19 (1957), 234–44.

dedicated to his beloved Queen of Navarre: other short pieces are devoted to friends at Lyons (Jean du Peyrat, Jean de Tournes, Jacqueline Stuard, etc.). Most of Des Périers's poetry is thus either of a personal or philosophic nature: he did not seek popular success and, although highly esteemed by his literary contemporaries, he wrote little in the light or impersonal vein that attracted musicians or music publishers aiming at a wider market. A few pieces were, however, considered suitable for music, like the set of three five-line *chansons*, each with the same rhyme scheme, the same opening pattern, and the same Petrarchist conceits: 'Par ton regard tu me fais esperer', 'Par ton parler me fais en toy fier', and 'Par ton amour tu m'apprens à aymer'.[104] The first of these was set for four voices by Claudin de Sermisy and published by Attaingnant in Paris as early as 1530,[105] thus antedating any version known to the editors or commentators of Des Périers's works. A three-voice arrangement of the same music attributed to Gosse was printed by Attaingnant in 1535.[106] All three poems also figure in a collection of five-voice chansons by Jacques Buus published in Venice by G. Scotto in 1550.[107]

The only other work of Des Périers known in a contemporary musical setting is his *Cantique de Moyse* (translated from Deut. 32), *Escoutez cieux et prestez audience*, which was printed with an official tune in the Genevan psalter in 1555 and in a four-voice setting by Philibert Jambe de Fer in Lyons in 1564.[108]

In 1558, fourteen years after the author's violent suicide, Robert Granjon published a collection of ninety of his stories in prose, under the title of *Les Nouvelles Recreations et Joyeux Devis de Feu Bonaventure Des Périers*. These owe much to Rabelais and to Marguerite de Navarre, as well as to older models, like Boccaccio and Poggio. The many references to music include one tale of a lady defending the propriety of the dance against a cynical theologian:

'If you were', said he, 'at a window or on a gallery, and saw afar in some great square a dozen or two people holding hands, jumping, turning, coming and going backwards and forwards, would they not seem crazy to you?' 'Yes indeed,' said she, 'if there were no beat.' 'I would still say so, even with a beat, if there were no drum or flute,' said he. 'I confess', said she, 'that it might look rather odd.' 'And so', said the learned doctor, 'do a pierced piece of wood and

---

[104] Des Périers, *Œuvres*, 187–8; ed. Lacour, i. 165.

[105] C. de Sermisy, *Opera omnia*, iv, no. 122.

[106] See D. Heartz, *Pierre Attaingnant, Royal Printer of Music* (Berkeley and Los Angeles, 1969), no. 65.

[107] J. Buus, *Il primo libro di canzoni francese a sei voci* (Venice, 1543), 6–8.

[108] Des Périers, *Œuvres*, ed. Lacour, i. 182. See Pidoux, *Le Psautier huguenot*, i, no. 213a; ii. 81, 144.

a bucket whose ends are covered with parchment have the power to make you find acceptable something which in itself seems crazy?' 'Why not?' said she, 'Don't you know how great is the power of music? The sound of instruments enters the person's spirit and then the spirit rules the body, which does nothing other than to show by signs and movements the disposition of the soul towards joy and sadness. You know that men who are sad look different from those who are happy and contented. Moreover, in all cases you must consider the circumstances—as you yourself preach every day. A pipe-and-drummer who plays alone would be like a preacher in the pulpit without a congregation. Dances without instruments or songs would be like an audience without a speaker. There is no point in rebuking our dances: you might as well cut off our feet and ears; and I assure you', said she, 'that if I were dead and I heard a violin, I would rise up and dance. Those who play tennis torture themselves much more, running after a little stuffed leather pellet, and they do it with such commitment that sometimes it seems as though they must be killing themselves; and although they have no musical instruments, like the dancers, they still consider it a marvellous pastime. Do you want to take away worldly pleasures? What you preach against voluptuousness, in truth, is not a case for abolishing pastimes, except for the unseemly ones; for you know quite well that the world cannot go on without pleasure; but that does not mean that we should take too much.' The doctor wanted to reply; but he was surrounded by ladies, who made him keep his place, fearing that they might take anything he said as an invitation to dance. And God knows that this was not the case.[109]

Although intriguing as evidence of the use of the violin, as well as the pipe and tabor, as an accompaniment for dancing in the early sixteenth century, this story does not specify the dance types, as does the fifth *Nouvelle*, which makes a passing reference to three Bretons who were fine dancers of *passepieds* and *triboris*.[110] This is curious as the first mention of the *passepied*, which enjoyed a great vogue at Louis XIV's court over a century later, and *trihory*, a Breton *branle* described in some detail in Arbeau's *Orchésographie* (Langres, 1589). Also of musical interest is the fourth *Nouvelle*,[111] telling of a master of arts from Picardy who, despite constantly being reprimanded for fighting, drinking in taverns, wenching, and gaming, kept his post as a bass in the choir of Reims cathedral because he sang so well.

The preface to the first edition of these stories claims that they were preserved through the 'diligence of some virtuous person', and that a certain amount of work was necessary before they could be published.

---

[109] B. des Périers, *Les Nouvelles Recreations* (Lyons, 1558), fos. 56ʳ–57ʳ, Nouvelle 38, 'Du docteur qui blasmoit les danses et de la dame qui les soutenoit'; ed. Lacour, ii. 158.

[110] Ibid., Nouvelle 5; ed. Lacour, ii. 29.

[111] Ibid., Nouvelle 4, 'Du bassecontre de Reims, Chantre picard et maistre es arts'; ed. Lacour, ii. 23.

The help in question probably came from the other poets and *raconteurs* in the Queen of Navarre's circle, notably Jacques Peletier and Nicolas Denisot. Peletier's efforts on behalf of his deceased friend may also account for the confusion of attribution surrounding a tract on the tuning of lutes and guitars, *La maniere de bien & justement entoucher les Lucs & Guiternes*, published by Enguilbert de Marnef in Poitiers in 1557.[112] The Romantic author and critic Charles Nodier (1780–1844),[113] who claimed to have seen an earlier edition by Pierre de Sainte-Lucie of Lyons dating from 1537, was convinced that this work was by Des Périers and rejected the ascription to Jacques Peletier and Elie Vinet, suggested in Antoine du Verdier's *Bibliothèque* (Lyons, 1585). This document is interesting from a musical viewpoint, since the writer mentions the new vogue for the guitar in mid-sixteenth-century France, attempts to trace the history of the instrument and its designation back to the ancient Greeks (on dubious philological grounds), and describes in great detail a system for fretting stringed instruments of any size. Plato is mentioned *en passant*, but the acknowledged technical authority is Aristoxenus. the final paragraph, with its apology to geometricians, might be considered to lend support to authorship of the mathematician-poet Peletier, who was also a frequent visitor to Lyons in the 1530s.

(ix) *Barthélemy Aneau* (c.*1500 1561*)

Like Champier, Barthélemy Aneau was a versatile and erudite humanist who played an important part in the cultural life of Lyons. Having studied classics and law with Wolmar in Bourges during the late 1520s, he joined the staff of Claude de Cublize, principal of the Collège de la Trinité[114] in Lyons some time before 1538. He himself was appointed Principal in May 1540, and in 1546 summoned the poet Charles Fontaine to fill his former post as regent in rhetoric. His views on education, like those of Rabelais, are remarkably liberal and enlightened. Unlike the rival Collège de Tournon, most of the Trinité's pupils were non-fee-paying day-pupils from the poorer classes: between 1540 and 1544 the Council paid Aneau an annual salary of 100 livres plus tuition fees of 2 sols 2 deniers a month for each student.[115] The syllabus included French reading, as well as Greek and Latin grammar,

---

[112] F. Dobbins, 'Des Périers' Treatise on the Tuning of Lutes and Guitars', in 'The Chanson at Lyons in the Sixteenth Century', i, App. 2.

[113] *Les Contes ... de B. des Périers*, ed. C. Nodier (Paris, 1861), 26–39; (repr. Geneva, 1967), 45–67.

[114] See Ch. 1, n. 18.

[115] Lyons, Archives communales, CC956, fo. 89[r].

rhetoric, morals, dialectic, and mathematics. Aneau did not believe in the birch, as did most of his contemporaries, and he gently encouraged his pupils to use their leisure time in games and singing, directed by the masters and regents:

Le jeudy, apres disner, [les élèves] auront depuis la reparaison jusques à la derniere leçon, l'espace de trois heures, lesquelles ilz employeront en toutes manieres de jeux liberaulx que leur prescripront mesmes leurs maistres et regentz, comme à jeux de nombre, de pellote et balles, à jeux de perciée, à chanter en musique . . . [116]

On Thursdays, after lunch, [the pupils] will have between the meal and the last lesson three hours, which they will use for all kinds of liberal games prescribed for them by their masters and regents, like number games, pelota [shuttlecock] and ball [games], ring games, and singing.

In the plays that Aneau himself wrote for the College, the role of music is unusally prominent. One example, a nativity play printed by Sébastien Gryphe in 1538, consists almost entirely of *noëls* that are *contrafacta* of well-known chansons: *Chant Natal contenant sept Noelz, ung chant Pastourel et ung chant Royal, avec ung Mystere de la Nativité par personnages. Composez en imitation verbale et musicale de diverses chansons. Recueilliz sur l'escripture saincte; & d'icelle illustriez* (Lyons, 1538). The title-page thus announces a 'Nativity Song containing seven noëls, a Pastoral song, and a Royal song with a Mystery Play about the Nativity to be acted. Composed in verbal and musical imitation of various chansons.'

The first five noëls form a kind of prologue. The opening *Noel ou Chant Spirituel*, representing the soul of Jesus Christ confessing the stain and ugliness of his sin (fo. a2^r), imitates the words of Marot's chanson *Pourtant si je suis brunette*, which was known in a four-voice setting by Claudin de Sermisy, printed in Lyons in the same year by Moderne;[117] a three-voice parody by Aneau's friend P. de Villiers was probably composed around the same time, although it was not printed until much later.[118] Aneau's pious text uses a technique similar to that of Beaulieu's spiritual songs, including the retention of the original's verbal incipit and rhyme-scheme, with marginal annotations indicating scriptural references and the addition of extra stanzas in the same form.

The same procedure is followed in the second piece, *Noel en suite de la royalle chanson, 'Doulce mémoire', en voix et parolles reduisant*

---

[116] Ibid., fo. 61^r.

[117] C. Marot, *Œuvres* (Lyons, 1538), Chanson 36; the music appeared in J. Moderne (publ.), *Le Parangon des Chansons: Tiers livre* (Lyons, 1538), no. 1; see C. de Sermisy, *Opera omnia*, iv, no. 127.

[118] See A. le Roy and R. Ballard (publs.), *Second livre de chansons à trois parties* (1578), no. 3.

en memoire à la pensée Chrestienne, le Benefice de Dieu envers l'homme (fo. a3^r), based on King Francis I's celebrated *épigramme* set by Sandrin and Layolle in musical collections published by Moderne in 1538.[119] Aneau again provides five stanzas, each beginning with the words *Doulce mémoire*, the first stanza remaining very close to the secular model; the original couplet is identical, and thereafter, merely by changing the odd word, he transforms the amorous ditty into a hymn of thanksgiving for the advent of Christ. The third noël, *Content desir qui cause tout bonheur* (like another parody in Beaulieu's *Chrestienne Resjouyssance*, 1546, no. 32), takes as its model an anonymous *quatrain* beginning with the words *Content desir qui cause ma douleur*, set by Sermisy in 1533.[120] Aneau appends four extra stanzas, as he does with the next piece, *C'est une dure departie Du filz de Dieu le createur* (fo. a4^v), again based on a secular chanson for four voices by Sermisy.[121] The fifth piece, *Noel en imitation de C. Marot, sur la lettre & le chant de la chanson 'J'ay le desir content'* (fo. b1^r), is also based on a setting by Sermisy.[122] Aneau attributes the model to Marot, although the poem, unusual for its construction in alexandrines, is not known in any editions of that poet's work; it was actually ascribed to Claude Chappuys in one manuscript source and to Francis I in three others.[123]

Next comes the *Chant pastourel* (fo. b2^r) in the form of a dialogue between three shepherds (Rogelin, Raguel, and Ruben) and a shepherd-ess (Rachel), the Angel's annunciation, and their consequent departure to witness Christ's birth. The model is Marot's chanson *Vous perdez temps de me dire mal d'elle*, known in four-voice settings by Sermisy[124] and by Arcadelt,[125] both published in 1538, the latter in Lyons. Aneau again appends four stanzas, divided between the four characters, although the first stanza, an ingenious, albeit archaic, transposition of Marot's original *chanson*, is given entirely to Rogelin (fo. b2^r):

> Vous perdez temps, pasteurs, & pastourelle
> Corner, muser, cornemuse meschante
> Tant de plaisir n'aurez pas autour elle,
> Comme a l'oiseau du ciel qui lassus chante
> Que le filz de Dieu naisce:
> A vostre advis rien n'est ce?

[119] See above, nn. 96–7.
[120] C. de Sermisy, *Opera omnia*, iii, no. 32.
[121] Ibid., no. 25.
[122] Ibid., no. 65.
[123] Paris, Bibliothèque nationale, MS français 2335, fo. 101^r (ascribed to Chappuys); MS fr. 1723, fo. 1^r; Chantilly, Musée Condé, MS 520, fo. 49^r; MS 521, fo. 103^r.
[124] C. de Sermisy, *Opera omnia*, iv, no. 168.
[125] *Le Parangon des Chansons: Tiers livre*, no. 25; see J. Arcadelt, *Opera omnia*, ed. A. Seay (Corpus Mensurabilis Musicae, 31; American Institute of Musicology, 1968), viii, no. 2.

N'est ce rien de sa grace?
Laissez moy ceste garce
Seule dancer la belle tire lire
Et me suyvez courans tous d'une tire.

    You are wasting your time, shepherds and shepherdess,
Playing your horns and bagpipes; wicked bagpipe,
You will not have as much pleasure from her company
As does the bird from heaven who sings above
That the son of God is born:
Does this mean nothing to you?
Does his grace count for nothing?
Leave that wench alone
To dance the lovely tire-lire
And come and follow me, running in a line.

This is followed by a dance on a popular tune: *Noel branlant sur le Chant 'Barptolemy, mon bel amy'* (fo. b4ʳ).

The ensuing 'Mystery of the Nativity of Jesus' (fo. c1ʳ) is also based on 'diverse tunes from several chansons' (*divers chants de plusieurs chansons*). Mary and Joseph sing in dialogue of the journey to Bethlehem and of the Immaculate Conception to the tune *Le plus souvent il m'ennuye*. The scene then shifts back to the shepherds for the Angel's annunciation, using 'the tune of the second verse of an old noel, and sung to a well-known *branle*, "Jolyet est marie", with a reprise and a coda based on *Gloria in excelsis Deo*' (*le chant du second couplet extraict d'ung ancien Noël. Et se chante sur le branle de 'Jolyet est marie' avec une reprinse: et une queue sur le 'Gloria in excelsis Deo'*) (fo. c4ʳ). As with the previous dance, this music is not known in any printed collection, although the *Jolyet* tune must have been popular, since it was used in a number of noëls by other poets.

The shepherds reply to the Angel and the scene shifts to the crib, where they sing together *Chantons Noël quand nous irons* (fo. d1ʳ) to the tune *Sonnez my doncq quand vous irez*. An anonymous four-voice setting of these words was printed in 1530, while a five-voice version by Willaert appeared posthumously.[126]

Next comes a *Chant royal* (fo. d1ᵛ) for six kings, beginning with the prophecy of David, *Ung Roy, ung Dieu, pour mort au bois souffrir*, and the dissimulation of Herod, *Si le travail vous prenez à plaisir*, before the three kings from the east present their gifts and tributes to the new-born king. The five eight-line stanzas and *envoy* are based on the chanson *Si mon travail vous peult donner plaisir*, ascribed to Sandrin

---

[126] Anon., RISM 1530⁴ no. 22; Willaert, RISM 1572², no. 33; *Le Roy & Ballard's 1572 'Mellange de Chansons'*, ed. C. Jacobs (Pittsburgh, Pa., 1982), no. 33.

by Attaingnant (RISM 1538[11], no. 13) but to Sermisy by Moderne (1538[17], no. 3).[127] In Attaingnant's collection the piece is followed by a responce, *Le doeul yssu de la joye incertaine*, which has the same rhyme-scheme and which ends with the line *Si mon travail vous peult donner plaisir*. Moderne also includes this responce, but does not respect the sequence, placing it much later in his collection (no. 23); however, he does ascribe the piece correctly to P. de Villiers, whereas Attaingnant first attributes it to Maillart, although his and other subsequent Parisian editions (1540[9], 1549[17], and 1551[4-5]) remedy this error.[128] Aneau uses this responce as the model for his final *Noël mystic, sur le chant 'Le dueil yssu'*, and his marginal annotations elucidate veiled references to the composer, as well as to himself, his home town, and his publisher (fo. d2[v]):

> Le jour yssu de lumiere incertaine
> Me mect aux yeulx à peu pres le plourer
> De l'endurer le bien passe la peine
> Oncques ne vy telle nuict esclairer
> O quel bonheur ha voulu procurer
> Que Dieu voulut corps virginal choysir:
> C'est double bien qu'il nous vient declarer
> Si son travail nous poeut donner plaisir.
>
> Noel, noel si hault qui l'air en tonne
> Non l'homme seul, mais tout animant dict
> Le grand Lyon son gros organ entonne   Lyon
> Noel, noel à haulte voix bondit,
> Ung chant plaisant fondé sur ung bon dict
> Le Rossignol vy lier par accords   Villiers
> Et ung Aigneau bailant luy respondit,   Aneau
> Noel chantant, et à criz et à cors.
>
> Le Gryphon d'or y ha planté sa gryphe   Gryphe
> Et maint noel engravé par escript:
> Pour demonstrer, que point n'est apocryphe
> Tout ce qui est chanté de Jesuchrist:
> Tout animant, tout homme, tout esprit   Omnis spiritus
> Donne louange á cest enfant nouvel: laudat dominum
> Parquoy chantons le chant que nous apprit   Psal. 150
> L'ange du ciel noel, noel, noel.
>
> The day that comes from uncertain light
> Almost brings tears to my eyes.

---

[127] Sandrin, *Opera omnia*, no. 7; C. de Sermisy, *Opera omnia*, iv, no. 147.
[128] L. Miller (ed.), *Thirty-six Chansons by French Provincial Composers (1529–1550)* (Recent Researches in the Music of the Renaissance, 38 (Madison, Wisc., 1981), 81–2.

In enduring it, pleasure outweighs pain
Never did I see such a bright night.
O what happiness he wanted to bring
When God chose that virginal body;
It is a double gift that he comes to announce
If his work can give us pleasure.
   Noel, noel, so loud that the heavens thunder;
Not only man, but every living creature speaks,
The great Lyon sounds its great organ,   Lyons
Noel, noel, aloud leaps forth.
A pleasing song based on good words.
The nightingale sees union in harmony,   Villiers [sees union]
And a bleating lamb responds,   Aneau [lamb]
Singing noel and crying out with all its heart.
   The golden griffin has dug in its claws   Gryphe [claws]
And engraved many noels in script;
To show that nothing is apocryphal
In anything that is sung about Jesus Christ;
All living creatures, all men, all souls   Praise the Lord
Give praise to this new-born child;   with all your spirit
For whom we sing the song taught us by   Psalm 150
The angel of heaven, noel, noel, noel.

Two years later, in 1541, the College presented another play by Aneau, this time a topical satire 'on the comparison of Paris, Rohan, Lyons, Orléans etc. and on the memorable events that have taken place since 1524'. Published in 1542 under the title *Lyon marchant*, it is a eulogy on the industry and prosperity of Lyons, expressed in allegorical form. After a prologue introducing the protagonists, Arion (symbolizing Francis I), enters astride a dolphin (representing the Dauphin François who was sent as a hostage to the Emperor Charles V to help obtain the release of his father in 1526). Arion plays 'on a lute or lyre a sad and lamenting song like *Doulce mémoire*, or some other'.[129] Sandrin's chanson thus continues its remarkable vogue, although, whereas Des Périers in 1539 considered it suitable for merry-making, Aneau now sees it as a sad and melancholy piece, perhaps because it recalled to him the Dauphin's death at Lyons in 1536.

Arising and laying his instrument aside, Arion now begins a speech, referring to a number of musical instruments and forms, including the archaic *aubade*, *lai*, *virelai*, and *bergerette*, quite in keeping with the

---

[129] B. Aneau, *Lyon marchant: Satyre Françoise. Sur la comparaison de Paris, Rohan, Lyon, Orleans et sur les choses memorables depuys Lan 1524. Soubz Allegories & Enigmes par personnages mystiques jouée au Collège de la Trinité à Lyon, 1541* (Lyons, 1542), fo. A3ʳ; repr. G. Veinant (Paris, 1831).

Rhétoriqueur style of the poetry (revealed for example in the word-play between *Mottel* in the seventh line, *mot tel* and *mortel* in the eighth, and *martel* in the ninth) (fo. A3ʳ):

> Je quicte tout, tabourins, & bedons
> Haulxbois, bourdons, fleuste, rebec, sonnete,
> Harpe, Angelic,[130] Luz, Manicordions,
> Ou accordions, Danses, & Tordions,
> Psalterions, Virginal, Espinete,
> Jeu d'orgue honneste, aubade, Chansonnete
> Bergeronnete, & Virelay, & Mottel
> Et tout mot tel, fors que le lay mortel,
> Que sans martel jadis forgea Tristan,
> Car esprouvé j'ay par trop maint triste an.

> I am leaving everything, fifes and drums,
> Shawms, drones, flute, rebec, hand-bell,
> Harp, angelica, lute, clavichords,
> Or accordions, dances, and tourdions,
> Psalteries, virginal, spinet,
> Honest organ, aubade, chansonnete,
> Bergeronnete, virelai, and motet
> And every such thing, except the deadly lai,
> Which Tristan used to forge without a hammer,
> For I have tried them all for many a sad year.

After two more *dizains* from Arion, Vulcan (representing war) enters from underground and noisily summons a gathering; this wakens Paris, asleep at the foot of a mountain, whilst the Lion, standing strong between two rocks, responds to the call, and all the characters descend on to the central stage, displaying their reaction to Vulcan's 'coup de matines' in a sequence of short interjections. A series of monologues follows, as each comments on recent events, such as the struggles with Charles V, the conquest of Milan, and loss of Ghent, the sorrowful death of the young Dauphin (allegedly poisoned by Sébastien de Montecuculo), the decapitation of Anne Boleyn and her brother, and the dislike of Pope Clement VII (Arion's 'faulx tyrant'—specifically identified in a printed marginal note). Arion also alludes to the cultural Renaissance following the Italian expeditions, praising the lyrical art of Greece with its hymns, psalms, paeans, and Pindaric odes, before

---

[130] The punctuation and capitalization in Pierre de Tours's 1542 publication of Aneau's play suggests that the *Angelic* was a separate instrument, perhaps a lute played like a harp, such as illustrated in M. Praetorius, *Sytagma Musicum*, ii (Wolfenbüttel, 1618, Pl. xxxvl, no. 2), rather than the double-necked 'angel lute' or 'angélique' found in late 17th-c. sources (see Ian Harwood, 'Angélique', *New Grove Dictionary*).

travelling on to Italy, where he is dazzled by the new poetic and musical forms, the dances, the grace of the people, and the beauty of their ornaments:

> Passay la mer: et vins en Italie
> Ou par mon art (qui toute joye allie)
> Sonnant sonnetz, Barzelettes, & Balles,
> Chansons, Strambotz, Pavanes, Madrigales
> J'acquis en brief la grace de la gent
> Beaulx ornements, bagues, or, et argent.   (fo. A7ᵛ.)
>   I crossed tha sea and came to Italy
> Where by my art (which every joy doth ally)
> Sounding sonnets, barzelettas and *balli*,
> Chansons, strambottos, pavanes, [and] *madrigali*
> I did in short acquire the people's grace
> Fine ornaments, rings, gold, and silver.

The identification of Italy with music at this early date could only have been conceivable in Moderne's Lyons. The *barzeletta* or *frottola* enjoyed only a limited vogue in France,[131] although the *strambotto* and its most celebrated exponents, Serafino, Tebaldeo, and Chariteo, had begun to affect a number of French poets, such as Scève and more especially Mellin de Saint-Gelais, who, like the *strambottisti*, was famed for his musical execution. The sonnet was beginning to arouse interest in France, but as yet only amongst a few poets, notably Saint-Gelais and Clément Marot; the first complete musical setting—Saint-Gelais' 'Au temps heureux', composed for four voices by Arcadelt—was published in 1539. The madrigal as a musical genre was still in its infancy (although Verdelot, Festa, Arcadelt, Berchem, and others already had a number of collections published by Gardane and Scotto in Italy), and as yet showed no signs of significantly affecting French musical collections or of threatening the long heritage of the chanson.

Lyon marchant ends with a contest for honour between the cities, but the result is a foregone conclusion. After holding forth on the hospitality given to all people, even foreigners and serfs, by Lyons, Verité offers a word of praise to the other contenders: 'Orléans is of great providence ... Paris is beautiful and is the final arbiter' (*Aurélian est de grand providence ... Paris est beau et le dernier Juge*). However, the refrain at the end of each stanza announces the outcome: 'But before them all strides merchant Lyons' (*Mais devant tout est le Lyon marchant*). Thus final triumph and glory is accorded to (fo. C2ʳ):

---

[131] D. Heartz, 'Les goûts réunis', in *Chanson and Madrigal, 1480–1530*, ed. J. Haar (Cambridge, Mass., 1964), 88–138.

Lyon marchant assis en son hault throne
Ayant le chef de haulx monts couronné
Comme Corinthe est de deux mers: du Rhodne
Et de la Saone il est environné.
De grand beaultez, & de richesse orné
Gardant du cueur de l'Europe l'entrée
Et marchissant sur diverse contrée
Qui n'est Lyon ne passant, ne couchant
Rampant, grippant sa proye rencontree
Mais devant tous est le Lyon marchant.

Merchant Lyons, seated on its high throne,
Crowned by the lofty mountains,
Like Corinth, encompassed by two seas—
The Rhône and the Saône.
Decorated with great beauty and richness,
Guarding the entrance to the heart of Europe
And bounding on diverse countries.
'Tis a Lion not passant or couchant, but
Rampant, gripping any prey it encounters:
Above all others strides merchant Lyons.

The success of such theatrical ventures was probably responsible for the Consulate's decision to employ Aneau, along with Guillaume du Choul and Maurice Scève, to provide emblems celebrating the visit of King Henry II and his wife Catherine de' Medici in 1548. Two years later he was placed in sole charge of the celebrations welcoming the new regional governor, Jacques d'Albon, and asked to provide 'ystoires et dictons': to this end he wrote the '[H]istoire d'Androdus qui premier aprivoysa le Lyon', an allegory, along the same lines as *Lyon marchant*, performed on a stage beneath a triumphal arch.[132]

Twenty years after the appearance of the *Chant Natal*, Godefroy Beringen printed another series of noëls presenting the Christmas story in dramatic dialogue with music, under the title: *Genethliac: Noel musical et historial de la Conception et Nativité de nostre Seigneur Jesus christ, par vers et chants divers* (Genethliacon: Musical and historical noël on the Conception and Nativity of our Lord Jesus Christ, with verse and tunes of various sorts). As with the *Chant Natal*, the title-page also announced as a sequel a *Chant royal pour chanter à l'acclamation des Roys* (*Chant royal* to be sung for the Kings' acclamation), as well as an *Aiglogue Sibylline de Vergil prophetisant l'enfantement de la Vierge & Nativité du Filz divin, Traduicte en decasyllabes François* (Sibylline Eclogue prophesying the Virgin birth and the Nativity of the divine Son, translated into French ten-syllable

---

[132] Lyons, Archives communales, BB 68, fo. 57ʳ and BB 71, fos. 186ᵛ–199ʳ.

lines). No author or composer is announced here, but a quatrain is appended to the title suggesting that the latter might be Du Tertre and the former Aneau:

> La Muse assise au chef du Tertre
> Coronné d'eternel rameau
> Par chants fait resonner la lettre
> Signée en la Foy de l'Aneau.
>
> The Muse, seated at the head of the Mound,
> Crowned with the eternal branch,
> With tunes resounds the words
> Signed in the Faith of the Lamb.

Furthermore, on the verso is a royal privilege for five years assigned to Aneau and, on the next page, a dedication to Marguerite de France, King Henry II's sister, again including a pun on the name 'Aigneau'. The following pages print a preface explaining that 'our fathers and ancestors, in the past and even more recently, reverently and joyfully celebrated Advent and Christmas by singing Noël in their homes with their families and servants, on long winter evenings, after dinner in front of the fire, passing the time innocently with joyful *chants Natalz* instead of lascivious chansons or scandalous gossip. For this honest purpose these *Noelz Evangeliques*, with new words and music, were composed in 1558...After the *chants de Noelz* is a *chant Royal* 'suitable for the feast of the Epiphany'.

One important difference between Aneau's two sequences of noëls is the fact that the later one abandons the use of existing music or *timbres* in favour of 'new music', specially composed for the new words. This change from adapting existing melodies to composing fresh music notated and printed along with the text is paralleled in the Protestant biblical dramas of Joachim de Coignac (*La desconfiture de Goliath* Geneva, 1551) and Louis des Masures (*David combattant*, *David triomphant*, *David fugitif*, and *Bergerie spirituelle*, Geneva, 1566), although the contrafactum principle returns in the anonymous *La Musique de David* (Lyons, 1566), which adapts the official Genevan psalm melodies or their four-part harmonizations by Goudimel.

Aneau's *Genethliac* begins with a dialogue between Damoetas (son of the Cumaean Sibyl) and Menalcas entitled 'Probleme pastoral ainigmatic en imitation du Vergilian Oximor'; this has no music but includes another punning reference to the author (p. 7):

> Di moy comment l'aigneau simple en nature
> Tua le loup et tollit tous les maux?
> Di moy comment parmi ces chams ruraux

Pourrait trouver quelque bergier habile
Les fleurs portans lettres des noms Royaux?

Tell me how the lamb, simple in nature,
Killed the wolf and took away all our sins?
Tell me how in these quiet meadows
Some clever shepherd might find
The flowers bearing the letters of the royal names?

The 'flowers' bearing the royal names refer to the ensuing songs, whose texts include anagrams printed in capitals mentioning the dedicatee Marguerite de France, her brother Henry II, his wife Catherine de' Medici and his mistress Diane de Poitiers, the dauphin François and his wife Mary Stuart, Antoine de Bourbon, King of Navarre, and his wife Jeanne d'Albret, François and Charles de Guise, respectively duke and cardinal of Lorraine, and Anne de Montmorency, Constable of France.

The play is arranged as a prologue, followed by sixteen scenes, each of which is described in an introductory rubric and illustrated by a woodcut, having a *chant* with strophic verse, usually divided between two or more characters. The notated music begins on page 8 with the annunciation, presented in dialogue between the angel Gabriel and Mary in six twelve-line heterometric stanzas. Only the Cantus and Tenor parts are printed in the one surviving copy (Paris, Bibl. nat., Cons. Rés. 85); however, Altus and Bassus parts may have been included in a separate book, as in the Beringen brothers' earlier publications of four-voice psalms by Bourgeois and Didier Lupi. A four-part arrangement is also suggested by the occasional fourths and frequent sixths between the parts, as well as by the rubrics; moreover, Chant XIII is marked 'Trio', although only the top voice is actually provided.

The first piece includes two strophes printed beneath the music, with five more appended on the two ensuing pages. The anonymous music in the transposed Ionian mode (F major) opens with a duple metre phrase in close imitation, repeated with a different ending for the second couplet; the ensuing syllabic phrase of folk-like character also begins in imitation, as do the third and fourth couplets; the next couplet is homophonic and concludes in triple metre, while the last repeated couplet begins with another imitative motif (akin to the third) and ends with a passage in coloration (see Pl. 2).

The remaining fifteen chants, depicting in dialogue the Visitation, Adoration, along with other episodes from the Nativity story, and the ensuing Virgilian Eclogue are of a similar nature. Aneau's verse has strophes of varied rhyme and metre in the manner of the noëls of François Briand (1512), Jean Daniel (c.1520–40), and Nicolas Martin (1555), all of whom were similarly involved with music and theatre.

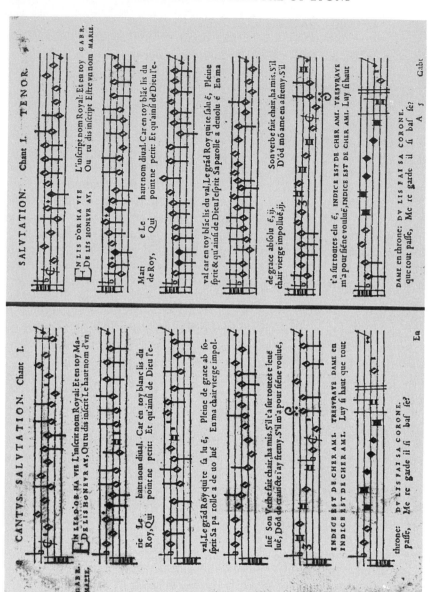

Pl. 2. Anonymous music (Cantus and Tenor parts) of the 'Salutation angélique' from Barthélemy Aneau's *Genethliac* (G. Beringen, 1559), pp. 8–9

The first strophe is usually set simply, having brief imitative openings or syllabic passages with short melismas at the cadences which faithfully respect the prosody, in a style similar to that of the contemporary metrical psalm. Most of the chants are in duple time, although the first, fourth, and tenth have sections in triple or compound time, while the ninth, a *branle*, is in compound time throughout. As with most Huguenot psalms, the main melodic interest is in the Tenor, with the Cantus often moving in conjunction in sixths or in imitation. Some of the tunes have a popular quality, while the forms are lucid and frequently repetitive in a variety of ways.

The *Chant Royal* (Chant XVI, pp. 50–2) has five eight-line strophes and an envoy, presumably sung to the second half of the music provided. The next piece is the *Genethliac ou Chant Natal, Aiglogue quatrieme de Vergil intitulé Pollion ou Auguste, extraict des vers de la Sibylle Cumane*, comprising 140 decasyllabic lines in consecutive verse, the first fourteen being set by Goudimel[133] in the same form that he and his contemporaries used when setting sonnets, with the music of the first quatrain repeated for the second. The final scene, the *Presentation de l'enfant au Temple, vers l'Archiprestre Sainct Symeon* (Chant XVII, pp. 61–3), has four decasyllabic quatrains, the first sung by Mary, the rest by Saint-Simeon, with music, ascribed to D. Lupi, paraphrasing the Nunc dimittis canticle. This, plus the textual and musical relationship of the *Cantique de la Vierge* (Chant III, pp. 14–15) to the Magnificat, may indicate that the play was intended to be enacted during Christmas Vespers.

Since music had long been an integral part of French drama, both sacred and secular,[134] it is appropriate here to briefly survey the development of the theatre locally. In 1435, thirty-three years after Charles VI established the Confrères de la Passion in Paris, a lay association was organized for the presentation of plays in Lyons; the *compagnons*, who may have included clerics, as activity centred on the Jacobins' Church, arranged the roles and the staging. In 1447 a Passion was performed by the monks at Saint-Bonaventure;[135] but apparently biblical subjects did not satisfy the youth, and ten years later the *clercs de la chancellerie du roy* performed a topical satire ridiculing the ladies' taste for luxury. This farce was censured by the town councillors, and during the following decade municipal authorization was required for dramatic enter-

---

[133] C. Goudimel, *Œuvres complètes*, xiii, ed. P. Pidoux and M. Egan (Boston, 1974), no. 71.

[134] See C. E. de Coussemaker, *Drames liturgiques du moyen âge* (Rennes and Paris, 1860); C. Brouchoud, *Les Origines du théâtre à Lyon* (Lyons, 1865); Brown, *Music in the French Secular Theater*.

[135] J.-B. Monfalcon, *Histoire de la ville de Lyon*, 2 vols. (Paris, 1847), i. 632.

tainments.[136] In 1475 the Consulat itself commissioned an 'ystoire', arranged as a series of dialogues with tableaux, for the ceremonial entry of Louis XI; but in general it remained opposed to such public spectacles. Thus in 1483 the *compagnons joueurs* played at the town gates to avoid the aldermen's jurisdiction,[137] although passion-plays were still performed in churches in 1485.[138] The situation improved with the presence of Louis XII in 1500, when the *clercs de la Bazoche* finally operated as a corporation from the Augustins' Church; although in Lyons they never enjoyed 'droit de juridiction', their leader having the title 'Prince' but not 'King'. In 1506 the Consulat granted a resident troupe of Florentine actors authorization to present a Saint Nicholas play at the Place des Terreaux[139] and in 1513 another, in praise of Pope Julius II, at the Puits de la Porcherie (now the Place Saint-Paul).[140] During the festivities in 1515 welcoming Francis I and Queen Claude, a citizen, dit Grenoble, was refused consent to erect a stage to perform 'certaine ystoire ou il blâmoit des membres du corps commun'. [141] But in August 1518, after considerable civic opposition, Pierre Molaris, the *Prince des bazochiens*, received permission to play a mystery lasting four days at the Place des Cordeliers.[142]

As the sixteenth century progressed, the long mystery play gave way to the morality and farce, presented in private halls rather than public squares. The first permanent theatre at Lyons was built in 1538 by Pierre Neyron, who converted three houses on the corner of the rue des Bouchers and the rue de la Martinière (now nos. 2, 4, and 6 of the rue Hippolyte Flandrin, near the Augustins' Church): the façade measured 23 metres and the internal capacity 60 square metres. The seating was arranged in three covered galleries for the wealthy bourgeoisie, and benches at floor level for the poorer citizens. The stage was constructed in three superimposed sections, the highest for heavenly scenes, the middle for earthly ones, and the lowest for infernal ones, thus providing opportunity for depicting the moral implications of the text by the technique of simultaneous representations).[143] The venture encountered problems, for Neyron died in 1541 and in September of that year, his son, Antoine, sold the premises to

[136] Lyons, Archives communales, BB 8, fo. 50ʳ, 25 May 1457.
[137] Ibid., BB 17, fo. 60ᵛ.
[138] Ibid., BB 19, fos. 50ʳ–55ʳ.
[139] Ibid., BB 25, fo. 17ʳ.
[140] Brown, *Music in the French Secular Theater*, 9.
[141] Lyons, Archives communales, BB 34, fo. 161ʳ.
[142] Ibid., BB 37, fos. 178ʳ–202ʳ.
[143] Paris, Bibliothèque nationale, MS français 12536; see O. Leroy, *Études sur les mystères* (Paris, 1837), 128.

Antoine Sigles, a German business man from Strasburg. However, according to Colonia, [144] a collection of plays written by Louis Chouquet and presented at Neyron's theatre was printed in 1542 under the title *Le tresexcellent et sainct mystère du vieil testament representé par personnages, auquel sont contenues les histoires de la Bible*. Some, like the anonymous mysteries printed in Lyons at this time, the *Sacrifice d'Abraham* (1539) and *Le Mystere de Sainte Barbe*,[145] incorporate a few songs for angels and shepherds; the second of these plays, which was probably adapted from a fifteenth-century original, includes Clément Marot's famous chanson 'Tant que vivray', sung by a loose woman 'with dissolute and lewd gestures of love'. *Le Gouvert d'Humanité*, one of several plays written by the notary Jean d'Abundance and printed around the same time in Lyons by Jacques Moderne, mentions 'tabourins et auboys' as the agents of Satan, playing for a dance performed by Temptation and Mortal Sin.[146]

The high moral tone of such mysteries presented on Sundays and feast-days was apparently not retained, and the theatre was closed in November 1548, after degenerating in response to the new vogue for licentious farce. In the same year Lyons encountered the new fashion in classical Italian theatre, with elaborate machines and musical *intermedi*, as Bibbiena's *Calandria* was presented by the Gelosi troupe, at the expense of the Archbishop, Ippolito d'Este, and the Florentine community, for the visit of Henry II and Catherine de' Medici. Brantôme recalls the novelty of the event in his memoirs as 'something never seen before and rare in France; until then people only spoke about farcers, the fools of Rouen, the players of the *Bazoche*, and other kinds of jesters and players of jests, farces, mummeries, and foolish things' (*chose que l'on n'avait encore vue et rare en France; car auparavant on ne parloit que de farceurs, des conards de Rouen, des joueurs de la Bazoche et autres sortes de badins et joueurs de badinages, farces, momeries et soteries*).[147]

In November 1551, despite his employers' pleas, Aneau resigned his post at the Collège de la Trinité to devote more time to writing. In the same year an anonymous pamphlet entitled *Quintil*, attacking Joachim du Bellay's *Deffence et illustration de la langue françoyse*, was published by Jean Temporal as an appendix to Sebillet's *Art Poétique* and reprinted separately in 1556. Its author, masquerading under the name

---

[144] *Histoire littéraire de Lyon*, ii. 430.

[145] L. Petit de Julleville, *Les Mystères*, 2 vols. (Paris, 1880), ii. 135, 486.

[146] P. Aebischer, 'Le Gouvert d'Humanité par Jean d'Abundance', *Bibliothèque d'Humanisme et Renaissance*, 24 (1962), 282–338.

[147] P. de Bourdeille, *Œuvres complètes*, ed. L. Lalanne, 11 vols. (Paris, 1858–78), iii. 256.

of Horace's friend Quintilius, is generally thought to be Aneau, or possibly his colleague Charles Fontaine.[148] The erudite, even somewhat pedantic, style is characteristic of the conservative playwright and poet, whose work was untouched by the revival of ancient drama or by the new Italian lyric poetry. The polemic springs to the defence of the old *formes fixes*, disdained by the Pléiade, claiming that their ingenious construction represented a tribute to the French language, while remaining faithful to the classical tradition. It derides Du Bellay's inconsistency in rejecting 'vulgarity' and demanding poetic elevation in one breath, and calling for the humblest musical instruments in the next:

Quel langage est ce, chanter d'une musette & d'une fluste? Tu nous as proposé le langage françois: puis tu fais des menestriers, tabourineurs & violeurs. Comme ton Ronsard trop et tres arrogamment se glorifie avoir amené la lyre Greque & Latine en France, Pource qu'il nous fait bien esbahyr de ces gros & estranges motz, 'Strophe' & 'Antistrophe'... Car qui demanderoit au plus savant de vous quel instrument est & fut 'Lyra' & la maniere d'en sonner ou jouer, & la forme d'icelle, nombre de cordes & accordz, et la maniere de chanter les vers dessus, ou sur la fluste, je croy que le plus habille se trouveroit moindre en cela que un petit Rebecquet & flusteur de vilage. Pource n'abaissez point la poésie à ménétrerie, voilerie & flagéolerie.

What language is this—to sing about a bagpipe and a flute? You propose a French language to us, then you go on about minstrels, drummers, and viol-players. Like your Ronsard, who boasts too much and very arrogantly that he brought the Greek and Latin lyre to France, really astounding us with those big and strange words, *Strophe* and *Antistrophe*... for if anyone should ask the most learned of you what instrument is or was the *Lyra* and how was it sounded or played, and what was its shape, the number of its strings and chords, and how were words sung to it, or on the flute, I bet that the most skilful would find less in this than a little village rebec- or flute-player. So do not reduce poetry to minstrelsy, viol-playing, or fluting.[149]

Aneau's own views on the comparative merits of rustic and sophisticated music are reflected in his *Imagination poétique*:

Soubz Timol Juge, un debat fut prins, entre
Pan le Pasteur et Phebus le bon chantre:
Lequel diroit meilleur chants, et plus beaux:
Phebus au Luc et Pan aux Chalumeaux.
Chascun des deux sonna son instrument,

[148] H. Chamard, 'La Date et l'auteur du Quintil Horatian', *Revue d'histoire littéraire de la France* (1898), 54; see also J. du Bellay, *La deffense et illustration de la langue françoise* (Paris, 1549), ed. H. Chamard (Paris, 1904; 2nd edn. 1948).

[149] B. Aneau, *Quintil sur le premier livre de la defence et illustration de la langue françoise* (Lyons, 1556), 202–3.

Phebus bien doux, et Pan bien haultement.
Le Roy Midas estant à l'audience:
En Juge fol donna brieve sentence.
    Et prefera la Musete hault quinant
De Pan, au Luc de Phebus doux sonnant.
Pour tel arrest, Phebus si luy feit naistre
    Oreilles d'Asne: affin de le cognoistre...[150]

    With Tmolus as judge a contest took place between
The shepherd Pan and the fine singer Phoebus [Apollo]
To find who sang the better and finest songs,
Phoebus with his lute and Pan with his *reed pipes*.
    Each of them played his instrument,
Phoebus very softly and Pan very loudly.
King Midas in the audience,
Like a mad judge gave his summary decision
    And preferred the noisy bagpipe
Of Pan to the lute of Phoebus.
For such a verdict, Phoebus so made him sprout
    Ass's ears for recognition.

The *Quintil* rejects the Pléiade's interpretation of classical lyricism and, on the authority of Horace, asserts that the ancients, like the moderns, gave their verses to professional minstrels for musical setting:

Car les poétes lyriques du passé, ne ceux du présent, ne chantoient, ne sonnoient, ne chantent, ne sonnent leurs vers...mais les composaient & composent en beaux vers mesurez, qui puys apres par les Musiciens estoient, et sont mis en Musique, & de la Musique és instrumens. Ce que bien donne à entendre Horace disant:

> Le menestrier qui de fleuste harmonique
> Sonne les vers du beau jeu pythonique,
> Premierement, avant que de tel estre,
> Apprins il a et revere son maistre.

Ou l'on peut voir, que je Joueur instrumentaire sonnoit és lieux & sacrifices d'Apollon les vers Pythiques, que longtemps par avent Pindar avoit composez.[151]

For the lyric poets of the past, and those of today, did not and do not sing or play their verse...but composed and compose in fine measured verses, which were and are then set to music by the composers and played to [the accompaniment of] musical instruments. This Horace clearly explained when he said:

> The minstrel who with harmonious flute
> Sounds the verses of the fine Pythian game,

---

[150] B. Aneau, *Imagination poètique traduicte en vers François des Latins & Grecz* (Lyons, 1552), 120.
[151] Aneau, *Quintil*, 204; cf. Horace, *Ars Poetica*, 414–15 (grotesquely misunderstood).

First, before being such,
Has learnt and revered his master.

From this we see that the instrumentalist played in the places of sacrifices to Apollo the Pythian verses that Pindar had written long before.

It admits that Mellin de Saint-Gelais (author of two of the three *chansons vulgaires*, 'Laissez la verde couleur' and 'O combien est heureuse', criticized by Du Bellay) was a rare exception to the rule:

> Et si vous autres me mettez en avant un Mellin Monsieur de Saint-Gelais, qui compose, voire bien sur tous autres, vers lyriques, les met en Musique, les chante, les joue, et sonne sur les instruments; je confesse et say ce qu'il sait faire, mais c'est pour luy... Et en cela il soustient diverses personnes, et est Poete, Musicien, vocal & instrumental... mais de telz que luy ne s'en trouve en la grande douzaine.[152]

And if you put forward the case of a Mellin Monsieur de Saint-Gelais, who composes his own lyric verses, better indeed than anyone else, sets them to music, sings them, plays them, and sounds them on instruments; I agree and know what he can do, but that is peculiar to him... And in this he is being different people, poet and musician, vocal and instrumental... but those like him are few and far between.

If the author of the *Quintil* was in fact Aneau, he conveniently forgets the noëls which in 1539 he had fitted to existing *timbres*, when insisting that music should be the handmaid of poetry:

> Car il n'est pas en usage (ce que tu dis autre part) que les Poetes composans chansons se assujectissent à suivre la Musique; ains au contraire les musiciens suyvent la lettre et le *subject* (qu'ils appelent) à eux baillé par les Poetes. Et qu'ainsi soit, j'en demande à Claudin, Certon, Sandrin, Villiers, et autres renommez Musiciens.[153]

For it is not usual (as you say elsewhere) that poets writing chansons subject themselves to following the music; on the contrary it is the composers who follow the letter and *subject* (as they call it) given to them by the poets. For evidence of this I would cite Claudin, Certon, Sandrin, Villiers, and other famous composers.

This was indeed normally the case; the composer respected verbal declamation, occasionally highlighting an individual word in the manner that was to characterize the new Italian madrigal. Yet after the old *formes fixes* were abandoned in favour of freer and more varied structures, there was an increasing realization of the need for characteristically musical forms whose exigencies sometimes override the verse-pattern and rhyme-scheme, while noëls, *voix-de-ville* and *chansons*

---

[152] Aneau, *Quintil*, 205.   [153] Ibid. 194.

spirituelles were often fitted to existing dances or popular songs.

Like many of his contemporaries in Lyons, Aneau was sympathetic to evangelical and even Calvinist ideas; he paid for these when he was assassinated in the Collège during an anti-Protestant uprising in 1561.

(x) *Charles de Sainte-Marthe (1512–1555)*

In June 1540, Charles de Sainte-Marthe received a teaching post at the Collège de la Trinité from Barthélemy Aneau, and in the same year published his *Poésie Françoyse* with Pierre de Sainte-Lucie. Since 1537, when his Calvinist sympathies ended his professorship in theology at Poitiers, Sainte-Marthe had travelled around Provence, Languedoc, and Dauphine. To judge from the poems he addressed to Dolet, Tolet, the Scèves, Pomponio Trivulzio, Marie-Catherine de Pierrevive, and others, he must have spent some time in Lyons.[154]

It was probably during this time that he met the composer named Villiers, whom his friend, Aneau, described as a nightingale in 1539. Sainte-Marthe dedicates a rondeau to this 'most perfect musician', defending music against uncouth and ignorant critics who decry it as 'fantastic science':

> Un tas de Sots lesquels ne scavent rien
> Osent blasmer sans propos la Musique
> Disant, que c'est science fantastique,
> Et de laquelle on apprend peu de bien.
>   Mais a lon veu aulcun homme de bien
> Qui advouast en raison juridique
>   Un tas de Sots:
>   Entre gents n'ont grace ne entretien
> On le cognoit à leur facon rustique
> Mais ne leur fault alterquer par replique
> Pas ne vallent un vieil efront de chien
>   Un tas de Sots.[155]

> A load of fools who know nothing
> Have the temerity to criticize music without justification,
> Saying that it is a fantastic science
> From which little good can come.
>   But have you ever seen a worthy man
> Who would admit as judicial evidence [the word of]
>   A load of fools:
> In company they show neither grace nor conversation.

---

[154] C. Ruutz-Rees, *Charles de Sainte-Marthe* (New York, 1910).
[155] 'A Villiers, Musicien tresparfaict', C. de Sainte-Marthe, *La Poésie Françoise* (Lyons, 1540), 97.

You can see this in their boorish manners,
But you should not get involved in answering them,
Not worth an old dog's snarl [a tinker's cuss] are
        A load of fools.

Villiers returned the compliment by setting two poems from the same collection: the first, 'Force d'Amour me veult souvent contraindre,' a *dizain* on the Petrarchist subject, 'Quel martyre c'est brusler d'affection et n'oser parler pour la descouvrir', was originally dedicated to the poet's poor but beautiful lady friend, Mlle Beringue de Loytaulde from Arles.[156] Villiers's four-voice setting first appeared in Lyons in the ninth book of Moderne's *Parangon des Chansons* (RISM 1541[8], fo. 18) and was reprinted the next year at Paris in Attaingnant's ninth book (1542[13] fo. 7[v]). The second poem, 'Rien n'est plus cher que cela qu'on desire,' another ten-line *épigramme*, on the neo-Platonic theme 'Qu'au bien d'Amour, rien n'est plus nuysant que jouyssance', was addressed to a certain Seigneur de Parnans.[157] Villiers's music appeared in 1543 in Moderne's eleventh book of chansons (now lost) and in Attaingnant's fourteenth (RISM 1543[11-12], fo. 4[v]). Only three further poems from the *Poésie Françoyse* were set as four-voice chansons, 'Le cueur loyal en amour' by L'Huyllier (1543[7-8], fo. 4[v]), 'Vous me changez pour ung aultre' by Brigard (1549[25], p. 3), and 'Les mesdisantz par leur meschant langaige' by Lachenet (1553[20], fo. 11[v]).

Early in 1541 Sainte-Marthe left Lyons for Geneva, but later that same year he was imprisoned as a suspected Lutheran in Grenoble. After his release in 1543 he returned to Lyons and, after spending some time in the service of the Duchess of Beaumont, he became *conseiller* and *maître des requestes* to Queen Marguerite de Navarre at Alençon. He contributed a number of *dizains* to a collection of amorous poems published at Paris in 1543,[158] but none of these was set to music.

(xi) *Maurice Scève (1501–1562)*

Maurice Scève, now generally considered the leading poet of the Lyons group, was fascinated by the philosophical aspects of contemporary music theory, particularly those related to the union of poetry and music. The musical symbolism of his *Arion* (1536), *Délie* (1544), *Saulsaye* (1547), and *Microcosme* (1562) and the polyphonic settings of

---

[156] Ibid. 75; see Ruutz-Rees, 278.
[157] Ibid. 13; see Ruutz-Rees, 319.
[158] N. Léonique *et al.*, *Les questions problématiques du pourquoy d'Amours Nouvellement traduict de l'Italien* . . . , (Paris, 1543).

his poetry are considered by V. L. Saulnier,[159] who while acknowledging his debt to Marsilio Ficino and Gregor Reisch, does not discuss Scève's view on the importance of numbers and geometry in the union of poetry and music, as expressed in at the end of the *Livre Second* of the *Microcosme*:

> De point, ligne, cerne, angle en divers corps formés
> Mesure la figure aux traits théoremés
> A disproportion pour se prospective
> Comme par contrepoints à Musique arriver
> Musique, accent des cieux, plaisante symphonie
> Par contraires aspects formant son harmonie: . . .

> From point, line, circle, angle formed in different bodies,
> The figure is measured with theorems
> With disproportion to obtain perspective
> As through counterpoint you attain music
> Music, sound of the heavens, pleasing symphony
> With contrary aspects making up its harmony: . . .

Saulnier's list of musical settings omits the eight-line 'Helas amour tu feis mal ton debvoir,' the sixth piece in the anonymous anthology *Le Petit œuvre d'Amour* (Paris, 1537, fo. A4^r), which may be attributable to Scève; this was set by Peletier in Attaingnant's sixth book of chansons (RISM 1539$^{15-16}$, fo. 6^v). The list also lacks 'En aultre part que là où ils aspirent' (*Délie*, no. 334), set for three voices by (Simon) Levrart and published in Louvain in Phalèse's third book of *Recueil des Fleurs* (RISM 1569^{11}). Moreover, it gives the first source of 'L'ardant desir du hault bien desire' (*Délie*, no. 82) as the second edition of Attaingnant's ninth book (1542^{13}), although Certon's setting of this *huitain* also appeared in the first edition (1540^{14}, fo. 4^v). Finally, its assertion that Moderne's collections include nothing by Scève is not strictly true, since the eighth book of *Le Parangon des chansons* (1541^7, fo. 18) includes Villiers's setting of 'Le veoir, l'ouyr, le parler, l'attoucher' (*Délie*, no. 41), which had been published by Attaingnant in Paris the previous year (1540^{13}, fo. 4^v). For a later printing in Lyons, see Pl. 9.

(xii) *Pernette du Guillet and the Ladies of Lyons*

The cult of feminism which characterizes literature in Lyons around the middle of the century was introduced by the Florentine emigrants of

---

[159] V. L. Saulnier, 'Maurice Scève et la musique', in *Musique et poésie au XVIᵉ siècle*, ed. J. Jacquot (Paris, 1954), 89–103.

the late fifteenth century. The idealized role of women in society, based on the model of Petrarch's Laura, permeates early sixteenth-century Italian lyric poetry, most notably Bembo's *Gli Asolani* (1505). Castiglione's *Il Cortegiano* (1528) requires the refined lady to be more than the impassive subject of chivalrous and gallant allusions: she should possess a knowledge of languages and the classics, compose epigrams and chansons, show musical accomplishments, especially on the lute and spinet, and be good and worthy company for her husband, whose virtue and learning she should admire. In the Lyons of Marie-Catherine de Pierrevive and Louise Labé, literary Platonism may represent an escapism from the low morals of a 'depraved' and decadent, luxury-loving society, as it did in Venice and at many of the French and Italian courts. This aristocratic preoccupation spread to the rich *bourgeoisie* who, in the absence of local nobility, were admitted to the royal court when it was held in the southern capital. Marie-Catherine de Pierrevive, celebrated for her charm, intelligence, and culture, opened her house to artists, poets, and musicians, while, following the example of King Francis I's sister, Marguerite de Navarre, a number of Lyonese ladies distinguished themselves in the arts, letters, and music; these ladies included Louise Perréal, whose painting and poetry are praised by Eustorg de Beaulieu; Jeanne Gaillarde, Marot's 'gilded feather'; Marguerite de Bourg, Tyard's 'Pasithée; Jacqueline Stuard, celebrated by Des Périers and Sainte-Marthe; and the Scève sisters, Sybille and Claudine, Marot's 'belles and bonnes sœurs lyonnaises'.

Even more remarkable was Maurice Scève's disciple, Pernette du Guillet, the 'gentille and vertueuse dame lyonnoise', whose *Rymes* were edited after her early death in 1545 by Antoine du Moulin and published by Jean de Tournes at the request of her husband.[160] This collection (comprising mainly *épigrammes* and stanzaic *chansons*), is discussed by Verdun Saulnier[161] and Victor Graham, whose modern edition gives the variant readings of the five *épigrammes* set to music, 'En lieu du bien que deux souloient prétendre', 'Je n'oseroys le penser veritable', 'Le corps ravy l'ame s'en esmerveille', 'Le grand desir du plaisir admirable', and 'C'est un grand mal se sentir offensé'.

It is notable that the first four musical settings were published in Lyons, the first two ascribed to F. de Lys and P. de Villiers respectively, in the sixth book of Moderne's *Parangon des Chansons* (RISM 1540[16]), with the next two, to Coste and F. de Lys, in the ninth book (1541[8]). All

[160] *Rymes de gentile et vertueuse dame, D. Pernette du Guillet Lyonnoise* (Lyons, 1545); ed. V. E. Graham (Geneva, 1968).

[161] V. L. Saulnier, 'Étude sur Pernette du Guillet et ses *Rymes*', *Bibliothèque d'Humanisme et Renaissance*, 9 (1944), 7–119.

three composers have special connections with Lyons, if only in that most of their work was printed there. However, the first two pieces were also printed in Paris in 1540, with the second and revised edition of Attaingnant and Jullet's second book of new chansons (1540[6], fos. 5[v] and 6[v]), the first piece being ascribed to Quentin rather than F. de Lys; in this book Attaingnant's chansons nos. 7–14 ('Doulce mémoire', 'Fini le bien', 'Ce qui souloit', 'En lieu de bien', 'Je ne le croy', 'Je n'oserois', 'Sy mon travail', and 'Le doeul yssu') follow each other in a significant and clearly pre-determined order, as pairs of poem and *response*, the latter beginning with the poem's last line and ending with its first, using apposite musical quotations. Thus it will be seen that 'En lieu du bien' must have been composed in response to 'Ce qui souloit en deux se despartir', a *huitain* ascribed to King Francis I in at least two contemporary manuscripts;[162] the music, attributed variously to Quentin and F. de Lys, begins with the theme of the last line of Sandrin's famous setting of the king's poem and ends with a variant of its opening melody (see Music Example 2). Attaingnant's sequence provides the first three *huitains* in the *Fleur de Poésie* anthologies published at Paris in the 1540s,[163] but the fourth, although designated 'responsif', uses only the first and last lines of Attaingnant's text, which was virtually identical to Du Guillet's 'En lieu de bien', altering the remaining lines and using only two rhymes.

The same procedure of musical reminiscence is used in Villiers's 'Je n'oseroys' (see Music Example 3), which quotes first from the close and finally from the opening of Sandrin's setting of the *huitain*, 'Je ne le croy et le sçay seurement' (1538[11] and 1540[9], fo. 6, 1538[15], fo. 28).[164]

Another *épigramme* by Pernette, 'Si le servir merite recompense' resembles the texts of two other contemporary chansons, 'Si le service est receu pour offence', a *quatrain* set by P. de Villiers in Attaingnant's first book of 1538 (1538[10], fo. 13[v]), and 'Si mon service a merité Recompense ou allegement', a *huitain* set by Crecquillon in Moderne's tenth book (1543[14], fo. 21), although there is a common model in Leone Ebreo's *Dialoghi d'Amore*.[165] Du Guillet's piece provides one of the notable examples of Platonism, although the poetess was also greatly influenced by images and ideas taken from Serafino and Chariteo.

[162] Dobbins, 'Doulce mémoire', 86–7.
[163] Anon., *La Fleur de Poésie Françoyse* (Paris, A. Lotrian, 1543), repr. in *Raretés bibliographiques* (Brussels, 1864) and *Collection erotica selecta* (Paris, 1909); *La Fleur de vraye Poésie françoyse* (Paris, P. Sergent, n.d.); *La Fleur de Dame Poesie Francoyse* (Paris, J. Bonfonds, 1548).
[164] See Sandrin, *Opera omnia*, no. 5.
[165] P. du Guillet, *Rymes*, ed. Graham, 29.

Pernette's fame did not match that of Louise Labé, 'la belle cordière', whose *Euvres* (comprising twenty-four sonnets, three elegies, and the *Débat de Folie et d'Amour*) were published by Jean de Tournes in 1555. Labé's Italianism is even more marked than Du Guillet's: the first sonnet in the published collection, 'Non havria Ulysse', is actually written in Italian, while the remainder are imbued with the spirit and style of Petrarch and his followers. For Scève and the Pléiade, Italianism and Platonism are essential ingredients for love poetry; and music is never far from the surface, as Apollo explains in the fifth discours of Labé's *Débat*:

Diray je que la Musique n'a été inventée que par Amour? et est le chant et harmonie l'effect et signe de l'Amour parfait. Les hommes en usent ou pour adoucir leurs desirs enflammez, ou pour donner plaisir: pour lequel diversifier tous les jours ils inventent nouveaus et divers instrumens de Luts, Lyres, Citres, Doucines, Violons, Espinettes, Flutes, Cornets: chantent tous les jours diverses chansons: et viendront à inventer madrigalles, sonnets, pavanes, passamesses, gaillardes, et tout en commemoraçion d'Amour.[166]

Shall I say that music was invented by love alone—with melody and harmony as the effect and sign of perfect love? Men use it to soften their passionate desires or to give pleasure: and in order to ring the changes every day they invent new and diverse instruments with lutes, lyres, citterns, douçaines (= curtalls), violins, spinets, flutes, cornetts: every day they sing different songs and they come to invent madrigals, sonnets, pavanes, passamezzi, galliards, and all this in the name of Love.

Like Pernette, Louise realized that the study of music, as well as language and literature, could aid the liberation of the female: her dedicatory epistle to Clémence de Bourges makes this point forcefully:

Mais ayant passé partie de ma jeunesse à l'exercice de la Musique, & ce qui m'a resté de tems l'ayant trouvé court pour la rudesse de mon entendement, & ne pouvant de moymesme satisfaire au bon vouloir que je porte à notre sexe, de le voir non en beauté seulement, mais en science & vertu passer ou egaler les hommes: je ne puis faire autre chose que prier les vertueuses Dames d'eslever un peu leurs esprits par dessus leurs quenoilles & fuseaus, & s'employer à faire entendre au monde que si nous ne sommes faites pour commander, si ne devo[n]s nous estre desdaignées pour compagnes tant es afaires domestiques que publiques, de ceus qui gouvernent & se font obeïr.[167]

But after spending part of my youth practising music, and having found the time left all too brief for the roughness of my understanding, and being unable myself to satisfy the good will I have for our sex, to see it surpass or equal men

---

[166] L. Labé, *Euvres* (Lyons, 1555); ed. A. Bosquet (Paris, 1960), 108.
[167] Labé, *Euvres* (Lyons, 1555), fo. a2ᵛ.

not only in beauty, but in science and virtue, I can do nothing other than plead with virtuous ladies to raise their minds above their distaffs and bobbins and to busy themselves in letting the world understand that while we are not made to give orders, we are not to be disdained as companions either in domestic or in public matters, by those who govern and who are obeyed.

None of Louise's poems is known in contemporary musical settings, the same being true of the much vaunted Clémence de Bourges, whose musical and linguistic attainments are extolled in a letter by Jean-Baptiste du Four, published in Roville's edition of Boccaccio's *Decameron* in 1555:

la quale accompagna si bene la voce con la mano che tocca gli instrumenti di musica, tanto nelle parole toscane che nelle franzese, et aggiunge tanta gratia all'arte che par' che de Palade sia stata chiamata per quarta compagna alle tre Grazie.[168]

who accompanies her voice so well, playing musical instruments with her own hands, [singing] Tuscan as well as French words, and she adds so much grace to the art that it appears that Pallas acclaimed her as a fourth companion to the three Graces.

In 1585 Antoine du Verdier wrote of her:

la perle des Damoiselles Lyonnoises de son temps employa sa jeunesse à l'exercice de la Poesie et de la Musique: et eut l'esprit accompaigné de tant de graces et le corps orné de tant de beautez, que le feu sieur de Peyrat, gentilhomme doué de toutes les bonnes parties qu'on sçauroit souhaiter, luy donna son cœur et se voua entierement à son service. Il feit une chanson sur le nom de sa Clémence que Francisco Roussel mit en musique à 4 parties, disant ainsi—O *que je vis en estrange martyre*.[169]

the pearl of the young Lyonese ladies of her day spent her youth in the practice of poetry and music: and her mind was endowed with so many graces and her body adorned with so much beauty that the late Sieur de Peyrat [son of the royal lieutenant of Lyons, he died fighting the Protestants at the siege of Beaurepaire in 1561], a gentleman endowed with all the good qualities one could wish, gave his heart to her and dedicated himself entirely to her service. He wrote a song on the name of his Clémence, which Francisco Roussel set to music for four voices, beginning 'Oh how I live in strange martyrdom'.

Roussel's setting of this *huitain* has not survived, although one by Didier Lupi Second published in Lyons (1559[19], p. 28) and another by Jacques Le Trot published in Paris (1560[3b] fo. 8[r]) have.

[168] See Picot, *Les Français italianisants*, ii. 13.
[169] A. du Verdier, *Bibliothèque* (Lyons, 1585), 182; ed. R. de Juvigny in *Les Bibliothèques Françoises . . .*, 5 vols. (Paris, 1772), iii. 394. See also C. de Rubys, *Histoire véritable de la ville de Lyon* (Lyons, 1604), 384.

The ascription 'Clem. de Bourges' is appended curiously to an organ intabulation by Jacob Paix (RISM 1583[23], no. 53) of Arcadelt's four-voice setting of 'Da' bei rami scendea', the fourth stanza of Petrarch's *canzone* beginning 'Chiare fresche e dolci acque'. The significance of this late ascription is unclear; but it might suggest that Arcadelt dedicated his madrigal, first published in 1542, to the Lyonese lady.

The musical gifts of Pernette, Louise, and Clémence de Bourges were shared by the mysterious lady celebrated under the pseudonym 'Panfile' by later Lyonnais poets such as Jean de Boyssières and Loys Papon. A long discourse in Papon's published works suggests that Panfile's singing and lute-playing belong to the time of Claude le Jeune, when *rechants* and echos were favoured in settings of strophic airs; the poem even mentions an 'academy', which might have been an echo of Baïf's Académie de Poésie et de Musique, rather than of any such establishment in Lyons:

> Mais alors qu'elle veut, d'un zelle plus actif
> Mesler a ces douceurz des tons qu'elle manie,
> D'une angelique voix, la celeste armonie
> Qu'elle appelle un Echo, de rechant de ses vers
> Qu'elle mesmé s'extase aux ayles de ses airs.
> Ceux a qui de ce leuth, les resonances plurent,
> Se pasment soubz les deux, surmerveillent, se meurent.
>   .   .   .   .
>
> Qui de son despinete, et qui de lyre thusque,
> Qui d'un harpe croyzée aux cordages ouverts
> Qui pour se resoudre en fondz ces rumeurs si divers
> Dont les Astres là haut cadencent leur extaze
> Des violles entonne une sonante baze,
> Pour aux graves bourdons des veines qu'elle tend,
> Remplir les fleuretis des autres qu'elle attend,
> Ce reste de renfort en cett' academie,
> Hausse et n'adoucit pas l'air de la mélodie.
> Ny toutz ces instrumentz qui degoysent leurs tons
> Les doigts, les archeletz qui meslangent leurs sons,
> Ne peuvent empescher de leur force qui pousse,
> Que ce leuth de s'entende en sa grace plus douce.[170]

> But while she wishes, with more active zeal
> To mingle the sweet sounds that she fingers,
> With an angelic voice, in the celestial harmony,
> That she calls an echo, with the reprise of her verse,
> That she herself enraptures on the wings of her airs.
> Those pleased by the resonances of this lute

---

[170] *Œuvres du chanoine Loys Papon* (Lyons, 1555), 2.

Faint under the [influence of the] two, and die in awe.

. . . .

[She] who with her spinet, who with her Tuscan lyre,
Who with a crossed harp with open strings,
Who to get to the bottom of those diverse rumblings
With which the stars above give rhythm to their ectasy,
With viols sounds a resonant bass,
To fill with the low [diapason] strings that she stretches,
The flourishes of others for whom she waits,
This remnant of comfort in this academy,
Highlights and softens not the air of her melody.
Nor all those instruments which spout their tones,
The fingers, the bows which mingle their sounds,
Cannot with their pressing strength prevent
This lute being heard with its sweeter grace.

(xiii) *Feminism, Platonism, and Lyricism in the Poetry of Lyons*

Charles Fontaine (1514–*c*.1568) figures as an ardent feminist and Platonist in *La Contr'amye de Court*, which champions the cause of ideal love against La Borderie's satire, *L'Amye de Court* (1541).[171] His first printed collection of poems, *La Fontaine d'Amours* (1545), the fruit of his recent Italian travels, reflects the influence of Petrarch, Serafino, and Sannazaro, but the later *Ruisseaux* (1555) are more overtly Platonist. These collections were published (by Jean de Tournes and Thibaud Payen respectively) in Lyons, where the poet resided from the late 1530s, accepting Aneau's offer of a teaching post at the Collège de la Trinité in 1541. No less that ten *épigrammes* from *La Fontaine d'Amours* were set to music, six by Dominique Phinot and four by Didier Lupi Second, all of them printed by the Beringen brothers in 1548.[172] The first seven lines of another poem in the same collection, beginning 'Resjouy toy, o populaire' and entitled 'Resjouyssance au commun peuple pour ceste Année 1545', was adapted and set by Corneille de Blockland (Montfort) under the title 'Resjouyssance au peuple pour l'an 1577' and published by Jean de Tournes in 1579. Fontaine's *Ruisseaux* includes an *odelette* in praise of the author by Hubert-Philippe de Villiers, whom in turn Fontaine compliments with a quatrain, recalling the 'science' of Charles de Sainte-Marthe's 'perfect musician':

---

[171] See R. L. Hawkins, *Maistre Charles Fontaine Parisien* (Cambridge, Mass., 1916), ch. 5.
[172] V. L. Saulnier, 'Dominique Phinot et Didier Lupi, musiciens de Clément Marot et des Marotiques', *Revue de musicologie*, 43 (1959), 61–80.

> Les Muses et la Musique
> Toutes deux sciences celestes
> Toutes deux se font manifestes
> En toy d'usance et théorique[173]
>
> The Muses [i.e. poetry] and music
> Both heavenly sciences,
> Both are made evident
> In you be practice and theory

The concurrence of Aneau, Saint-Marthe, and Fontaine at the Collège de la Trinité around 1540 would suggest that all three authors were referring to the same musician called Villiers. Moreover, the survival of musical settings of 'Le deuil yssu', cited by Aneau, and of two poems by Sainte-Marthe, would seem to indicate that this was the 'P. de Villiers' named in the publications of Moderne in Lyons and Attaingnant in Paris. However, the specification of the names Hubert Philippe in Fontaine's collection, and in a number of translations and other literary works from the 1550s and 1560s, including an *Aer funèbre* for Prince Louis de Condé (1569), which presents three-part music in a quite different monodic or *voix-de-ville* style (see Pl. 13), may mean that the poet-musician was a younger relative. Thus it is possible that 'P. de Villiers' was not the Pierre de Villiers mentioned as a canon at Cambrai Cathedral in 1516,[174] but this same Philippe or Hubert-Philippe Villiers, who in his later years became known as a poet. However, the success and reputation of P. de Villiers as a composer of polyphonic chansons, motets, and masses in the 1530s and 1540s would appear to contradict the apologetic tone adopted by Hubert-Philippe in explaining why he had the 'presumption' to write his own music for the Prince of Condé's funeral air, instead of calling on 'the most excellent French composers' whom he 'knew well'.

Fontaine's friend, Guillaume des Autelz (1529–c.1581),[175] also emerges as a feminist and Platonist in his *Repos de plus grand travail* (Lyons, 1550). His next collection of poetry, the *Amoureux repos* (Lyons, 1553), comprising mainly odes and sonnets in the manner of the Pléiade, includes a lament on the death of Clément Marot sung to the tune of Saint-Gelais' 'Laissés la verde couleur' (fo. B4ʳ), as well as a lyrical piece dedicated to his cousin and neighbour, Pontus de Tyard, which abounds in the new lyrical imagery, with references to Ronsard, Du Bellay, Plato, and Pythagoras:

---

[173] *S'ensuyvent les Ruisseaux de Fontaine* (Lyons, 1555), 334.
[174] F. Lesure 'Villiers, P. de', *Die Musik in Geschichte und Gegenwart* (Kassel, 1966), xiii. 1643.
[175] M. L. Young, *Guillaume des Autelz* (Geneva, 1961).

Il faut que mon pouce accorde
Un tel son, dessus sa corde,
(Puis que de ton saint honneur
Je veulx estre le sonneur)
Que rend, quand plus s'evertue
La Vandomoyse tortue,
Ou le doux Luth Angevin.

   .   .   .   .   .   .

Mon Dieu quelle soif de gloyre
Luy fait dessous Platon boyre
Ce vin puissant gracieux
Quelle sienne faim devore
Du renaissant Pythagore
Les nombres religieux.[176]

My finger must tune
A similar sound upon its string,
(For of your saintly honour
I would be the player),
As is made more laboriously
By the lyre of Vendôme [i.e. Ronsard]
Or the sweet lute of Angers [i.e. J. du Bellay].

   .   .   .   .

My God what thirst for glory
Makes him drink under Plato
This potent gracious wine.
What hunger of his devours
The sacred numbers
Of the reborn Pythagoras.

He goes even further in a sonnet prefacing the *Vers liriques* published after the third book of Tyard's *Erreurs* (Lyons, 1555):

Premierement ta Muse Hermodienne
Ne resonna qu'ennuiz, soupirs & pleurs:
Continuant en apres tes Erreurs
Tu ne chantas qu'en note Lydienne.
   Nous attendions ore une Ionienne
Resjouissance, en fin de tes malheurs:
Et revoici de nouvelles douleurs,
Tousjours ta lyre est Simonidienne.
   Donq Pasithee ha le cueur d'une roche:
Ou ton desir de sa vertu n'approche:
Ou bien dequoy, dequoy donq te pleins tu?
   De ce vilain vulgaire qui te pique!

---

[176] G. des Autelz, *Amoureux repos* (Lyons, 1553), fo. E4ʳ.

Quoy? notre sainte escole Socratique
Asservit elle au vain bruit la vertu?[177]

First of all your Mercurian muse
Sang only of troubles, sighs and tears
Continuing after your *Erreurs*
You only sang in the Lydian vein.

We were waiting to hear the Ionian
Rejoicing, after your misfortunes:
And here are new sadnesses,
Your lyre is still Simonidian.

So Pasithée still has a granite heart,
Still untouched by your desire for her virtue;
But what really are you complaining about?

That vulgar villain who piques you!
What? Does our sacred Socratic school
Subject virtue to vain gossip?

Another local poet with feminist leanings was Labé's friend Claude de Taillemont,[178] whose *Discours des Champs Faez à l'honneur & exaltation de l'Amour & des Dames* (Lyons, 1553) includes pieces addressed to Jeanne de Navarre, Duchess of Vendôme, and to Queen Catherine de Medici; other poems follow Petrarch, Scève, and the Pléaide in portraying the ideal woman in personal or abstract terms, with music often enhancing her beauty. In the first discourse we learn that the assembled company were capable of singing polyphony:

Thélème et moy allasmes au jardin cueillir le rameau d'olive, duquel feismes un chapeau: et estans de retour, le mismes en presence de la compagnie, sus la teste, chantans à quatre parties ce couplet (p. 36):

> De vertus environée
> Couronnée
> Soit Eumathe, la gentille

Thélème and I went into the garden to pick olive branches with which we made a crown: and when we returned to the company we put it on her head, singing this verse in four parts:

> With virtue surrounded
> Crowned
> Let kind Eumathe be

The company might not rival the sweet natural harmony of the bird who (p. 40):

---

[177] P. de Tyard, *Erreurs amoureuses*, iii (Lyons, 1554), fo. 12^r.

[178] See J. Texte, 'Note sur la vie et les œuvres de Claude de Taillemont', *Bulletin historique et philologique* (1894), 406–20.

commenca à desgorger un chant à doux et harmonieux, que comme ravis, demourans longtemps sans nous bouger, n'estant moins ebahis de la privauté de telle beste que de son chant incongneu.

began to utter a song so sweet and harmonious that we remained for a long time in ectasy without moving, being no less astounded by the liberty of such a creature than by its strange song.

But they sang chansons from music books and danced to the sound of the lute, beneath a great leafy oak (p. 43):

au pié d'un gros chesne feuillu, chantasmes avec livres de musique plusieurs chansons Puis, ayans quelque peu dansé au son du luc . . .

The 'damoiselle parfaite' later sings her amorous verse 'with a sweet and harmonious voice' (pp. 52–3), while in the second discourse Thélème sings a quatrain to the accompaniment of a viol and is followed by Thimoe, who sings another to the lute. The author is then persuaded to sing a third quatrain, before Thélème brings out a *huitain* which all three sing together with instruments (pp. 138–9). Thus Taillemont describes the kind of environment in which many similar courtly chansons published in Paris and Lyons were performed.

Another collection of lyrical pieces by Taillemont, *La Tricarite plus quelques chants, au faveur de pluzieurs Damoezelles* (Lyons, J. Temporal, 1556), is dedicated to Jeanne de Navarre and other ladies. This collection is also notable for its orthographic experiments (explained in the Preface) and its attempt at French elegiac in quantitative metre, although no musical settings are known at present. The collection reflects the position of Lyons in the forefront of grammatical and orthographic experimentation, following the publication there of Dolet's treatise on translation and French punctuation (1540) and Meigret's on spelling (1542) and grammar (1550), the latter arousing fierce opposition in Aneau's *Quintil* (1551) and Des Autelz's *Replique . . . aux furieuses défenses de Louis Meigret* (1551).[179]

(xiv) *Guillaume de La Taissonnière* (c.1530–c.1590)

Of the younger contemporaries of Scève, whose works were published in Lyons, only Taillemont was a native of the city: most hailed from nearby towns—Guillaume des Autelz from Valence, Pontus de Tyard and Claude de Pontoux from Chalon, Philibert Bugnyon and Guillaume de La Taissonnière from Mâcon. Like Jacques Peletier du Mans, La

---

[179] See F. Brunot, *Histoire de la langue française*, 2 vols. (Paris, 1906), ii. 93–123.

Taissonnière later distinguished himself as a mathematician;[180] but he first appeared in print as a poet with his *Amoureuses Occupations*, published in Lyons in 1555. The lyricism of this collection is clear from the dedicatory sonnet to the young ladies of Chanien and Estours (p. 2):

> Toujours le luth que voz mains cinabrines
> Vont pincetant ne vous tient occupées:
> Toujours la Soye en toiles mi-coupées
> Vous n'enlacez d'eguilles damasquines,
>   Ni voz chansons clerement argentines
> En mille pars de fredons recoupées,
> Ne sont toujours de voz goziers chantées
> Bien qu'elles soent de ce tant les plus divines.
>   Quand donc par fois voz esprits prendront cesse
> De ces labeurs trompeurs de la paresse
> Je vous suplye ouir l'amoureus son
>   Sortant du creus de mon ame offencée
> Par la fureur d'une amour élancée
> Dedans le fort forcé, de ma raison.[181]

> The lute plucked by your cinnabar hands
> Does not occupy you all the time:
> Nor the silk, cut up into strips,
> Which you sew with your damascene needles,
>   Nor does the clear singing of silvery chansons
> In myriad parts with semiquaver diminutions
> Come all the time from your throats,
> Although they be amongst the most divine.
>   When therefore some time your minds do cease
> These labours to deceive idleness,
> I beg you to hear the amorous sound
>   Coming from the depth of my soul
> Assailed by the fury of a love that springs
> From the strong fortress of my mind.

Transalpine influence is also evident in the twenty-nine *strambotz* (pp. 9–19), all of which have the same rhyme scheme (a b a b a b c c), including another piece referring to the new lyre (p. 13):

> Son argentin, musicale armonie
>   Graves acors nettement prononcés
> Luth resonant quand celle te manie
>   Qui me tient tant mes soleils asconcés,
> Connois tu point que de pitié munie

[180] See Du Verdier, *Bibliothèque*, 510–11.
[181] G. de La Taissonnière, *Amoureuses Occupations* (Lyons, 1555), p. 2.

Elle ait regret de mes travaus passés?
Ainsi disoit fondant en tristes pleurs,
  Au luth de cell' qui causoit mes douleurs.

Silvery sound, musical harmony,
  Grave chords clearly articulated,
Lute resounding when you are played
  By the one who holds me so entranced,
Don't you know that, filled with pity,
  She was sorry for my past suffering?
So she said, melting in sad tears,
  To the lute of the one who caused my sadness.

The other main poetic genres represented in the collection, *Sonetz*, *Chantz*, and *Odes liriques*, are equally lyrical and sometimes show the author's preoccupation with music, as for example the sonnet described as 'Chanson envoyée à Mademoiselle de Mésez' (p. 31):

Tu pourras bien te vanter d'une chose
Douce chanson comblée de bonheur
Puis que tu vas pour réjouir le cœur
De celle en qui la vertu se repoze
  Tu pourras (si dire ainsi je l'oze)
Crier tout hault, musicale douceur
Qui se disoit de poésie sœur
N'a plus le bruit, ains est du tout forclose
  Car cette-la qui n'heut onc connoyssance
De la musique & d'ou vint sa naissance
De ses accors rend les cœurs si contens
  Qu'Apollo méme, ou Phœbus de sa lire
Ne sceurent onc que c'est que de bien dire,
Au pris de celle ou aller tu pretens.

You can certainly be proud of one thing,
Sweet chanson full of happiness,
Since you are going to gladden the heart
Of the lady in whom virtue reposes.
  You may (if I dare to say so)
Cry out loud, sweet music
Who claimed to be the sister of poetry,
Has fame no more but is debarred from everything.
  For the lady who never had any knowledge
Of music or where it came from,
With her harmony makes hearts so happy,
  That Apollo himself, or Phoebus with his lyre
Never knew what eloquence was
Compared to the lady to whom you make bold to go.

It is curious that the only poem from the *Amoureuses Occupations* that figures in a contemporary polyphonic chanson anthology is an *épigramme*, with the conventional French octave rhyme-scheme (a b a b b c b c), entitled 'De l'absence d'elle' (p. 62). It begins with the line 'Quelque rigueur qu'on puisse recevoir' and was set by (Laurent) Caron, a singer at Péronne, and printed in Nicolas du Chemin's fourteenth book of chansons in Paris (1560³ᵃ, fo. 11ʳ). However, the lyricism of the entire collection is symbolized in its penultimate poem, a sonnet addressed to the Milanese lutenist Giovanni Paolo Paladino, who published two books of lute music in Lyons in 1549 and 1560.[182]

An epithalamium written for the second marriage the Baron of Saint-Amour, Louis de La Baume, in 1574 and published in La Taissonnière's *Attifet des demoiselles* (Paris, 1575) was set to music in Corneille de Blockland's *Jardin de Musique*, printed in Lyons in 1579 by Jean de Tournes. Blockland also appends two poems by La Taissonnière addressed to his book's dedicatee, Gabrielle de Dinteville, Baroness of Bohan (fo. P2ᵛ):

> De Montfort, qui as l'heur, ou l'oreille m'abuse,
> D'envoyer des accords à la posterité
> Qui ne vieilleront point par le temps limité,
> Et de les faire plaire à la dixieme Muse,
>   Je ne sçay de quel roy fut en ton ame infuse
> La vigueur d'un esprit de si grand rarité,
> Que pour te faire honneur d'un los bien merité
> J'ay faute de sçavoir & besoin d'une excuse.
>   Mais je sçay bien, Montfort, que tu ne pouvois mieux
> Qu'à celle qui congnoit la musique des cieux
> Addresser ces chansons d'une gentile audace:
>   C'est elle qui pourroit charmer cest Univers.
> Par sa voix nompareille à chanter ces beaux vers,
> Et qui est icy bas une quatrieme Grace.

>   Montfort, you have the good fortune, unless my ear deceives me,
> Of commiting to posterity harmonies
> Which will not age with the passing of time,
> And of making them please the tenth Muse.
>   I know not what ray infuses your soul
> With a vigorous spirit of such great rarity,
> That to honour you with well-deserved praise
> I lack the knowledge and need an excuse.
>   But I know well, Montfort, that you could find no better person
> To whom to address these chansons with their pleasant boldness

---

[182] F. Lesure and R. de Morcourt, 'G. P. Paladino et son "Premier Livre" de luth (1560)', *Revue de musicologie*, 42 (1958), 170–83.

Than this lady who knows the music of the heavens:
  She is the one who can charm the universe
By singing these fine verses with her peerless voice,
And who is a fourth Grace down here.

His second eulogy of Montfort is a *dizain* (fo. P3ʳ):

Montfort, qui fais profession
Des quatre fureurs principales,
Et qui en toutes quatre egales
Les plus grands de ta nation:
Tu n'as pas faict election
Soulement de science digne,
Ains aussi de beauté divine
A qui tu voüës tes labeurs,
Qui surpasse toute ame insigne,
Comme toy, de mesmes fureurs.

Montfort, who manifests
The four principal furies,
And who is in all four equal
To the greatest of your nation:
You have not only chosen
A worthy scholar,
But also a divine beauty,
To whom you dedicate you labours.
She, like you, surpasses every notable soul
With the same furies.

In his *Erotasmes de Phidie et Gélasine* (Lyons, 1557)[183] the jurisconsult Philibert Bugnyon celebrates La Taissonnière's lyricism with an ode (p. 69):

Un Orphée bondissant
Aux fredons de sa cithare,
Si doucement ne sépare
Les Soeurs, du Mont florissant,
  Que de ta grecque Tortue
Tu fais bravader çà-bas
Les Mâconnises aux bals,
Ou tout gent coeur s'évertue.
  Quand je voy gaucher tes doigts
Dessus le plan de tes cordes,
Qu'en pinsetant tu accordes,
Avecq' le doux de ta voix:
  Il me semble que j'entend

---

[183] P. Bugnyon, *Erotasmes de Phidie et Gélasine* (Lyons, 1557); ed. H. Vaganay (Mâcon, 1900).

Un musical Amphion,
Un Phébus, un Arion,
Qu'en mer le Dauphin attend . . .

   An Orpheus leaping
To the semiquavers of his cithara,
Does not so sweetly separate
The Sisters, from the flowering mountain,
   As you do with your Greek lyre [i.e. lute]
Enlivening down here
The ladies of Mâcon at their dances,
In which all noble souls participate.
   When I see the fingers of your left hand
Controlling the pattern of your chords,
Which you pluck with in tuneful accompaniment
To the sweet sound of your voice.
   I seem to be hearing
A musical Amphion,
A Phoebus, an Arion
For whom the Dolphin waits at sea . . .

Bugnyon also addressed a sonnet to Simon Joly, the composer of a collection of twenty motets for four voices and one for five paraphrasing Psalm 50 (*Miserere mei*), published in Lyons by the Beringen brothers in 1552, with a dedication to François de Tournon, Cardinal Archbishop of Lyons and subsequently Bourges, where Joly was organist in 1559.

(xv) *Pontus de Tyard (1521–1605)*

Tyard was born at Bissy-sur-Fley near Chalon-sur-Saône in 1521 or 1522. He studied at Paris, but spent most of his life near Lyons, in the Mâconnais; he was a canon at Mâcon cathedral in 1552 and, after serving Henry III as *valet de chambre* and reader in astronomy, geography, mathematics, and philosophy between 1569 and 1578, was appointed Bishop of Chalon. A disciple and friend of Scève, he was later accepted as the philosopher of Ronsard's group. His earliest poetry, the *Erreurs amoureuses*, published by Jean de Tournes in three books (1549, 1551, and 1554),[184] reveals a neo-Platonism and a neo-Petrarchism typical of both the Lyons poets and the ensuing Pléiade. The collection comprises mainly sonnets, the favourite form of the Pléiade; but the six poems set to music (all from the first two books) include three stanzas from two 'Chants' ('Mon oeil au trait de ta beaute', 'Alors mes pensers

---

[184] P. de Tyard, *Erreurs amoureuses*, ed. J. A. McClelland (Geneva, 1967).

constumiers', and 'Je suis contrainct d'aimer'), the first stanzas of two 'Chançons' ('Caverneuse montagne') and 'Puisque je voy que mes afflictions', and two 'Epigrammes' ('Ce m'est un mal que je n'eusse pensé' and 'La grande ardeur de mon affection').[185] 'Caverneuse montagne' was set for four voices by the Parisian organist Antoine Cartier (1557[9], fo. 4[r]) and adapted as a monodic *voix-de-ville* by Jean Chardavoine (Paris, 1576, fo. 183[r]); the other poems were set for three or four voices by Pierre Clereau in two books published in Paris between 1559 and 1575.[186]

In the *Continuation des Erreurs Amoureuses* (Lyons, 1551), the poet's mistress, Pasithée (recently identified as Marguerite de Bourg, a lady distinguished in the literary circles of Lyons),[187] is praised for her accomplishment on the lute and guitar, as well as her graceful dancing and poetic composition. In his 'Chant à son Leuth'[188] Tyard compares the inspiration derived from his beloved's beauty to the eloquent lute-playing of Alberto da Ripa and Mellin de Saint-Gelais:

> Chante et de toy rien qu'elle ne resonne
> Y employant la mieux parlante corde
> Que touche Albert ou que Saingelais sonne.

> Sing [lute], and from you let only [my goddess's beauty] resound,
> Using the most expressive string
> That Albert touches or that Saint-Gelais sounds.

After translating Ebreo's *Dialoghi d'amore*, the bible of Platonism for the poets of Lyons, in 1551, Tyard began the first of his own philosophical dialogues to instruct Pasithée in the new learning, *Solitaire Premier, ou Prose des Muses et de la fureur poétique* (Lyons, 1552).[189] Here Pasithée enchants her admirer with he Ode, measured in the Italian manner and sung to the lute, while the poet tells of the moral effects of music and of he common origin and destiny of poetry and music, before ending the work with the choral harmony of Apollo and the three Graces. But the musical symbolism of Tyard's first philosophical discourse is given a fuller expression in his sequel, *Solitaire Second ou Prose de la Musique*.[190] This discourse could have been of little didactic

---

[185] P. de Tyard, *Œuvres poétiques* (Paris, 1573); ed. C. Marty-Laveaux (Paris, 1875), 16, 37, 74–6, 70, 19, and 47; *Erreurs amoureuses*, ed. J. A. McClelland, 103, 140, 204, 197, 107, and 157.

[186] M. Cauchie, 'Les Chansons à trois voix de P. Cléreau', *Revue de musicologie*, 9 (1927), 77–91; F. Lesure and G. Thibault, 'Le Musicien P. Cléreau et ses sources poétiques', *Bibliothèque d'Humanisme et Renaissance*, 16 (1954), 366–70.

[187] M.-M. Fontaine, '*Un cœur mis en gage*, Pontus de Tyard, Marguerite de Bourg et le milieu lyonnais des années 1550', *Nouvelle revue du seizième siècle*, 2 (1984), 69–89.

[188] *Erreurs amoureuses*, ed. McClelland 246–8.

[189] P. de Tyard, *Solitaire Premier*, ed. S. F. Baridon (Geneva, 1950).

[190] P. de Tyard, *Solitaire Second* (Lyons, 1555), ed. C. M. Yandell (Geneva, 1980).

or practical value to musicians, unlike the new spate of vernacular works following Loys Bourgeois' *Droict Chemin de Musique* (Geneva, 1550). It was rather an attempt to relate music to a general philosophy, akin to metaphysics and astrology, and to reinterpret Classical ideas from a humanist standpoint. Tyard discusses musical terminology, notation, and instruments, but is really more interested in the effects of music on man (and beast), which he illustrates in detail. His only real original ideas are those on the mnemonic virtues of music and the considerations for adapting rhyme, metre, and tune to subject-matter. Like Plutarch and Champier, he disdains professional musicians and follows the, by now conventional, Platonist and Pythagorean theories of Ficino and his followers. Yet *Solitaire Second* deserves detailed discussion here, since it represents the longest exposition of the Lyonnais poets' attitudes to music, linking the more fragmentary philosophies expressed by Champier, Dolet, and the earlier humanists with those of the Pléiade.

Tyard follows Dolet and Champier in recognizing music as the representative of symmetrical perfection and the 'image of the whole Encyclopaedia', reminding us that he had already (in his *Solitaire Premier*) tried to show that 'Music contains every discipline'. The views of Plato's *Republic* on the importance of music and gymnastics in the education of the philosopher are reflected in the section on 'corporal and spiritual exercises'; just as jousting, racing, jumping, fencing, etc. are seen as beneficial for the body:

la Musique servoit d'exercice pour reduire l'ame en une parfette temperie de bonnes, louables et vertueuses meurs, emouvant & apaisant par une naïve puissance & secrette energie, les passions & afeccions, ainsi que par l'oreille les sons estoient transportez aus parties spirituelles: qui fut occasion prestée aus premiers Poëtes & Theologiens de l'acompagner de Poësie, au nom de fureur sous la charge des Muses...[191]

Music served as exercise to put the soul into a perfect temper of good, praiseworthy, and virtuous morals, moving and calming the passions and affections by a instinctive power and secret energy, just as sounds were carried to the spiritual parts by the ear: this gave the early poets and theologians the opportunity to accompany it with poetry, in the name of fury under the aegis of the Muses...

Solitaire later elaborates on the ethical powers of music, and in the section devoted to modes (pp. 103–12), he follows Glareanus' *Dodecachordon* (Basle, 1547) in viewing the Dorian as 'the simplest and purest mode, suitable for the expression of gravity' and the

---

[191] Ibid. 11; ed. Yandell, 75.

Phyrgian as apt for the expression of 'anger and irritation'. He goes on to repeat a contemporary anecdote about the effects of the 'perfect' playing of the lutenist Francesco da Milano at a feast in Milan attended by his friend Jacques des Contes de Vintemille,[192] who told him how Francesco's first notes had interrupted the post-prandial conversation and how the listeners were soon carried away by the graceful melancholy of his fantasia, before a more vigorous continuation restored their spirits. Tyard describes the audience's reaction in some detail and thus anticipates the story of Claude le Jeune's impact at Baïf's Académie told in Artus Thomas's *Philostrate* (Paris, 1611, i. 282); however, both accounts are no more than modern variations on the traditional myth of Timotheus and Alexander, already elaborated by Rabelais. Tyard also describes the courageous effects of military music and bellicose instruments (drums, fifes, flute, trumpet, *trompe*, and horns), the power of the *chanson rustique* to relieve the ploughman's toil, and of the lullaby to quiet a crying child.

Solitaire Second asserts that music signifies 'Universal Philosophy, the state of the whole World and its components, divided into *Musique mondeine* and *Musique humeine*'. Boethius' classification of *musica mundana, musica humana*, and *musica instrumentalis* is somewhat confused by combining the last two. Tyard goes on to define music theory as (pp. 12–13):

la science qui considere avec sens & raison, la difference des sons graves & aiguz, ou bas & hauz, donnant le moyen de bien & harmonieusement chanter: à quoy est requis que l'on sache distinctement toutes les especes de Harmonie, & puis que l'on soit industrieusement exercé à entonner & exprimer disertement les voix en toutes mutacions, sous une mesure tousjours bien observee, tellement que son propre suget est un chant harmonieusement recueillant en soy des paroles bien dites, mesurees en quelque gracieuse cadence de rime, ou balancees en une inegale egalité de longue ou brieve prononciacion de sillabes.

the science which with sense and reason considers the difference between low and high sounds, or [between] soft and loud, providing the means of singing well and harmoniously: for this it is necessary to know clearly about species of harmony, and then to practise assiduously to intone and express the notes fluently in every mutation, with a carefully regulated measure, so that its proper subject is a melody that harmoniously encompasses words which are well-spoken, measured with some graceful rhythmic cadence, or balanced in an unequal equality of long or short pronunciation of syllables.

[192] Vintemille, rescued from the siege of Rhodes in 1522, was brought to Lyons by Georges de Vauzelles and acquired a reputation as a translator and poet in French and Latin before his death in 1582. An English translation of Vintemille's account of Francesco's playing is given in C. Field, 'Fantasia', *New Grove Dictionary of Music*, vi. 381.

In reply to the question, 'What is music?', he varies the definition (p. 14):

Musique est une disposition de sons proporçionnables, séparez par propres intervalles, laissant aus sens & à la raison une vraye preuve de sa consonance.

Music is a disposition of proportionate sounds, separated by proper intervals, leaving real proof of its consonance to sense and reason.

As a response to the enquiry, 'What is harmony and consonance?', Tyard paraphrases Champier (p. 15):

Harmonie contient du moins deus consonances et consonance n'est autre chose qu'un accord. Comme on diroit, une quinte est un acord ou consonance, ou (dira quelqu'autre) une double: mais si vous sonnez dessus la quinte une quarte, ou une quinte entre les deus extremes de la double, c'est une harmonie composee de deux consonances, assavoir Diapenté, qui sinifie quinte, et Diatessaron, qui sinifie quarte.

Harmony contains at least two consonances and consonance is nothing other than an agreement. As one might say, a fifth is an agreement or consonance, or (as some other will say) so is an octave. But if you sound a fourth above the fifth, or a fifth between the two extremes of the octave, that is a harmony consisting of two consonances, namely *Diapente*, which means a fifth, and *Diatessaron*, which means a fourth.

The ensuing section attempts an explanation of intervals and genera, expanding upon Boethius (*De Musica*) and Gafori, whose writings he may have known through Jean Grolier and whose influence is assessed in Cathy Yandell's modern edition of *Solitaire Second* (pp. 21–47).

The only engraved musical example is included in a chapter describing ancient notation using Greek letters, which Tyard acknowledges as a variation on Boethius, based on an old manuscript in his possession. He illustrates the system with a strophe of an ode, presumably of his own composition, indicating to Pasithée that she already knows the tune, which is then given again in modern notation.[193] To her subsequent question about how long each syllable should be, Solitaire replies that 'our language is less perfect than Greek or Latin, in which this concern is removed by the length and brevity of syllables observed by orators and poets. However, usage and learned men could offer some rules here which would remove doubt and give our poetry the perfection required'. This expectation of remedy seems to anticipate the later solution of Baïf's Académie, to whose *musique mesurée* the rhythm given by Tyard would appear to conform.

As a poet anxious for verbal clarity Tyard preferred monophony or monody to polyphony: he concurs with Aneau in admitting the

---

[193] See *Solitaire Second*, 27; ed. Yandell, 98.

superiority of the words over music. Thus in reply to the question 'Who is worth more in music, the operator of one voice (*Phonasce*) or the assembler of several (*Symphonete*)?' he writes:

si l'intention de Musique semble estre, de donner tel air à la parole, que tout escoutant se sente passionné et se laisse tirer à l'afeccion du Poëte: celui qui sçet proprement acommoder une voix seule, me semble mieus ateindre à sa fin aspirée: vu que la Musique figurée (ou chose faite) le plus souvent ne raporte aus oreilles autre chose qu'un grand bruit, duquel vous ne sentez aucune vive eficace. Mais la simple & unique voix, coulée doucement, & continuée selon le devoir de sa Mode choisie pour le merite des vers, vous ravit la part qu'elle veut.[194]

If the intention of music seems to be to give a tune to words, so that anyone hearing it will have his passions roused and will let himself be drawn to the poet's affection, he who can properly accommodate a single voice seems to me better able to achieve the end to which he aspires, in view of the fact that figured music (or *res facta* [i.e. polyphony]), usually conveys to the ear nothing but a great noise, for which you cannot effectively feel anything. But the simple, single voice, sweetly flowing and continuing according to the need of its mode chosen to enhance the verse, delights the part it wants to.

The Ancients, he claims, declaimed their lyric verse thus, simply and monodically, achieving secret power through the judicious choice of mode. Just as earlier he lamented the passing of the elevating union of music and poetic fury, he now regrets the decline of the status of music from being in ancient times the most important science required for the institution of good morals to a reputation of sloth and effeminate activity:

Plus encores me déplait le change fait du rang lequel anciennement elle tenoit premier entre les sciences necessaires pour l'institucion de bonnes meurs à une reputacion d'inutile oisiveté et exercitation efeminée.[195]

Here he also laments the emergence of the vagabond singer (*chantre vagabond*) and mercenary minstrel (*mercenaire menestrier*), unworthy of the name of musician, later claiming that he has the 'greatest difficulty finding a single tune suitable to his verses, let alone a three- or four-voice setting, the common practice familiar to innumerable [contemporary] singers':

J'ay avec plus de peine recontré un seul chant propre à mes vers, qu'escrit les vers, tels qu'ils sont, ni contr'assemblé trois ou quatre parties: reconnoissant en ce dernier un vulgaire usage, familier à infiniz chantres.[196]

---

[194] Ibid. 133; ed. Yandell, 214.
[195] Ibid. 10; ed. Yandell, 74–5.
[196] Ibid. 133; ed. Yandell, 214.

He saw the real problem, however, not so much that it was impossible
to fit notated music to his words, but that the French language was not
measured quantitatively, and that the musicians, who were for the most
part illiterate (just as most poets were generally unmusical), paid little
heed to the matter, even when setting sacred Latin texts:

Non toutefois, que je croye estre impossible d'accommoder proprement la
Musique figurée aus paroles, ni que je desespere de ce tems: mais la difficulté
de notre langage non encores mesuré en certaines longueurs ou brievetez de
sillabes, & le peu d'egard que je voy y estre pris par les Musiciens, qui tous, ou
la plus part, sont sans lettres, & connoissance de Poësie: comme aussi le plus
grand nombre des Poëtes mesprise, & si j'ose dire, ne connoit la Musique, me
fait creindre que tard, ou rarement, nous en puissions voir de bons & naturels
exemples. J'enten assez que les Musiciens ecclesiastiques (desquelles la
maniere de proceder n'est en tout semblable à celle que je vous ay deduite)
pensent avoir l'image de la plus diligent observaçion: si toutefois ils sont decuz
ou en tout ou en partie, aus personnes doctes & curieuses de cete discipline
j'en remis le jugement.[197]

Not however, that I think it impossible to fit figured music [i.e. polyphony] to
words, nor that I despair of these times: but the difficulty of our language,
which is not yet measured with definite long and short syllabic quantity, and
the scant regard I see paid to this by musicians, all, or most of whom, are
illiterate and ignorant of poetry: just as most poets despise and, dare I say, are
ignorant of music, makes me fear that only lately and rarely do we find any
good and natural examples. I quite understand that ecclesiastical musicians
(whose way of proceeding is not at all the same as that I have described to
you), think that they reflect the most diligent observation: whether, however,
they are mistaken in whole or in part I defer judgement to those learned and
interested in this discipline.

He again anticipates Baïf in seeking 'a Mode of singing, a way of writing
verse with feet and appropriate metres, as I believe the ancient Greeks
and Horace... very interestingly observed (*une Mode de chanter, une
façon de vers composée en piez & mesures propres: comme je croy les
anciens Grecs & Horace... avoir trescurieusement observé*);[198] and he
may have spurred on the younger poet when he wrote:

Bien voudróy je que quelqu'un plus hardi, & plus que moy sufisant, entre-
print, & vint à chef d'un art Poëtique aproprié aus façons Françoises: je
requerrois qu'il prescrit des loix Musicales: nommées lois anciennement,
pource que selon leur disposicion, laquelle il n'estoit permis d'enfreindre, la
Mode de chanter & la façon des rimes estoient gardees inviolablement: joint
que les premiers, privez de la commodité des lettres, ausquelles ils pussent
fier la conservacion de leurs loix, les chantoient, & ainsi les montroient aus

---

[197] Ibid.; ed. Yandell, 215.   [198] Ibid. 155; ed. Yandell, 243.

jeunes, à fin que le plaisir du chant, rechanté souvent, les imprima plus tenamment en la memoire. Je requerrois donq (veu je dire) qu'à l'image des Anciens (si bien leurs Spondees, Trochees, Embateries, Orthies & telles autres façons sont loin de l'usage de tous, & de la connoissance de peu) noz chans ussent quelques manieres ordonees de longueur de vers, de suite ou entremellement de Rimes, & de Mode de chanter, selon le merite de la matiere entreprise par le Poëte, qui, observant en ses vers les proporcions doubles, triples, d'autant & demi, d'autant & tiers, aussi bien qu'elles sont rencontrees aus consonances, seroit dine Poëte-musicien & témoigneroit que la harmonie & les Rimes sont presque d'une mesme essence.[199]

I would very much like someone bolder and more able than I to instigate and direct a poetic art of an authentic French kind. I would expect him to prescribe musical rules: they were called rules in early times because according to their arrangements, which could not be contravened, the mode of singing and the kind of rhyme [= rhythm?] were inviolably kept: added to this, the primitives, lacking the convenience of letters [= notation] to which they could entrust the preservation of their rules, sang them and thereby showed them to the young people, so that the pleasure of singing, oft repeated, more clearly imprinted them in their memory. I would like to say that, in imitation of the Ancients (even if their Spondees, Trochees, Anapaests, *pedes orthii* [= a Greek foot of five short syllables] and other choices are far from commonly used and are known to few), I would expect our songs to use some ordered ways of measuring verse, in succession or interspersed with rhymes [= rhythm?] and a mode of singing selected according to the requirements of the subject chosen by the poet, who by observing double and triple proportions, as many and half [*sesquialtera*] as many and a third [*sesquiquarta*], as long as they are matched to the consonances, will be a worthy poet-musician and will show that harmony and rhyme [= rhythm] are almost essentially the same.

Solitaire Second closes with a chapter on 'The composition and use of the monochord', demonstrating different consonances by proportions, with an engraving of a line-drawing of the instrument: the publisher, Jean de Tournes, apologizes for any proportional inaccuracies, resulting from his having to scale down Tyard's original drawing. It is symptomatic that Tyard should follow Boethius in choosing the didactic monochord, like Ptolemy and, later, Ficino, who similarly illustrates the 'tetrachord'[200] rather than the more practical lute and guitar of Aneau or the viol and flute of Philibert Jambe de Fer. Solitaire also quotes Boethius and Glareanus as authorities in the last section, although many of Solitaire's philosophical ideas derive from the neo-Platonist writings of Ficino,[201] even if some of these were transmitted through local

---

[199] Ibid. 155–6; ed. Yandell, 244.
[200] See M. Ficino, *Opera* (Basle, 1576), 1453.
[201] See P. O. Kristeller, *The Philosophy of Marsilio Ficino* (New York, 1943), 307.

sources such as Champier and Dolet. V. L. Saulnier[202] identifies Tyard's 'very old book ... given to me by ... Maurice Scève' as Gregor Reisch's encyclopaedic *Margarita Philosophica* (Basle, 1535), which he considers *Solitaire*'s principal source of inspiration. Scève was welcomed into Tyard's 'docte et musicale solitude' at Bissy and figures as one of the interlocutors in his third philosophical treatise, *Discours du temps, de l'an, et de ses parties* (Lyons, 1556), which includes a dialogue involving music, ending with the entry of singers and musicians to provide relaxation.

*   *   *

In his farewell to Lyons in 1536, Clément Marot reflects the earlier views of Jean Lemaire when he prays for the survival of 'the amorous air of that great city'. This might be interpreted as a plea for the continued flowering of Lyonese literature; for as Michelet observed, 'In Lyons the inspiration of poetry was not nature but love.'[203] If music was 'the food of love', and indeed Labé's Apollo considered it even the 'invention of love', it inevitably enjoyed great honour in the Golden Age of the city's literature. Its role may, however, have been more mystical and idealized because of its importance in the universe of Plato, the model for so many of the local school of poets:

Nowhere perhaps were Platonist theories more honoured than in the Lyonese poets of the period. In the great city of Lyons, opulent and given over to trade, both persistent and impassioned, inclining despite everything towards mysticism, a poetic school was formed with a character all its own.[204]

Platonism proved to be as significant a force in the southern capital's culture and intellectual life as the theological humanism of Erasmus, Luther, Le Fèvre, and Calvin was in its religious development. Despite the growth in Protestantism, Marot, Dolet, and Des Périers emerge as sceptical free-thinkers rather than Zwinglians, Lutherans, or Calvinists. But even in Lyons censure and persecution eventually affected tolerance and intellectual liberty, while atheistic Platonism was suppressed or adapted to conform with orthodox religious ideas.

---

[202] 'M. Scève et la musique', 90.
[203] J. Michelet, *Tableau de la France* (Paris, 1861), ed. C. Morazé (Paris, 1962), 134.
[204] L. Petit de Julleville, *Histoire de la langue et de la littérature française*, 8 vols. (Paris, 1897), iii. 129.

3
Musical Activity in Lyons

(i) Royal Visits, Official and Private Engagements

THE literary evidence may exaggerate the role of music in everyday life since, as we have seen, Platonist poetry endowed it with a mystical aura. However, there is abundant documentation of professional musical activity of the type spurned by the philosophers, as well as clear evidence that the gifted literary ladies did not enjoy a monopoly of amateur endeavours. The surviving archival documents, a fraction of the original, include mainly municipal accounts and notarized contracts recording payments, receipts, and official commissions concerning professional musicians and instrument-makers. Naturally there is more information on the official trumpets and drums, whose payments are regularly recorded in the civic accounts (CC 373–1590) and on the formal ceremonies—particularly banquets, receptions, and festivities arranged by the town council for the king or other visiting potentates. The present chapter by no means represents a complete record of the city's musical activity, but it reflects the picture provided by contemporary chronicles and descriptions of great events, the findings, both published and unpublished, of local archivists (notably Henri Coutagne and Georges Tricou), the summary catalogues of extracts from the civic and departmental (Rhône) archives compiled by F. Rolle, A. Steyert, G. Guigue and others between 1865 and 1962, as well as the results of local searches undertaken by me in 1968–70 and more recently by Laurent Guillo.

As related in ch. 1, the presence of the royalty and aristocracy during the Italian campaigns boosted the artistic life of Lyons. Two biographies of the famous knight, Bayard (Pierre du Terrail), by Symphorien Champier and Jacques de Maille, give a colourful general description of some of the ceremonies and pastimes which took place in the city around 1500: Maille's account, for example, mentions the visit in 1494 of the Duke of Savoy to Charles VIII at Lyons, 'where he stayed, whilst his princes and gentlemen enjoyed life, with jousts and tournaments every day, and in the evening dances and balls with the local ladies who were beautiful and graceful'.[1] The archives sometimes provide more

---

[1] J. de Maille, *La Vie de Bayard*, ed. J. Roman (Paris, 1878), 15–16.

detail on the music provided for these occasions. For example, they show that on 26 March 1503 a drummer, a rebec-player, a lutenist and an organist were paid two gold écus (worth £3. 10s.) 'according to rates agreed by the town councillors' to perform at a banquet given at the residence of the Archbishop (Charles II de Bourbon) in honour of the visit of Philippe le Beau, Count of Flanders, for the betrothal of his son Charles (later the Emperor Charles V) to Louis XII's two-year-old daughter, Claude:

Aux instruments, c'est assavoir: Jehan de la Senaz tabourin, Guillemin joueur de rebec, Jehan Barete joueur de lut et Poncet joueur des orgues qui jouerent audit Banquet par tauxacion de MM les conseillers—deux escus d'or valant 3 livres 10 sols.[2]

The same civic archives report payment to several musicians, including the instrumentalists Jean Berault, Robert Gabriel, Guillaume [de la Mœulle] de Genève, Jacques Girard, and the drummers Benoît, Goujellin, La Monnoye, and Le Chat, for playing at 'un festin de banquet' presented in February 1548 for four Swiss ambassadors and their retinue on their return from court, where they had attended the baptism of Princess Claude. They also document the remuneration of Antoine Froyssard, Simon d'Ayme, Thomas Vigne, Barthélemy Gottefroide, and Julio Cursio for playing their musical instruments at a banquet which the town prepared for the visit of Henry III in 1581.[3]

Contemporary reports indicate that music also accompanied the solemnities of ceremonial entries, like the arrival on 14 August 1506 of the new Archbishop of Lyons, François de Rohan, who was accompanied in the procession to the cathedral by the singer and canon Rolin de Semur, while the clergy sang *Inter natos mulierum*. Another account of this event states that the choir sang *Te Deum laudamus* in clear and resonant voice and that later in the cathedral one of the choir sang *Humilate vos ad benedictionem*, to which the chorus responded *Deo gratias*. Neither the French nor the Latin report, however, offers any details of the music used in the two allegorical *histoires* performed for this occasion at the Porte de Bourgneuf and on the steps of Saint-Jean.[4]

More *histoires* were performed during the ceremonies greeting Francis I in July 1515; but while even the expenditure on costumes worn by the young ladies representing the symbolic characters is recorded,[5]

[2] Lyons, Archives communales, CC 556, fo. 11ᵛ.

[3] Lyons, Archives municipales, CC 977, no. 25, fo. 4ʳ, and CC 1341.

[4] C. O. Reure, *L'Entrée à Lyon de François de Rohan* (Lyons, 1900), 22; M. C. Guigue, 'L'Entrée de F. de Rohan', *Bibliothèque de l'École des Chartes*, 63 (1902), 339–51.

[5] Lyons, Archives communales, CC 66, pièce 11.

there is no mention of payment to musicians, either in the archives or in a separate contemporary account of the festivities.[6]

The release and return of Francis I's sons, following the Peace of Cambrai, was celebrated between 8 and 10 July 1530 with 'moralitez et histoires figurez' and a *Te Deum* sung at the cathedral and a procession preceded by 'trumpets and shawms playing very melodiously poly-phonic musical chansons that were very good to hear'. The printed account of the proceedings closes with 'a fine, new Chanson written and composed for the joyful advent of our lords, the royal children', sung to the tune of 'Quand me souvient de la poulaille'.[7]

Puis que la belle fleur de lyo
A produict si noble amytié
De quoy les deux lyepars jolys
Ont faict telle solennité
Vive le noble roys Françoys
Et sa noble maiesté
Ilz sont amys à ceste fois
Vive le noble roys Françoys

Les ans dorés sont revenuz
Selon le cours du firmament
Car saturne & dame venus
Ont cest' année gouvernement
Chantons tous amoureusement
Françoys: bourguignons d'ung accord
Et vivons amoureusement
Sans jamais avoir nul discord
Qui est celuy tant soit parfaict
Qui sceut reciter par ses ditz
La grant triumphe qu'on a faict
A bayonne des deux petis
Quant à moy je soutiens & dis
A brief motz pour le faire court
Que c'est ung droit paradis
Maintenant de haute la court.

Since the beautiful lily
Has produced such noble friendship
From which the two pretty leopards
Have made such solemnity
Long live noble King Francis
And his noble majesty.

[6] Wolfenbüttel, MS 86.4 extravagantium; see G. Guigue, *L'Entrée de François I* (Lyons, 1899).
[7] *Les Nouvelles venues à Lyon de la reception de nos seigneurs les Daulphins et duc Dorleans en France* (Lyons, 1530), fo. A8ᵛ.

They are friends now.
Long live noble King Francis.

The golden age is back again
Following the course of the firmament,
For Saturn and Venus
Are governing this year.
Let us all sing with love,
French and Burgundians in one accord.
And let us live in love
Without ever any discord.
Who is he so perfect
That can recite with words
The great triumph achieved
At Bayonne by the two youngsters.
As for me I support them
And with brief words pay them court.
It is really paradise
Now that we have our noble court.

Although the suggested *timbre* is not known in any polyphonic setting, Attaingnant's *Trente et six chansons musicales* (1530^4, fo. 10^r) includes an anonymous quatrain with the same rhyme-scheme and metre— 'Quand me souvient du temps passé'—whose melody would be appropriate. Another account of these peace celebrations at Lyons (published five years later) again mentions the 'trompettes clerons & auboys' which led the civic procession on 7 July, adding a description of another civic procession to Saint-Nizier on the following day:

lendemain viij de juillet fut faicte procession generale en laquelle furent portées toutes les banieres: et clerons, et entre les mendiens et seculiers les auboys et aultres instrumens sonnant doulcement et ainsi devotement alla à sainct Nizier rendre graces à Seigneur d'icelle eureuse delivrance.[8]

on the next day, 8 July, there was a general procession in which all the banners were carried; and in front of the procession were the trumpets and clarions, while between the mendicants and seculars were shawms and other instruments playing sweetly; and thus it went to Saint-Nizier to give grace to our Lord for this happy delivery.

On the following Sunday, 10 July, another procession was led by *trompettes* and *clerons* and followed by 'les auboys, saquebuttes et aultres instruments sonnant doulcement et melodieusement'. In the evening there were poems and theatrical entertainments, including an

---

[8] *La grande & triumphante entrée des enfans de France & de madame Alienor seur de l'Empereur* (Lyons, 1535).

aquatic spectacle with a ship bearing masquers and singers 'faisant merveilles de chants'.

On May 27 1533, the new queen, Eleanor of Austria (sister of Charles V) entered Lyons in a great procession behind the town's aldermen, who were preceded by twelve liveried trumpeters and followed by more instrumentalists—*trompettes, saquebuttes et clerons*. The hasty preparations and the poor state of municipal finances (after the *Grande Rebeine* riots and the rebuilding of fortifications) did not prevent lavish entertainment. Jean de Vauzelles organized mysteries and literary inventions, while the Florentine painter and architect Salvatore Salvatori took charge of the decoration. However, it is not known who was responsible for the music which figured in an aquatic spectacle and a ballet, although archival records mention Anthoine Baraillon from Forez leading a band of sixteen *trompètes et aulxboys*. Baraillon and his companions may have been involved only in the procession, but the printed report also mentions a melodious tune played on a shawm by a mermaid sitting astride a dolphin on the river[9] and the dancing of the nymph's 'spectacle' accompanied by minstrels:

dans ledict bois avoit une compaignie de dames à deulx visaiges, qui la en dansant piteusement à une triste dance que les menestriers jouoient, tournoyoient certains satyres vestuz de leurs couleurs, et forme[s] ainsi qu'ilz sont painctz et troublaient toute la dance, au sort quant une belle dame vestue d'ung satin blanc et troussée en chasseresse, avec son arc et trousse arrivoit, elle faisoit si grand peur ausd' Satyres, qu'ilz s'en fuyoient, et alors lesd' dames dansans tournoient leurs joyeulx visaiges: et dansoient fort joyeusement, & puis quant lad' dame qui se nommoit Diana s'en esloignoit, revenoient lesd' Satyres qui de rechief troubloient la dance en sorte qu'elles rep[re]noient leur triste visaige, et melancholique dance, et cela feust continué jusques à ce que la Royne fust au devant dud' eschaffault à laquelle fust cecy reverement prononcé par Diana:

> Vostre seul veoir et regard gracieux
> Nous rend o Royne ainsi trestous joyeulx
> Comme voyez, quant Diana la chaste,
> Vient deschasser ce que la danse gaste
>   Celle qui dance.
> La triste dance avons longtemps dansé
> Et en langueur nostre temps dispensé
> Mays maintenant par ta doulceur et grace,
> Tous reprendrons nostre joyeuse face.[10]

in the aforementioned wood was a company of two faced ladies touchingly dancing a sad dance that the minstrels were playing, turning round some

---

[9] *L'Entrée de la Royne faicte en l'antique et noble cité de Lyon* (Lyons, 1533), fo. B2ʳ.
[10] Ibid., fo. C2.

satyrs, dressed in their colours and formed as they are painted, who were disturbing the whole dance. When a beautiful lady arrived, dressed in white satin and skirts tucked up like a huntress, with her bow and [arrow-]case, she frightened the said satyrs so much that they fled; and then the dancing ladies turned round [to show] their happy faces and danced very joyfully; but when the said lady whose name was Diana went away, the aforementioned satyrs returned and again disturbed the dance, so that the ladies again assumed their sad faces and melancholy dance: and this was continued until the queen was in front of the aforementioned platform, whereupon these words were reverently pronounced by Diana:

> Your look alone and gracious glance,
> O Queen, makes us all so happy,
> As you see, when chaste Diana
> Chases away whatever is spoiling the dance
>   She who is dancing.
> The sad dance for a long time we danced
> And in langour our time did spend,
> But now by your sweetness and grace
> We shall all assume again our happy faces.

As well as being involved in the dramatic entertainments performed during the royal entries, the student actors of the law schools, the *Basochiens*, organized their own festivities, such as the annual Ascension-Day pilgrimage to the Île-Barbe.[11] The priest, Philibert Girinet, describes one of these pilgrimages in a Latin eclogue, mentioning the previous evening's firework display on the river accompanied by the blare of 'loud' instruments—trumpets, sackbuts and shawms:

> Inde dedere sonum stridentes aere recurvo
> Vocali clangore tubae, lituique sonori.
> Hic quoque rimosas hominum penetrabat ad aures
> Tibicen varius, mulcens concentibus auras.[12]

> Then were heard strident sounds from the curved bells
> Of clangorous noisy trumpets and clarions.
> Here also mens' cracked ears were penetrated by
> The versatile piper, soothing the air with harmonious music.

The boat journey along the Saône the following day corresponds in many details to Des Périers's description of 1539, although Girinet's

[11] A. L. Fabre, *Études historiques sur les clercs de la Bazoche* (Paris, 1856); id., *Les Clercs du Palais* (Lyons, 1875); M. Audin, *La Bazoche et les clercs du Palais* (Lyons, 1909); Brown, *Music in the French Secular Theater*, 30–40.

[12] P. Girinet, 'De Petri Gauteri pragmaticorum Lugdunensium principe electione idyllion' in *Bucolicorum auctores 38...Farrago...eclogarum*, ed. G. Cousin (Basle, 1541), 742; French translation in C. Breghot du Lut, *Le Roi de la Basoche* (Lyons, 1838), 19.

account may in fact refer to a similar pilgrimage two years earlier. The penultimate stanza, in Virgilian manner, describes a banquet followed by a concert, with 'soft' plucked stringed instruments and unaccompanied voices in harmony, with dances and games to end:

> Vocales alii pulsabant pectine neruos:
> Assa [Ast] alii modulos concordes uoce canebant
> Parte alia numeros diffundit tibia dulces
> Buxea: non pauci genialia nabla frequentant.
> Talibus, atque aliis se oblectant. Deinde relictis
> Consurgunt mensis cuncti, uinoque, cibisque
> Distenti; fremitus, laetaeque per atria uoces
> Ampla uolant: strepitu ingenti tectum omne repletur.
> Hinc alii subeunt: umbras, et amoena uireta,
> Fragrantes alii hortos, prata alii herbida calcant.
> Pars festas ducit choreas, pars desidet herba
> In molli, dura exercet pars membra palaestra.
> Contendunt alii plenis dulcedine ludis.[13]

Some played tuneful strings with the plectrum, others sang harmonized music [motets] unaccompanied. Elsewhere the boxwood flute sounded its soft measures, while a number [of people] resorted to the genial *nabla* [harp]. With such (things) and others they enjoyed themselves. Then, leaving the tables, they all got up together, filled with wine and food. There was a roar, and happy voices flew through the spacious halls and the whole house was filled with a great noise. From here some went into the shade and on to the pleasent lawns, others to the fragrant flower gardens, while others trod the grassy meadows. Some led festive dances, or sat down on the soft grass, or exercised their limbs in the tough *palaestra* (wrestling-ground). Others competed in games full of pleasure.

For the entry of the new Archbishop of Lyons, Ippolito II d'Este, on 17 May 1540, the poet Maurice Scève collaborated with the Florentine painter Benedetto dal Bene in providing *moralitès*, *mistaires*, and *ystoires*. Scève again acted as 'conducteur et ordinateur des ystoires et triumphes' ('director and coordinator of the tableaux and triumphs') for the most magnificent entry of the sixteenth century, that of King Henry II and his wife Catherine de' Medici in September 1548.[14]

The elaborate preparation for this great reception included the importation of trumpets, fifes, and drums from surrounding areas, as well as from the royal band. Five trumpeters—Jehan Bret, Nicolas Fazin (Fuzy), Christophe Gonet, Françoys Gordet, and Andrè Noeret—came

---

[13] Girinet, 'De Petri Gauteri', 746.

[14] M. Scève, *La Magnificence de la superbe et triumphante entrée de la noble et antique cité de Lyon faicte au treschrestien Roy de France* (Lyons, 1549); ed. G. Guigue, *La Magnificence...Relations et documents contemporains* (Lyons, 1927); G. Paradin, *Mémoires de l'histoire de la ville de Lyon* (Lyons, 1573), 320–51.

from Chambéry on 13 September and were paid 80 livres tournois (20 sols each per day) for being on hand and serving in the royal entry. A sixth, Michel Noeret, played only for the six days of the festivities and was paid 5 livres 2 sols (17 sols per day).[15] Three more—Pontet Bandin, Loys and Jacques Chazelles—summoned from Montbrison by Pierre Bret, were paid at a lower rate (51 livres for twenty days, which included two days' allowance for travelling).[16] The five royal trumpeters—Dominique de Brangues, Disdier le Doulx, Loys Chausson, Guillaume Chasseau, and Françoys Mesnyer de Vivonne— also offered their services and received the customary payments.[17] The five trumpeters from Lyons were paid separately according to their specific duties: thus Bonaventure Marquet, Guillaume Congnet, Jehan Valfo, and Francoys Boydard received 2½ livres tournois each, and their leader Pierre Bret 3 livres, for playing on the Saône the day before the King's departure.[18] The five drummers, 'Benoist Bellon et ses compagnons', received only 9 sols each for playing during the same aquatic spectacle, while four *taborineurs* and two *fiffres* summoned from Montbrison—André Thevillon, Benoist de Lachault, Claude Vial, and Laurens Babotte, Jehan Cousturier, and Antoine Fournier— received 2 écus each for participating in the entry processions of the first two days and in addition were provided with taffeta tunics for the occasion.[19] 5 livres were also paid to each of the *capitaines des mestiers* for their six fifes and drums, the bill totalling 100 livres.[20]

The Consulate charged two of their number, Antoine Bonyn and Jean de La Porte, to organize shawms and cornetts playing on raised platforms at the Bourgneuf and Saint-Eloy gates; the composer Charles Cordeilles, along with Charles Pyrouet (or Perryet), and seven other shawm-players were accordingly paid 9 écus.[21]

Festivities began after lunch on Sunday, 23 September in the suburb

---

[15] Lyons, Archives municipales, BB 67, fo. 251^v; CC 981, nos. 1–9.

[16] Ibid., CC 981, no. 8.

[17] Ibid., BB 67, fo. 252^v.

[18] Ibid., CC 981, nos. 2–3.

[19] Ibid., BB 68, fo. 173^v; CC 981, no. 5.

[20] Ibid., CC 981, no. 6.

[21] Ibid., BB 68, fo. 172^v; CC 981, no. 1, fo. 109^r. These payments seem generous, considering that the same archives record carpenters, masons, and labourers receiving only 8 sols tournois per day. Between 1540 and 1544 journeyman printers were paid 35 sols per day, while Aneau, as principal of the Collège de la Trinité, received a monthly stipend of 100 sols plus fees of 2 sols 2 deniers from each student. At the same time a loaf of white bread cost about 7 deniers (1 livre = 20 sols = 240 deniers; 1 écu = 5 sols). Baudrier's *Bibliographie lyonnaise*, x, quotes the wholesale prices of books printed by Macé Bonhomme in Lyons as between 2½ and 19 sols each. The inventory of Jean de Badonvilliers, who died in 1544, gives a contemporary valuation of second-hand music-books and instruments in Paris with, for example, a bound collection of chansons printed by Attaingnant assessed at 20 sols parisis (= 25 sols tournois): see F. Lesure, 'Un amateur de musique au début du xvie siècle', *Revue de musicologie*, 25 (1953), 79–81.

of Vaise, where the governor, Monseigneur de Saint-André, presented to the King first the local gentlemen, then the Genoese and Florentine delegations in pairs, and finally the representatives of the clergy. The ensuing procession included some seven thousand men, led by mounted archers and followed by the guilds (*bandes des mestiers*) in seven groups, three abreast, with each group led by fifes and drums, the representatives of the foreign Nations, Luccan, Florentine, Milanese, and German, public and ecclesiastic officials, and the prominent families of Lyons in three groups—*Notables, Enfants à pied*, and *Enfants à cheval*. After a display of fencing and other armed combat, the infantry, led by fifes and drums, and the cavalry, led by twelve mounted trumpeters, took their place in the procession. Next came the municipal corps, the gentlement and ladies of the royal Chamber, the King's Swiss guard with its own fifes and drums, the cardinals of Ferrara, Guise, Vendôme Lorraine, and Bourbon, the King himself, the royal princes, the Knights of the Order, and finally another detachment of archers.

As the vast cortège passed through the Bourgneuf Gate, decorated with allegorical figures and panegyric inscriptions, fauns and satyrs gambolled to the music of 'diverse instruments such as shawms, douçaines, sorduns, and cornetts', provided by Cordeilles and his colleagues. Six cornetts also played at Pourcelet on a platform beneath a triumphal arch representing the Temple of Honour and Virtue, decorated with musical figures, with Fame blowing a trumpet and Virtue escorted by nymphs playing the lyre and flute. After an oration in the cathedral and the official reception arranged by Archbishop Ippolito, the King was led to a luxuriously decorated landing-stage on the Saône to witness 'boundless merry frolics with jousting, combats, and other aquatic diversions with various musical instruments, all amazingly entertaining'.

Queen Catherine and her retinue, which included Marguerite de Navarre, followed the same procedure the following day, although, after the Archbishop's reception, the festivities concluded with a ball rather than a repetition of the aquatic spectacle.

The next afternoon the King and Queen embarked in their gondolas to witness a *naumachia* 'accompanied by the sound of fifes, drums, trumpets, and clarions'.

On Wednesday evening the court was entertained in the hall of Saint-Jean with the tragicomedy *La Calandria* by Bernardo Dovizi, Cardinal Bibbiena. The play, an imitation of Plautus, was one of the most successful of early sixteenth-century dramas, being performed first at Urbino during the festivities organized by Castiglione in 1513, then at Leo X's Rome for Isabella d'Este in 1514, and at Ferrara, again for

Isabella d'Este, in 1520;[22] Archbishop Ippolito, who along with the Florentine community organized the 1548 production, may have witnessed the Ferrara performance in his youth. The piece was a favourite with the Florentine *Cazzuola* group,[23] who staged it several times for the Medici, but it was the *Gelosi* troupe who were responsible for the Lyons performance. Brantôme, who attended, wrote:

on dit qu'il despendit en la représentation plus de 10,000 escus, ayant faict venir, à grands coust et despens, des plus excellens comediens et comedientes d'Italie.[24]

it is said that he [Archbishop Ippolito II d'Este] spent more than 10,000 crowns on the production, bringing the finest actors and actresses from Italy.

The citizens must have already been familiar with Italian theatre since there had been a troupe of Florentine players resident at Lyons earlier in the century. The décor was also designed by Italians, Nannoccio dal Bene (then in the service of Cardinal François de Tournon) and Zanobi.

Scève's account does not give many details, but the publisher Roville also issued a description of the festivities in Italian, with a 'particular description of the Play whose recital was arranged by the Florentine nation in honour of his Christian Majesty'.[25] This tells us that the hall was sumptuously decorated and illuminated, with twelve allegorical statues, half in togas and crowned with laurels representing six Florentine poets and half armed in the classical manner representing ancestors of the Medici family, 'restorers of Greek and Latin literature, architecture, sculpture, painting, and other fine arts after the neglect of the Gothic age'. The Memoirs of Guillaume Paradin indicate that the play's five acts alternated with allegorical musical interludes representing the 'Seven Ages' and stress the novelty of the Florentine dramatic song and recitative:

avec la recreation de diversité de la musique changeant selon les sept aages intervenans aux intermedes des actes accompaignez de Apollo chantant et recitant au son de sa Lyre, plusieurs belles rithmes Toscanes à la louange du Roy: et sans oublier une nouvelle mode, et non encore usitée aux recitemens des Comédies, qui fut qu'elle commença par l'advenement de l'Aube qui vint traversant la place de la perspective et chantant sur son chariot trayné par deux coqz et finit aussi par la survenue de la Nuict converte d'estoilles . . .[26]

---

[22] Castiglione describes the first performance in a letter to Ludovico Canossa; see B. Castiglione, *Tutte le Opere* 1, ed. G. La Rocca (Verona, 1978), 1067–73. It is also mentioned by Vasari, *The Lives of the Painters, Sculptors and Architects*, trans. A. B. Hinds, 4 vols. (London, 1927), ii. 297.

[23] Vasari, *Lives*, iv. 34–7.

[24] Bourdeille, *Œuvres complètes*, iii. 256.

[25] *La Magnifica & triumphale entrata* . . . (Lyons, 1549): ed. G. Guigue, *Magnificence*.

[26] Paradin, *Mémoires*, 346–7; Guigue, *Magnificence*, 69.

with the entertainment of varied music, changing according to the seven ages, intervening as *intermedi* between the acts, accompanied by Apollo singing and reciting to the sound of his lyre several fine Tuscan rhymes in praise of the King; and not forgetting a new mode not previously used in the recitals of plays, which began with the advent of Dawn who came across the perspective set singing on a chariot drawn by two cocks and finished also with the arrival of Night covered in stars . . .

The lyrical portions of the text are printed, but the music has not survived; moreover, nothing is known of the composer, Piero Mannucci or Mannucciqua, organist for the Florentine Nation at the Church of Notre-Dame de Confort after the death of Francesco Layolle. It is therefore impossible to know whether Apollo's singing to the lyre was in any way similar to the later Florentine *stile recitativo*.

The *intermedi* were certainly different from those of the first performance, decribed by Castiglione as consisting of four ballets, two *moresche* and two *branles*, followed by an *épilogue* recited by Cupid explaining their significance as the triumph of love over conflict and discord, before the hidden music of four voices and four viols combined in a prayer to love. They were closer to those written by Francesco Corteccia for Antonio Landi's comedy *Il Commodo*, performed during the festivities for the wedding of Duke Cosimo de'Medici and Eleanor of Toledo at Florence in 1539.[27] Corteccia's music was published in part books by Antonio Gardano at Venice, in the form of homophonic madrigals rather than that of monodic recitatives or arias, the same being true of a piece used in Francesco d'Ambra's comedy *Il Furto*, performed at Florence in 1544 and published in Corteccia's first book of madrigals in Venice two years later.[28]

The Italian report of the Lyons production describes the first *intermedio* with Dawn on a chariot drawn by two cocks, combing her long golden hair and singing this canzona (p. 92):

> Io son nuntia del sol, che la prim'hora
> Imperlo & egli indora
> Spenga il cielo ogni stella,
> Rend'al mondo i color che'l vespro invola,
> Ch'homai gelata & sola
> All'opre usate appella
> Ciascun la casta Aurora
> E'nvita a sospirar chi Amore adora.

---

[27] A. Minor and B. Mitchell, *A Renaissance Entertainment* (Columbus, MO., 1969); see also F. Ghisi, *Feste musicali della Firenze medicea* (Florence, 1939), 49–64.

[28] Ghisi, *Feste*, 65–8.

> I am the messenger of the sun, who at dawn
> Am set in pearl and he in gold.
> Let the sky extinguish all the stars,
> Give back to the world the colours which evening steals.
> For now, frozen and alone,
> Chaste Aurora calls back to work,
> And invites everyone who worships love to sing.

The song was accompanied by two spinets and four transeverse flutes (*flauti d'Alamagna*), recalling the instruments—*gravicembalo, organo, flauto, arpa*, and *voci a uccegli*—used to accompany 'Vattene almo' sung by Dawn in the 1539 *Intermedi*.[29]

Apollo appears next, with a lyre (viol) in his left hand and a bow in his right, followed by four ladies, one of whom stands next to him. (*questo tenendo la lyra nella sinistra & l'archetto nella dextra, era seguitato da quatro donne delle quale una gli stava a canto*). After the ladies' music, Apollo introduces himself, smoothly playing and singing six hendecasyllabic octave stanzas, beginning (p. 94):

> Phebo son io, per cui s'alluma il giorno
> Per cui splende la luna & l'alte stelle...
>
> I am Phoebus [Apollo], through whom day is lit,
> Through whom the moon and the stars in the heavens shine...

The introduction of the Four Ages—iron, bronze, silver, and gold—closes the first *divertissement*.

After the Prologue and first act of *Calandria*, the second *intermedio* presents the first Iron Age, *l'Età del Ferro*, accompanied by *Crudeltà* (Cruelty), *Avaritia* (Avarice), and *Invidia* (Envy), reciting a complimentary stanza to the King:

> Invitissimo Henrico, io prego humile
> Che voi non me scacciate, ohime, dal regno...
>
> Most invincible Henri I beg you humbly
> Not to drive me out of the kingdom...

This is taken up and sung by four voices with a *sonata* played by four viols and four transeverse flutes (p. 97):

laqual cosa segui sempre alla fin di tutti à quattro li atti, dico di passare alcuni simili personaggi i quali erano la maggior parte ritratti di alcun folle buffoni & nani che seguitano il corte, i quali personaggi mentre che passavano era dentro da quatro voci cantato in musica quei versi, che poco innanzi haveva recitati l'Eta del ferro & nel medesimo tempo sonata la medesima musica da quatro violini da gamba & da quatro flauti d'Allamagna.

---

[29] Minor and Mitchell, *A Renaissance Entertainment*, 224.

these things always followed at the end of each of the four acts, that is the passage of similar characters, mostly drawn from some of the fools, jesters, and dwarfs who follow the court, and while they passed four voices behind the scene sang to music those verses which the Iron Age had recited just before and at the same time the same music was played on four bass viols and four transverse flutes.

After Act II the third interlude introduces the Bronze Age (*l'Eta del bronzo*) with *Fortezza* (Strength), *Fama* (Fame), and *Vendetta* (Vengeance). Another eulogy to Henry beginning 'I who was of bronze, The Age of proud Henry' (*Io che del bronzo fui L'Eta de altero Henrico;* p. 98) is taken up as a madrigal by four singers accompanied by three crumhorns and a trombone:

Et qui ritiratisi con le compagne da parte, per la cagione che gia vi ho detto, fu subito dentro da quatro voci cantata in musica il sopra detto madrigale & da tre storte & un trombone nel medesimo tempo sonato.

And when they had left with the ladies, for the reason I spoke of earlier, the aforementioned madrigal suddenly from within was sung to music for four voices, with three crumhorns and a trombone playing at the same time.

In the fourth interlude, the Silver Age (*l'Età d'argento*) is accompanied by *Cerere* (Ceres), *Pales*, and *Agricultura*. Another paean to Henry (p. 99):

> Io que l'Eta d'argento
> Son, valoroso Henrico, humil vi chieggio . . .

> I who of the Silver Age
> Am, valorous Henry, do humbly petition . . .

is performed in a manner approaching monody, the single voice being accompanied by seven foundation instruments:

Qui taciutasi, furono subito dentro i medesimi versi cantati in musica da una voce sola accompagnata da cinque liuti, un violone da gamba & una spinetta . . .

When this ended we immediately heard the same verses from within, sung to music by one solo voice accompanied by five lutes, a large bass viol, and a spinet . . .

After Act IV the Golden Age (*l'Età dell'Oro*), escorted by *Pace* (Peace), *Justitia* (Justice), and *Religione* (Religion), recites another poem of praise (p. 100):

> L'Eta mi chiamo Aurata & vengo a voi
> Gran Re, per esser vostra . . .

> I am called the Age of Gold and I come to you
> Great King, to serve you . . .

This was repeated to music for five voices, three trombones and two cornetts:

Come l'Eta dell'Oro hebbè detto i sopra scritti versi & che dentro furono cantati in musica da cinque voci & nel medesimo tempo sonati da tre tromboni & due cornetti . . .

When the Golden Age had spoken the verses written above, and they had been then sung within, with music for five voices played at the same time by three trombones and two cornetts . . .

At the end of the play Apollo returns with his lyre, accompanied by the Golden Age and his acolytes to sing another paean (p. 101):

> Invitissimo Henrico, alte novelle
> Rimandato da Giove, al fin vi porto . . .
>
> Most invincible Henry, great news
> I bring you sent from Jove . . .

Further praises ensue and the Golden Age presents a lily to the Queen before Night enters on a chariot, singing a *canzona* accompanied by two spinets, four transverse flutes, and four bass viols (p. 105):

> Colei son'io, che con somnifer'ali
> Furo il lume a i mortali . . .
>
> I am she who flys on the wings of sleep,
> Shutting out the light from mortals . . .

The spectacle concludes as it began with the release of birds (p. 105):

Mentre che ella cosi cantava si viddono volare sopra della scena alcuni di quelli uccelli che hanno in odio il sole, & dentro s'udi contrafare la voce loro.

While she sang thus, some birds that shun the sun were seen flying above the stage, while from within their voice was imitated.

The printed account states that all the music was composed and the instruments 'concerted' by the organist of Notre-Dame (de Confort), who like his predecessor, Francesco Layolle, was probably a Florentine: 'Tutti le musiche furono composte & gli strumenti consertati da Messer Piero Mannucciqua, organista della natione Fiorentina in Nostra Dama' (p. 105). No Pietro Mannucci or Mannucciqua is known as an organist or composer in Florence or Lyons at the time, although he may be identical with the organist 'Me Pierre' mentioned in the archives in 1561 (see below, App. III(*i*)). The reporter or printer may have garbled the name of one of the musical Animuccia family from Florence, whom Paolo Mini in his *Difesa della citta di Firenze* (Florence, 1578, p. 180) praises along with the Aiolli, Corteccia, and Rampollini as 'well-known organists'.

The dramatic entertainment was so much to the king's liking that it was repeated for the Court on Friday evening, while a third performance on Saturday was arranged for 'the gentlemen of the Consulate and other citizens who had not been able to get into the first performances'.

On Thursday (27 September), the royal party was regaled by another nautical spectacle on the Saône, with the trumpets, clarions, shawms, cornetts, and drums on the galleys joining the artillery in enlivening the atmosphere. The musicians no doubt included Benoist Bellon and four others in his fife-and-drum band who were paid 45 sols for playing at a third aquatic spectacle on Sunday, 30 September, when a galley built for the Cardinal of Ferrara caught fire. After hearing High Mass on Sunday the royal party left on Monday, 1 October, well satisfied with their week of festivities.

Musicians continued to be in demand for minor festivities, such as the banquets given for the Swiss ambassadors in 1547 and 1548, which included 'several entertainments with instrumentalists and acrobats playing the farces of Hercule Matachin'.[30] One document[31] specifies some of these instrumentalists as the shawm- or violin-players Guillaume de Genève and Jacques Giraud, with the fife-and-drum players Guillaume de la Monnoye, Jehan Benoît, Claude Goujellin, and Benoît Le Chat.

A number of other festivities involving music are mentioned in the chronicle of Jean Guéraud.[32] They include an official reception on 19 January 1551 given for Guéraud's nephew, Jean Tignat, lieutenant-general, with *trompettes & hautboys*, and a grand dinner at the Hôtel de Ville on 7 July 1552, when the *Basochiens* entertained the guests with the help of fifes, drums, shawms, trumpets, and violins. Guéraud also indicates that shawms and violins regularly played at weddings, mentioning for example the ceremony at St Paul's on the morning of 12 February 1554 for the daughter of Jean Paffiz (who played an important part in the organization of the 1548 *Entrée*) and the draper Leonard Ponnard, which was accompanied by a band of shawms. In the same year the Archives report the payment of 22 sols 9 deniers to six violins for playing at the festivities for the marriage of Antoinette Poulein.[33]

Guéraud also relates that shawms accompanied the celebration of the baptism of a velvet-worker at Saint-Pierre les Nonnains on 3 January 1562.

The fashion for Italianate masques or mummeries is reflected in

[30] G. Tricou, 'Les Musiciens lyonnais et le Roy des Violons', *Revue musicale de Lyon*, 1 (1903–4), 148.

[31] Lyons, Archives communales, CC 977, no. 25, fos. 3^r–4^r.

[32] Guéraud, *Chronique lyonnaise*.

[33] Lyons, Archives communales, Charité E 164, p. 49.

Guéraud's *Chronicle* for 1552 (p. 67), which mentions a 'mommerye' presenting the story of Pluto and Proserpine organized by the Florentine community, with a second, involving Jupiter, Pallas, Mercury, Venus, and Pan, mounted by prominent Luccan gentlemen. Both of these presented different *entrées* and employed musical instruments. Guéraud also describes another lavish example, devised and produced by Barthélemy Alexandron and financed by the Florentines, to celebrate the wedding of Laurent Capponi and Hélayne Guadaigne in April 1554; this used musical instruments as well as costumes to differentiate its protagonists, Asia, Africa, and Europe, anticipating an exotic trend that recurs in French *opéra-ballet* two centuries later (p. 73):

this mummery was the most magnificent and excellent thing ever seen in Lyons. Its subject and device was the three parts of the world—Asia, Africa, and Europe—[represented as] two queens and a king ... The first queen, [dressed] partly in French, partly in Italian and partly in Spanish fashion, was accompanied by footmen, and soldiers similarly [dressed], with players of instruments like German drums, flutes, and violins, in all twenty or twenty-five people attired in her livery. Then came a Moorish King dressed in Estiopian [Ethiopian] and Indian fashion of wonderful richness with his footmen all dressed in crimson satin, golden silk, and other rich drapery, with a dozen or about fifteen of the strangest instruments possible, all well tuned to each other, and in short this was the finest and richest display seen in Lyons within living memory.

The second queen ... was Africa, dressed partly in Turkish fashion and partly in the Egyption fashion of the Barbary Coast, with her footmen in Turkish costume with long yellow straw-coloured damask robes, playing little copper drums and cornets inverted in a strange way [serpents or cornetts with upturned bells] ...

He further describes (p. 112) another masque designed by Alexandron, organized by the Count of Roussy to conclude a jousting tournament (*jeu de la bague*) in March 1555, celebrating the four seasons and the twelve months of the year, with lavishly costumed dancers accompanied by

twelve instrumentalists, all different, representing the twelve months, entering in the order of the year, so that one of the seasons entered and led in with him three of the months playing their instruments; and then when they had all entered, the four seasons, who were dressed as two men and two women, each took a woman from the [assembled] company and danced a *branle* in the round, while the twelve months all playing their instruments surrounded them, dancing in a way that made the order look very good. This was one of the most inventive masques ever seen ...

Guéraud (pp. 209–10) also refers to the week's festivities following the announcement of the peace of Cateau-Cambrésis in April 1559, although with less detail than the official printed accounts, which describe the celebrations beginning on Thursday, 13 April with the aldermen and prominent citizens attending a thanksgiving ceremony at the cathedral, with a *Te Deum* sung by Benoît Bautier, *vicaire-general* to the new Archbishop, Cardinal François de Tournon, and the clerical procession led by the royal trumpets and followed by the municipal band:

the three trumpets sent by the King for the proclamation of the said peace, wearing livery of blue taffeta with the escutcheon of France on the front and back, and on their trumpets the coats of arms of the Princes to whom they belonged, the King of France, King Philip, and the Prince of Savoy, the former being accompanied by the town trumpeters and followed by the great band of shawms playing wonderfully well.[34]

Guéraud, however, mentions that the next morning (Friday, 14 April), eight trumpets led the public rejoicing at the Hôtel de Ville and Place du Change, where 'the Florentines had paid for the shawms and were distributing gifts' (p. 209). He also describes the eight trumpets accompanying a public procession to the Cordeliers' church, where High Mass was sung on Sunday, as well as the High Mass sung at Notre Dame de Confort, the next day, followed in the evening by a firework display at the Saint Sebastian Gate accompanied by a 'great band of violins and trumpets playing most melodiously'.

The printed accounts (pp. 15–18) also indicate that on Thursday the 20th, the violins again joined the trumpets and shawms, playing continuously on the scaffolds placed around a great monument to Mars, Minerva, Mount Parnassus, and Pegasus, complete with the Hippocrene fountain spouting wine and water, erected by the printers in the square in front of Notre-Dame de Confort: they further describe a *naumachia* on the Saône on Sunday the 23rd as 'more impressive to the ear than to the eye', with its 'trumpets, drums, shawms, and variety of martial and musical instruments mixed in confusion'.

Charles IX, accompanied by his mother Catherine de' Medici and by Henri de Navarre, visited Lyons on 13 June 1564 in order to restore royal authority a few months after the pacification of Amboise had ended the first of the religious wars. In the wake of the violent upheavals of 1562, Catholics and Protestants shared the town's government, each party being represented by twelve aldermen. Assenting to the edict of Amboise, the aldermen accepted the King's nominee, the Marshal of Vielleville, as governor on 9 June 1564. Fearing

---

[34] *Triomphes, pompes et magnificences faicts à Lyon* (Lyons, 1559), 6. For another description see *Le Discours du grand triomphe fait en la ville de Lyon pour la Paix faite & accordée entre Henry second . . . & Philippe Roy des Espagnes & leurs aliez* (Lyons, 1559).

a riot in the royal presence, the new governor banned workers' meetings, so that guilds did not enjoy their customary place in the procession, while Protestants and Catholics marched together with the *enfants de la ville*. But compared with the magnificence of 1548, this entry was a relatively poor affair, reflecting the decline in the town's pride and wealth. Claude de Rubys noted:

The Entry showed the effects of the poverty and destitution of the time and was neither sumptuous in its costumes nor ingenious in its theatrical apparatus and perspectives.[36]

The programme was ambitious enough, but lack of finance limited the results. The organizer was the lawyer Antoine Giraud, whose account was published in Paris,[37] although, curiously, not in Lyons. The decoration was entrusted to a certain Maître Thomas, assisted by Pierre Cruche or Eskrich, and the musical entertainment was arranged by Philibert Jambe de Fer.[38] The municipality's fee of 26 écus d'or soleil, to be shared amongst all the musicians, singers, and instrumentalists, was modest in comparison to that paid to Cordeilles and his colleagues in 1548. Nevertheless, music accompanied the customary eulogistic allegory, as described in the printed account:

The nine Muses . . . sitting on various seats in a theatre built in perspective . . . began to strum their various musical instruments with very great charm; and this melody was accompanied by another harmony from musicans, placed in the concavity [pit] of the upper theatre; in melodious voices they sang with excellent music the following canticle:

> Chante du siècle d'or les divines douceurs
> Lyon tresgenereux, chante l'heur des Gaulois
> Francs de crainte des Loups les Agneaux seront seurs
> Car en sainte bonté la Paix fera les Lois.
>
> Cy après tu vaudras mieux que tu ne valois,
> Riche d'un jeune Roy jà de mœurs tout chenu:
> Dy donc le recevant: O Charles de Valois,
> Mon prince, o siècle d'Or, tu sois le bien venu.[39]
>
> Sing of the divine gentleness of the Golden Age
> Most generous Lyon, sing of the happiness of the Gauls,

[35] *Triomphes, pompes et magnificences faicts à Lyon pour la Paix* (Paris, 1559).

[36] C. de Rubys, *Histoire véritable de la ville de Lyon*, 402.

[37] *Discours de l'entrée du tres illustre . . . prince, Charles de Valois, neuvième . . . en sa renommée et fameuse ville de Lyon* (Paris, 1564); ed. V. de Valoux and A. Steyert, *L'Entrée de Charles IX à Lyon en 1564 avec pièces justificatives et figures . . .* (Lyons, 1889). See also V. Graham and W. Johnson, *The Royal Tour of France by Charles IX and Catherine de' Medici* (Toronto, 1979).

[38] See G. Tricou, 'Philibert Jambe de Fer', *Revue musicale, 3* (1903), 511–13; F. Lesure, 'L'Épitome musical de Philibert Jambe de Fer (1556)', *Annales musicologiques*, 6 (1963), 341–86 at 342–3.

[39] Valoux and Steyert (eds.), *L'Entrée de Charles IX*, 20.

Free from the fear of Wolves, Lambs will be secure,
For in saintly good, Peace will legislate.

Hereafter you will be worth more than you were,
Enriched with a young King already aged in manners;
Say then, when you greet him, 'O Charles de Valois,
My Prince, o Golden Age, welcome.'

When this canticle was over, the same musicians 'poured forth a wonderful, delightful sound which greatly pleased his Majesty's ear' with various kinds of instruments.

On another stage at the Saint-Eloi gate was a second allegorical tableau portraying a 'young King crowned, daintily strumming a lute and walking over an old man in disgrace who rather grumpily held a lute whose strings he broke, making a pitiful face'. The King evidently enjoyed the entertainments offered and remained in the town for twenty-five days.

The next public event of note was the celebration of the victory at Jarnac marked on 4 August 1569 by a procession of the military personnel and all the parishes of Lyons, along with the collegiate churches, followed by a great number of choirboys and prebendaries singing and 'psalming' with the canons of Saint-Nizier and Saint Paul. The municipal archives report that the Archbishop's secretaries from the Chapter of Saint-Jean were accompanied by a band of violinists, with organ, shawms, and *cornetz à bouquin* playing magnificently and that a street-altar (*reposoir*) was erected in front of the house of the Governor François Mandelot:

et là furent faictes louanges à Dieu en musique vocalle nouvelle de chant et de lettres dont voyez la Teneur:

L'honneur premier de l'insigne victoire
Venant de Dieu se rend à sa grandeur
A notre Roy est la deuxieme gloire
Auquel prudence a si bien servy l'heur
Qu'il est des siens plus rebelles vainqueur,
Et prest à vaincre une armée estrangere.
Mais ne se peult qu'une louange entiere
Ne donne actainte au cueur des Lyonnais
D'un duc royal qui croissant sa lumiere
A debellé l'ennemy des Françoys
Dieu donne au Roy pour redoubler nos voix
L'achevement selon nostre priere.[40]

and there praises were given to God through new vocal music with melody and words of this tenor:

The foremost honour of notable victory
Coming from God is due to His greatness.

[40] Lyons, Archives communales, BB 80, fo. 115^r.

To our King is due the second glory,
To him whose good fortune has been so well served by prudence,
That he has triumphed over his most rebellious subjects
And is ready to defeat a foreign army.
But an entire laudation can only
Touch the heart of the people of Lyons
When a royal duke, increasing his glory,
Has defeated the enemy of the French.
May God grant the King, to redouble our voices,
The success we pray for.

The account does not mention the composer of this tribute to royal victory. But there is no evidence of direct court involvement and it may therefore be assumed that local musicians were again commissioned, perhaps including Philibert Jambe de Fer, who had directed the musical proceedings for the Consulat in 1564 and was experienced in setting such conventional decasyllabic verse.

The 'Symphonies pour un reposoir' by M. A. Charpentier and others of later generation may have been anticipated by the instrumental music performed at another stop on the processional route:

Devant le lougis de M. le president Larcher y eust un aultre reposoir du CORPUS DOMINI. Auquel lieu, après les prieres ecclesiastiques ne manqua point la musique organique et instrumentale de hautbois et cornetz à bouquin avec une allegre armonie et armonieuse allegresse.[41]

In front of President Larcher's house there was another altar for the CORPUS DOMINI. Here, after the church prayers, there was no lack of organ music and instrumental music for shawms and cornetts with joyful harmony and harmonious joy.

The religious struggles affected the ceremonial of Lyons during the ensuing decades and the town became increasingly provincial. The limited festivities welcoming the, as yet, uncrowned King Henry III from Poland on 6 September 1574, included a polyphonic mass sung in the cathedral,[42] but could not boast any musical spectacle to match the *Ballet des Polonais* in Paris. Pomp and pageantry were, however, revived to a limited extent, at the end of the century, with the entries of Henry IV in 1595 and in 1600,[43] the latter in the company of the new Queen, Marie de'Medici.

[41] Ibid.

[42] *L'ordre tenu à l'arrivée du treschrestien roy de France et de Pologne Henry de Valois troisième de ce nom faicte à Lyon . . .* (Lyons, 1574).

[43] P. Matthieu, *L'entrée de . . . Henry IIII, roy de France et de Navarre en sa bonne ville de Lyon, le IIII septembre l'an MDXCV* (Lyons, 1595); id., *Les deux plus grandes, plus célèbres et mémorables resjouissances de la ville de Lyon* (Lyons, 1598); *L'entrée de . . . Marie de Medicis, Reine de France et de Navarre en la ville de Lyon le 3 decembre 1600* (Lyons, 1600). See also Lyons, Bibliothèque municipale, MS 1449, and Archives communales, AA 21, no. 8; AA 144, nos. 12 and 16.

It is thus clear that music played an important part in many public aspects of urban life. The royal entries are well documented, as are a host of other regular but unofficial public festivities and processions, both religious and secular. The carnivals and burlesque cavalcades, like the 'Chevauchée de l'âne', the 'Fête du cheval fol', the 'Tirer l'oie', the 'Fête des pains bénis', and the 'Dimanche Gros', probably used music in the same manner as the Florentine *feste* and *charivari*. Certainly the *chevauchées* of 1566 and 1578 employed many instruments, including violins, shawms, trumpets, fifes, and drums.[44] The waits also played for guild activities, as well as for private commissions like the banquets, serenades *(aubades)*, and weddings described by Guéraud and others.

(ii) *Musicians Mentioned in the Archives of Lyons*

The names of over two hundred musicians and instrumentalists are tabulated below in App. I–III, providing some evidence of an active musical life in the city throughout the sixteenth century. There is, however, little correspondence between the names cited in the archives and those figuring in the music that was copied or printed in the city. Only eleven composers—Francesco and Allemano Layolle, Guillaume de La Mœulle, Charles Cordeilles, Loys Bourgeois, Philibert Jambe de Fer, François Roussel, Giovanni Paolo Paladino, Richard Crassot, Paschal de L'Estocart, and Jehan de Maletty—are mentioned in the archives, and none of these is known to have been a native of Lyons. Like Cordeilles, La Mœulle, Paladino, and the Layolles, most of the names are recorded as instrumentalists: 30 as drummers, 25 as trumpeters, 12 as lutenists, 11 as violinists, 8 as shawm-players, 6 as flute-players, 6 as rebec-players, and 26 as organists.

While there is evidence that most professional instrumentalists were illiterate and incapable of deciphering mensural notation, if not tablature, the specific mention of waits playing 'chansons faictes et musicalles', as well as the publication of a few crude polyphonic compositions by Cordeilles and La Mœulle in the *Parangon des chansons*, suggests that some apprenticeships may not simply have been concerned with technical mastery and the imbuing of an aural improvisatory tradition, but also with some of the more sophisticated aspects of figural music.

[44] *Recueil faict au vray de la Chevauchée de l'Asne en la ville de Lyon* (Lyons, 1566), repr. Lyons, 1829; Rubys, *Histoire véritable*, 499; C. Noirot, *L'Origine des Masques, Mommerie, Bernez...* etc. (Langres, 1609), ed. C. Leber (Collection des meilleurs notices et traités particuliers relatifs à l'histoire de France, 9; Paris, 1826), 147–68; H. J. Martin, *Entrées royales et fêtes populaires à Lyon* (Lyons, 1970), 46–59.

It is interesting to compare figures for the various instrumentalists with the corresponding ones for the instrument-makers in App. IV, remembering that the former represent only professional players, designated as such. Thus it seems that the surviving documents do not always truly reflect amateur interest and practice at the time. For example, few flute players are listed *flûteurs* or *joueurs de flûte*, whereas the real popularity of the instrument throughout the century is clearly illustrated in contemporary iconography, in the number of manufacturers, and in the importance accorded to both types of flute— German (transverse) and nine-holed (recorder)—in Philibert Jambe de Fer's treatise *Épitome musical* of 1556 and Simon Gorlier's *Livre de tabulature de flutes d'Allemand* of 1558. Similarly, the mention of only one spinet-player (Jean Clement, *fl.* 1569–98) is less representative than the archival references to three manufacturers, or the publication of Gorlier's *Premier livre de tablature d'espinette* of 1560. It is interesting that the organist Nicolas Bontemps was never mentioned as a spinet- or clavichord-player, although he actually manufactured *manicordions*. Likewise, we find no specific reference to guitar- or cittern-players (Varin's designation as 'cytharedus' is ambiguous), despite the publication of further tablature-books by Gorlier, perhaps because such instruments were usually played professionally by the same men who played the lute.

The documents do, however, reflect contemporary practice and fashion. The references to the shawm-players all occur in the second quarter of the century and all indicate municipal employment as waits. They also show that most of these players were proficient on a second instrument: thus Anthoine Baraillon is described both as 'chef des hautbois' and 'trompette', while Cordeilles, Peroyet, and their seven 'compagnons haultboys' were paid for playing both 'cornetz et haultboys' during the royal festivities of 1548. Jacques Girard played the fiddle as well as the shawm; but Antoine Pellat must have only been a part-timer, since he is also described as a carpenter. Similarly, the only specialist cornettist mentioned, Luc Gentil, was also one of the two listed cornett-makers.

The large number of trumpet-players listed reflects their civic duties. Two were regularly employed by the municipality to signal the opening and closing of the city gates at dawn and dusk from a tower on the Fourvière Hill, and to accompany town criers in promulgating the town Council's public announcements. Additional players were enlisted in times of trouble to sound alarms from the ramparts or church towers; but in 1548, when the Council required twelve trumpeters for the celebration of Henry II's *entrée*, only four could be mustered in Lyons itself, five more being imported from Chambéry and three from Montbrison. Similarly, seven *trompettes estrangiers* were brought in for Charles IX's *entrée* in 1564.[45] The municipality also regularly employed drummers, including two to precede the town guard.[46] It seems that in peacetime the position of drummer did not carry much kudos or remuneration; in 1503 Robin de la Marre claimed exemption from taxation as 'a mere drummer', while Robert de Balsac's morality play *Le droict chemin de l'hôpital*, published with Symphorien Champier's *Nef des Princes* in 1502, included 'vieux tabourins' who were in need of charitable aid. On the other hand, the property owned and taxes paid by Gabriel Chardon between 1528 and 1572 suggest considerable wealth.

Many instrumentalists combined music-making with other earning occupations. Thus the flautists Mathelin de La Noue, Jacques Pillon, Michaud Raffin, like the cornettist Luc Gentil, were also manufacturers. The lutenists Julio Burgnesi, Nicolas Juli, and maître Simon also made and sold instruments, while Jean Ferrand was a pastry-cook Loys de Luxembourg made 'moles de quarte' and Jean Paule Paladin was involved in trading at the fairs. Amongst the organists, Antoine and Jean Lebfevre and Francisque des Oliviers were responsible for building or repairing organs, as well as playing them, while Nicolas Bontemps also made clavichords and Jehan Duprey sold confectionery. Amongst the violinists Rambert Badouille was also listed as a painter or illuminator. Jean Bertaud 'menestrier' was a miller and vinegar-maker; the shawm-player Antoine Pellat was also a carpenter, while the drummers Barthélemy Bonsens, Robin de La Marre, and Benoît Genevy were registered as 'espinglier' (pin-maker), crossbow-stringer, and painter respectively. Simon de La Vanelle was variously referred to as 'trompetier', 'faiseur de trompettes' and 'graveur' (engraver); but to judge from his nickname, 'Treze Mestiers' (Thirteen Trades), the trumpeter-sergeant Simon Pajard (or Pojoud) must have broken all records as a 'jack of all trades'.

The corporations and associations which organized instrumentalists in Paris do not seem to have been as important in Lyons. An attempt to impose a 'Roy des violons' and to restrict professional recognition and engagements in 1518 seems to have failed,[47] and while it is difficult to ascertain of the exact implications of the word 'compagnons' used for Cordeilles, Peroyet, and the shawm-band, or for Benoît Bellon and his

[45] Lyons, Archives communales, C 1112, fo. 35r.
[46] E. Vial, *Institutions et coutumes lyonnaises* (Lyons, 1903), 17–28, 171–246.
[47] Lyons, Archives communales, CC 650. Tricou, 'Les Musiciens lyonnais', 148–50.

fellow drummers in 1548, it seems as though players were usually paid individually rather than as bands.

The large number of organists may be somewhat misleading, reflecting the detailed local research devoted to Layolle and his successors, aided by the records for the replacement or renovation of the organs at three churches.[48] In view of the proscription of the organ from the Lyonese liturgy, a tradition long maintained at the cathedral, it can be assumed that some of the organists were not permanently employed and only played portative organs for particular occasions. There certainly seems to have been no permanent organ in the cathedral before 1841, although the archival references to Francesco Layolle (1523–38), Piero Mannuciqua (1548), Mathieu de Fleurs (1559–62), Philibert Ydeux (1570), and the part-timer Jehan Duprey (1595) suggest that the Florentine congregation in the Dominican church of Notre-Dame de Confort maintained continuous succession. The Luccans' chapel in the Franciscan church may have enjoyed similar privileges, although the organ, destroyed by the Huguenots in 1562, was not replaced for thirty years. While the claim of F. J. Fétis's *Biographie universelle* (Paris, 1844) that Aleman Layolle was organist at Saint-Nizier remains unsubstantiated, there is evidence for Loys de Vela being employed at Saint-Paul in 1556.[49]

On the other hand, the number of lutenists recorded does not reflect the instrument's popularity with amateurs in the way that the number of *luthiers* does. One lutenist (Varin) was curiously designated 'cytharedus', while another (Loys de Luxembourg) also played the harp. The earliest of the lutenists, Gaspar Hoste (*fl.* 1489–99) was German, and, to judge from the names, at least two of the others (Jean Paule Paladin and Francesco Veggio) were Italian, and one (Edentos) Spanish or even perhaps Scottish (= Edington?).

A significant number of these instrumentalists and manufacturers were Italian, particularly Milanese, as were many of those employed by the French court after 1502, when Louis XII brought back from Milan a band including six shawms and sackbuts. With the additional evidence provided by the names of the authors of instrumental publications, it seems that Italians, and to a lesser extent Germans and Jews, played an important role in instrumental music in France during the sixteenth century, just as French and Flemish singers and composers did in vocal music in Italy at the time.

[48] G. Tricou, *Documents sur la musique à Lyon au XVIe siècle* (Lyons, 1899); J. Baffert, 'Les Orgues de Lyon du xvie au xviiie siècle', *Cahiers et mémoires de l'orgue*, 11 (1974), 1–85.

[49] N. Dufourcq, *Documents inédits relatifs à l'orgue français* (Paris, 1934), 173, cites archival records indicating that a Monsieur Devella was successively organist in Aix (1585), Riez (1589–99), Avignon (1602), and Nîmes (1603).

The references to six rebec-players (including one Italian and one Scot) all date from the first half of the century. The terminology is also chronologically significant, with no 'rebecquet' or 'joueur de rebec' mentioned after 1547 and no 'violon' before that date. All of the eleven violinists were active during the last third of the sixteenth century and at least three of them were Italians. The violins attributed to Gaspard Duiffoproucart (Tieffenbrucker, 1514–71) are probably apocryphal, and none are depicted in Pierre Woeiriot's engraved portrait of 1562 (see Pl. 3). The first clear reference to a violin-maker (Turquey) does not appear until 1594. But only one viol-player is actually specified, and Gabriel Sourcin is styled 'basse de violon'. The viol, like the lute, spinet, and flute, was essentially an amateur instrument, whilst the violin and rebec, like the shawm, cornett, trumpet, and drums, were normally played by professionals. This fact is underlined not only by the large number of makers and dealers for these instruments, compared to the rarity or complete absence of shawm-, cornett-, trumpet-, and drum-makers, but by the surviving printed music and instruction books. Thus Jambe de Fer's *Épitome musical* (Lyons, 1556), p. 62, describes only the flute, recorder, and viol, stressing the amateurs' preference for the viol over the violin:

We call viols those [instruments] that gentlemen, merchants, and other virtuous people use for their leisure . . . The other kind are called violin and this is the one commonly used for dancing, and with good reason, for it is easy to tune and easy to carry, which is very necessary, especially when conducting a wedding or mummery.

(iii) *Instrument-Makers*

In the course of the sixteenth century Lyons became an important centre for the manufacture of musical instruments, with the number of archival references to makers and dealers increasing as the century progressed. The impetus derived mainly from the expansion of the trade-fairs, which handled the sale of a wide variety of locally made instruments, including *cistres* (citterns), *cornemuses* (bagpipes), *flûtes d'allemands* (transverse flutes), *flûtes à neuf trous* (recorders), *guiternes* (guitars), *hautbois* (shawms), *luths* (lutes), *violles* (viols), and *violons* (violins).[50] Nicolas de Nicolay's *Description générale de la Ville de Lyon* (Lyons, 1573), confirms this variety, observing that 'many people

---

[50] See Brésard, *Les Foires de Lyon*, 180–92; also Lyons, Archives communales, AA 151, fo. 71ʳ; BB 19, fo. 202ᵛ; BB 24, fos. 476–8; BB 32, fos. 237–41; BB 33, fo. 128ʳ; BB 34, fos. 25ᵛ, 45ᵛ, 53ᵛ; BB 38, fo. 142ᵛ; BB 54, fo. 67ᵛ; BB 58, fo. 88ʳ; BB 64, fo. 44ᵛ; BB 73, fos. 97ʳ, 100ʳ, 115ʳ; BB 76, fos. 94ʳ, 178ʳ, 265ʳ; BB 81, fo. 12ʳ; BB 82, fo. 115ʳ; BB 87, fo. 135ʳ; BB 89, fo. 86ʳ; BB 97, fo. 62ʳ.

Pl. 3. Pierre Woeiriot's engraving of Gaspard Duiffoproucart (1562)

were engaged in making viols, violins, citterns, guitars, lutes, flutes, recorders, shawms, bagpipes, and other sorts of musical instruments' (p. 161), indicating also that cases for these instruments were made 'in the style of Lyons, Paris, Rouen, and other places' (p. 173).

Listed in App. IV are the names of forty-five instrument-makers or dealers (in many cases these were identical) active in sixteenth-century

Lyons. While this list by no means represents all such activity in the city, it allows some general conclusions to be drawn. One is that such a high number in proportion to a population of around 50,000 certainly suggests a wider market than that provided by the city itself. Another is that it illustrates the demand for certain instruments. Thus it shows the popularity of the lute, outstripping that of all other instruments, with no less than fifteen names associated with its sale or manufacture, although at least three of these names (Flac, Helmer, and Lejeune), are also referred to as guitar-makers, while Woeiriot's 1562 engraving of Duiffoproucart shows him surrounded by a twelve-string harp, a four-course guitar, a five-string viol, as well as various lutes (see Pl. 3). We find only one maker (Vinatte, 1568–72) specializing exclusively in viols and one (Turquey, 1594) in violins, while the demand for gut strings is reflected in the mention of no less than four string-makers, active between 1580 and 1599, and of two dealers specializing in the sale of lute-strings in 1569.

Whereas all the references to *luthiers*[51] most of whom were foreigners (six German and two Italian), date from the second half of the century, the spinet-makers and one *manicordion*-maker were active in the first half and all seem to have seen French. Only one of the three organ-builders who restored the organs at the churches of the Florentine and Luccan communities in Notre-Dame de Confort (1570) and Saint-Bonaventure (1593) and in the city hospital (1576) was from Lyons.[52] The 'magnificent' organ in St Paul's installed around 1500 was sold by auction in 1539, following a promise to the cathedral chapter that members of the collegiate church would no longer perform polyphony, but would follow the official monophonic chant;[53] moreover, since Loys de Vela was registered as organist at St Paul's in October 1556 it seems that the tradition of polyphonic and instrumental music there was revived at least momentarily.

Three of the eight listed flute-makers were from the Rafi family (recorded variously as Raffin, Raphin, Rapin, or Ruffin); the most famous, Claude (son of Michaud) was honoured in verse by Marot and Baïf, while his recorders and flutes were prized by players and collectors long after his death in 1553. Only one cornett-maker

---

[51] H. Coutagne, 'Gaspard Duiffoproucart et les luthiers lyonnais du xvie siècle', *Mémoires de l'Académie des Sciences, Belles-lettres et Arts de Lyon*, 3 (Paris and Lyons, 1893), 418–81; G. Tricou, 'Duiffoproucart et Lejeune luthiers', *Revue musicale de Lyon*, 1 (1903–4), 89–91.

[52] While Jean Lefebvre and his son Antoine later worked in Toulouse and Bordeaux, Francisque des Oliviers also built organs in Beauvais (1531), Amiens (1550), Tours (1551), Troyes (1555), and Dijon (1560 and 1584), according to Dufourcq, *Documents inédits*, 68 and 392.

[53] Lyons, Archives du Rhône, Fonds ecclésiastiques, actes capitulaires de Saint-Paul, 13 G 40, fo. 94r; 13 G 42, fo. 270v.

(Flachières, 1556–8) is found, although the cornettist Luc Gentil was listed as an instrument-maker and -dealer. No makers of shawms or bagpipes are mentioned, although bagpipes were illustrated in Aneau's *Genethliac* (1559) and Nourry's *Noelz nouveaulx* (c.1530). Moreover, it is clear that shawms were played during the Chevauchée de l'âne in 1566 and sold at the fairs. The flute- or trumpet-makers may have handled this trade, as the *luthiers* no doubt did for the unmentioned citterns and vielles (hurdy-gurdies). The absence of drum-makers remains, however, quite inexplicable.

(iv) *Singers*

With ecclesiastical archives suffering considerable damage during the French Revolution, surviving records mention few singers. Most of these were connected with the principal churches, six with the collegiate church of Saint-Nizier (one—Nicolas Roillet or Rouillet—was designated 'chantre, procureur et receveur' and another—Jean Mellier—'procureur général'), five with the cathedral (including one 'sous-maistre de chœur') one with Saint-Paul (a 'sous-maistre des enfants'), and one with Fourvière. Three were simply designated 'manécantant' (chorister), one '*cantor*' and three 'chantre'—without naming the relevant churches. One 'chantre', Claude Vial (1573), may be the same person as the 'taborineur' who played for the royal entry of 1548, while another, Tristan Dronin (1540–82), was also variously described as 'musicien', 'joueur d'instrument', and 'violeur'.

There is considerable evidence that polyphony, like instrumental playing, was officially proscribed from the liturgy of Lyons during the sixteenth and seventeenth centuries. The Archbishop of Lyons, Primate of France, was head of a conservative diocese, the first Christian community established in Gaul, and one that had proudly maintained its Gregorian rite unchanged since the eleventh century. The hierarchy generally supported this conservatism and resisted innovation. Around 1530 Symphorien Champier noted:

l'eglise de Lyon est immuable et quod non suscepit novitates. Parquoy en icelle on ne chante que plain chant sans aucune chose faicte, ny orgue, ny aultres instruments quelconques.[54]

the church of Lyons is immutable and does not support innovations. That is why here only plainchant is sung without any polyphony, or organ, or any instruments whatsoever.

[54] S. Champier, *L'Antiquité* (repr. Lyons, 1884), 98–9.

Another report published in 1559 congratulates Lyons, like Utrecht, for excluding polyphony and banning trumpets, cornetts, and other strident instruments from its services:

Unde illarum magis constantiam admiror Ecclesiarum, quae istum praevidentes divini cultus abusum, semel musicam illam choro maluerunt excludere, uti Traiectensis et quod audio, Lugdunensis: quam illarum veneror magnificam, quae ipsi et putant, et jactant adeo, maiestatem, qua Dei chorum omni phonascorum syntagmate, vocum omnis generis discrimine, imo et tubarum clangore, cornutorum [*cornettorum* in 1575 edition] stridore, alloque strepitu vario.[55]

Hence I admire the steadfastness of the churches which, forseeing the abuse of the divine worship, prefer to exclude this music from the chorus, as in Utrecht, and I hear, Lyons; I respect less the magnificent [music] of those that have decided themselves to cast aside majesty, and all those choirmasters who break up God's phrases with all kinds of voices and with the clangorous sound of trumpets and strident cornetts, and with various other rackets.

Similarly, the *Ordonnances* published by the Cardinal Archbishop Pierre d'Espinac in 1578 proclaim (p. 13):

Ne voulons autre chant, autres choses nouvelles ny autres cérémonies estre gardées en nostre diocèse que celles qui sont reçeues et approuvées en nostre Eglise cathédrale de Lyon, laquelle ne reçoit, comme dit saint Bernard, aucune nouveauté, et si, en chant, office et cérémonie, c'est la première de toutes les Eglises de la chrétienté ... sous prétexte de musique ne faut entremesler ny chanter chansons publiques et prophanes en l'église.

We do not want any other chant, any novelties, or other ceremonies to be kept in our diocese except those that are received and approved in our Cathedral Church of Lyons, which, as St Bernard said, accepts no novelty, and so, in its chant, office, and ceremony, it is the first of all the churches in Christendom ... on the pretext of music we should not intermingle or sing public or secular songs in church.

The same attitude still prevailed in the seventeenth century, with the canons permitting only plainsong and encouraging simplicity, the priests, clerks, and choirboys learning to sing the entire psalter by heart.[56] A *Mémoire du Chapître primatial de Lyon* published in Paris in 1776 records that in 1528, as part of a revival of ecclesiastical chant, the Cathedral Chapter ordered a revision and reprinting of graduals and antiphonaries:[57] this may relate to the *Graduale* published by Garnier

---

[55] W. van der Lindt, *Panoplia Evangelica* (Cologne, 1559), 422; rev. edn. Cologne, 1575, 408.

[56] J. de Saint-Aubin, *Histoire ecclésiastique de la ville de Lyon* (Lyons, 1666), 93.

[57] Quoted in Baudrier, *Bibliographie lyonnaise*, ii. 373.

and Gobert in 1531, the *Responsoriale* by Septgranges, also in 1531, and various missals and psalters printed during the next decade.[58]

However, it was difficult for the seat of the primacy of France permanently to ignore polyphonic embellishment, especially when it maintained a large clerical organization, resembling in many ways that of the Chapelle royale. From the eleventh century the office of *maître du chœur* was responsible for the choice of clerks, disciplinary punishments, and the organization of ceremonial. Below him was the *sous-maître* or *chapelain des douze*, and next in line the *maître d'enfants* (*magister puerorum*), who was surely a musician. Although the names of all sixteenth-century *maîtres du chœur* are recorded,[59] the principal being François de Saçoncy (1503–10), Jean de Talaru (1511–30), Christophe de Levis (1531–52), and Claude de Talaru (1551–69), little is known about the lesser offices. But evidence of polyphonic performance is restricted to occasional reports, like that of the chapter of Saint-Just in 1489 which specifies singing in 'organum' and counterpoint ('Cantores vero in organo et contrapuncto decantaverunt'[60]), or those of masses sung illicitly in St Paul's.[61] Polyphonic masses were also performed in the cathedral on special occasions, such as the visit of Louis XII and Philippe le Beau,[62] whose chapels sang together on 2 April 1503, and the reception for the crown prince Henry III on 8 September 1574.

The Florentine and Luccan communities maintained chapels in the Dominican and Franciscan churches which were not subject the chapter's prohibitions against polyphony. It is unfortunate that the registers of the Dominican church of Notre-Dame de Confort have not survived, for Florentine merchants and bankers who established their parish there, after their transfer from Geneva in 1466, endowed a chapel dedicated to St John the Baptist, patron saint of Florence, installing a sumptuous organ before 1514, employing Francesco de Layolle to play it from the early 1520s. The church, conveniently situated in the printers' quarter, may have witnessed many of the masses and motets composed by Layolle and published by Etienne Gueynard or Jacques Moderne, all three of whom lived and worked in the nearby rues Raisin and Mercière.[63] With their Dominican liturgical

[58] These are listed ibid. ii. 373–9, xii. 5, and in R. Amiet, *Inventaire générale des livres liturgiques de Lyon* (Paris, 1979).

[59] J. Beyssac, *Les Chanoines de l'église de Lyon* (Lyons, 1914).

[60] See J. Forest, *L'École cathédrale de Lyon* (Lyons, 1885), 333.

[61] Ibid.

[62] L. P. Gachard, *Collection des voyages des souverains des Pays-Bas* (Brussels, 1876), 290–4.

[63] See Pl. 1, reference H. For a more detailed map see S. F. Pogue, *Jacques Moderne; Lyons Music Printer of the Sixteenth Century* (Geneva, 1969), Fig. 1.

aspects, their simple counterpoint and their dedication to a Florentine patrician, the Mass Propers, published in 1528 by Gueynard, could have been designed for a new polyphonic chapel, intended as another ornament reflecting the glory of the transplanted Tuscans' prosperity.

While the spread of Protestantism during the second half of the century encouraged wider amateur performance of psalm melodies and simple harmonizations, the religious struggles no doubt damaged the Catholic tradition: at all events chant-books, as well as organs, were destroyed, for example in the Franciscan monastery of Saint-Bonaventure,[64] during the Huguenot uprising in 1562.

[64] P. Bazin, *Quelques remarques sur le Grand Couvent de Saint-Bonaventure* (Lyons, 1563), 34.

4

Music Copied and Printed in Lyons

(i) Manuscripts

WHILE the musical life of Lyons is illuminated by a study of its literature, chronicles, correspondence, and archives, its most valuable testimony is the music copied or printed in the town, even if this testimony is incomplete and in need of careful assessment. With no continuous demands from a resident court or polyphonic chapel, the vast production that made Lyons an important centre for music publication in the sixteenth century exceeded the requirements of the local aristocracy and bourgeoisie, serving a wider national, and even international, market through the fairs and other commercial outlets. Some idea of the circulation of manuscript and printed music may be gleaned from the surviving correspondence of the immigrant banking and trading families, such as the Capponi, Manelli, and Strozzi, which refers to motets and songs (*canti* or *canzoni*) by Layolle, Arcadelt, Festa, and others sent between Lyons, Florence, Rome, and Venice and performed at home by amateurs and professionals alike.[1]

The relatively poor survival rate of manuscripts copied in France during the late fifteenth and early sixteenth centuries obscures our view of music in the provinces, as well as in the courts of Charles VIII, Louis XII, and Francis I. Foreign sources of this period include a few four-part songs referring to Lyons, such as the anonymous 'Il estoit ung bon homme,' found in a manuscript copied between 1492 and 1516 in Florence, perhaps for Giuliano de'Medici.[2] The same song is found in a parchment choir-book copied around 1500 in Paris for René II de Vaudémont, Duke of Lorraine, or his son around 1500 and in four part-books copied around 1520 in Florence.[3] Similarly, 'Rej[o]uissez vous bergeres, belles filles de Lion' is found, ascribed to Mouton, in a choir-book copied in Florence, probably by a French scribe around

---

[1] R. Agee, 'Ruberto Strozzi and the Early Madrigal', *Journal of the American Musicological Society*, 36 (1983), 1–17; id., 'Filippo Strozzi and the Early Madrigal', *Journal of the American Musicological Society*, 38 (1985), 227–37.

[2] Cortona, Biblioteca del Comune e dell'Accademia Etrusca, Cod. 95–6, fo. 21[r] (Superius and Contratenor part-books) and Paris, Bibliothèque nationale, MS nouv. acq. fr. 1817, fo. 24[r] (Tenor).

[3] Paris, Bibliothèque nationale, MS fr. 1597, fo. 61[v], and Florence, Biblioteca Nazionale Centrale, Magl. XIX, 164–7, fo. 42[v]. A modern edition of the chanson is published by Rouart et Lerolle (Paris, n.d.).

1520, and reappears anonymously in a set of part-books copied, probably in Bruges, for the merchant Zeghere de Male in 1542.[4] These cases are similar to Mouton's four-in-one canon 'En venant de Lyon et bon, bon, bon',[5] printed by Antico in Venice in 1520 and by Attaingnant in Paris in 1528.

Recent discoveries and studies of manuscripts in Copenhagen, Uppsala, and Lyons suggest that Lyons was the centre of a flourishing trade in music-copying, with access to a wide international repertoire, as well as to more provincial sources.

The first of these manuscripts, found in the Royal Library of Copenhagen, MS Ny Kgl. Samling 1848, 2°, is an enormous choir-book containing 278 pieces (23 duplicated), with 151 polyphonic chansons, 44 motets, 14 Magnificats, 3 complete masses, and several fragments and other textless pieces, including 8 German Lieder, composed between around 1450 and 1525. According to Hendrik Glahn,[6] the Danish library purchased this manuscript from Sotheby's of London in February 1921, along with other non-musical manuscripts which had belonged to Jean-Baptiste Marduel (1763–1848), a priest at the cathedral in Lyons and later at the church of Saint-Nizier. In 1833 Marduel donated his collection to the Jesuits, who in 1867 moved it to a new library in the rue Sainte-Hélène. More tangible evidence of Lyonese provenance is provided by the manuscript's paper, which has eight different watermarks, most of them identical with others found in documents from the Archives Municipales of Lyons between 1517 and 1524. These dates confirm the '1520' marked on the new binding that was added around 1800. Another clue to provenance is provided by the scribal signature 'Charneyron' on pages 356–7 and 448–50, which Peter Woetmann Christoffersen[7] suggests was that of Claude Charneyron, a priest at Villefranche (sur Saône) near Lyons in 1540.

Dr Christoffersen describes the manuscript as the private collection of a professional copyist, consisting of ten independent fascicles no longer bound in their original order, storing pieces for later use, or left over after manuscripts already sold, together with three small booklets and two separate bifolia. Five hands are discernible, although two

[4] Florence, Bibl. Naz. Centrale, Magl. XIX, 117, fo. 42ᵛ and Cambrai, Bibl. municipale, MSS 125–8, fo. 126ᵛ; ed. H. M. Brown in J. Haar (ed.), *Chanson and Madrigal, 1480–1530* (Cambridge, Mass., 1964), 155–62.

[5] Facsimile in D. Heartz, 'A New Attaingnant Book and the Beginnings of French Music Printing', *Journal of the American Musicological Society*, 14 (1961), 9–23; modern edition in F. Dobbins (ed.), *The Oxford Book of French Chansons* (Oxford, 1987), no. 6.

[6] H. Glahn, 'Et fransk musikhåndskrift fra begyndelsen af det 16. århundrede', *Fund og Forskning i Det kgl. Biblioteks samlinger*, 5–6 (1958–9), 90–109.

[7] P. W. Christoffersen, 'Musikhåndskriftet Ny Kgl. Samling 1848 2, Det Kgl. Bibliotek, København' (diss., Copenhagen, 1978).

predominate, the second of which was perhaps that of a student, who copied some material from the main scribe.

The manuscript's repertoire is eclectic and chronologically widespread, containing old three-part chansons by Morton and Hayne alongside others by Ockeghem, Compère, Josquin, and Agricola, as well as more recent ones by Févin, Jacotin, and Sermisy, the latter including three-voice versions of some pieces published in four parts in Attaingnant's 'New chansons' of 1527 or 1528; it also contains some recent four-part masses by Gascongne and L'Héritier. The composers actually named in the manuscript are Alexandre (Agricola), Dulo[t], Tomas Jannequin, Maistre Jaques d'Anvers (Barbireau), Maioris, Mirus, Johannes de Sancto Martino, Richaffort, and Ysaac. Some of its pieces are found elsewhere in sources attributed to Bedingham, Morton, Dufay, Hayne, Mureau, J. Fresneau, Busnois, Ockeghem, Bonnel, Brumel, Févin, Compère, Josquin, Adam von Fulda, Prioris, Hesdin, Sermisy, Clément Janequin, and Willaert, as well as in others which were published anonymously in Venice and Paris (RISM 1501, 1520[6], and [1528][7]; 1529[4]). The most frequently represented composers are Compère (with sixteen or seventeen pieces) and Agricola (fourteen or fifteen, seven of them attributed in the manuscript).

While there is no direct evidence of Compère residing in Lyons, he no doubt visited the town with the French King Charles VIII during the Italian campaigns of 1494–5, and he could have been there again with Louis XII, for instance at the meeting with Philip, Count of Flanders, in 1503. Agricola may also have visited Lyons on the last of these occasions. Josquin and Ghiselin, who were in Lyons in 1503, are each represented by two chansons, although only Ghiselin's are actually ascribed. These pieces could not have been copied directly into the manuscript at that time, since watermarks on the oldest paper correspond to others found in archival documents dating 1517–19. The presence of the anonymous four-part chanson 'Tous nobles cueurs venes veoyr Magdaleine' (p. 185), referring no doubt to Madeleine de la Tour d'Auvergne, who married Lorenzo, Duke of Urbino, at Amboise in 1518 and died the following year,[8] suggests a *terminus ante quem* for the fascicle comprising the present pages 135–88, which include four three-voice chansons found in RISM 1529[4] as well as several three-voice versions of four-part pieces by Sermisy and his contemporaries, which must date from Francis I's reign (1515–47). The inclusion of the anonymous three-part chanson 'Sur le pont de Lyon', adapting the traditional text and melody of 'Sur le pont d'Avignon', may confirm the

---

[8] A. Seay, 'Two Datable Chansons from an Attaingnant Print', *Journal of the American Musicological Society*, 26 (1973), 326–8.

paper's evidence that the manuscript originated in Lyons between 1517 and 1525, when the queen Mother Louise of Savoy and the French court were resident in Lyons.

The attribution of the chanson 'Nous bergiers et nous bergeres' (p. 419) to 'Tomas Jannequin' corresponds to that found in a contemporary Florentine manuscript (Florence, Biblioteca Nazionale Centrale, Magl. XIX. 117, fo. 73ᵛ). 'Haquinet', named as the composer of two three-voice and two four-voice motets, may be a local figure, like 'Mirus', composer of the three-voice chanson 'Aquillon, serpentin, dangier'.

'Mirus' may even be identical with 'Le Mire', one of the few named composers in another manuscript now belonging to a Scandanavian library which may have been copied in Lyons around the same time. Certainly the repertoire of Uppsala, Universitetsbiblioteket, Vokalmusik i Handskrift 76a is very similar to the Copenhagen manuscript's, containing a collection of mainly polyphonic chansons, with a minority of sacred pieces, composed in the late fifteenth and early sixteenth centuries and copied by two main and several subsidiary scribes. The composers represented include Agricola, Brumel, Compère, Mouton, Ninot le Petit, and Prioris, who may all have had passing connections with Lyons, although the most substantial contribution was that of Févin, whose six attributed chansons match the number of pieces ascribed to Hayne in other sources. Ten of Uppsala'a sixty-eight pieces are also found in the Copenhagen manuscript. On the evidence of the paper (widely used in southern France during the first decade of the sixteenth century), some of the chanson texts, and additional annotations, Howard Mayer Brown[9] tentatively suggests that this manuscript may have been copied in Toulouse or some other part of south-western France, perhaps for Pierre Robin, president of the royal court in Languedoc. He also indicates, however, that the binding includes a legal document mentioning a certain Radulphus, 'Filius Petri quondam lugdunensis diocesis abhac hora in Anthea' (Radulphus, son of Peter, from the diocese of Lyons, now living in Anthea). Here 'Anthea' may signify Ampuis, a small town on the Rhône, twenty miles south of Lyons. Another possible link with Lyons may be the inclusion of the anonymous two-voice *prosa* for the dead, 'Langentibus in purgatorio' (fo. 68ᵛ), which is similar to one with an added third voice found in some fragments recently recovered from the binding of a copy of Petrus de Natalibus Venetus, *Catalogus sanctorum* (Lyons, J. Huguetan, 1542), in the municipal library of Lyons (MS 6632).

[9] H. M. Brown, 'A "New" Chansonnier of the Early Sixteenth Century in the University Library of Uppsala: A Preliminary Report', *Musica disciplina*, 37 (1983), 171–233.

Dr Christoffersen describes these fragments as consisting of twenty-three folios (310 × 200 mm.) cut from a larger codex on paper with a watermark representing a water-wheel, found frequently on archival documents in Lyons between 1495 and 1531, as well as on one sheet in Copenhagen 1848.[10] He discerns four hands and lists the contents as a three-voice introit 'Puer natus est nobis' (fo. 1[r]), three four-part masses (fos. 1[v]–11[v]), the two-part 'Lugentibus in purgatorio' with a third voice added in a later hand (fo. 12[r]), twelve two- and three-part textless pieces, probably part of one or more longer works (fos. 13[v]–16[r]), five plainsong invitatories and antiphons in the seventh, sixth, fifth, and fourth tones, variously marked 'feria secunda pascha', 'de Sancto Stephano', and 'Nativitate' (fos. 16[v]–20[r]), and finally a textless three-in-one canon (fo. 20[v]).

A later manuscript, which may have been copied in Lyons around 1560, is a set of four quarto part-books containing seventy-four chansons by Arcadelt, Certon, Crecquillon, Sandrin, Sermisy, Villiers, and others, with seven *chansons spirituelles* by Didier Lupi, Gardane, Janequin, and Le Gendre. After being in the possession of the Fuggers of Augsburg, the part-books passed into the possession of the Emperor Ferdinand III in 1656 and are now in the Österreichische Nationalbibliothek in Vienna (Mus. Hs. 18811). The *civilité* script and tear-drop notation are very similar to those found in the music published in Lyons by Robert Granjon. Moreover, no fewer than seventeen of the pieces are found in Granjon's two *Trophée de Musique* collections (RISM 1559[14–15]), albeit with differences in layout and orthography. The inclusion of two of Guillaume Guéroult's *chansons spirituelles* with music by Didier Lupi Second, as well as his setting of Jean du Peyrat's 'O que je vis en estrange martire', may be another indication of Lyonese origin. There is further physical evidence to support this hypothesis, which is developed in a doctoral study of the manuscript by Jerry Call of the University of Illinois.[11]

(ii) *Printed Collections*

If the case for Lyons being a flourishing centre of music-copying remains unproven, there is no doubt that the town was an active and

---

[10] P. W. Christoffersen, letter to the author dated 13 Nov. 1986, indicating that the watermark is similar to C. M. Briquet, *Les Filigranes*, 4 vols. (Paris, 1907; repr. Amsterdam, 1968), no. 13453 (dated 1503–15).

[11] J. Call, 'A Chansonnier from Lyons: The Manuscript Vienna, Österreichische Nationalbibliothek, Mus. Hs. 18811' (doctoral thesis, Univ. of Illinois of Champaign-Urbana in progress).

significant centre for music-publishing during the sixteenth century. Music printed from woodblock in Lyons can be traced back to missals published by Numeister, Hus, and other German immigrants of the 1480s. Italian influence is more evident in the liturgical incunabula of Boninis, Chaussard, Mareschal, Giboletus, Sachon, and Topié, as in their sixteenth-century successors Bevilacqua, Davost, Despreaulx, Fradin, Giunta, Gueynard, Gryphe, Huguetan, Lescuyer, Osmont, Payen, Septgranges, and Veycellier.[12] While this initial activity may not have been significantly greater than that of some other cities in Germany, Italy, and France, it is clear that after Petrucci's introduction of a process for printing music from type by multiple impression around 1500 and of Attaingnant's less costly process of printing by single impression in the late 1520s, Lyons rivals Venice and Paris as an international leader in the publication and distribution of polyphonic music, before giving way to Antwerp and Louvain in the second half of the sixteenth century.

More than a hundred books containing mensural music, mostly polyphonic chansons, psalms, and motets (see below, App. V), were printed in Lyons between around 1525 and 1592. Many others have been lost, as can be seen from the contemporary catalogues of booksellers and collectors such as Antoine du Verdier and Ferdinand Columbus, who purchased some fifteen thousand books, including one hundred and seventy musical editions, for his library in Seville during his travels around Europe between 1514 and 1536. In her study of the musical editions in the Columbine library, Catherine Weeks Chapman[13] notes some twenty-two music books bought in or published in Lyons between 1531 and 1536, a number which far exceeds the nine whose present whereabouts are known. The twenty-two are listed below, with the acquisition number in Columbus's register and the description given in his alphabetic listing, followed by identifying or supplementary notes:

5091   'Francisci de Layole': Septem psalmi penitentiales in cantu [in] 8° [including] *Domine ne in furore tuo* [purchased in 1535][14]

5582   'Francisci de Layole': motetti n°. 12 [including] *O clara virgo xpi gloriosa* L[yon] [in] 8° [British Library, K. 8. 6. 7 (5)]

---

[12] K. Meyer-Baer, *Liturgical Music Incunabula: A Descriptive Catalogue* (London, 1962); Baudrier, *Bibliographie*, ii. 22, 41, 155, 373–9; xii. 5.; R. Amiet. *Inventaire général des livres liturgiques du diocèse de Lyon* (Paris, 1979); L. Guillo, 'Recherches sur les éditions musicales lyonnaises de la Renaissance' (doctoral thesis, Paris, École pratique des Hautes Études IVᵉ section, 1986), 59–61.

[13] C. W. Chapman, 'Printed Collections of Polyphonic Music Owned by Ferdinand Columbus', *Journal of the American Musicological Society*, 21 (1968), 32–84.

[14] See F. D' Accone (ed.), *Music of the Florentine Renaissance*, 6 (Corpus Mensurabilis Musicae, 32; American Institute of Musicology, 1973), 60–132.

5583   'Francisci de Layole': Motetti n°. 12. 5 vocum L[yon] [in] 8°
[including] *Suscipe verbum virgo maria quod tibi*

7622   'Francisci de Layole': Motetti n°. 12 trium vocum L[yon] [in] 8°
[Purchased probably in Perugia in 1530]

9198   'Jo. Mouton': Missa de cantes cantilenam et luculi cantum.
L[yon] [in] 8° [beginning] 'Chirie'

9199   Canson novelle francoise n°. 11 a trois e[t] a4 e[t] a5. *Las je me
playns mauldite soit fortune* et est regis francie. L[yon] [in] 8°
[The piece cited refers to a quatrain by King Francis I set for
four voices by Sermisy and published in Attaingnant's first book
of chansons. Columbus lists two more copies (nos. 5168 and
13748); 9199 was probably purchased at Turin in 1531, 13748 at
Lyons in 1535]

9208   'Francisci de Layole': Motetti cum 5 vocibus n°. 12 in 4^{or}
partibus et p[rim]^a est *Ego in foelix* et ulti[m]^a est *Ave verum*.
L[yon] [in] 8° [Purchased in Turin in 1530]

9209   'Francisci de Layole': Motetti ex vocibus paribus 12 rerum.
P[rim]^a est *Ave Maria* et ulti[m]^a *Virgo Maria*. L[yon] [in] 8°
[Purchased in Turin in 1531]

9210   Clementis Genichin Sperantis modulatio in dimidio folio. 2°

9251   'Francisci de Layole': Motetti novi li[br]° p[rim]° n°. 12. Ultimus
est *Memor esto* L[yon] [in] 8°. Celorum candor splenduit novum
sydus emienit in cantu. [Purchased in Turin in 1531]

9339   Missarum solemnium totius anni[:] contrapunctus seu musica
figurata super plano cantu L[yon] 1528 [15]

13451   Misse 10 p[rim]^a p. mombi [= P. Moulu] *De s. stephano*. 10^a. F.
de Layole *De salutaris hostia* cum tribus motetis. L[yon] 1531
[in] 2 [= folio] [= *Liber decem missarum*, Lyons, Moderne,
RISM 1532^8]

13523   Chanson in language provensal cum cantu d'organo. [In] 8°
Maudit sia tant de [Purchased in Lyons in September 1535] [=
Chansons nouvelles en lengaige provensal]

13734   Moteti del fior in 4^{or} volumine li[ber] p[rimu]^s h[abe]t 32 el
p[rim]° est *O regem celi* et ulti[m]^a *O admirabile commercium*
L[yon] 1532 [= *Motetti del fiore*, Lyons, Moderne, RISM 1532^{10}]

13757   Chansons de la coronne libre premier et sunt 23. p[rim]^a *Je
veulx laysser* et ulti[m]^a *Sus l'herbe brunete* et est layole [in] 8°

[15] See D. A. Sutherland (ed.), *The Lyons Contrapunctus* (Recent Researches in the Music of the
Renaissance, 31–2; Madison, Wisc., 1976).

[A three-voice setting of the last chanson was printed by Antico in Venice in RISM 1520[6]]

13758 Canciones con plures vocum duarum in 2 volumine et p[rim]ª est *Qui tollis peccata* [de] Richafort ulti[m]ª est *Pleni sunt* [de] Layole [in] 4°

13762 Psalmi penitentiales per Loiset Pieton [in] 8° [Purchased in Lyons in 1535][16]

13765 Fleur des chansons a4 parties n°. 23. P[rim]ª *C'est une dure departie* et ulti[m]ª *Vivra tousjours en soucy* [in] 8° [Settings of both named chansons by Sermisy were printed by Attaingnant in 1528–9]

13766 Psalmi penitentiales cum 5 vocibus. P[rim]ª *In te domine speravi* ultimus *Nunc dimittis et ego is [sic] felix et peccavimus contra* a4 parties [in] 4°

13770 Missarum trium liber p[rimu]ˢ *Conditor alme syderum* de Layole 2ª *Quam pulchra es* de Pieton 3ª *Jamais amoureux bien* de Jo. He[s]din [in] 8°

13772 *Memor esto* sex vocum discantus He[s] din[in] 8° [rimu]ˢ et discantus secundus in 4 dimidiis folliis [in] 8° [A six-voice setting of *Memor esto* printed at Nuremberg in 1553 is ascribed to Layolle][17]

13953 Chansons 13 ulti[m]ª est *Pis ne me peul[t] venir que l'ay* [An anonymous four-voice setting of this *huitain* was printed by Attaingnant in RISM 1530[5]]

Although perhaps purchased in Lyons, the Columbus books numbered 9210, 13757, 13765, 13772, and 13953 were probably not published there, having repertoires or titles more readily suggesting Paris or Venice. However, the others no doubt include the town's earliest polyphonic publications, one of which is almost certainly the Tenor part-book, bound together with four similar octavo part-books containing masses and motets printed by woodcut in Venice by Andrea Antico for Andrea Torresano in 1521 (RISM 1521[1–5]). The physical similarity and proximity of these books led Catherine Weeks Chapman to surmise that Antico, whose activities between 1522 and 1533 are unknown, may have gone to Lyons, perhaps along with his fellow Istrian Jacopo Moderno or with the Florentine Jacopo Giunta, nephew

---

[16] Guillo, 'Recherches', 36–40; see, R. Clark (ed.), 'The Penitential Psalms of Loyset Piéton' (M. Mus. thesis, London, 1986).

[17] See F. D'Accone (ed.), *Music of the Florentine Renaissance*, 5, no. 20.

of his erstwhile partner Luc'Antonio Giunta of Venice. But in a recent study of the London Tenor, [18] Laurent Guillo claims that the ornamental initials and other features in the three text founts are identical with those used by the obscure Antoine du Ry, active in Lyons as a printer for Simon Vincent and Jacopo Giunta between 1515 and 1534, and that the state of wear in the initials suggests a date between July 1523 and April 1525. The fleur-de-lis typographical mark on the title-page of the Tenor is similar to others used by many printers, especially Italians (including Dorico in Rome, RISM 1531[4]), as well as Trot, Vincent, J. Giunta, and Moderne in Lyons.

While the part-book's twelve motets are unattributed, at least one, the penultimate five-voice *Ave virgo sanctissima*, was later reprinted by Ulrich Neuber in Nuremberg in 1568 with ascription to Francesco Layolle.[19] With the second motet in the book having the text *O clara virgo Christi*, specified in no. 5582 of the Columbus catalogue, it seems almost certain that this collection was the set of twelve by Layolle published in Lyons (see Pl. 4). Five more octavo sets of twelve motets by Layolle listed by Columbus (nos. 5583, 7622, 9208, 9209, and 9251) may have been issued by the same printer as a series, similar to the series of Antico and Torresano in 1521. So too may Layolle's penitential psalms,[20] although Loyset Piéton's penitential psalms (no. 13762) were printed in the early 1530s by Jacques Moderne, like the mass and motet anthologies entered by Columbus as nos. 13451 and 13734.

The Columbus catalogue entry 13523 must refer to the *Chansons nouvelles en lengaige provensal*, a small undated octavo book of multi-stanza poems in Provençal, preceded by melodies in black notation on a four-line stave (see Pl. 5). These chansons were probably written by the *basochiens* of Aix-en-Provence between 1518 and 1531. On the evidence of typography and ornament, the only extant copy (Paris, Bib. nat., fonds Rothschild, IV. 6. 179) has been variously attributed to Claude Nourry, to the heirs of Barnabé Chaussard, to Moderne, and to Antoine Blanchard.[21]

---

[18] L. Guillo, 'Les Motets de Layolle et les Psaumes de Piéton: Deux nouvelles éditions lyonnaises du seizième siècle', *Fontes artis musicae*, 32 (1984), 186–91; see also Guillo, 'Recherches', ii, Annexe IV.

[19] F. D'Accone, *Music of the Florentine Renaissance*, 5, no. 6; no. 36 presents the Tenor's final five-voice motet, *Stabat mater* (scored from a later manuscript copied in Padua, where it is again unattributed).

[20] Restored from later German copies in F. D'Accone, ibid. 6, 60–132.

[21] *Chansons nouvelles en lengaige provensal*, fac., ed. E. Picot (Mâcon, 1909); ed. F. Pic (Beziers, 1979). Chaussard used the same title-page illustration in a collection of farces (British Library, C20 d4): see E. Picot, *Catalogue des livres composant la bibliothèque de feu M. le Baron James de Rothschild*, 5 vols. (Paris, 1884–1920), i, no. 1021; v, no. 191; J. T. Bory, *Recherches sur l'imprimerie à Marseille* (Paris, 1858), 129; Pogue, *Jacques Moderne*, 240.

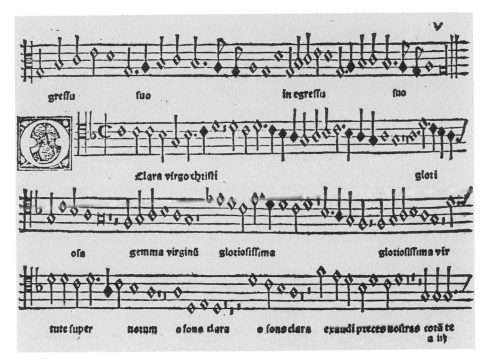

Pl. 4. Tenor part of 'O clara virgo christi', motet for four voices cited in the catalogue of Ferdinand Columbus as one of twelve by Layolle published in Lyons c.1525 (British Library K. 8. b. 7 (5))

The first dated publication of polyphonic music surviving from Lyons is the *Contrapunctus seu Figurata Musica Super Plano Cantu Missarum Solennium Totius Anni*, a large folio choir-book containing thirteen mass Propers and three motets ascribed to F. de Layolle.[22] The collection is unique in combining a plainchant Tenor or Bass, notated in neumes on a four-line stave, with three other polyphonic voices on five-line staves. Printed by Bernard Garnier and Guillaume Gobert, and sold by Étienne Gueynard at his shop near Notre-Dame de Confort, the work has a five-year royal privilege dated August 1528, with a dedication to the Florentine consul, Bernardo Altovita, dated September 1528. Garnier, designated in the dedication as 'typographus', may have been responsible for the text in moveable type, whereas Gobert, designated 'item chalcographi' ('one of the engravers'), probably did the woodcuts for the initials, miniatures, and music.[23]

[22] Edited by Sutherland in *The Lyons Contrapunctus*.
[23] The typography is described in detail in Guillo, 'Recherches', i. 15; ii, no. 9.

Pl. 5. First song from *Chansons nouvelles in lengaige provensal* (*c.*1530)

Garnier's dedication claims to have 'selected music by all the first-rate masters from the classical age to our own and, like a busy bee, taken the best pieces from their works, applying them like the juices of the finest flavour in this book and in others that, God willing, I will print in the near future'. However, the consistency of the music suggests a single hand, presumably that of Layolle, named as composer only for the three motets appended at the end. Layolle, who served as organist at Notre-Dame de Confort, the church of the Florentine community in 1528, was certainly familiar with the book's sponsor, the Florentine emigrant banker Bernardo Altovita, who was also the dedicatee of the *Sette salmi penitentiali*, written by the composer's friend Luigi Alamanni and published in 1526. Layolle could have heard the *Choralis constantinus* and other Proper settings by Heinrich Isaac in Florence during his youth, before moving to Lyons, where he became the key figure on the musical scene during the 1520s, composing the lion's share of the polyphonic music purchased there by Columbus, and later acting as editor for Jacques Moderne's first collections of mass ordinaries and motets.

A second dedication from 'the same Printers to the Reader' indicates that the *Contrapunctus* was only their 'first offering, satisfying the greater and commoner need, before progressing to works in which the most famous musicians can offer their own models and imitations'. Garnier and Gobert used their choral-note fount again for the last time in February 1531, when they published the first printed gradual for the Lyonese liturgy, the *Graduale ad usum et ritum ecclesie Lugdunensis*.[24] This was quite different from the more elaborate polyphonic project emanating from the Florentine community and its church in Notre-Dame de Confort.

(iii) *Jacques Moderne*

Gueynard died in 1529, and the true sequel to his polyphonic *Contrapunctus* was the *Liber decem missarum*, a collection of ten mass ordinaries and three motets published in 1532 by Jacques Moderne. There are a number of clues connecting Gueynard's enterprise with Moderne's: the title-page of the 1532 masses uses a border found in a Bible published by Gueynard, while Moderne's dedication to Charles d'Estaing, apostolic notary and canon at the cathedral of Lyons, uses the same type-face and ornamented initial as the address to Altovita in the *Contrapunctus*.[25] Francesco Layolle, named as the composer of the three motets at the end of the *Contrapunctus*, again figures prominently, contributing two masses and three motets in the *Liber decem missarum*, acting as Moderne's musical editor here and in several collections of motets printed before his death around 1540. The decorated initials, ornamental borders, and layout of Moderne's musical pages emulate the *Liber quindecim missarum* printed in 1516 in Rome by Andrea Antico and Antonio Giunta. Antonio's uncle, Luc'Antonio Giunta, who also collaborated with Antico in various musical publications, including a collection of chansons printed at Venice (RISM 1520[6-7]), had previously worked with Gueynard on a missal for Roman usage[26] published in Lyons in 1508, while another member of the Giunta family, Jacopo, who published from premises at Lyons in the rues Mercière and Thomassin from 1519, collaborated with Antoine du

---

[24] Ibid. i. 48.
[25] Pogue, *Jacques Moderne*, 39–40, 71–2.
[26] See Baudrier, *Bibliographie*, xi. 166–262.

Ry and later commissioned Moderne to print Alciati's *Emblems*[27] in 1545. Moderne's publishing address was the rue Mercière, while Gueynard had operated in the same neighbourhood, in the heart of the printer's quarter near Notre-Dame de Confort, the chapel of the Florentine community. Gueynard's printer Bernard Garnier and Moderne both lived nearby in the rue Raisin during the 1520s. Guillo[28] also indicates that the British Library copy of Moderne's *Liber decem missarum* includes the letters 'BG' and 'D. AL. B' stamped on the binding, suggesting that they represent Bernard Garnier, who might have been involved in its printing, and Lord Altovita, Bernardo, the dedicatee of the *Contrapunctus*.

There is thus considerable evidence linking Antico, Du Ry, Gueynard, the Giuntas, and Moderne, and it may be no coincidence that Moderne began his music printing on the expiry of Gueynard's privilege. Moderne's later connections with Italian printers include his reprinting twenty *ricercari* from Andrea Arrivabene's *Musica Nova* (Venice, 1540) and his close copies of two books of masses by Morales printed in Rome by Valerio Dorico in 1544. Meanwhile, his own motet publications were acknowledged in the title and content of Gardane's *Fior de Mottetti tratti dalli Mottetti del Fiore* (RISM 1539[6] and 1539[12]).

Attaingnant published his *Chansons nouvelles* (RISM 1528[3]) in Paris four months before Gueynard's *Contrapunctus* appeared in Lyons. His first royal privilege was not granted until 1529, but in June 1531 he obtained a further six-year privilege, which claimed that he had 'invented and brought to light the way and industry of cutting, casting, and printing the said notes and characters, both of music and polyphony, as of the aforementioned tablatures for lutes, flutes, and organs', expressing concern that competitors would exploit his invention.[29] He may well have been thinking specifically of Jacques Moderne, who could have copied the single-impression secret by direct or indirect means, having already proven himself a skilled counterfeiter in the best Lyonese tradition.[30] At all events, by 1532 Moderne had succeeded in mastering the new technology, and during the rest of Francis I's reign he remained the only printer in France exempt from Attaingnant's privilege, monopolizing music-publishing in Lyons. Antoine Gardane, who may have served an apprenticeship with Moderne in Lyons, es-

---

[27] Pogue, *Jacques Moderne*, 30–2, 190, 233, 255; Baudrier, *Bibliographie*, vi. 77, 354–8, 380–2, 403–84; see also A. A. Renouard, 'Notice sur la famille des Junte et sommaire de leurs éditions jusqu'en 1550', in *Annales de l'imprimerie des Alde* (Paris, 1934); T. W. Bridges, 'Giunta', *New Grove Dictionary of Music*.

[28] Guillo, 'Recherches', i. 51.

[29] Heartz, *Pierre Attaingnant*, 173–5; id., 'A New Attaingnant Book', 9–23.

[30] Pogue, *Jacques Moderne*, 40–1.

tablished his music-printing business in Venice and used the new single-impression method from 1538. The Avignon publisher Jean de Channey issued four books of masses, lamentations, hymns, and Magnificats by Carpentras in 1532 and charged the bookseller Constantin Fradin[31] to seek a publishing privilege from Francis I during his visit to Lyons in 1533. This was not apparently granted, although De Channey employed the old, more costly, double- or triple-impression method of Petrucci and his emulators, using a unique type with rounded noteheads cut by Étienne Briard.

Samuel Pogue's excellent monograph on Moderne[32] lists and analyses one hundred and forty-eight editions, over a third of which include music, signed by or attributed to the printer from Istria, showing that his musical repertoire was largely original, contemporary, and independent, if eclectic, serving a wide European market and representing a wide variety of composers and patrons. The only significant omission from Pogue's bibliography is the *Davidici Poenitentiales Psalmi* of Loyset Piéton, a set of four unsigned and undated large octavo partbooks (170 × 110 mm.) preserved in the collegiate church archives in Castell'Arquato, erroneously listed in RISM (P2344) as a publication of Attaingnant. Its musical typography is clearly identical with that used by Moderne until 1544, even if its smaller format is unique. Guillo[33] notes that the ornamental initials are identical to the Italianate ones used in the 1528 *Contrapunctus*, suggesting that Bernard Garnier may have assisted in Moderne's early publications, like this one. At all events, the book was purchased in Lyons by Columbus in the autumn of 1535 (no. 13762), along with a set of pentitential psalms for four voices by Layolle (no. 5091) and one for five voices by an unnamed composer (no. 13766).

Moderne's musical publications comprise the bulk of his output in volume and significance. Before 1544 most of these publications were anthologies of motets and chansons by internationally famous contemporary composers, with a minority by lesser-known local figures, issued in two series: the *Motetti del Fiore* (1532–42) comprising eight books, and the *Parangon des Chansons* (1538–44) eleven.[34] The first book of the *Difficile des Chansons* (c.1540) contained only pieces by

---

[31] See P. Pansier, *Histoire du livre et de l'imprimerie à Avignon du XIVᵉ au XVIᵉ siècle*, 3 vols. (Avignon, 1922), iii. 124–6; for Channey's connections with Lyons see Baudrier, *Bibliographie*, x. 291–304.

[32] Pogue, *Jacques Moderne*. Reviewed by the present author in *Journal of the American Musicological Society*, 24 (1971), 126–31.

[33] Guillo, 'Les Motets de Layolle', 189.

[34] F. Dobbins, 'Jacques Moderne's *Parangon des Chansons*: A Bibliography of Music and Poetry of Lyon, 1538–1543', *Royal Musical Association Research Chronicle*, 12 (1974), 1–90.

Janequin, while the second (RISM 1544[9]) was another mixed anthology. After 1532 Moderne issued one more folio anthology of masses and motets (RISM 1547[2], repr. 1548[1]) and one containing Magnificats (1550[4]). The later books were mostly devoted to a single composer: two to masses by Pierre Colin (1542 and 1554), two to masses by Morales (1545 and 1551), two to *Canzoni* by Layolle (c.1540) and one to *Canzoni* by Petrarch set by Matteo Rampollini. As well as one monophonic collection of noëls (c.1535), two books of plainchant masses (1557), and two old musical treatises (1540 and c.1557), there were three lute tablatures by the Venetian Francesco Bianchini (c.1547), the Milanese Giovanni Paolo Paladino (c.1549) and the Hungarian Bálint Bakfark (c.1553). The latter was exceptional in that it was the only one of Moderne's musical publications to carry a dedication (to the Archbishop of Lyons, François de Tournon) and a three-year privilege signed by J. Tignat, the royal lieutenant, protecting this one book against other printers and booksellers in Lyons, specifically perhaps Jean Pullon de Trin, who printed a similar tablature by Paladino in 1553. However, without the official protection enjoyed by Attaingnant in Paris, Moderne had exercised a complete monopoly of music-printing in Lyons until the accession of Henry II in 1547.

(iv) *Godefroy and Marcellin Beringen*

Moderne's first serious rivals in music-publishing at Lyons were the Beringen brothers, Godefroy and Marcellin, Protestants of German origin operating between 1545 and 1559 from premises in the rue Mercière.[35] After printing many books on the classics, law, and medicine, they turned their attention to music in 1547, issuing two books of psalm paraphrases by Clément Marot, set for four voices by Loys Bourgeois.[36] The second of these carried a five-year privilege signed on behalf of the new King on 4 August 1547. In the same year the brothers printed a collection of thirty motets for five voices by Dominique Phinot dedicated to the Genoan merchant Lucca de Grimaldo, and in the following year a collection of seventeen motets and lamentations for six to eight voices dedicated to the Archbishop of Besançon, François Bonvalot.[37] In 1548 they issued two books of polyphonic chansons by Phinot, dedicated respectively to Nicolas Bave and

---

[35] Baudrier, *Bibliographie*, iii. 31–55.
[36] See Douen, *Marot et le psautier huguenot*, ii, no. 25; Pidoux, *Le Psautier huguenot*, ii. 35–7.
[37] See D. Phinot, *Opera omnia*, ed. J. Hofler and R. Jacob (Corpus Mensurabilis Musicae, 59; American Institute of Musicology, 1972–82), i–ii.

César Gros, Italian merchants living in Lyons, with a third book by Didier Lupi dedicated to various Luccan merchants and bankers also living in Lyons.[38] The 1547 privilege was used for a sixth time for a collection of *chansons spirituelles* by Guillaume Guéroult set to music for four voices by Didier Lupi and dedicated to the Count of Gruyère.[39] A collection of fifty psalms translated by Clément Marot, with the official Genevan melodies, was published without privilege or dedication in 1548 and revised in 1549 (Pidoux, 48/II and 49/I). The brothers turned again to Lupi in February 1550 for thirty four-voice settings of psalms translated by Gilles d'Aurigny, dedicated to the Lyonese banker Nicolas Baillivi and still protected by the 1547 privilege (Pidoux, 49/III). Their next extant musical publication, dated 1552 but still issued under the 1547 privilege, was a collection of Latin psalms set for four voices by Simon Joly,[40] organist of the cathedral of Saint-Étienne at Bourges, dedicated to Cardinal François de Tournon, Archbishop of Bourges and Lyons.

Marcellin Beringen probably died sometime between 1552 and 1554, since only Godefroy's name appears on the title-pages of the four-part *Pseaulmes LXXXIII de David* by Loys Bourgeois in 1554 (Pidoux, 54/II) and Barthélemy Aneau's *Genethliac* in 1559.

Baudrier's *Bibliographie lyonnaise*[41] cites an inventory of printing material ceded by Godefroy Beringen to Guillaume and Jacques Reynaud on 2 September 1556, listing not only Granjon and Gara- mond types but 'Noctes grandes d'Allemaigne', 'Noctes petites gloses d'Allemaigne', and 'Nocte de Lovain à longue queue', which presumably refer to music-type. In fact the music-type that the Beringens employed for all fourteen surviving publications is identical with that used by Johannes Petreius at Nuremberg between 1536 and 1541 (see Pl. 6). Guillo[42] indicates that this type was also used in Geneva by Jean Gérard and Adam and Jean Rivery in 1550, by Simon du Bosc and Guillaume Guéroult in 1556, and by Michel Blancher in 1562, as well as by Heinrich Peter for Glarean's *Dodecachordon* in Basle in 1547 and by Tielman Susato in Antwerp in 1552. He further suggests that the 'large German notes' mentioned in the 1556 inventory were identical with those used in Lyons by Macé Bonhomme in 1555 and by Antoine Cercia in 1562, while the 'Louvain note[s] with long stem[s]', used by Pierre

---

[38] V. L. Saulnier, 'Dominique Phinot et Didier Lupi'.

[39] Pidoux, *Psautier huguenot*, ii. 4, no. 48/III; M. Honegger, 'Les Chansons spirituelles de Didier Lupi et les débuts de la musique protestante en France' (doctoral thesis, Paris, 1970).

[40] F. Lesure, 'Une œuvre inconnue d'un compositeur inconnu: Simon Joly (1552)', *Revue de musicologie*, 47 (1961), 198–9.

[41] Baudrier, *Bibliographie*, iii. 31.

[42] Guillo, 'Recherches', 127.

Pl. 6. Cantus of Didier Lupi Second's 'Souvent ie veulx baiser' from the *Tiers livre* (G. and M. Beringen, 1548). Munich, Bay. Staatsbib. 4 Mus. pr. 52/12.

Phalèse and his heirs between 1552 and 1674 were also used in a book of madrigals printed by Antoine Cercia in 1567.

(v) *Macé Bonhomme*

Whereas music represents a significant proportion of the total output of Moderne (55 out of 84 signed editions) and Beringen (13 out of 62), other printers made only exceptional excursions into the musical field during the second half of the century. Thus Macé (Matthieu) Bonhomme,[43] active in Lyons between 1535 and 1563 except for two years following the printers' strike of 1539 (when he moved his business to Vienne and then Avignon), obtained a ten-year privilege to print a single collection of monophonic *noëls* and *chansons* by Nicolas Martin from Savoy in 1555.[44] (See Pl. 7.)

[43] Baudrier, *Bibliographie*, ii. 185–8; iii. 117–18, 167–70; iv. 304–7; ix. 235–7; x. 185.
[44] N. Martin, *Noelz et Chansons nouvellement composez tant en vulgaire Françoys que Savoysien dict Patoys* (Lyons, 1555, repr. 1556); ed. J. Orsier (Paris, 1879); ed. C. Gardet (Annecy,

Pl. 7. Last song and privilege from Nicolas Martin's *Noelz et Chansons* (M. Bonhomme, 2nd edn., 1556). Lyons, Bibl. municipale Rés. 356 050.

Like the aforementioned *Chansons nouvelles en lengaige provensal*, these multi-stanza poems (many in Savoyard patois are preceded by monophonic melodies; but Bonhomme prints the music in white void notation on a five-line stave with a variety of clefs, using the single-impression method. The same type, which Guillo[45] suggests came from the Beringen sale, reappears in a Missal for the liturgy of Lyons printed by Corneille de Septgranges for Jacopo Giunta[46] in 1546 and in a monophonic psalter printed by Antoine Cercia in 1562.

(vi) *Michel du Bois*

Born in Villiers-sur-Arthie in the Oise, and probably apprenticed in Paris, Michel du Bois went to Geneva in 1537, publishing there several

1942, repr. 1973); see also J. Orsier, 'Un poète musicien au XVIᵉ siècle, N. Martin, ses noels et ses chansons', *Revue de la Renaissance*, 9 (1908), 181–203.

[45] Guillo, 'Recherches', i. 127; ii, no. 31, Type no. 127.
[46] Facsimiles in Dobbins, 'The Chanson at Lyons', fos. 177ᵛ and 211–14.

theological works, including the first French edition of Calvin's *Institution de la Religion Chrestienne*. He was one of a number of Protestant printers whose activity was divided between Lyons and Geneva and who suffered religious persecution accordingly. He left Calvin's city in 1541, moving to Lyons, where he worked with Antoine Vincent and Jean Frellon,[47] who in 1553 ceded his press and materials to him. Two years later Du Bois published, without privilege, a collection of a hundred and fifty psalms paraphrased by Clément Marot, Jean Poitevin, Maurice Scève, Claude le Maistre, Estienne Pasquier, and others, with monophonic melodies added by Philibert Jambe de Fer (see Pl. 8).

Royal letters patent were issued at Blois on 3 February 1556 for the publication of Philibert Jambe de Fer's treatise *Épitome musical*, which Du Bois printed on 28 April 1556, with a dedication to Jean Darut and Georges Obrech, Protestant merchants living in Lyons. On his return to Geneva in October 1557, Du Bois was sent before the Consistory and imprisoned for three days for having been 'polluted by idolatry' during his stay in Lyons. However, he was restored to the *bourgeoisie* in March 1559, and was permitted to return to Lyons to collect his belongings.[48] His name appeared on the title-page of forty-one psalms translated by Théodore de Bèze and set for four voices by Philibert Jambe de Fer with a dedication to the banker Georges Obrech, signed on 20 April 1559 in Lyons, although this cannot be taken as proof that it was in fact printed there. Indeed, at about the same time Du Bois published (probably in Geneva), two books of motets by Clemens, Crecquillon, and others (RISM 1559[4-5]), using a Latin form of his name, M. Sylvius (RISM 1559[4-5]). These form the third and fourth volumes of an undated series, employing the same music-type, the first two being signed by another Genevan printer, Jacob Arbillius (cf. RISM 1558[8]). Although a couple of pieces by Goudimel are included in the third volume, these motets use Catholic Latin texts, mainly set by Netherlandish composers, particularly Clemens non Papa and Crecquillon. In September 1560 Du Bois shared an edition with Pierre Davantes in Geneva, presenting eighty-three psalms by Marot and Bèze, using the orthodox melodies annotated with a new mnemonic devised by Davantes.[49]

Du Bois died shortly afterwards, for on 28 January 1561 Davantes and Jacques d'Arbilley (almost certainly the Jacob Arbillius who shared the

---

[47] Baudrier, *Bibliographie*, v. 157–67, 226–41.

[48] P. Chaix, *Recherches sur l'imprimerie à Genève de 1550 à 1564* (Geneva, 1954), 176; Pidoux, *Le Psautier huguenot*, ii. 105 and 110.

[49] Details on the publications and activities of Du Bois are provided in Pidoux, *Le Psautier huguenot*, ii. 85–121, and Guillo, 'Recherches', i. 128–31.

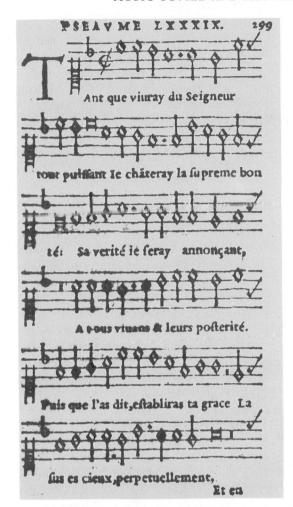

PSEAVME LXXXIX. 299

Ant que viuray du Seigneur

tout puiſſant Ie châteray la ſupreme bon

té; Sa verité ié feray annonçant,

A t-ous viuans & leurs poſterité.

Puis que l'as dit,eſtabliras ta grace La

ſus es cieux,perpetuellement,
Et en

Pl. 8. Psalm 89 translated by
Jean Poitevin with music
adapted by Philibert Jambe de
Fer (M. du Bois, 1555)

1558–9 motet series) requested the Genevan Council to be released
from the guardianship of his children.[50]

Davantes, who died on 31 August of the same year,[51] packed a variety
of humanist endeavour into his short life, establishing a reputation
under the pseudonym Antesignanus as a doctor, philologist, and printer.
Born at Rabastens-de-Bigorre near Tarbres in 1525, he was in Lyons in
1554, sharing a royal privilege to publish a biblical commentary with
the aforementioned Macé Bonhomme, and editing texts by Clenardo,

[50] Geneva, Archives d'Etat, Registres du Conseil pour les affaires des particuliers, 12, 2ᵉ partie,
fo. 92ʳ.
[51] Ibid., Registre des Morts, 4, p. 39.

Hippocrates, and Terence.[52] He settled in Geneva early in 1559 and may have assisted in completing the melodies for the 1562 psalter.[53] On 25 May 1560 he received a three-year privilege from the Council to publish 'a new musical invention upon the Psalms'. This probably refers to his 'new and easy method for singing each strophe of the Psalms without going back to the first', illustrated in an edition of eighty-three psalms printed by Du Bois, with an explanation in the preface.[54] This mnemonic system, based on numbers rather than solmization syllables, was later adopted in Jean-Jacques Rousseau's *Projet concernant de nouveaux signes pour la musique* (Geneva, 1781).

(vii) *Robert Granjon*

Robert Granjon, the famous typecutter and disciple of Claude Garamond, was active as a bookseller at the Cloz Bruneau in the rue Saint-Jean de Latran in Paris from March 1545; but by 1546 he was already making annual trips to Lyons,[55] where he supplied matrices to Jean de Tournes and Sébastien Gryphe.[56] Having obtained a royal privilege to print tablatures for lute, guitar, and other instruments in February 1550, on 23 December he signed a contract of association with another Parisian printer, Michel Fezandat (Faisandat), renewing it on 9 November of the following year.[57] One of the products of the partnership was *Le troysiesme livre contenant plusieurs Duos et Trios... nouvellement mis en tablature de Guiterne par Simon Gorlier, excellent joueur*, dated 1551, bearing Gorlier's dedication to 'Françoys Pournas Lyonnois, seigneur de la Pimente, son singulier amy'. Another was *Le premier livre de Chansons, Gaillardes, Pavannes, Bransles, Almandes, Fantaisies reduictz en tabulature de Guiterne par Maistre Guillaume Morlaye joueur de Lut*, which is dated 1552.[58] This date is curious, since Granjon and Fezandat dissolved their association on 27 December 1551.[59] Fezandat returned to his previous address in the

[52] Baudrier, *Bibliographie*, i. 119; ii. 357; iii. 287, 455; vii. 180, 229–39; viii. 308, 359, 371, 401–2; x. 241, 251–3, 263–4; xi. 454.

[53] P.-F. Geisendorf, *Le Livre des habitants de Genève* (Geneva, 1957), i. 151; Guillo, 'Recherches', 84.

[54] Douen, *Clément Marot et le psautier huguenot*, ii. 490–502; Pidoux, *Le Psautier huguenot*, ii. 118–19.

[55] E. Coyecque, *Recueil d'actes notariés relatifs à l'histoire de Paris*, 2 vols. (Paris, 1905–23), ii, nos. 3427 and 4170.

[56] See Baudrier, *Bibliographie*, i. 284; ii. 49–64, 429–31.

[57] Paris, Archives nationales, Minutier central des notaires, 110, 15–16; see also Coyecque, *Recueil d'actes notariés*, i, nos. 1699–2785.

[58] Heartz, 'Parisian Music Publishing under Henry II', *Musical Quarterly*, 46 (1960), 448–67; Brown, *Instrumental Music*, 1552₅.

[59] Coyecque, *Recueil*, no. 5985.

Hôtel d'Albret and formed a new partnership with the royal lutenist, Guillaume Morlaye, who on 13 February 1552 obtained a new privilege to print the works of his teacher, Alberto de Ripa, while Granjon assumed the firm's responsibilities at Lyons and settled in the town. The will of the engraver, Bernard Salomon, dated 19 October 1559, shows that his daughter Antoinette was married to Granjon, who was designated 'master printer, citizen of Lyons'. Subsequent notarized documents usually refer to Granjon as 'bourgeois de Paris', although between 1561 and 1577 he possessed a house in the rue Grolée in Lyons.[60]

On 26 December 1557 Granjon secured an exclusive royal privilege for his newly invented 'lettres françoises d'art et de main' a cursive type first used in Innocenzo Ringhieri's *Dialogue de la Vie et de la Mort*, translated by Jean Louveau.[61] Plantin used the new type at Antwerp in 1558, as did Philippe Danfrie and Robert Breton at Paris in 1559;[62] but Granjon retained the exclusivity at Lyons until Antoine Volant and Thomas de Straton reprinted Ringhieri's *Dialogue* in 1562. On 2 July 1558 a decree by the seneschal's court expressly forbade Simon Gorlier to use a cursive script like Granjon's.

Gorlier, who had previously furnished Granjon with musical material, was now a rival, for on 2 December 1557 Granjon formed an association to print music with Guillaume Guéroult and Jehan Hiesse. These two were to provide the music for Granjon to print and to share the cost of materials and labour. Guéroult complained that Granjon was printing and selling books privately and refused to pay the 6 livres 4 sols which was assessed as his third share in the cost of paper and printing for 'two leaves of music … received from a child from Marseilles'; this must refer to the undated Tenor part-book of the chansons by Barthélemy Beaulaigue—the Superius, Contratenor, and Bassus books being dated 1559. Granjon counter-claimed that his partners were not providing him with enough material fully to employ his presses, and the seneschal court's verdict of 14 June, 1558 was proclaimed in his favour. The relevant documents, reproduced and discussed by Claude Dalbanne,[63] provide invaluable information on contemporary music-printing, showing for example that fifteen hundred copies of Beaulaigue's chansons were printed, and that, with paper costing 45 sols per ream, the return on each book was 2 sols 6 deniers.

[60] Baudrier, *Bibliographie*, ii. 53–4.
[61] H. Carter and H. Vervliet, *Civilité Types* (Oxford Bibliographical Society Publications, NS, 1965), 27–33.
[62] G. Thibault, 'Un recueil de musique imprimé en caractères de civilité par R. Breton', *Bibliothèque d'Humanisme et Renaissance*, 2 (1935), 302–8.
[63] C. Dalbanne, 'R. Granjon, imprimeur de musique', *Gutenberg-Jahrbuch* (1939), 226–32.

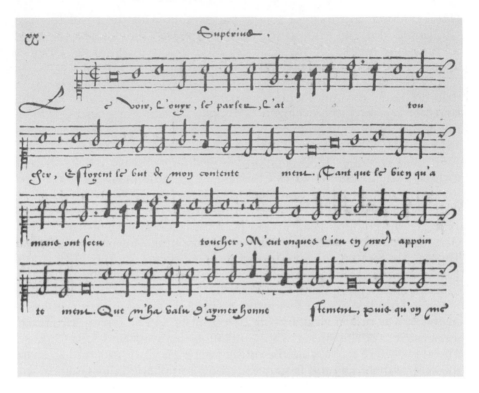

Pl. 9. (*above and opposite*) R. Granjon's music-type and *civilité* script. Superius of Villiers's four-voice setting of Maurice Scève's 'Le veoir, l'ouyr' from the *Premier Trophée de Musique* (1559). Paris, Bibl. nat., Rés. Vm^7 192.

Granjon did not last long in Lyons as a publisher: no books in his name survive after 1562, and his five music sets are all dated 1559:

1. CHANSONS NOUVELLES | composées par Barthelemy Beaulaigue excellent Musicien. | Et par luy mises en Musicque à quatre parties, | et en quatre Livres. | SUPERIUS | A LYON, | De l'Imprimerie de Robert Granjon | MV^{c}lix | Avec privilege du Roy

2. MOTTETZ NOUVELLEMENT | mis en musicque à quatre, cinq, six, sept & huit parties, | en quatre Livres: par Barthelemy Beaulaigue | excellent Musicien | SUPERIUS | (etc. as above)

3. Le PREMIER TROPHEE | de Musicque, composé des plus harmonieuses & excellentes | Chansons choisies entre la fleur & composition des plus fameux | & excellens Musiciens, tant anciens que modernes, | Le tout à quatre parties, en | quatre volumes . . . (etc. as above). (RISM 1559[14]) (see Pl. 9).

4. Le SECOND TROPHEE ... (etc. as 3.) (RISM 1559[15])

5. QUARANTE ET NEUF | Psalmes de David ... traduitz en rime françoise par C. Marot, et mis | en musique à trois parties selon le chant | vulgaire par Michel Ferrier de | Cahors en Quercy | TENOR | A LYON | De l'impression de Robert Granjon | MV[c]lix | Avec privilege du Roy

All five collections use the single-impression technique, but Granjon devised tear-shaped note-heads, resembling those cut by Étienne Briard for Jean de Channey's publications of Carpentras's music, a choice which may have resulted from his partner Guéroult's relations with the Arnoullet family, who earlier had employed De Channey.

After 1562 Granjon moved to Antwerp. In 1571 he was again in Paris, but by 1575 he was back in Lyons. He was still listed as a citizen there in 1577, although in the following year he moved to Rome, where he remained for the rest of his life. Just as his *civilité* letters and rounded music-type were subsequently used in Lyons by Thomas de Straton, many other kinds of music-type cut by Granjon are found in later publications from Lyons by Gorlier, De Tournes, and Bonhomme.

(viii) *Simon Gorlier*

Having prepared a book of guitar intabulations for Granjon and Fezandat in 1551, the lutenist Simon Gorlier obtained his own ten-year royal privilege on 17 February 1557:

Il est permis à Symon Gorlier imprimer ou faire imprimer par tel Imprimeur ou Libraire que bon luy semblera, tous livres en Musique nouvellement par luy composez ou à ses frais et despens recouvertz; soit en Musique verbale, vocale, ou istrumentale, Théorique, Praticque, Diatonique, Chromatique, Enharmonique, et Tabulatures de toutes sortes d'istruments Musicaux . . .

Simon Gorlier is permitted to print or have printed by any printer of his choice those books of music newly composed by him or acquired at his expense; whether they be of verbal, vocal, instrumental, theoretical, practical, diatonic, chromatic, enharmonic music, or tablatures for all kinds of instruments . . .[64]

According to the *Bibliothèque* of Antoine du Verdier (Lyons, 1585, p. 1136), four tablatures were duly printed:

1. Premier livre de Tablature de flustes d'Aleman (impr. à Lyon par luy mesme, 1558) (in 4)
2. Premier livre de tablature d'espinette, contenant Mottetz, fantasies, chansons, Madrigalles & Gaillards (impr. à Lyon par ledict Gorlier 1560) (in 4)
3. Livre de tablature de Guiterne (impr. de mesmes) (in 4)
4. Livre de tablature de Cistre (impr. de mesmes) (in 4)

These cannot be mere figments of the bibliographer's imagination, since the spinet tablature was known to be in the possession of the younger Raimund Fugger (1528–69).[65] However, Gorlier's only surviving publication is a tablature by the Milanese lutenist, Giovanni Paolo Paladino (RISM 1560[27]; Brown 1560[3]), which appears to be no more than a reprint with substitute title-page of an earlier Lyons edition, for the colophon on fo. 40[v] reads: 'Stampato in Lione per Giovan Pullo de Trino, a l'instantia di M. Giovan Paulo Paladino'[66] (see

---

[64] Quoted from *Livre de tablature de luth de M. Jean Paul Paladin* (Lyons, 1560), fo. 1[v].

[65] See R. Schaal, 'Die Musikbibliothek von Raimund Fugger', *Acta musicologica*, 29 (1957), 126–37.

[66] Lesure and Morcourt, 'G. P. Paladino', 170–83; G. P. Paladino, *Premier livre de tablature de luth* (1560), fac. edn., Geneva, 1983; mod. edn. M. Renault and J. M. Vaccaro, Corpus des luthistes français (Paris, 1986).

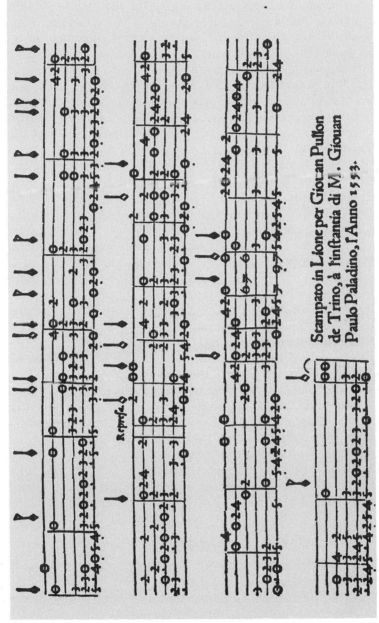

Pl. 10. End of closing *Gagliarda* and colophon from J. P. Paladin's lute tablature (S. Gorlier, 1560) Vienna, Österreichische Nationalbibliothek, Musiksammlung S.A. 77. D.13.

Pl. 10). Du Verdier does not list any entry for Jean Paule Paladin, but instead mentions 'Antoine François Paladin, Milanois' as the composer of 'two books of lute tablature containing several *chansons spirituelles* printed in Lyons by Simon Gorlier in 1562' (*Bibliographie*, p. 75). A catalogue compiled in 1625 by Georg Draud[67] follows Du Verdier here, as with the four aforementioned books. Other 'ghosts' catalogued by Du Verdier and Draud include Gorlier's 'Livre de Musique à quatre ou cinq parties en cinq volumes (impr. à Lyon) (in 4)' and the 'Chansons & Voix de ville à 4 parties' (A Lyon par S. Gorlier, 1561) (in 8)' by Aleman Layolle, 'Musicien & Organiste à Lyon'. Layolle's book is also listed amongst the 'Libri Venales 1550–1670' (fo. 358ᵛ) of the Plantin Archives in Antwerp.

One book of Gorlier's which survived until the present century is *LA LYRE | CHRESTIENNE | avec la Monomachie de David | & Goliath, & plusieurs autres | chansons spirituelles, Nouvel | lement mises en Musique per A. de Hauville*. Baudrier's *Bibliographie*[68] includes a facsimile of the title-page dated 1560, although Du Verdier and Draud both cite an edition of 1566. Guillaume Guéroult wrote the preface and four of the poems, while Antoine de Hauville supplied the music.

Like Granjon's, Gorlier's output as a music-printer does not appear to have lasted more than a few years, although notarized documents[69] prove his continued residence and publishing activity in Lyons until 1584. On 27 June 1565 he is still described as a bookseller, as he was on 23 April 1582, when he is reported as owing 50 écus to another publisher, Jean Pillehotte, for the purchase of printing merchandise, and on 7 June 1584, when he owed 45 livres for paper and printing merchandise to Hughes Barbou. However, he is no longer referred to as a musician or 'excellent player', as he had been in his guitar-book of 1551. Perhaps he was disheartened by the criticism of Loys Bourgeois, who called him 'trougnon d'espinette ('spinet stalk') in his lampoon, *Responce à la seconde Apologie de Simon Gorlier, faite contre Louis Bourgeois*,[70] printed in 1554.

(ix) *Antoine Vincent and the Genevan Psalter*

The advance of Protestantism, which reached its peak at Lyons in the early 1560s, is reflected in a spate of psalm publications, many containing only the official Genevan melodies, but a few presenting

[67] G. Draudius, *Bibliotheca exotica* (Frankfurt, 1625), 209–10.
[68] Baudrier, *Bibliographie*, ii. 47.
[69] Ibid. 46–9.
[70] A. Pirro, *Les Clavecinistes* (Paris, 1924), 25–6.

polyphonic settings. The trend set earlier by immigrants such as the Beringen brothers and Michel du Bois was supported by Calvin, who recognized the value of a propagating press.[71] The most devout prefaces were reserved for the publications issued directly under the aegis of Calvin and the Genevan council; but with psalms selling well throughout France, the 25 per cent profit margin may have been an even stronger incentive for the printers of Lyons than their missionary zeal. Many publishers were anxious to seek exclusive rights for one version or another, basing their claims for privileges on novelty of disposition, presentation, format, or notation.

Some of the printers resident in Geneva had subsidiaries or associates at Lyons, in some cases handling printing, in others distribution. This situation developed as a reaction to royal edicts of 1548 and 1551 banning the sale in France of books printed in Geneva.[72] Few of the names which appear on the psalm collections published in Lyons were independent agents: a number worked for Antoine Vincent, who in October 1561, obtained for his son Antoine II a ten-year privilege from Charles IX, granting exclusive rights to publish and distribute the newly completed psalter throughout the whole of France, although he reliquinshed the markets of Paris in 1562 and Arras in 1563.[73] In various documents the younger Vincent is described as 'bookseller, son of Antoine, merchant bourgeois and citizen of Lyons'. Baudrier describes the elder Vincent as 'one of the most zealous Protestants in Lyons' and refers to his association with the German Frellon brothers in the city as early as 1542.[74] On 22 December 1561, during the Catholic reaction to the Protestant uprising, Vincent's books were collected and burned on the Pont de Saône,[75] and in 1567 he, along with the Gabianos and Sennetons, was named as a rebellious and seditious Protestant by the royal lieutenant general, René de Birague. He died in 1568, after seven months' imprisonment.

Orentin Douen[76] listed twenty-six editions of *Les Pseaumes mis en rime Françoise par Clément Marot & Théodore de Beze* published on Vincent's behalf in 1562. Most of these were printed in Geneva by Blanchier, Bonnefoy, Cercia, Courteau, Jean de Laon, Jaquy, and other members of the 'communion'[77] or in Paris by Royer, Breton, La Mothe,

---

[71] E. Droz, 'Antoine Vincent et la propagande protestante par le Psautier', in *Aspects de la propagande religieuse* (Geneva, 1957), 276–93; Pidoux, *Le Psautier huguenot*, ii. 128–30.

[72] E. Haag, *La France protestante*, 10 vols. (Paris, 1846–59), *pièces justificatives*, pp. 17–29.

[73] See Pidoux, *Le Psautier huguenot*, ii. 123, 130–1, 138.

[74] Baudrier, *Bibliographie*, i. 167; v. 157–268.

[75] C. de Rubys, *Histoire véritable de la ville de Lyon*, 413.

[76] Douen, *Clément Marot*, ii. 93–115.

[77] Pidoux, *Le Psautier huguenot*, ii. 129–36.

Le Roy et Ballard, Du Puy, and Le Jeune; but at least three were issued at Lyons by Antoine Cercia (using the same music-type as Bonhomme did in 1555), François Gaillard, and the famous Jean de Tournes (both using a Granjon type introduced by Gorlier in 1560).[78] By 1561 De Tournes had already printed a sextodecimo edition containing only the ninety psalms paraphrased by Clément Marot and Théodore de Bèze, with the approved melodies, which had mostly been issued in Geneva by 1556. In 1563 he published an octavo edition of the complete psalter for Antoine Vincent; this, like his previous editions, used a musical type cut by Granjon, found in the *Instruction* printed by Gorlier at the beginning of Paladino's lute-book of 1560. This type was also employed in further editions of the complete psalter printed by Macé Bonhomme for Jean Mareschal in 1563 and by Symphorien Barbier for Antoine Vincent in 1564, and in many others issued in Lyons and Geneva during the next eighty-five years.[79] De Tournes also printed a quarto edition of the complete psalter in 1563, using another music-type, again probably cut by Granjon, and found in editions by Bonhomme of the same year and in many others published in Geneva between 1562 and 1658.[80]

Unsigned sextodecimo editions of the complete psalter, including prayers by Augustin Marlorat following each psalm, were issued in Lyons in 1563 and again in 1564, using Granjon's tear-drop notation and *civilité* type purchased by Thomas de Straton in 1561. Similar sextodecimo editions, including Marlorat's prayers, were published by Gabriel Cotier and Nicolas Perrineau in 1564 and 1565,[81] with a letter indicating the solmization syllable before each note, following a precedent introduced by Pierre Vallette to facilitate the learning of the new melodies in the *Octanteneuf Pseaumes*[82] printed by S. du Bosc in Geneva in 1556. An unsigned sextodecimo and an octavo edition published by Charles Pesnot, both issued, with Marlorat's prayers, in 1563, are unique in using the melodies of Loys Bourgeois's 1547 harmonization, rather than the official Genevan ones for the Lord's Prayer and the Creed: this may indicate a particular Lyonese orientation. All these editions have the same musical type, which Guillo[83] identifies as belonging to Macé Bonhomme.

In some cases the psalms were published in conjunction with the Genevan translation of the New Testament, as were Jean de Tournes's

---

[78] Guillo, 'Recherches', ii, nos. 53–5.
[79] Ibid., nos. 51 and 60 (including illustration of type).
[80] Ibid., Types nos. 130–1.
[81] Ibid., nos. 62, 67, and 68.
[82] Pidoux, *Le Psautier huguenot*, ii. 94–8.
[83] Guillo, 'Recherches', ii, nos. 64 and 65.

and Jean Mareschal's quarto editions of 1563, like Gabriel Cotier's and Symphorien Barbier's sextodecimos of 1564; in others they appeared with translations of the whole Bible, as in Pierre Michel's printings for Claude Ravot, Laurens Clemensin, and Elie Le Prieur, all issued in folio in 1566. The De Tournes and Pesnot octavos of 1563, like the Perrineau, Cotier, and Barbier sextodecimos of 1564, also include a *Calendrier historial*, while most editions of all sizes issued after 1561 include the Calvinist catechism, the *Prières ecclesiastiques*, and the *Confession de foy des Églises de France*. Thus, as in Geneva, the monophonic psalms were distributed as part of a complete vade-mecum, supplying all the official texts for the Huguenot faithful. Guillo[84] also lists three pamphlets of Calvinist propaganda, including music printed in Granjon's tear-drop notation: the *Complainte faitte à Dieu* with three *chansons spirituelles*, one of which is noted (Lyons, 1561), *L'Épistre que le prophete Jeremie envoya* (Geneva, 1562), and the *Confession de la foy chrestienne* (n.p., n.d.) which employs the Genevan melody for Psalm 119.

(x) *Antoine Cercia*

Although the monophonic psalm dominated music-publishing in Lyons in the 1560s, a few printers continued to issue simple polyphonic versions. In January 1562 Philibert Jambe de Fer secured a privilege from King Charles IX to set the recently completed 'Psautier entier'. The results appeared in two quarto part-book editions issued in Lyons in 1564, the first signed by Antoine Cercia with Pierre de Mia and the second (which has fewer errors and which appends a setting of a sonnet written by the Parisian doctor Rassé de Neux for Charles IX) signed by the composer himself in association with Pierre Cussonel and Martin la Roche. The typography is different in both editions, the first using the common Granjon type, like Bonhomme's and De Tournes's,.. while the second introduces a new one, although, according to its colophon, it too was printed by De Mia.[85]

Cercia's ornamented initials reappear in 1567, with a larger musical type (probably the 'long-stemmed Louvain notes' mentioned in Beringen's inventory, used by Phalèse from 1552) in a larger quarto book of four-voice Italian madrigals by Giovanni Antonio di Mayo.

Cercia, who was born at La Guillotière near Lyons, married the daughter of the printer Jean Moylin in 1539. He later settled in Geneva, where he was registered as an 'habitant' on 16 August 1554, and where

[84] Ibid., nos. 49, 57, and 58.
[85] Pidoux, *Le Psautier huguenot*, ii. 127; 143–4, nos. 64/III and IV.

he was active as a printer and bookseller between 1558, when he
reprinted a collection of anonymous *Chansons spirituelles* and applied
to the Council for a three-year privilege to use a 'large type... to print
the psalms to help old people', and 1562, when he was registered as
one of the 'communion' permitted to publish the new Psalter. Baudrier
cites no documents relating to his activity at Lyons, but according to the
title pages of the Jambe de Fer and Mayo collections, he was in the
town between 1564 and 1567, before reappearing in Geneva in 1568–9.
Guillo also ascribes to Cercia's Lyons period a monophonic psalter
printed without specified location in 1562 and *La Musique de David*, a
biblical drama published by Jean Saugrin in 1566.[86]

(xi) *Thomas de Straton*

Jambe de Fer found a rival providing polyphonic settings of the new
psalter in the person of the 'excellent musician' Richard Crassot, whose
four-voice settings of the complete Genevan psalter were published in
Lyons by Thomas de Straton in 1564 and reissued by Jean Huguetan
in 1565.[87] De Straton began his printing career as an apprentice to
the Arnoullet press in the early 1550s; he was one of the 'extremely
frightened workers' who in 1553 fell foul of the Inquisition by printing
Michel Servet's *Christianissimi Restitutio* under the auspices of Guéroult
at Vienne. In 1561 he joined the bookseller Antoine Volant in pur-
chasing punches from Robert Granjon to reprint Innocenzo Ringhieri's
Dialogue, and it is probable that the music-type which he used during
this period was also cut by Granjon.[88]

Du Verdier's *Bibliothèque* (1585) lists Straton's lost quarto edition of
Philibert Jambe de Fer's settings of 'les 22 Octonaires du Psalme 119 de
David traduits par Jean Poitevin (1561)', but not his *Premier livre de
chansons spirituelles...par divers Auteurs & excellens musiciens*, which
has survived.[89] The latter is based on Didier Lupi's collection of 1548,
suppressing six pieces but adding ten new ones by Arcadelt (2),
Janequin (2), Maillard (1), Certon (1), Jambe de Fer (1), and anonymi
(3). These are retained in a later edition issued in Lyons by Benoît
Rigaud (RISM 1568[9]). De Straton and Rigaud print all four voices in the
same sextodecimo book, with the Altus and Bassus on the recto folios,

---

[86] Guillo, 'Recherches,' ii. 142–6; Pidoux, *Le Psautier huguenot*, ii. 108, 129–30.

[87] Douen, *Clément Marot*, i, no. 136; ii. 113–16; Guillo, 'Recherches,' ii, nos. 72 and 76. See also
L. Guillo, 'Les Psaumes de Richard Crassot', *Le Mot Dit*, i (1986), 36–41.

[88] See Baudrier, *Bibliographie*, i. 410; Guillo, 'Recherches', i. 138–40.

[89] Du Verdier, *Bibliothèque*, ed. Juvigny, iii. 194; Pidoux, *Le Psautier huguenot*, ii. 87–8 and
126.

an arrangement not used since the quarto books of Attaingnant's second series of chansons (e.g. RISM 1536$^{3-6}$). There is no trace of De Straton after 1564 and he may have died in the plague which devastated Lyons in that year. At all events, Crassot turned to Jean Huguetan to reprint his psalms in 1565, announcing the same ten-year royal privilege on the title-page and adding only a single woodcut ornament at the end.

(xii) *Jean de Tournes*

A simple homophonic style similar to that of Lupi's *chansons spirituelles* pervades the anonymous four voice settings of *Vingtsix Cantiques chantés au Seigneur par Louis des Masures Tournisien*, printed in four octavo part-books by Jean de Tournes in 1564. A new preface to the second edition suggests that the poet Des Masures was in Lyons during the St Bartholomew's Day Massacre in 1572 and narrowly avoided the fate of his friend Claude Goudimel, who may have provided the music for these *Cantiques*, as well as for the eleven choruses in his three biblical dramas.[90]

The De Tournes dynasty was almost solely responsible for maintaining the musical output of the Lyons press during the latter part of the sixteenth century, producing at least twelve editions between 1561 and 1587. The first Jean de Tournes (1504–64) was apprenticed to Sébastien Gryphe before establishing his own press in 1542; entering a partnership with Guillaume Gazeau in 1547, he was appointed Royal Printer in 1559 and earned a reputation for fine typography and illustration with the aid of the engravers Bernard Salomon and Georges Reverdy. Embracing Calvinism in his late years, he produced at least four different editions of the Genevan monophonic psalter between 1561 and 1563, as well as the four-voice settings of Des Masures' Canticles in 1564, when he died in the plague which claimed the lives of a quarter of the population of Lyons. On his death the business passed to his son Jean II, who suffered pillage, confiscation, and fines after the Catholics resumed control of the city council in 1567–8, but who remained in Lyons until 1585, when he finally moved to Geneva.

While Aleman Layolle's *chansons* and *voix de ville*—along with Giovanni Antonio di Mayo's madrigals—represent the only secular music printed at Lyons in the 1560s, there was a limited revival during the Catholic upsurge following the St Bartholomew's Day Massacre in

---

[90] F. Dobbins, 'Notated Music in French Plays of the late Sixteenth Century', paper read to the Society for Renaissance Studies, London, 1982; the *Cantiques* are included in Goudimel, *Œuvres complètes*, xiv. 85–102; see also Guillo, 'Recherches', ii, no. 78.

1572. In that year the younger Jean de Tournes (1539–1615) published *L'excellence des Chansons musicales composees par M. Jaques Arcadet . . . Recueillies & Reveues par Claude Goudimel*, with spiritual texts substituted for the secular ones set by the Catholic composer who had died at Paris four years earlier. No copy survives, but it is listed in the catalogues of Cless, Willers, and Draud,[91] along with a 1587 edition, whose title is identical save for the qualification 'tant propres à la voix qu'aux instrumens' (appropriate for both voices and instruments). An edition dated 1586, preserved at the Bayerische Staatsbibliothek, contains forty-four contrafacta of secular texts which had appeared in various books between 1538 and 1565. The same catalogues also mention the publication by the younger Jean de Tournes in 1581 of *La Musique contenant plusieurs chansons françoises à quatre, cinq et six parties* by Gilles Maillard.

Concrete evidence of Jean de Tournes II's music-printing survives in LE II LIVRE DU | JARDIN DE MUSIQUE, | Semé d'excellentes & harmonieuses chansons & voix de ville. | * | Mises en musique a quatre parties, par Corneille de Montfort | dit de Blockland, Gentilhomme Stichtois[92] of 1579. The same 'Imprimeur de Roy' also issued Blockland's didactic *Instruction fort facile pour apprendre la Musique Practique* in 1573; a new edition in 1587, like the second edition of the Arcadelt and Goudimel contrafacta, was presumably printed in Geneva, as were the *Thresor de Musique* (1594) and *Cinquante pseaumes* of Lassus (RISM 1597[6]), a collection of three-voice motets by Jan Tollius (1597), a set of Italian translations of the psalms adapted to the Genevan melodies by Francesco Perrotto and dedicated to Queen Elizabeth of England (1603), and another anonymous collection of sixty psalms in Italian translation with the Genevan melodies. A third Jean de Tournes was responsible for reprinting Claude le Jeune's *CL Pseaumes* in Geneva in 1617 and 1627.[93]

Two sets of octavo part-books containing new four- and five-voice chansons by the late Claude Goudimel and old ones by the great Orlande de Lassus were assigned to Jean Bavent in 1574 (RISM 1574[1–2]), with a dedication to Joseph du Chesne, doctor, poet, and diplomat living in Geneva, signed by Pierre Enoch of Geneva. Nothing is known of Bavent, but his music-type (cut by Granjon) and ornamen-

[91] J. Clessius, *Unius seculi eiusque virorum literatorum monumentis . . . ab 1500 ad 1602* (Frankfurt, 1602), 539–40; B. Fabian (ed.), *Die Meßkataloge des sechzehnten Jahrhunderts*, 4 vols. (Hildesheim, 1972), i. 463; Draudius, *Bibliotheca exotica*, 208–10.

[92] Fac. edn. by L. Guillo and M. Chomarat (Lyons, 1983).

[93] Cartier, *Bibliographie des éditions des de Tournes*, nos. 717 and 742. See also Guillo, 'Recherches', i. 146–9, ii, nos. 53, 60, 61, 71, 84–7, 91–6.

tal initials are identical with those used by the De Tournes press (see Pl. 11). Guillo suggests that Bavent was a pseudonym and Lyons perhaps a fictitious address, devised to evade the problems of Protestant publications in France after the St Bartholomew's Day Massacre.[94]

(xiii) *Clément Baudin and Gasparo Fiorino*

Clément Baudin was active as a bookseller and exporter associated with the Senneton firm,[95] publishing literary works in Lyons between 1556 and 1577. The only surviving music publication signed in his name is the first book of five-voice madrigals by the Luccan composer Regolo Vecoli (RISM 1577[10]).[96] This has music-type identical to that used by Nicolas du Chemin in Paris between 1554 and 1567 and by Jean II de Tournes in Lyons in 1581. The dedication to the Luccan gentleman Lorenzo Buonvisi, patron also of madrigals by Bastini (1567), Baccusi (1579), Dorati (1579), and Isnardi (1581), speaks of 'queste prime compositioni, c'ho fatto di Musica' ('these first musical compositions of mine'), and was signed at Lyons on 10 November 1576 (see Pl. 12).

Regolo's second book, published in Paris by Le Roy & Ballard in 1586 (the year in which the composer won a prize at the annual musical competition at Évreux in Normandy), bears a dedication to a Luccan lady and mentions 'quelli infortunii che affliggono hora Lione', suggesting that the composer had suffered during the town's religious conflicts.[97]

A collection of *Canzonelle alla napolitana*,[98] containing verses addressed to many of the prominent ladies of Lyons, composed and published in the city in 1577 by Gasparo Fiorino, musician to Cardinal Luigi d'Este of Ferrara, with a dedication to Lucretia Buonvisi, does not include any music, unlike similar collections printed in Venice between 1571 and 1574.

(xiv) *Charles Pesnot and Barthélemy Vincent: Lyons or Geneva?*

Another associate of the Senneton firm with Protestant sympathies, Charles Pesnot, operated as a bookseller with branches at Frankfurt and

---

[94] Guillo, 'Recherches', i. 148; ii, nos. 86–7.

[95] Baudrier, *Bibliographie*, v. 20–34.

[96] E. Vogel, A. Einstein, F. Lesure, and C. Sartori, *Bibliografia della musica italiana vocale profana pubblicata dal 1500 al 1700*, 3 vols. (Pomezia, 1977), ii. 1769–70; Guillo, 'Recherches', ii, no. 89.

[97] F. Lesure and G. Thibault, *Bibliographie des éditions d'A. le Roy & R. Ballard* (Paris, 1956), 47.

[98] Guillo, 'Recherches', ii, no. 90.

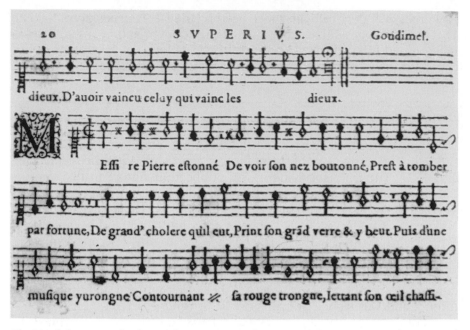

Pl. 11. (*above and opposite*) Jean Bavent's typography: Goudimel's 'Messire Pierre' from *La Fleur des Chansons . . . Premier livre* (1574)

Geneva, publishing a number of books in Lyons under the sign of the salamander, between 1555 and 1580.[99] After issuing a sextodecimo edition of the monophonic *Psautier* for Macé Bonhomme in 1563, he appears as publisher of three books of chansons, mainly of the 'spiritual' kind favoured by the Protestants, dated 1578, and one of psalms paraphrased in Latin verse by George Buchanan, dated 1579, all set by Jean Servin. It has been suggested that these were all published in Geneva, where Servin lived between 1584 and 1596, and that the printer gave a false address on the title-pages and dedications to facilitate circulation in France.[100]

    All four use the same type and ornament as the five books of music[101]

[99] Baudrier, *Bibliographie*, iii. 122–82.

[100] E. Droz, 'Simon Goulart, éditeur de musique', *Bibliothèque d'Humanisme et Renaissance*, 14 (1952), 266–76 at 271; Guillo, 'Recherches', i. 114.

[101] P. de L'Estocart, *Premier livre des Octonaires de la vanité du monde à trois, quatre, cinq et six parties* . . . (1582); ed. H. Expert, *Les Monuments de la musique française au temps de la Renaissance*, x (Paris, 1929); *Second livres des Octonaires* . . . (1582); ed. J. Chailley and M. Honegger, ibid. 11 (Paris, 1958); *Cent ringt et six quatrains du Sieur de Pibrac . . . de nouveau mis en musique à deux, trois, quatre, cinq et six parties* . . . (1582); *Sacrae cantiones quatuor, quinque, sex et septem vocum . . . liber primus*; *Cent cinquante Pseaumes de David . . . par C. Marot et T. de Besze . . . à 4–8 parties* (1583); fac., ed. P. Pidoux and H. Holliger (Kassel and Basle, 1954).

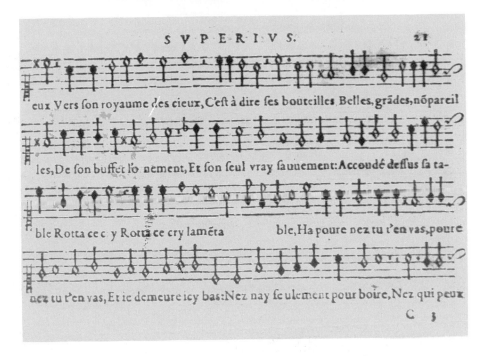

by Paschal de l'Estocart which were published by Antoine's eldest son Barthélemy in Lyons in 1582–3. These include a complete set of psalms simultaneously issued by Eustace Vignon at Geneva; the only differences between the Geneva and Lyons editions are the title-pages and the substitution of prefatory sonnets by L. de Chambrun and L. de La Haye in the latter for a sonnet and an anagrammatic Latin piece by Jean de Sponde in the former. Both editions use identical music-type and ornament, including at the end of the Superius, Contra, and Tenor part-books a six-line poem dedicated to 'L'Estocart and his printer Jean de Laon'.[102] This type and ornament were also used for Jean Le Royer's quarto part-books of Simon Goulart's contrafacta of Ronsard sonnets set by Guillaume Boni and Antoine de Bertrand and for Goulart's edition of the *Theatrum musicum* containing motets by Lassus which appeared in Geneva between 1578 and 1580. It thus appears that Charles Pesnot and Barthélemy Vincent merely provided a French outlet for music printed in Geneva.

---

[102] See Guillo, 'Recherches', i. 113–16.

AL NOBILISSIMO ET MOLTO MAGNI-
FICO SIGNOR', ET PADRONE MIO OSSERVANDISSIMO,
IL SIGNOR LORENZO DEL SIGNOR GIO. BVONVISI,
GENTIL'HVOMO LVCCHESE.

OVENDO io dare alla stampa queste prime compositioni, c'hò fatto di Musica, non senza mia molta fatica, & studio, mi sono r.soluto donarle, & dedicarle à V.S. non táto per gl'oblighi infiniti, che io le tengo, quato per il molto giuditio, & sue rare qualita, per le quali quegli ancora che solo la conoscano, se gli confessano obligati. Le riceua V.S. (se non sono quali meriterebbe) con quello animo, co'l quale altre volte non si è sdegnata fauorirme tanto, che m'ha hora fatto ardito presentandogliele, di ornarle di cosi chiaro nome, & io pregandogli da nostro signor ogni contento, viuero sempre suo. Da Lione alli 10. Nouembre 1576.

Di V. S. molto Magnifica.

Seruitore affettionatissimo & oblighatissimo

Regolo Vecoli.

Pl. 12. (*above and opposite*) Dedication and first page of the *Canto* part from R. Vecoli's first book of five-voice madrigals (C. Baudin, 1577) Munich, Bayerische Staatsbibliothek 4 Mus. pr. 4417

(xv) *Jean Pillehotte*

The proselytizing spirit persists in the Jesuit Michel Coyssard's *Paraphrases des hymnes et cantiques spirituelz pour chanter avecque la doctrine chrestienne*, printed by Jean Pillehotte in 1592 (RISM 1592[6]),[103] as in the anonymous psalms, hymns, and motets printed by Jean Didier in 1610 (RISM 1610[11]). Pillehotte, who, like Didier, used the same Granjon type as De Tournes and others, also printed a musical treatise by Coyssard in 1608. A more flamboyant Catholic style finally emerges with the airs, chansons, noëls, and madrigals by Guédron, Gastoldi, and others in *Amphion sacré*[104] printed with contrafact texts in Lyons by Claude Cayre for Louis Muguet in 1615 (RISM 1615[7]).

---

[103] Baudrier, *Bibliographie*, ii. 224–364; A. Gastoué, *Le Cantique populaire en France* (Lyons, 1924), 262; Guillo, 'Recherches', i. 179–87; ii, no. 97.
[104] Baudrier, *Bibliographie*, iv. 97; Guillo, 'Recherches', i. 188–90; ii, no. 100.

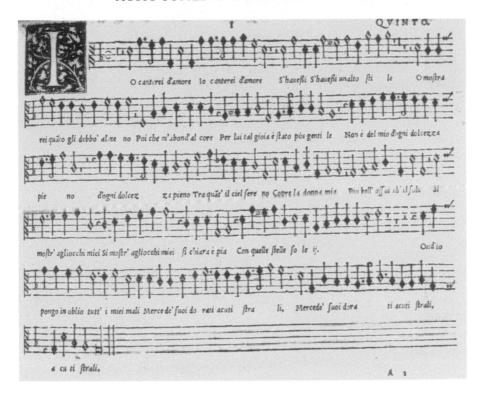

The summary table of these musical publications in Appendix F shows a concentration of activity in the second third of the sixteenth century, which corresponds to the Golden Age in the city's literary history. Another feature that parallels the literary scene is the high proportion of books of Italian music (Fiorino, Layolle, Mayo, Rampollini, Vecoli, Paladino, Bianchini), compared to the output of presses in other parts of France. After Moderne there were no significant rivals to the busy music presses of Du Chemin and Le Roy & Ballard in Paris, Phalèse & Bellère in Antwerp and Louvain, or the Gardanes and Scottos in Venice. Apart from the surge of psalm publication during the period of Protestant government, music-printing is represented largely by the sporadic efforts of literary publishers such as Granjon, De Tournes, Rigaud, Pesnot, and Pillehotte. Indeed, after the flight of persecuted Huguenot printers following the Catholic restoration and repression during the last third of the century, Geneva, which had previously relied on the superior technology of Lyons, became more important as a centre for music-publishing. The decline in Lyonese music-publishing corresponds to the decline in importance of its trade-fairs, another result of the religious upheavals, which effectively removed the city from the literary and musical map in the seventeenth century.

5

Composers in Lyons

(i) Publication and Correspondence

THE city's official documentation rarely specifies the activities of composers as such, although it occasionally mentions their names as musicians or instrumentalists (App. I–III). The evidence for their presence, if not residence, often comes instead from letters, including foreign correspondence, from references by local poets, and from music copied or printed in the town.

The evidence of publication must, however, be treated with great caution, since the inclusion of a few pieces in anthologies containing music by a variety of composers cannot be taken as proof of direct collaboration, or even concurrence, between composer and printer, at a time when there was rarely any effective means of protecting an individual composer's work. Nevertheless, a new edition entirely or predominantly devoted to a single living composer normally entailed his permission and often his personal supervision. Francesco de Layolle, whose work rarely appeared in publications outside Lyons, seems to have acted as Moderne's musical editor until his death; and he was perhaps succeeded in this capacity by P. de Villiers.[1] The Beringen brothers enjoyed the co-operation of Loys Bourgeois, Dominique Phinot, and Didier Lupi when printing their music in the late 1540s, while Nicolas Martin personally expressed his gratitude to his publisher, Macé Bonhomme, in 1555. The lutenist Bálint Bakfark journeyed to Lyons in 1553 to have his music printed by Moderne, probably at the suggestion of his old patron François de Tournon, now Archbishop of Lyons. The same Archbishop had similarly encouraged Simon Joly, organist of Saint-Étienne at Bourges, to publish his Latin psalms in Lyons in 1552, even if such an orthodox Catholic could hardly have approved of the publication being undertaken by the Protestant Beringen press. The Milanese lutenist Giovanni Paolo Paladino may also have gone to Lyons originally to publish his music in 1549, and he remained there until his death in 1566.[2] But the printer Robert Granjon relied on his publishing partners, Guillaume Guéroult and Jehan Hiesse, to pro-

---

[1] Pogue, *Jacques Moderne*, ch. 6.
[2] Lesure and Morcourt, 'G. P. Paladino', 172–3.

vide him with musical material, and it is unlikely that he called in either Barthélemy Beaulaigue, the choirboy from Marseilles, or Michel Ferrier from Cahors to supervise the printing of their music.

The composer Philibert Jambe de Fer secured his own royal privilege to prevent unauthorized printing of his four- and five-voice settings of the Huguenot psalter in 1562, and collaborated directly with his publishers in Lyons two years later.[3] The printer Jean de Tournes II brought in Claude Goudimel to edit a collection of spiritual contrafacta of chansons by the recently deceased Arcadelt in 1572, and in the following year was assisted by Corneille de Blockland, who lived near Lyons, first at Saint-Amour, then at Lons-le-Saulnier. Blockland may also have helped the mysterious Jean Bavent in publishing two books of old chansons by Lassus and Goudimel. Jean Servin's dedications in the four books of chansons published by Charles Pesnot between 1578 and 1579 were all signed at Lyons, although this may have been a commercial deception, like the address given on the title-pages of four books by Paschal de l'Estocart printed in Geneva by Jean de Laon.

Before the advent of music-printing at Lyons in 1528, the picture of musical activity is somewhat obscure, with the few surviving manuscripts of arguably local provenance containing no repertoire of obviously local origin. Yet even in the absence of archival evidence it is certain that some of the musicians in the service of Louis XII and Francis I, if not the entire *chapelle royale*, visited Lyons during the Italian campaigns. Louis XII set up court in the town between 1499 and 1504, returning in 1507 and 1511–12, whilst Philippe le Beau, Count of Flanders, and his retinue came in 1503[4] and probably again en route for Spain in early 1506. Margaret of Austria also visited Lyons, especially during the years of her marriage to Philibert II le Beau, Duke of Savoy (1501–4), when she resided at nearby Pont d'Ain. Francis I and his court made Lyons their base of operations for the Marignano campaign in 1515, returning in 1522 and again in 1524 in preparation for a new offensive, while his mother, Louise of Savoy, remained in the town during the next two years, acting as regent after the French defeat at Pavia.

(ii) *Le Petit, Brumel, and Mouton*

Occasionally foreign correspondence indicates the presence in Lyons of composers represented in external musical sources. A curious case is

---

[3] Pidoux, *Le Psautier huguenot*, ii. 127 and 144.

[4] Gachard, *Collection des voyages*, 290–4; cf. G. van Doorslaer, 'La Chapelle musicale de Philippe le Beau', *Revue belge d'archéologie*, 4 (1934), 21–58, 139–66; E. Van der Straeten, *La Musique aux Pays-Bas*, 8 vols. (Brussels, 1867–88), vi. 96–102.

that of the 'Le Petit, maître à Lion' who sent a new motet to Lorenzo il Magnifico in Florence between 1469 and 1492, suggesting that it might be suitable for his chapel.[5] Was this the Jean Petit alias Balthasar, singer in the Sistine Chapel between 1488 and 1501,[6] or Joannes Petitto, singer in the Santissima Annunziata church in Florence between 1488 and 1493, or even Jean Le Petit, attached to the choir-school at Langres Cathedral[7] from 1506 to 1529? No music is ascribed to 'Petit' or 'Le Petit' in Lyonese sources, although there are no less than thirteen pieces attributed to Ninot le Petit in the Florentine chansonnier Biblioteca di Conservatorio di Musica, MS Basevi 2442, which was probably compiled around 1527 for the banker Filippo Strozzi (1488–1538), who, after being involved in the republican plotting against the Medici, sought refuge in Lyons.[8] The fact that the Strozzi family brought some of their music to Lyons is confirmed by an inventory of their possessions[9] left at Lyons in 1547.

Antoine Brumel probably became acquainted with Lyons between 1487 and 1492, when he was master of the six *pueri cantores* at the cathedral of Saint-Pierre in Geneva. After resigning a similar post at Notre-Dame in Paris in November 1500, he served Duke Philibert of Savoy in Chambéry, before appearing in Lyons in July 1505. The state archives at Modena preserve correspondence between Alfonso I at Ferrara and Sigismondo Cantelmo, Duke of Sora, in Lyons, inviting Brumel to spend the rest of his life in the Este service for a salary of 150 ducats per annum: 50 ducats, payable at Lyons, were sent to cover the musician's travelling expenses in the following December.[10]

There is no documented evidence confirming the presence of Jean Mouton, who might have visited Lyons on his way from Amiens to Grenoble in 1501, on his way back the following year, or during one of the sojourns of Anne of Brittany or Francis I, whom he subsequently served. One of his four-voice canons printed by Antico in Venice in 1520 (reprinted by Attaingnant in Paris in 1528 and by Rhau in

[5] B. Becherini, 'Relazioni di musici fiammenghi con la corte dei medici', *La Rinascita*, 4 (1941), 84–112 at 94.

[6] For the most up-to-date biography of Ninot Le Petit, see *Johanni[s] Parvi Opera omnia*, ed. Barton Hudson (Corpus Mensurabilis Musicae, 87; American Institute of Musicology—Hänssler-Verlag, 1979), pp. xi–xiii. Hudson believes that the handwriting of a letter written by Ninot rules out identification with the Lyonese Le Petit.

[7] F. d'Accone, 'A Documentary History of Music of the Florentine Cathedral and Baptistry during the 15th Century' (Ph.D. diss., Harvard University, 1960), 202–3; Lesure, 'La Maîtrise de Langres au xvie siècle', *Revue de musicologie*, 52 (1966), 202–3.

[8] H. M. Brown, 'Chansons for the Pleasure of a Florentine Patrician', in *Aspects of Medieval and Renaissance Music: A Birthday Offering to Gustave Reese*, ed. J. LaRue et al. (New York, 1966, 2nd edn. 1978), 56–66.

[9] Agee, 'Filippo Strozzi and the Early Madrigal', 228.

[10] Van der Straeten, *La musique aux Pays-Bas*, vi. 96–102.

Wittenberg in 1545) begins with the line 'En venant de Lyon';[11] however, Mouton may have chosen these words merely to correspond to the monorhyme verse ending with his own name, the model perhaps being another text with the same opening found in the monophonic chansonnier, Paris, Bibliothèque nationale, MS fr. 12744.[12] According to the catalogue of the library of Ferdinand Columbus (no. 9198), Mouton's 'Missa de cantes cantilenam et luculi cantum' was printed in Lyons; but this is hardly more significant, since publication must have occured several years after the composer's death in 1522. Moderne printed his mass 'Quem dicunt homines' in 1532 in his first book and two of his chansons in 1538–9; but far more of Mouton's music appeared in Venice, Paris, and Antwerp.

(iii) *Agricola, Josquin, and Ghiselin*

Mouton may have accompanied Queen Anne and her husband, Louis XII, during the extended periods that the French court spent in Lyons in 1503 and 1504. There he could have encountered Alexander Agricola and Pierre de la Rue, who probably accompanied, Philippe le Beau, when he visited the city for the betrothal of his son, Charles, to Claude, the infant daughter of Louis XII. Philippe's chapel sang mass at the cathedral on 23 March and again on 2 April, this time combining with the French royal chapel,[13] which included Johannes Prioris with perhaps the Févin brothers, Antoine de Longueval, Hilaire [Daleo], and Pierre Moulu. Ten days later the Mantuan ambassador to the French court reported that Johannes Ghiselin and Josquin des Prez had arrived from Paris in a fine carriage and that they had spent the night at his residence before going on to Ferrara.[14] The music composed and sung on these and other similar occasions may be reflected in the poetry of Jean Lemaire and in music found in manuscripts elsewhere, like Moulu's 'Mater floreat florescat' and 'Vulnerasti cor meum' copied in the Medici Codex (the latter also being printed by Moderne in 1532).

(iv) *Francesco de Layolle*

The situation changes significantly after the introduction of music-printing in 1528. A key figure in this new development was Francesco

---

[11] Heartz, 'A New Attaingnant Book', plates IIIa–b; ed. Dobbins, *Oxford Book of French Chansons*, no. 6.

[12] G. Paris and A. Gevaert. *Chansons du XVe siècle* (Paris, 1875), no. 88.

[13] See above, n. 4.

[14] C. Gottwald, 'Ghiselin', *New Grove Dictionary of Music*. vii. 340.

de Layolle or dell'Aiolle (1492–c.1540),[15] the leading composer on the musical scene of Lyons during the two decades that he lived there. He left his native Florence around 1518, perhaps following his friend Andrea del Sarto, who was commissioned to paint an *Assumption of the Virgin* for the chapel which the Florentine Bartolomeo Panciatichi had built in the Dominican church of Notre-Dame de Confort in Lyons. A new chapel was completed there in 1523, at the expense of another wealthy ex-patriate Florentine, the banker Tomasso Guadagni, and the young organist may have been brought in to boost the musical establishment for the increasingly prosperous Italian community. At all events, he was clearly living in Lyons by August 1522, when his friend and compatriot the republican poet and diplomat Luigi Alamanni wrote from exile to Battista della Palla in Florence, stating that he could only be reached through Layolle. The musician set a *canzone* fragment ('Lasso la bella fera') and a madrigal ('Infra bianche rugiade') by Alamanni, as well as two poems ('Gite sospir dolenti' and 'Rompi del empio cor'), by Filippo Strozzi. But, despite his close contact with these and other republican exiles such as Antonio Brucioli and Zanobi Buondelmonte, and the tone of some of the motets which he composed or selected for publication by Moderne, there is no evidence that Layolle was directly involved in the anti-Medici plots of 1522, 1527–8, or 1537.

Layolle's presence in Lyons between 1523 and 1538 is confirmed in several civic taxation records (see Appendix III(i)), including one of 1528 which specifies his position as organist at Notre-Dame de Confort. In the same year he contributed three motets to a book of mass Propers published by Etienne Gueynard, with a dedication to Bernardo Altovita, consul for the Florentine community in Lyons. Four years later he acted as editor for a book of mass ordinaries printed by Jacques Moderne, who during the next eight years published the bulk of his music (75 *canzoni*, 11 chansons, 35 motets, and 3 masses, as well as other books of motets and penitential psalms, now lost, listed in the catalogue of Ferdinand Colombus.

(v) *Conseil, Arcadelt, Verdelot, and Piéton*

Papal records of payment from the time of Clement VII indicate that Johannes Consilium (Jean Conseil) was in Lyons in October 1525.[16] This

---

[15] Pogue, *Jacques Moderne*, 34–41; F. D'Accone, *Music of the Florentine Renaissance*, 3–4; D. A. Sutherland, 'Francesco de Layolle (1492–1540): Life and Secular Works' (Ph.D. diss., University of Michigan, 1968).

[16] H.-W. Frey, 'Regesten zur päpstlichen Kapelle unter Leo X. und zu seiner Privatkapelle', *Die Musikforschung*, 9 (1956), 139–56 at 145.

was probably a short visit (coinciding with that of Francis I's chapel) rather than any extended sojourn, as would seem to be confirmed by the inclusion of the name 'Consilion' amongst the older composers in Rabelais's *Quart Livre*. The later attribution to 'Consilium' by Moderne of just two motets, one of which (*Nigra sum*) was ascribed to L'Héritier and to Willaert in other sources, does not in itself seem sufficient to support the contention of Suzanne Clercx[17] that Conseil, like Arcadelt and Verdelot, was in Lyons after leaving Florence between 1527 and 1532. Moderne's printing of nine motets by Arcadelt and eight by Verdelot between 1532 and 1539 may simply be the result of their earlier or indirect contact with Francesco de Layolle, who probably edited Moderne's earlier collections of sacred music. The same may be true for Loyset Piéton, who had seven motets and a whole set of penitential psalms published by Moderne in the 1530s.

(vi) *Other Franco-Flemish composers*

Samuel Pogue[18] lists Moderne's composers by 'probable country of origin', although his case for Hanenze, L'alleman, Naich, and James being French is dubious. James may have been Scottish, although the one chanson ascribed to him (1543[14], fo. 23) was attributed to 'Lupus' by Attaingnant (1542[14-15], fo. 16[v]), Du Chemin (1551[4-5], fo. 30[v]), and Granjon (1559[14], p. 40). Nevertheless, if Pogue's assessment that sixty-six per cent of the 134 composers named by Moderne were 'French' seems a slight overestimate, his figure of twenty-eight per cent for 'Franco-Flemish' contributors (fourteen per cent of whom worked in Italy) is probably more accurate. Pogue's analysis of Moderne's repertoire of 810 musical works, excluding Piéton's penitential psalms, also shows that Layolle, with 107 pieces, provided more than twice as many as his nearest rivals, Rampollini (50) and Colin (40). While the anthologies give prominence to Villiers (37), Layolle (36), Fresneau (21), and Coste (16), supporting the case for their Lyonese connections, they also favour some composers of international fame who had no other lasting links with Lyons, like Gombert (29), Claudin de Sermisy (19), Maillard (17), Sandrin (16), Arcadelt (16), Certon (14 or 15), Willaert (13), Janequin (12), Mornable (12), Jacquet (12), Lupi (12), Lupus (10), Richafort (9), Verdelot (9), Crecquillon (9), J. L'Héritier (9), Buus (8), Piéton (7), Courtois (6), Manchicourt (6), Benedictus (5), and Le Heurteur (5). The figures in parenthesis refer to Moderne's ascriptions, which were not invariably accurate or consistent with those of

---

[17] S. Clercx, 'Archadelt', *Enciclopedia della musica* (Milan, 1963).
[18] Pogue, *Jacques Moderne*, 59–60 and 342–3.

other publishers. For example, two of the eleven pieces attributed to 'Jennequin' in the *Parangon* series—'Laras tu cela Michault' (RISM 1538[17], no. 13) and 'Je prens en gré la dure mort' (1540[16], no. 25)— were ascribed by Attaingnant to Bon Voisin (1538[12], no. 13) and Clemens (1539[15-16], no. 11) respectively.

The problem of distinguishing between *Doppelmeister* is often formidable. Moderne ascribes nine motets and one mass to 'Lupus', five motets to 'Jo. Lupi', two motets and at least six chansons simply to 'Lupi'. By attributing works variously to 'Lupus' and 'Lupi' within the same books (1532[12]) and (1539[11]), Moderne presumably intended to distinguish between at least two different composers. 'Lupus' seems usually to indicate the Flemish composer, Wulfaert Hellinck, (*c*.1496– 1541), who lived in Bruges, since four of the ten pieces published by Moderne are specifically attributed to Hellinck in later sources. The Mass 'Ferrarie Dux Hercules', ascribed to Lupus, is more problematical. If it was intended for the marriage of Ercole II and Renée, daughter of Louis XII, in 1528, four years before it was printed in the *Liber decem missarum* (1532[8]), it might have been composed by the Lupus who was in Ferrara in 1518–19. If it is by Hellinck, it may be that the composer stopped at Lyons to publish some of his recent work on his return from Ferrara to Bruges, as Clément Marot did later on his journey from Ferrara to Paris in 1536. The five motets specifically ascribed to 'Jo. Lupi' are almost certainly by Jennet le Leu, master of the choirboys at Cambrai Cathedral, for they reappear in Attaingnant's *Io. Lupi, Chori Sacrae Virginis Mariae Cameracensis Magistri, Musice Cantiones* in 1542; however, the two motets 'Domine quis habitabit' and 'Alleluia ego dormivi', published in 1539 with the simple designation 'Lupi', are not found in the Paris edition, and Moderne's omission of the prefix 'Jo.' seems not to be significant. The six chansons ascribed to Lupi in the later books of the *Parangon* were probably by the Cambrai composer; three of them had previously been printed by Attaingnant, two ascribed to 'Lupi' (1530[1], no. 17, and 1540[14], no. 13) and one—'Ma povre bourse' (1539[3], no. 1)—to 'Beaumont' (1530[3], no. 1); one of the remaining three *unica* begins with the Charles V's motto *Plus ultra* (1540[16], no. 9). It is unlikely that any of Moderne's pieces were by Didier Lupi Second, whose secular and sacred chansons and psalm settings were published by the Beringen brothers in 1548.[19]

---

[19] On the Lupus/Lupi composers, see B. J. Blackburn, 'The Lupus Problem' (Ph.D. diss., University of Chicago, 1970), and 'Johannes Lupi and Lupus Hellinck: A Double Portrait', *Musical Quarterly*, 59 (1973), 547–83. The authorship of the 'Italian Lupus' pieces has now been complicated by Richard Sherr's discovery that Lupus Hellinck was in Rome in 1518; see his introduction to *Selections from Bologna, Civico Museo Bibliografico Musicale, MS Q 19 ("Rusconi Codex")* (Sixteenth-Century Motet, 6; New York, 1989), pp. xi–xii.

The situation with regard to 'Jacquet' is also confused: two of the
eleven motets that Moderne attributed to him are *unica* and five are
first editions. 'Aspice domine quia factus est' (1532^9, no. 2) is found in
several manuscript and later printed sources with the specification
'Jacquet da Mantua'; but 'In illo tempore dixit Jesus' and 'Murus tuus'
(1542^5, nos. 17 and 25) were published by Gardane at Venice with
ascription to 'Jachet (de) Berchem'.[20] The ambiguity is curious in view
of the fact that Moderne clearly specifies 'J.' or 'Ja. Berchem' for six
chansons that he printed between 1540 and 1543, half of them appearing also in Attaingnant's seventh book (RISM 1540^{13}).

The 'Benedictus' designated as the composer of five motets, one—
'Plangite pierides' (1538^2, no. 22)—a lament on the death of Erasmus,
and another—'Et Francia foelix'—a paean to King Francis I, must refer
to Benedictus Appenzeller, then based in Brussels as choirmaster in
the service of Mary of Hungary, Charles V's sister and regent in the
Netherlands.[21]

While Pogue discusses the possibility of Nicolas Gombert visiting
Lyons,[22] he does not consider the case for another musician in the
service of the Emperor Charles V in Brussels, Thomas Crecquillon,
whose chansons were printed for the first time in the tenth and eleventh
book of Moderne's *Parangon*, shortly before Susato's rival press was
established at Antwerp in 1543. Political independence may be seen in
the inclusion of so many works by other Netherlanders who worked
within the imperial orbit, like Antoine Barbe (one chanson), Joannes
Courtois (five motets and one or more chansons in the lost *Parangon*
XI), Pieter Maessins (two Latin graces at the end of the eighth book)
Pierre de Manchicourt (five motets and one chanson), Rogier Pathie
(chansons in *Parangon* I and XI), Nicolas Payen (one chanson), and
Joannes Richafort (seven motets, one mass, and one Magnificat). The
intermittent conflict between the Valois and Habsburg dynasties did not
affect Moderne's repertoire in Lyons as much as it did Attaingnant's in
Paris. The greater freedom of the southern city, later seen in the
unhampered publication of vernacular psalms, permitted the inclusion
of Benedictus' lament for Erasmus and Lupi's chanson based on Charles
V's device, which would certainly not have suited the royal printer of
Francis I. The two monarchs spent most of their reigns waging war with

---

[20] Pogue, *Jacques Moderne*, 129 and 177; see also A. M. Bautier-Regnier, 'Jachet de Mantoue',
Revue belge de musicologie, 6 (1952), 101–19; G. Nugent, 'The Jacquet Motets and Their Authors'
(Ph.D. diss., Princeton University, 1973); G. Nugent, 'Jacquet of Mantua', *New Grove Dictionary of
Music*, ix. 456–7.

[21] G. G. Thompson, 'Archival Accounts of Appenzeller, the Brussels Benedictus', *Revue belge de
musicologie*, 32–3 (1978–9), 51–70.

[22] Pogue, *Jacques Moderne*, 61.

one another or manœuvring diplomatically to achieve supremacy in the delicate balance of power. The *entente* ensuing from the Peace of Cambrai (1529) was interrupted by Charles's invasion of Provence in 1536, but four years of peace followed the treaty signed in 1538, and during this time Moderne published more music by the Netherlanders.

As seen in the cases of Conseil, Arcadelt, Verdelot, and Jacquet, Moderne's press also proved a convenient outlet for both French and Flemish composers working in Italy. A number of these, such as Carpentras, Conseil, Andreas de Silva (who provided Moderne with four new motets), the Poitevin Hilaire Penet, and the Savoyard Costanzo Festa (who each provided one motet), were in the service of the Medici Popes Leo X (1513–21) and Clement VII (1523–34). Adrian Willaert, choirmaster at St Mark's from 1527 until his death in 1562, had seven motets published at Lyons (six for the first time), as well as three *ricercari* (including one *unicum*) and three old three-voice French chansons.

While the presses of Venice and Rome increased their output of secular Italian madrigals from the 1530s on, the demand for French chansons (especially the three-voice variety, which was popular between 1520 and 1536) fell proportionately after the Valois withdrawal from political and military adventures in the peninsula,[23] although Janequin's chansons remained commercially attractive, and the *bicinia* of Gardane and Gero ran through several editions after 1539. Even when the cheaper single-impression technique was introduced at Venice in 1539, there is evidence that French music-books were still imported and that few chansons were published in Italy. Thus Jachet Berchem, whose madrigals were printed in Venice from 1536 on, looked to Lyons and Paris for the publication of his chansons; and although two books of five- and six-voice secular and spiritual chansons by Jacques Buus, organist at St Mark's from 1541, were printed in Venice in 1543 and 1550, he had previously relied on Moderne for the publication of seven four-voice chansons.[24]

Ernoul Caussin, choirmaster at the Steccata church in Parma between 1534 and 1548, was also directed to Moderne for the publication of five motets between 1539 and 1542, before his own collection appeared in Venice in 1548. If the two motets of Jehan du Boys and the two motets and one chanson of Maître Jhan are added to the total, it will be seen that French emigrants in Italy provide approximately ninety pieces,

[23] A. M. Bautier-Regnier, 'L'edition musicale italienne et les musiciens d'outremonts au xvie siècle (1501–63)', in *La Renaissance dans les provinces du nord* (Paris, 1956), 27–49.

[24] H. M. Brown, 'The Chanson Spirituelle, Jacques Buus and Parody Technique', *Journal of the American Musicological Society*, 15 (1962), 145–63.

more than ten per cent of Moderne's repertoire, whereas they contribute little over five per cent of Attaingnant's.[25] The two printers' figures for composers working in the Low Countries are more akin: 108 pieces (13½%) for Moderne, compared to about 200 pieces (10%) for Attaingnant. The main divergence between their repertoires arises from the fact that Attaingnant took more than half his music from musicians who held posts in or around Paris, most of them at the Chapelle Royale or Sainte-Chapelle. But his output also shows a nationalistic tendency, with as many pieces by musicians active in the French provinces as by composers working within the Habsburg orbit. He includes few Italian settings (one each by Claudin and Janequin, one anonymous, and one by Costanzo Festa), with nothing by German or Spanish composers. Moderne, on the other hand, printed three whole books of Italian madrigals as well as a number of motets, masses, and Magnificats by musicians from Spain and Germany.

(vii) *Moderne's Italian, Spanish, German, and Hungarian Composers*

Since the musical resources of the cathedral and other churches in Lyons could not match those of the royal chapel and capital, Moderne was compelled to cast his net wider than his Parisian competitor. The fact that more than a quarter of his production was provided by Italian composers reflects both local taste—notably the prominence and artistic generosity of the Florentine community—and local talent, led by Layolle and the lutenists, supported by the industrious instrument-makers. However, another influential factor was Lyons's commercial enterprise, the trade-fairs providing an ideal base for the international distribution of music-books and instruments.

The eclecticism of Moderne's repertoire is seen in the inclusion of music by three Spaniards, three Germans, as well as several Italians. Morales is represented by two separate volumes of masses published in 1545 and 1551, and, in the anthologies, by five Magnificats (RISM 1550[4]) and four motets (RISM 1539[11] and 1542[5]). Luys de Narváez has one motet in each of the last-mentioned collections, while Mateo Flecha provides the only secular Spanish song printed in Lyons, 'Oyd los vivientes' (1544[9], fo. 2). German composers are represented by Mathias (Eckel) and (Leonard) Paminger, each of whom contributes one five-voice motet to the third book (RISM 1538[2]). Although his motet collections include music by only two Italians, Francesco de Layolle and Costanzo Festa, Moderne devotes two whole books of madrigals to

---

[25] Heartz, *Attaingnant*, 96–100.

Layolle and one, containing seven complete *canzoni* by Petrarch set for three, four, five, and six voices, to Matteo Rampollini (d. c. 1554), a Florentine who had contributed to the wedding music for Duke Cosimo and Eleanor of Toledo, printed by Gardane in Venice in 1539.

Nowhere is Moderne's internationalism seen more clearly than in the range of instrumental music that he published. Antoine du Verdier's *Bibliothèque françoise* (Lyons, 1585) records that in 1536 Moderne printed a *tabulature d'epinete* by Guillaume de Brayssingar, who he describes as a German organist in Lyons. While no trace of Brayssingar or Brayssing has been found in the Lyons archives and no copy of the book survives, F.-J. Fétis confirmed its existence in the second edition of his *Biographie universelle* in 1860, claiming that it contained *ricercari, fantaisies,* and variations on themes by the most famous composers of the time. While this may be pure invention, it is plausible the Moderne would have emulated the keyboard publications of Attaingnant issued in Paris a few years earlier.

Whether or not Moderne took the dances in his sole collection of music for instrumental ensemble, the undated *Musicque de Joye*, from Attaingnant,[26] he certainly copied twenty of its twenty-two 'phantaisies instrumentales' (by Willaert, Giulio Segni, Guillaume Colin, Girolamo Parabosco, Nicolaus Benoist, and Girolamo Cavazzoni) from the *Musica Nova*[27] published by Andrea Arrivabene in Venice in 1540.

Moderne's Italianate orientation is further underlined by the fact that his three surviving lute-books use Italian, rather than French, tabulature. This may reflect the demand of his customers or the preference of his arrangers; the latter include the Venetian Francesco Bianchini, who dedicated his book containing one *fantasia*, six chansons, three psalms, and six dances to François Gouffier, Bishop of Béziers (RISM 1547[27]), as well as the Milanese Giovanni Paolo Paladino, whose similar collection of two fantasias, five chansons, and five dances was published without any dedication in 1549. A larger collection of lute-music was printed in Lyons at Paladino's request by Giovanni Pullon de Trino in 1553 and reprinted by Simon Gorlier in 1560; this, taken with a sonnet published in his honour by the poet La Taissonnière in 1555, archival records of his buying an estate with a vineyard in the parish of Saint-Vincent in 1553, still in his possession in 1556, and a seneschal decision on his

[26] Seven are found in P. Attaingnant, *Danseries à 4 parties: Second livre* (1547), ed. R. Meylan (Paris, 1968), nos. 2, 7–9, 17, 25, and 37.

[27] H. C. Slim (ed.), *Musica Nova, Venice, 1540* (Monuments of Renaissance Music, 1; Chicago and London, 1964).

[28] Lesure and Morcourt, 'G. P. Paladino'; L. Guillo, 'Giovanni Pado Paladino à Lyon', *Revue de musicologie*, 73 (1987), 249–53.

estate dated 4 September 1565, announcing his recent death without heirs, confirms the fact that Paladino lived in Lyons for many years.[28] The seneschal verdict refers to him as a 'merchant operating at the fairs of Lyons', as well as an 'instrumental player from Milan', indicating that he left debts to various Florentine, Milanese, and German merchants. Thus it seems that Paladino, like Guillaume Morlaye in Paris, supplemented his earnings as a lutenist by international trading.

The rival lute-music publication of Giovanni Pullon may have influenced Moderne in securing a three-year privilege from Jean Tignat, Henry II's lieutenant-general in Lyons, to print a collection of four ricercars, four Latin motets, six French chansons, and six Italian madrigals by the Hungarian lutenist Bálint Bakfark[29] in January 1553. It was the sole music-book printed by Moderne with a privilege, and this only offered protection against other printers in Lyons. Bakfark included a prefatory dedication to François de Tournon, Cardinal Archbishop of Lyons, expressing gratitude to his patron for bringing him from his distant native land. In fact, during this period Bakfark remained in the service of the Polish court, travelling to Lyons in 1552, via Wittenberg and Augsburg, in order to publish his music.

Although the poetry of Des Périers indicates that the lutenist Alberto da Ripa was in Lyons, probably with his employer Francis I, in 1539, none of his music was printed there. However, including Gorlier's 'ghosts', nine tablature-books were published between 1547 and 1562, a period which corresponds to the city's golden age of literary lyricism.

(viii) *Local and Provincial Composers*

Moderne's output was primarily motivated by demand and, despite the export trade through the fairs and the number and prestige of the Italian community in Lyons, most of his customers must have been French. So were most of his contributors; indeed, notwithstanding the aforementioned differences, nearly half his music came from the same composers who dominated Attaingnant's output, particularly Janequin, Claudin, Sandrin, Maillard, Certon, and Mornable. This is not to say that he pirated the Parisian publication: the many *unica* and first editions deny this, whilst even the twenty per cent of his repertoire which duplicates Attaingnant's shows variants in layout, detail, ornamentation, and even attribution, suggesting that he received most of his music quite independently. Moreover, a significant amount (around one-third)

---

[29] O. Gombosi, *Der Lautenist Valentin Bakfark: Leben und Werke, 1506–1576* (Musicologia hungarica 1; Budapest, 1935, 2nd edn. 1967); E. Haraszti, 'Un grand luthiste du xviᵉ siècle: Valentin Bakfark', *Revue de Musicologie*, 9 (1929), 159–76.

came from composers active in Lyons or in the French provinces, many of them not represented in Parisian publications.

The ties between Lyons and Avignon, another Italianate city and nominally a papal enclave, were traditionally strong, and it is significant that, while not attempting to pirate Jean de Channey's sacred publications, Moderne should print two lively chansons (1541[8]) by the native Provençal, Elzéar Genet (alias Carpentras), revealing a new facet of the priest-composer's character. He also issued nine motets (eight of them original) by Jean L'Héritier, who moved from Rome to Avignon in the service of the Cardinal legate François de Castelnau between 1538 and 1540, as well as two masses, two motets, and nine chansons by Antoine Gardane, who may also have come from Provence. Moderne does not, however, appear to have published any music by Loys d'Avignon, organist at Lyons between 1515 and 1533.

The writings of the poet-musician Eustorg de Beaulieu provide abundant information on the problems, relationships, and attitudes of a minor musician struggling to establish himself and to make a living in Lyons and to come to terms with the new religious ideas there. But he was in the town for only a short time between 1534 and 1537, and made little impact as a composer, publishing just three songs with Moderne before departing for Switzerland.

(ix) P. de Villiers

A composer of more substance was P. de Villiers, who figures more prominently than any other in Moderne's musical anthologies, with at least thirty chansons, five motets, two madrigals, and one mass, printed between 1532 and 1543. Between 1536 and 1548 Attaingnant in Paris also ascribes to 'Villiers' or 'De Villiers' some thirty-one chansons, fourteen of which had already appeared in Lyons. The fact that Moderne included a chanson in local dialect,[30] two Italian pieces, and at least four *épigrammes* by poets living in Lyons (two by Charles de Sainte-Marthe, one by Pernette du Guillet, and one by Maurice Scève) already hints at close links with Lyons during the 1530s. This is confirmed by the fact that Villiers's name is mentioned not only by Rabelais, but also by the three writers associated with the Collège de la Trinité in the late 1530s and early 1540s—Aneau, Fontaine, and Sainte-Marthe—suggesting that he may have have taught music there. This would give added significance to the symbolism of Villiers's canonic mass subtitled 'Trinitas in unitate' (RISM 1540[1], fo. 101[r]; see Music Example 5).

---

[30] Pogue, *Jacques Moderne*, 387–92.

Villiers may have visited Augsburg, a city closely connected with Lyons through the fairs and the book-trade, in the early 1540s, since his seven-voice motet, 'Sancte Stephane', printed by Moderne (RISM 1542[5], praises a prominent prelate of the city, whose cathedral was also named after St Stephen.[31] Three years later Philipp Ulhard of Augsburg published the four-voice lament 'Tundite vos Musae lachrymas' (RISM 1545[2], fo. 22[r]) with an ascription to 'Piere Vuilliers'.

Twelve more chansons were attributed to Villiers or De Villiers in Parisian collections between 1547 and 1553, after Moderne had ceased publishing chanson collections; but one new piece ('Venus avoit son filz Amour perdu') was printed later in Lyons by Robert Granjon (1559[14], p. 43).

Despite this prolific output and abundant literary reference, the exact identity of Villiers remains mysterious. The name is a common one throughout France, with several mentioned in Lyons during the sixteenth century, none of them, however, readily identifiable with the 'P. de Villiers' specified by Moderne. Without the Augsburg publisher's specification, the composer might be considered identical to the writer-musician Hubert-Philippe de Villiers, who translated into French Italian books by Innocenzo Ringhieri, Girolamo Parabosco, and an anonymous soldier at the Siege of Metz published in Lyons between 1553 and 1556, with dedications to Marguérite de Bourbon, Duchess of Nevers, her secretary, Martin de La Herbaudière, and the Governor of Lyons, Jean du Peyrat. A book of verse that Hubert-Philippe wrote under the title *Le Trophée d'Anthoine de Croy* (J. Saugrin, Lyons, 1557) describes the author as secretary to the Prince of Condé, Louis de Bourbon, champion of the Huguenot faction. A further collection of his poetry, entitled *Le Limas d'Ubert Philippe de Villiers*, was printed by the Parisian music-publisher Nicolas du Chemin in 1564, while another, entitled *L'Erynne françoyse de la France affligée*, survives in manuscript (Oxford, Bodleian, Rawl. poet. 244), with a binding containing an anonymous canonic chanson, 'Qui ne l'aymeroit', which had appeared in a collection of chansons published by Antico in Venice in 1520. But more significant is an *Aer funèbre sur la mort lamentable . . . de Loys de Bourbon, Prince de Condé . . . par Ubert Philippe de Villiers, Secretaire dudit Sieur Prince*, printed in 1569 with a typography similar to that used at the time by some of the Protestant presses of Lyons (see Pl. 13).

This lament is set to music as a dialogue for one boy and three men, representing France and Heaven, in a modern *voix-de-ville* style, including some crude parallel harmony, quite unlike that found in the

---

[31] The *prima pars* has been edited ibid. 393–401; on Villiers, see also 64–7.

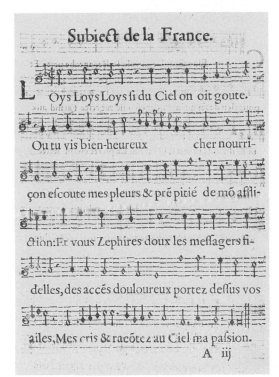

Pl. 13. Fist page of music from Hubert Philippe de Villiers's *Aer funèbre* (1569) Paris, Bibl. nat., Rés. Yf 1654

chansons ascribed to Villiers in earlier collections. Moreover, the *Aer* includes a preface in which the author apologizes for daring to write his own music rather than asking any of the 'finest French composers' whom he knew well (fo. A1ᵛ):

Ne m'accuse, je te pry, de presumption ou temerité, si moy-mesmes ay mariée la Musique à mes vers, estant ainsi que les plus excellens Musiciens de la France (desquels j'ay ce bien d'estre familierement conneu et de la plus part aimé) me soulageants en cecy eussent encor de beaucoup enrichi et illustré mon poème par la douce gravité de leurs accords; car tout ainsi qu'une belle robe accroit souvent une beauté, aussi la Musique proprement joincte et accommodée au vers rend les nombres de beaucoup plus agreables. Mais souvien toy d'autrepart, que comme la mere assottée de son enfant ne luy trouve bien-seant quelque accoustrement, pour riche qu'il soit, venant d'autre main que la sienne: aussi aveuglé peut estre de ma propre affection, ay estimé qu'autre que moy ne pouvoit mieux approprier la Musique aux deux subjects de cest Aer funebre: le premier desquels (qui est la France) se doit lamentablement chanter seul sans harmonie d'accords par une voix puerile, et le second (qui est le Ciel) à voix muées et gravement ...

Do not blame me, I beg you, for presuming or daring to match my own music to my verses, when the finest French musicians (with whom I am well acquainted and for the most part liked), easing my feelings in this, might have enriched and illustrated my poem by the gentle gravity of their chords: for just as a beautiful dress often increases beauty, so music properly joined and adapted to the verse makes the numbers much more agreeable. But remember too that the mother besotted with her child does not find becoming any clothing, no matter how rich it be, coming from any hand but her own: thus blinded perhaps by my own affection, I thought that no one but I myself could better adapt music to this funeral air's two subjects, the first of which (that is France) should be sung as a lamentation alone without any chordal harmony by a boy's voice, and the second (that is Heaven) gravely by mature voices . . .

This does not sound like the experienced and accomplished composer of many fine polyphonic chansons and motets. Yet there is evidence that this was the same Villiers associated with the poets of the Collège de la Trinité in Lyons, in the fact that one of those poets, Charles Fontaine, in his *Ruisseaux* (Lyons, 1555), specifies the name 'Hubert-Philippe de Villiers' as the author of a dedicatory epistle and as the dedicatee of an epigram praising his embodiment of the 'two celestial sciences' of poetry and music. The mention of 'science' links this epigram with Charles de Sainte-Marthe's *rondeau* to 'Villiers, Musicien tres perfaict', whom one must assume to have been the composer who set two of Sainte-Marthe's poems to music (see above, p. 77). It remains possible, however, that Hubert-Philippe was in fact the son or some other younger relative of P. de Villiers.

(x) *Loys Henry, G. Campis, and Cassa sol la*

A number of composers whose names occur occasionally in Moderne's publications but not elsewhere may have local connections. But the quest for information on these minor figures has so far proved largely unrewarding. Guéraud's Chronicle[32] reports on 1 July 1559 that a 'Louys Henry, son of the late Marc Henry and of my niece Catherine Bessy' became a monk at the Célestin monastery: it is possible that this was the Loys Henry who wrote 'Qui veult estre joly' in the second book of the *Difficile des Chansons* (RISM 1544[9], fo. 16[r]). However, the name Henry occurs frequently in the Lyons archives: Guillaume and Jean Henry were aldermen between 1527 and 1560, while a Jehan Henry, listed as an instrument-player in 1581, may be identical with Jean Henry (the elder) 'maître joueur d'instruments' in Paris in 1552.[33] But the name was

[32] *La Chronique lyonnaise de Jean Guéraud*, 136.
[33] F. Lesure, 'Les Orchestres populaires à Paris vers la fin du XVIe siècle', in *Musique et musiciens français du XVIe siècle* (Geneva, 1976), 143–60 at 144–5.

also common throughout France: indeed, a Louis Henry was mentioned as 'maître de la psallette' at Angers in 1536 and as a friend of Janequin.[34]

G. Campis, represented by two chansons in *Parangon* V (1539[20], fos. 7–8), might be related to Jannot de Campis the printer, active in Lyons twenty years earlier,[35] or to Henrico de Campis the singer and music-publisher active contemporaneously in Ferrara (cf. RISM 1539[7]). Similarly, Cassa sol la, composer of two chansons in *Parangon* II (1538[16], repr. 1540[15], fos. 16 and 20), may be related to Luigi Cassola, whose serenade poetry was favoured by contemporary madrigalists.

(xi) *Pierre Colin*

The list of music published at Lyons (App. V) shows that until 1540 anthologies were favoured, but after 1545 collections devoted to a single composer or intabulator. The transition is seen in the output of Moderne between 1540 and 1544, with series like the *Parangon des Chansons* and *Motteti del Fiore* giving way to entire volumes by Francesco de Layolle, Pierre Colin, and Matteo Rampollini. Colin, who was choirmaster at Autun in Burgundy between 1550 and 1561, may have had some connection with Lyons in the 1540s, since his book of eight masses, eight motets, and Magnificats, printed by Moderne in 1542, was dedicated to Charles d'Estaing, Canon of Saint-Jean. Twelve more of his masses appear in the *Liturgicon Musicarum* (1554, repr. 1556) dedicated to the deacons and canons of Autun; but by this time his sacred works had also been published in Venice, Antwerp, Paris, Nuremberg, and Geneva. Moderne, who introduced more of Colin's music than any other printer, was the first to include his motets in anthologies (RISM 1539[11] and 1542[5]), although Attaingnant printed more of his chansons.[36]

(xii) *Gabriel Coste, Henry Fresneau, P. de La Farge, and F. de Lys*

Although Fétis (*Biographie universelle*, 1860) claimed that the composer designated 'G. Coste' in sixteen chansons and two motets printed by Moderne between 1538 and 1543 was a Gaspard Coste, chorister at Avignon cathedral in 1530, no record of any such chorister has been discovered; moreover, Fétis proved unreliable in confusing this musician with Gasparo Costa, an organist active in Italy at the end of the

---

[34] J. Levron, *C. Janequin, musicien de la Renaissance* (Grenoble and Paris, 1948), 85–8.

[35] Baudrier, *Bibliographie*, xi. 212–16.

[36] See W. C. Lengefeld, 'The Motets of Pierre Colin (fl. 1538–1565)' (Ph.D. diss., University of Iowa, 1969); M. Oakley, 'The "Liber Octo Missarum" of Pierre Colin' (M. Mus. Thesis, London, 1987).

century. In the index of his *Musicque de Joye* (RISM 1550[24]), Moderne
lists a ricercar by 'Gabriel Costa', while giving the usual designation, 'G.
Coste', above the music. If no record of Gabriel Coste has yet been
found in the archives, the name Coste was quite common in Lyons: a
Jehan Coste, mentioned in 1515 as a 'tailleur d'ystoires', was again
employed for the 1548 royal entry, while a Louis Coste, 'affaneur', was
paid 3 écus 45 sols for working the bellows of the organ at Notre-Dame
de Confort for fifteen months from 3 March 1595.[37] An indication
of Lyonese connections is suggested by the fact that Coste set two
stanzas from Des Périers' *Voyage à Notre-Dame de l'Isle*, as well as an
épigramme by Pernette du Guillet and six lines (441–6) from Héroët's
Parfaicte Amye printed in Lyons by Dolet in 1542.[38] Only one of Coste's
chansons (a setting of Clément Marot's 'Je ne sçay combien la haine
dure') appeared in Paris (RISM 1540[13], no. 13).

One motet and twenty chansons were ascribed to 'H. Fresneau' in
Moderne's anthologies. The name Henry Fresneau is actually specified
in the second volume of *Le Difficile des Chansons* (RISM 1544[9]), which
presents no less than thirteen of his pieces, including two anecdotes
about the sexual adventures of 'Ung Cordelier' and 'Ung Jacobin', both
perhaps of local significance. Another piece—'Montez soubdain que la
beste ne rue'—published in the seventh book of *Le Parangon des
Chansons* (RISM 1540[12], fo. 21), may refer to the Chevauchée de l'âne, a
festivity regularly celebrated in Lyons. One awkward text set in the fifth
book of the same series (RISM 1539[20], no. 8), 'Mignons qui suivés la
route du dieu d'amours', may be no more than a publicity jingle,
advertising a travelling troupe of officially sanctioned actors. Like other
composers of polyphonic music (e.g. Pierre Regnault dit Sandrin),[39]
Fresneau may have been connected with theatrical entertainment; certainly his knowledge of the popular repertoire is attested in a *fricassée*
(RISM 1538[17], no. 1), quoting from over a hundred chansons.[40] He
specialized in novelty pieces, composed in a catchy style with rapid
syllabic patter, and it is easy to see how 'Le jeu m'ennuye' ascribed to
Fresneau in Moderne's sixth book of chansons (1540[16], fo. 9) could
be attributed to Janequin in Attaingnant's twenty-third book several
years later (RISM 1547[10], no. 8).[41] Attaingnant further ascribes two of
Fresneau's pieces from the *Difficile des Chansons* ('Ung laboureur sa

---

[37] Lyons, Archives communales, CC 21, BB 67, fo. 178[v], and Rhône, Arch. dép. E (Not. Bégule).
[38] A. Héroët, *La Parfaicte Amye* (Lyons, 1542), 18; ed. F. Gohin (Paris, 1909), 26.
[39] See Brown, *Music in the French Secular Theater*.
[40] F. Lesure, 'Éléments populaires dans la chanson française du début du xvie siècle', in *Musique
et poésie au xvie siècle* (Paris, 1954), 169–84.
[41] Clément Janequin, *Chansons polyphoniques*, ed. F. Lesure and A. T. Merritt, 6 vols. (Monaco,
1965–71), iv, no. 127.

journée commençoit' and 'Thenot estoit en son cloz resjouy', RISM 1544[9], nos. 13 and 14) to 'Sanserre' (RISM 1545[10], nos. 5 and 13). The uncertainty of the Parisian publisher is underlined by the fact that, after attributing 'Par ton Amour, hélas je suis laissée' to Fresneau in his eighteenth book (RISM 1545[13], no. 2), he reprinted the same piece with ascription to 'Guyon' in the very next book (1546[12], no. 14). The Parisian publisher was clearly less familiar with Fresneau than was Moderne, and, apart from a single chanson in his third book—'A bien compter ma joye abandonnée' (RISM 1538[12] and 1540[10], no. 23)— which had already been published in Lyons (1538[17], no. 22), he ascribed to Fresneau only four pieces, all printed between 1545 and 1547. Only one further piece by Fresneau appeared in Paris, in Du Chemin's eleventh book (RISM 1554[21], no. 3).

Between 1532 and 1547 Moderne issued eight motets and two chansons by P. de La Farge, distinguishing this composer from La Fage who contributed a setting of the psalm 'Super flumina Babilonis' to his first book of five-voice motets. (1532[9], no. 2). While the latter was probably the Jean de La Fage represented by one chanson and twelve other motets in Florentine, Roman, Venetian, and Parisian sources between 1519 and 1535, as well as the musician mentioned in a noël by the Angers organist Jean Daniel (c.1530) and in the Prologue to Rabelais' *Quart livre* (see above, Ch. 2 p. 36), the name La Farge does not appear in any sources outside Lyons. He may be identical with 'Me. Pierre de La Farge, chanoine de l'Eglise Collégiale de St. Just à Lyon, habitant dans le cloître de lad(ite) Eglise', whose will was attested by the town's royal notary, Jean Roy, on 18 August 1559. The will itself has been lost, but a copy made in 1760 is preserved at the Bibliothèque municipale (MS 2623). Doubts, however, arise from the fact that the will described La Farge as 'personne noble' and 'licentié en droit', without mentioning any musical distinction or occupation.

The case of 'F. de Lys', who contributed seven chansons to the *Parangon* series between 1539 and 1543, remains shrouded in mystery. The designation was probably a pseudonym: the fleur-de-lis was not only the French royal device, but was also used by a number of Italian printers such as the Giuntas, the Trot and Tinghi families, and by Buglhat, Campis, and Hucher of Ferrara (cf. RISM 1539[7]), as well as by Moderne in Lyons. A Lyonese connection is suggested by the fact that two of the texts set by F. de Lys are by Pernette du Guillet, although one of them, 'En lieu du bien' (see Music Example 2) is ascribed to 'Quentin' in Attaingnant and Jullet's second book (RISM 1540[9], fo. 5[v]). Apart from this chanson and one motet, 'Vir inclitus Vincentius', printed in Moderne's third book (1539[10]) and reprinted in Venice (1539[12], 1545[4], and 1564[6]), no other music by F. de Lys appeared outside Lyons.

(xiii) *Guillaume de La Mœulle*

Guillaume de La Mœulle (de la Mole) is represented by one chanson each in seven different books of the *Parangon* series between 1538 and 1543 and another arranged for lute in Bianchini's tablature of 1547. (See Music Example 9) Having served as secretary to Pierre de La Baume, the last bishop of Geneva, La Mœulle was granted citizenship under the republican government on 28 January 1517.[42] He appears next in Lyons listed as 'Guillaume la Mole, dict de Genesve' instrumentalist resident in the Fourvière district of Lyons in 1545, and on (28 February 1548 as 'Guillaume de Genesve', instrumentalist employed by the town council to play, with other violins and shawms, for a banquet offered to four Swiss ambassadors and their entourage returning from the baptism of Princess Claude.[43] When on 12 October 1553 he succeeded Loys Bourgeois as the singing-teacher appointed by the Calvinist council of Geneva, Guillaume was described as 'ancien bourgois de ceste cité.'[44] His salary of 12 florins 2 sous per quarter in Geneva does not seem to have been sufficient for his needs, since he was constantly asking for advances.[45] Attempts to supplement his salary led to trouble, for on 9 April 1555 he was summoned before the Consistory to answer charges that he had used his violin to play dances and other worldly vanities, in association with a certain 'maistre Abel'; the latter may be the composer of the first known polyphonic setting of a psalm translated by Marot, 'Estant assis aux rives aquatiques', printed by Moderne at Lyons in 1540. One of the witnesses called to give evidence specifically mentioned that she saw 'ung rebet et notes de basse dansses' and that the late-night revelry was being conducted by Maistre Guillaume himself. La Mœulle denied the charges, first claiming that he had played only to amuse a sick child, then that he only played psalms, along with 'chansons spirituelles et fantaisies', and that he had neither led nor seen any dancing. But he was duly admonished for having 'mené de dances et d'aulbades'. The same censure recurred the following February, after La Mœulle had been engaged to play dances, as well as psalms, on his rebec for a wedding. A month later a petition from the singers and musicians to be allowed to play violins and other instruments to accompany psalm-singing was refused on the grounds that it encouraged vanity.[46]

[42] See A. Covelle (ed.), *Le Livre des bourgeois de l'ancienne République de Genève* (Geneva, 1897), 185.

[43] F. Rolle *et al.* (eds.), *Inventaire sommaire des archives communales*, 3 vols. (Paris, 1865–87), i. 61 and iii. 215.

[44] Geneva Archives d'État, Registres du Conseil 47, fo. 163ᵛ; see P. Pidoux, *Le Psautier huguenot*, ii. 60.

[45] Pidoux, ibid. 60–1, 67–8; pl. 2 shows La Mœulle's signature on a receipt dated 6 March 1555.

[46] Ibid. 77 and 89–90.

These documents not only reflect the Calvinist attitude towards music (the same attitude which probably discouraged Marot and many others from remaining in Geneva), but suggest the kind of activity that earned La Mœulle and other musicians a living in Lyons. Guillaume died in poverty at an advanced age in September 1556, after suffering an illness and seeing his wife imprisoned for infidelity.[47]

The only music by La Mœulle printed outside Lyons was a collection of psalms, canticles, and spiritual songs with texts by Guillaume Guéroult, published by the latter with Simon du Bosc in Geneva in 1554. Although the title-page claims that these pieces were 'set for one to four voices mostly by La Mœulle', the music printed in this edition is entirely monophonic; moreover, in the last section, containing *chansons spirituelles*, most of the tenors are identical with those of Didier Lupi printed by the Beringen brothers in Lyons six years earlier. A copy in Cambridge University Library is bound together with a collection printed in the same typography, containing five *chansons spirituelles*, purportedly by the cornett-player Claude de La Canesière, nicknamed 'Le Chantre', and four fellow Protestant students from Lausanne, who were imprisoned at Lyons in May 1552 and, after an harangue with the Franciscan and Dominican friars, burnt at the stake a year later.[49] Although no attribution is published, it is possible that La Mœulle provided the published melodies for these songs.

(xiv) *Loys Bourgeois*

Loys Bourgeois was born in Paris and, according to Douen,[50] quoting from a now mislaid document in the Geneva Council's Registers, was summoned to Geneva in 1541. Certainly by 1545 he was well established as a singer and *maistre des enfants* at Saint-Pierre.[51] His first music appeared in Lyons in the fifth book of Moderne's *Parangon des Chansons* (1539–40), and his relations with the Beringen brothers in Lyons continued between 1547 and 1554. In August 1552 he sought three months' leave from his duties in Geneva to visit Lyons for the publication of his most recent psalm-settings. In December the Genevan Council refused his request for a further two-month extension of absence, terminating his employment at the end of March 1553 and paying his wife, Jeanne, his arrears of salary to join him in Lyons.[52] In

[47] Ibid. 78–81 and 89–91.

[48] Ibid., no. 54/IV.

[49] See Crespin, *Recueil de plusieurs personnes qui ont constamment enduré la mort*, fo. 375ʳ (rev. edn., 1556), fos. 434ʳ–438ʳ.

[50] Douen, *Clément Marot et le Psautier huguenot*, ii. 615.

[51] P. A. Gaillard, *Loys Bourgeois* (Lausanne, 1948), 51–88.

[52] Pidoux, *Le Psautier huguenot*, ii. 55–8.

May 1553 he signed a contract to give music lessons to a member of the Lyons bourgeoisie,[53] and in 1554 Godefroy Beringen published his *Pseaulmes LXXXIII de David*. In the same year Bourgeois became embroiled in a heated polemic with the publisher-musician Simon Gorlier,[54] quoting the names of Layolle, Jambe de Fer, François Roussel, and all 'maistres de chapelle' to support his argument that it was advantageous to study Greek and mathematics to be a good musician. He is later mentioned in the city archives[55] as a 'maître musicien' living in the rue de Flandres in 1557. However, by May 1560 he had taken up residence in the rue de Hautejeuille at Paris, and his daughter Suzanne was baptized there in the church of Saint-Cosme.[56] Just two months before this Nicolas du Chemin printed 'Si je vivois deux cens mille ans' (RISM 1560³ᵃ, fo. 12ʳ), the first secular chanson by Bourgeois to appear in twenty years.

The popularity of Bourgeois' psalm-settings, however, seems to have endured, for Antoine du Verdier's *Bibliothèque françoise* (p. 792) mentions *83 Psaulmes de David en Musique (fort convenables aux instrumens) à quatre, cinq et six parties, tant à fin que ceux qui voudront chanter avec elle à l'unyson ou à l'octave accordent aux autres parties diminuées. Plus le Cantique de Simeon, les commandemens de Dieu, les prieres devant et apres le repas. Et un canon à quatre ou à cinq parties, et un autre à huit* printed in Paris by Antoine le Clerc in 1561. This volume, now lost,[57] was probably a revised, expanded version of the Lyons edition of 1554, with the five-, six-, and eight-part pieces added. Du Verdier's explanation that the psalm melody was borne in the tenor, so that the amateur singer could join in at the unison or octave with the more elaborate added voices, epitomizes Bourgeois's role as a popularizing pedagogue, attempting to reconcile professional (Catholic) polyphony with congregational (Calvinist) monody. The meeting-point was homophony, as illustrated by the fifty simple four-voice psalms published by the Beringen brothers in Lyons in 1547.[58] Like Beaulieu's *Chrestienne Resjouoissance*, which appeared a year earlier, the book's dedicatory epistle (to André Chenevard)[59] faith-

[53] L. Guillo, 'Recherches', i. 82.

[54] L. Bourgeois, *Responce à la seconde Apologie de Simon Gorlier* (Lyons, 1554); cf. Pirro, *Les Clavecinistes*, 25–6.

[55] Loose unnumbered notes by G. Tricou in Lyons, Bibliothèque municipale, MS 6118.

[56] Paris, Bibl. Nat. MS nouv. acq. fr. 12124, no. 7664; see F. Lesure, Review of P. A. Gaillard, *Loys Bourgeoys* (Lausanne, 1948), *Revue de musicologie*, 39 (1948), 97–8.

[57] A copy is listed in C. F. Becker, *Die Tonwerke des 16. und 17. Jahrhunderts* (Leipzig, 1855), col. 65.

[58] Thirty-seven of these are edited in K. P. Bernet Kempers, *37 Psalmen in vierstemmige bewerking van Loys Bourgeois uit 1547* (Delft, 1937).

[59] Reprinted in Pidoux, *Le Psautier huguenot*, ii. 35–6.

fully echoes the Calvinist attitude to music, expressing disdain for 'dissolute chansons', while attempting to justify polyphony or at least the addition of 'trois parties concordantes opposant note contre note' to the 'subject' or 'chant commun'. This epistle, somewhat apologetically, announces a freer second volume, referring no doubt to *Le Premier livre des pseaulmes composé par Loys Bourgeois en diversité de Musique*, also published by the Beringen brothers in 1547.[60]

As 'maître des enfants' in Geneva, Bourgeois's task had been to train choristers to lead congregational singing rather than to entertain a silent audience; however, his missionary zeal for music proved stronger than that for Calvinism, and his *Droict chemin* (Geneva and Lyons, 1550)[61] provided the first didactic manual on singing and sight-reading written in the French language. Although indebted to Glareanus, Gafori, and others, the book showed a considerable simplification in theory and practice, introducing the concept of *solfège* and abandoning the archaic Guidonian hand.

As seen in the cases of Beaulieu and La Mœulle, the Protestant administrations in Switzerland did not generally favour instrumental music, mainly because of its 'lascivious' connection with dancing and secular entertainment. But Bourgeois was eager to vindicate its acceptability and insisted that the psalms of 1547, 1554, and 1561 were most suitable for instruments. Moreover, in the preface to the *Droict chemin* (fo. A2[r]) he expressed the intention of writing a book on instrumental performance: 'Je reserve à parler de la diversité des tons, de quelques proportions inusitées de nostre temps, des Canons, ensemble de la composition de Musique, au livre que j'ay deliberé de faire touchant la maniere de jouer des instrumentz...' (I shall save talking about different modes, certain proportions not used today, canons, and the composition of music for the book I have decided to write on how to play instruments).

Although on his return to Paris, Bourgeois reverted to the composition of secular chansons ('that effeminate music, which is intended to express the voluptuousness or langour of love'; *Pseaulmes cinquante*, Lyons, 1547, fo. A2[r]), the possibility that his Protestantism may have caused his death in the massacre at Vassy in 1562 is consistent with the fate of others (among them Aneau and Goudimel at Lyons) and with the fact that nothing by Bourgeois appeared after 1561.[62]

---

[60] *Loys Bourgeois. 'Le premier livre des Psaumes'*, ed. P. A. Gaillard (Monuments de la musique suisse, 3; Basle, 1960).

[61] L. Bourgeois, *Le Droict chemin de Musique* (Geneva, 1550); facs., ed. P. A. Gaillard (Documenta musicologica, 1; Kassel and Basle, 1954).

[62] For further biography, see Gaillard, *Loys Bourgeois*.

(xv) *Pierre Clereau, Benoist, and Charles Cordeilles*

The fifth book of Moderne's *Parangon* (RISM 1539[20]) also includes three chansons ascribed to 'P. Clereau', who, like Bourgeois, does not figure in the collections published by Attaingnant. The composer was no doubt the Pierre Clereau who was choirmaster at Toul between 1554 and 1557, and who published six masses, two motets, and numerous chansons, both sacred and secular, in Paris between 1554 and 1570. But apart from a certain penchant for setting Italian verse and the poetry of Tyard, there is nothing to connect him with Lyons.

The need for caution in establishing identities is seen in the case of Benoist. Two four-voice chansons in the third book of Moderne's *Parangon* (1538[17], nos. 9 and 12) are ascribed to 'Benoist', and a motet in the fourth book of the *Motteti del Fiore* (1539[11], no. 19) to 'N. Benoist'. One of the chansons—'Je suis tant sien'—is found with two others in a manuscript in the Bavarian State Library (MS Mus. 1503a, nos. 1–3), the third piece ('Loyal amant') reappearing in a collection printed by Kriesstein at Augsburg (1540[7], no. 25), all being ascribed to 'N. Benoist'. An instrumental ricercar published in Andrea Arrivabene's *Musica Nova* at Venice in the same year (1540[22], no. 7) specifies 'Nicolo Benoist', transcribed as 'Nicolaus Benoist' in Moderne's edition ([c.1550][24]). It is reasonable to suppose that all these works are by the same composer. However, a collection of *Chansons spirituelles* published in Geneva by Du Bosc and Guéroult (RISM 1555[17], p. 29) ascribes one piece, 'Dont vient hélas qu'iniquité abonde' to '*M.* Benoist', the initial perhaps being a typographical error. In fact, the name Benoist was common throughout France, and Nicolas du Chemin was consistent in attributing two more similar four-voice chansons, 'Si je congnois que l'on ayme' (1550[11], p. 14) and 'Elle s'en va de moy tant regretée' (1550[12], p. 24) to 'Ph. Benoist'.

The 'C. Cordeilles' who contributed three chansons to Moderne's sixth book (1540[16], nos. 4, 8, and 18) and one to the seventh (1540[17], no. 21) is surely 'Charles Cordeilles meneur d'aulboys' who, with Charles Peroyet, organized the shawm-playing for the tableaux at Saint-Éloy and Bourgneuf during the entertainment for Henry II in 1548. None of his music was printed outside Lyons, which is not surprising in view of his lack of skill in part-writing. However, his melodies of these four chansons are effective enough, suggesting that, as a wait, he might have been trained in improvisation and perhaps in deciphering instrumental tablatures rather than in polyphonic composition.

(xvi) *Philibert Jambe de Fer*

Loys Bourgeois's lampoon[63] of 1554 implies that Philibert Jambe de Fer, like Francesco de Layolle and François Roussel, was a choirmaster, presumably at a church in Lyons, although this has not been confirmed by archival evidence. Jambe de Fer published only one motet, 'Salve salutaris victima', a prayer for the new king Henry and his government, in Moderne's *Harmonidos Ariston* (RISM 1547[2] and 1548[1], fo. 33[v]; See Music Example 4.); The orthodox hierarchy could hardly have approved of his predilection for vernacular psalm-settings, evidenced in at least four collections published in Lyons between 1555 and 1564, despite his support from King Charles IX.[64] It seems, moreover, that Jambe de Fer's activities were not restricted to music; on 4 September 1555 he is mentioned in the Chronicle of Jean Guéraud as an associate of a gaming-house, and in a notarized document dated 15 April 1561 as a 'musician and licensed broker'.[65] Such worldly pursuits seem inconsistent with the Calvinist sentiments expressed in the fervent preface to his four- and five-voice homophonic settings of the *CL Pseaumes*, with the official Genevan tune presented simply in the Tenor or Superius, published by Antoine Cercia and Pierre de Mia in 1564.[66]

The title-page of the four- or five-voice *Psalmodie de XLI Pseaumes royaux* (published by Michel du Bois in 1559 with a dedication to the Lyonese banker Georg Obrech) gives Philibert's birthplace as Champlitte in Burgundy.[67] Fétis's claim that he collaborated directly with Jean Poitevin at Poitiers in 1549 is based on bibliographers' ghosts; the earliest surviving editions of Poitevin's psalm paraphrases contain no mention of musical setting.[68] More curious is the fact that Jambe de Fer's only known secular chanson, the courtly 'Femme qui honneur veult avoir', was printed in Paris in Du Chemin's tenth book (RISM 1552[4], no. 7), and that he seems to have taken no active part in the festivities for the royal entry in 1548, as he did in 1564. André Pirro[69] claimed that Jambe de Fer was associated with Martin Bran, a 'spinet-player famous during the earliest times of the Reformation' martyred by the opponents of the new religion in 1552. The composer was certainly resident at Lyons in 1553, when he used the services of the notary

[63] See above, n. 54.
[64] Pidoux, *Le Psautier huguenot*, ii. 85–7, 114–16, 138–9, 143–5; Guillo, 'Recherches', ii, nos. 30, 37, 50, 73–4.
[65] See Lesure, 'L'*Épitome musical*', 342.
[66] Pidoux, *Le Psautier huguenot*, ii. 138–9.
[67] Ibid. 114; Guillo, 'Recherches', ii, no. 37; see also P. A. Gaillard, 'Die *Psalmodie de XLI Psealmes royaux*', *Jahrbuch für Liturgik und Hymnologie*, 2 (Kassel, 1956), 111–12.
[68] Guillo, 'Recherches', i. 76–81.
[69] Pirro, *Les Clavecinistes*, 25.

Chaliard. He quite clearly remained there until 1564, when his four-
and five-voice settings of the new Psalter were printed, and when he
and his musical colleagues received 65 of the total 16,000 livres spent
on the festivities greeting Charles IX. He married twice and died
around 1566, leaving no children, although his second wife's nephew
was the musician Martial des Bargues, whose heirs organized string-
bands at Lyons until the eighteenth century.[70]

(xvii) *Dominique Phinot*

It is unfortunate that the eleventh book of Moderne's *Parangon*[71] is no
longer preserved in the Brussels library for, amongst other things of
interest, it includes at least one chanson by 'Finot', no doubt the
Dominique Phinot who published two books of chansons and two
books of motets with the Beringen press a few years later. The 'molto
magnifico Signor Lucca de Grimaldo' to whom Phinot dedicated his
first book of motets was probably the same member of the Genoan
family involved in banking and shipping to whom Ruffo's second book
of five-voice madrigals was addressed in 1554 (Lucha Grimaldi); but
there is no evidence that Lucca ever resided in Lyons, where some
members of the Grimaldo family were involved in importing and insur-
ance. The same is true of the dedicatee of Phinot's second book of
motets, the much travelled François Bonvalot, Archbishop of Besançon,
who was sent on diplomatic missions to Paris, Geneva, and Rome by the
Emperor Charles V. However, Phinot's dedications to 'noble et vertueux
seigneur Nicolas Bave' (probably the Genoese merchant involved in the
festivities for Henry II's *entrée* in the same year)[72] and to his 'great
friend, César Gros' (sieur de Saint-Joire, who lived near the Pêcherie
and served the municipality as alderman on several occasions between
1553 and 1571)[73] do suggest that the composer spent some time in
Lyons. Moreover, as well as three texts by Maurice Scève, and six by
Charles Fontaine, teacher at the Collège de la Trinité in the 1540s,
Phinot set the *épigramme* which Marot wrote after his departure from
Lyons in 1537:

On dira ce que l'on vouldra	Say what you like
Du Lyon et sa cruauté:	About Lyons and their cruelty;
Tousjours ou le sens me fauldra	If I were always sensible
J'estimeray sa privauté	I would have to admire their privacy.

---

[70] Tricou, 'Philibert Jambe de Fer'; see also id., 'Les Musiciens lyonnais', 148.
[71] Pogue, *Jacques Moderne*, 180, no. 39.
[72] Guigue, *La Magnificence*, 181–2.
[73] Saulnier, 'Dominique Phinot et Didier Lupi'.

J'ay trouve plus d'honnesteté	I find more honesty
Et de noblesse en ce Lyon	And nobility in these Lyons
Que n'ay pour avoir frequenté	Than I do in the million
D'autres bestes ung million.	Other beasts that I know.

An anonymous *épigramme* set by Phinot, and also by Du Tertre (in Du Chemin's second chanson book of 1557), 'Frerot un jour aux Cordeliers estoit', may refer to the Franciscan church in Lyons, with a painting of St Francis in the choir: '. . . il voit là Un sainct Françoys painct au dessus de Dieu. Il entre au c[h]œur et s'arreste au milieu . . .'.

Nothing is known of the composer's early life, although he is described by Jerome Cardan as 'Gallus'. The name Phinot is fairly common in Savoy, and it is perhaps significant that Duke Emmanuel-Philibert stayed with Phinot's friend and patron, Cesare Grosso, during his visit to Lyons in October, 1559.[74] Phinot's first motets appeared in anthologies printed in Venice by Gardane (RISM 1538[4] and 1539[13]), in Ferrara by Buglhat (1538[5]), in Strasburg by Schoeffer (1539[8]), and in Nuremberg by Petreius (1540[6]); but these disparate publications are less significant than the two whole volumes printed in 1547–8 by the Beringens.[75] Gardane's collections also include two Italian madrigals (1541[16], repr. 1546[19] and 1561[10], repr. 1569[18]) and two masses (1544[1] and 1544[5]). The only information on Phinot's career that has so far come to light suggests that he was in the service of Guidobaldo II della Rovere, Duke of Urbino, between 1545 when he received a payment from Ercole d'Este II, Duke of Ferrara, and 1555 when he was funded for clothes and provisions in Pesaro.[76] Although his activity seems to have been restricted to northern Italy, it is likely that he journeyed to Lyons in the late 1540s to supervise his four publications for the Beringen press. There is, however, no evidence that he participated in the music organized for the royal visit in September 1548, and it is also difficult to envisage who in Lyons would have performed his many responsorial five-voice motets, let alone the grand double-choir pieces in eight parts.

(xviii) *Didier Lupi Second*

The Beringen brothers printed three books attributed to Didier Lupi Second, one containing secular chansons,[77] the others four-voice settings of *chansons spirituelles* by Guillaume Guéroult[78] and psalms

---

[74] Ibid. 64.

[75] For the edition of Phinot's music, see Ch. 4 n. 37.

[76] R. Jacob, 'Dominique Phinot', in *Cultural Aspects of the Renaissance: Essays in Honour of Paul Oskar Kristeller* (Manchester, 1976), 425–39.

[77] See n. 73.

[78] Honegger, 'Les Chansons spirituelles de Didier Lupi Second'.

paraphrased by Gilles d'Aurigny. The wording of the dedication of Lupi's secular chansons to various Luccan merchants and bankers suggests that the composer had only recently arrived in Lyons—perhaps from Lucca. The inclusion of five recent texts by Marot (four published in 1547 and a fifth not appearing until 1550) indicates that Lupi must have set these pieces quickly. Four texts by Charles Fontaine (whom Aneau had appointed regent at the Collège de la Trinité in 1540), as well as Lupi's later composition of a piece for Aneau's *Genethliac*, might indicate some connection with the Collège at a time when Villiers seems no longer to have been active in Lyons.

Lupi must have also worked quickly and closely with Guéroult to complete and publish the *Premier livre de chansons spirituelles nouvellement composées par Guillaume Gueroult, mises en musique par Didier Lupi Second* in 1548. The ninth piece—'Susanne un jour'—proved especially popular and was often reprinted; moreover, its tenor was borrowed for other polyphonic arrangements by some thirty different composers.[79] Indeed the whole book—the first collection devoted entirely to newly composed *chansons spirituelles*—was a considerable success, going through at least seven more editions: two at Lyons (by T. de Straton in 1561 and by B. Rigaud in 1568), one at La Rochelle, and no less than four at Paris. It is odd that after the sudden activity that produced three books within three years, nothing more by Lupi should appear until 1559, when two single pieces were published in anthologies.

No archival or literary evidence for Lupi's presence in Lyons has yet been found, although he no doubt collaborated directly with Guéroult, who worked in Lyons and Vienne as a corrector for the Arnoullet press between 1547 and 1553, and, after taking refuge in Geneva, returned to Lyons in 1557, joining Granjon and Hiesse in their music printing venture.[81] The care with which the Beringen brothers specify the lengthy appellation 'Didier Lupi Second' suggests that they were aware of the confusion caused by the musical 'Wolf pack'. Similarly, Granjon's *Premier Trophée de Musique* of 1559 ascribes one chanson, 'Honneur sans plus' previously published in 1542 by Attaingnant and in 1543 by Moderne (with attribution to 'Ja. James') to 'Lupus', but another 'O que je vis en estrange martire' to 'Lupi second'. The text of the latter was, according to Du Verdier's *Bibliothèque* (p. 182), written for Clémence de Bourges by the Sieur du Peyrat, son of the royal governor of Lyons.

[79] See K. J. Levy, '*Susanne un jour*: The History of a 16th-Century Chanson', *Annales musicologiques*, 1 (1953), 375–408.
[80] G. Becker, *Guillaume Guéroult et ses chansons spirituelles* (Paris, 1880).
[81] See Baudrier, *Bibliographie*, x. 98–100; see also above, Ch. 4. n. 63.

This Lyonese connection is confirmed by the inclusion of a four-part piece by D. Lupi for the presentation scene at the end of Aneau's *Genethliac musical* (G. Beringen, 1559, Chant XVII), and by the fact that all the music definitely attributable to this composer was printed in Lyons, mostly in three collections issued by the Beringen brothers, with dedications to local dignitaries. The *Tiers livre contenant 35 chansons* (the *third* book of secular chansons published by the Beringen brothers, the previous two being composed by Phinot) includes a dedicatory epistle from Lupi to Antoine and Jean-Baptiste Barthélemy, Joseph Cinamy, Jerosme Michel, Joseph Arnolfin, Alaman Orsuccio, and Vincent Carniccion, a group of merchants and bankers originally from Lucca but later active or resident in Lyons.[82] The dedication acknowledges 'benificence' received by the composer from these 'great men' since his arrival and promises something else to come 'in a higher style'. This may refer to the *Psalmes trente... traduictz en vers françois par Giles d'Aurigny*,[83] which carries a dedication dated 15 February 1550 to the banker and 'bourgeois de Lyon', Nicolas Baillivi, whose name occurs frequently in the town archives between 1554 and 1569 and to whom a *Chant pastoral* by Louis des Masures was addressed in 1559.

Lupi's dedicatory epistle apologizes for the 'profane chansons unworthy of a Christian man' which he had set a year earlier at the behest of some of his friends and expresses the hope of 'healing the wound with the same stick that inflicted it', following the advice of his 'best friends' by setting these 'newly translated psalms, fervently expressing the love of God' rather than 'intemperance and luxury'. Curiously, it then refers to the composer having presented his 'first book' of lascivious chansons to the same dedicatee. This might signify that the *Tiers livre* was really Lupi's third book of secular chansons, or that the dedication, although signed by the composer, was actually written by the publishers, so that the first book would refer here to Phinot's first book of chansons, dedicated to 'Nicolas Bave', who could be the same as Nicolas Baillivi. The reference to a 'higher' style might, however, apply to the *Chansons spirituelles* of 1548, dedicated to the Count of Gruyère, to whom Guéroult had also addressed his first book of emblems and his chronicle of emperors.[84] The *Chansons spirituelles* also include a prefatory sonnet by the composer, dedicated simply to music-lovers; its first eight lines were set for three voices by Jean de Castro in 1574.

[82] See Guillo, 'Recherches', ii, no. 22.
[83] See ibid., no. 26.
[84] See ibid., no. 24, and Baudrier, *Bibliographie*, x. 123 and 132.

(xix) *Antoine de Hauville and Simon Gorlier*

Lupi's associate Guillaume Guéroult also wrote the preface and four texts for a collection of *chansons spirituelles* entitled *La lyre chrestienne* set by Antoine de Hauville[85] and published in 1560 by Simon Gorlier. Hauville's two-voice settings of Marot's graces, 'O souverain pasteur' and 'Père eternel', were published at the end of Richard Crassot's four-voice psalms in 1564 and reprinted in 1565. His only other surviving pieces were two secular chansons printed in Paris, the four-voice 'L'amy certain' in Marie Attaingnant's first book (1553[20], fo. 12ᵛ) and 'Herbes et fleurs' in Le Roy and Ballard's *Mellange* (1572[2], fo. 10ᵛ)

Gorlier had himself acquired a considerable reputation as a lutenist in the early 1550s and, according to Antoine du Verdier's *Bibliothèque* (1585), published a *Livre de Musique à 4–5* of his own composition. Between 1553 and 1554 Gorlier was involved in a polemic with Loys Bourgeois, who ridiculed his lack of humanist education as being typical of a mere instrumentalist and inferior to that of choirmasters or singer-composers like Bourgeois himself, Layolle, Jambe de Fer, and Roussel:

> Nous autres qui chantons et composons en musique . . . avons esté aprins en grec, arithmétique et géométrie pour parvenir là. Je m'en rapporte à Roussel, Jambe-de-Fer et Layolle (qui te monstreroyent ta leçon) et à tous maistres de chapelle.[86]

> We others who sing and compose music . . . have been taught Greek, arithmetic, and geometry to reach this point. I refer to Roussel, Jambe de Fer, and Layolle (who could teach you a lesson) and to all choirmasters.

(xx) *François Roussel*

This lampoon suggests the presence in Lyons of the composer François Roussel, who had been choirmaster at the Julian Chapel in St Peter's in Rome in the late 1540s. That he extended his soujourn in Lyons is suggested by a report nominating 'M[aîtr]e musitien M[aîtr]e Francoys Roussello' as an expert witness for Philibert Jambe de Fer in a suit against the printers Tribillet and Jean d'Ogerolles in March 1561.[87] The expert witness called for the opposition was 'M[aîtr]e musitien M[aîtr]e Helye Gachoux'; Antoine du Verdier's *Bibliothèque* (1585) records an edition of *Les cent cinquante psalmes* printed in 1560 by d'Ogerolles which may have been the book disputed by Jambe de Fer. Du Verdier's

---

[85] See Baudrier, *Bibliographie*, ii. 46–8.
[86] Bourgeois, *Responce à la seconde Apologie*, cited in Pirro, *Les Clavecinistes*, 25.
[87] Guillo, 'Recherches', ii, document 33.

catalogue provides further evidence for Roussel's presence in Lyons, by reporting that 'Francisco Roussel' set a poem addressed to Clémence de Bourges by Jean du Peyrat in the 1550s, while his *Antithesis de la paix et de la guerre* includes a preface dated 4 August 1568 dedicated to Guillaume de Gadagne (Guadagni), military commander, Seneschal of Lyons, and son of the wealthy Florentine banking family, praising his musical patronage:

vous estes le Mœcenas des hommes studieux: ce qu'entre plusieurs autres Francisque Roussel, docte & excellent musicien a experimenté. Comme donques, en recognoissance de voz singuliers benefices envers soy, il a voué à vostre Seigneurie, partie de ses compositions musicalles (qui esgallent, ou peu s'en faut, l'harmonie des neuf cieux, & lesquelles seront fort bien receues de la Posterité.) aussi je vous donne (sans comparaison) ces miens Vers...[88]

you are the Maecenas of studious men: this has been experienced by, among many others, Francisque Roussel, learned and excellent musician. In recognition of the singular beneficence you accorded him, he has dedicated to your Lordship some of his musical compositions (which very nearly rank with the harmony of the nine heavens and which will be very well received by posterity): so I offer you (without comparison) these verses of mine...

The compositions in question are not known. But a collection of chansons for four to six voices published by Le Roy & Ballard[89] at Paris in 1577 includes and was prefaced by sonnets dedicated to Jacques de Savoie, Prince of Nemours, who had been governor of Lyons between 1562 and 1571. Roussel's first published chanson, a setting of the first stanza of 'Qui veut avoir liesse' from Marot's *Adolescence Clémentine*, appeared at Lyons in Granjon's *Second Trophée de Musique* (1559[14]), although it was reprinted with six others at Paris in the same year (1559[13]). With a penchant for Ronsard and Baïf, his later chansons, include no texts by the Lyons poets.

Roussel worked again in Rome between 1562 and 1575, during which time Dorico published two books of his madrigals. Antoine Gardane also issued a volume of his madrigals in Venice in 1562, while many others were included in various anthologies. These Italian publications, as well as the manuscript and archival sources, give his name as 'Francesco Rosselli', 'Roscelli', or 'Rosello.'[90] Such inconsistency in transliteration might suggest that he was French; although Le Roy & Ballard's 1577 book specifies 'Francoys Roussel', Du Verdier's designations 'Francisco' and 'Francisque' imply an Italian origin.

---

[88] A. du Verdier, *Antithesis de la paix et de la guerre* (Lyons, 1568), 4.
[89] Lesure and Thibault, *Bibliographie*, 41 and 184–5.
[90] G. Garden, 'François Roussel: Sa vie et son œuvre' (doctoral thesis, Paris, 1972).

(xxi) *Alamanno Layolle*

Alamanno Layolle apparently did not succeed his father Francesco as organist at Notre-Dame de Confort, the position being held by Piero Mannucciqua in 1548 and by Mathieu de Fleurs in 1559. He was, however, mentioned in 1551 as a *joueur d'instrumens* living in the rue Saint-Jean, and in the following year as a 'Musicien et organiste à Lyon', in a marriage contract with Léonette Bastier, daughter of the owner of the house where his father had spent his last years.[91] Antoine du Verdier's *Bibliothèque* lists his four-part *Chansons & Vaudevilles* published by Simon Gorlier in 1561, with a Tenor part that Fétis's *Biographie universelle* claimed included a prefatory note indicating that he was organist at Saint-Nizier; but no archival record has yet been found to substantiate this or even to suggest that there was a permanent organ in the church during the sixteenth century. In 1565, a few years after his wife's death, Alamanno moved to Florence, leaving his daughter, Andrée, in Lyons in the charge of his sister Marguerite. This daughter's marriage contract refers to 'the late Aleman Layolle, citizen of Florence' in December 1571, and a will was registered on his behalf in March 1576, although recently discovered evidence suggests that he lived on in Florence until 1590.[92] Moderne printed none of his music, and in the absence of Gorlier's collection, only six three-voice madrigals published in Florence by Marescotti (RISM 1582[8]) and a manuscript containing keyboard arrangements of famous old chansons and madrigals and of the sixth of the Florentine *Intermedii* by Malvezzi and Cavalieri for Grand-duke Ferdinand's wedding at Florence in 1589 are known.

(xxii) *Nicolas Martin*

In 1555 and 1556 Macé Bonhomme printed and reprinted a monophonic collection of noëls and chansons, some in French, some in Savoyard patois, with words and music by Nicolas Martin. The title-page described Martin as 'Musicien en la Cité saint Jean de Morienne en Savoye'. Joseph Orsier[93] gave his date of birth as 1498, and claimed that he left Saint-Jean-de-Maurienne for Chambéry and subsequently Lyons after being dismissed from his post at the cathedral by the new Archbishop, Jerôme Ricevali, who disapproved of his 'chansons follettes'. This

[91] Tricou, *Documents sur la musique à Lyon*, 28–30.

[92] F. D'Accone, 'The *Intavolatura di M. Alamanno Aiolli*', *Musica disciplina*, 20 (1966), 151–74.

[93] Martin, *Noelz et chansons*, ed. Orsier; see also Orsier, 'Un poète-musicien au xviᵉ siècle, Nicolas Martin, ses Noëls et ses chansons (1498–1566)', *Revue de la Renaissance*, 9 (1908), 181–203.

accords with Angley's recollection that a motet by Martin was sung 'en fort belle musique' at Saint-Jean.[94] The composer-poet could not have remained long in Lyons, since he turns up again in Maurienne, organizing a mystery play to divert the people of Saint-Jean during an epidemic, in March 1565: a copy of the town council's deliberations suggests that Martin was expert in such matters:

De la benoiste passion a esté dict que les esleus parleront et communiqueront avec Maistre Nicolas Martin pour entendre de luy comme l'on fera les rooles du mistere d'icelle voué à jouer par personnaiges à la dicte presente cité . . .[95]

It has been decided for the blessed passion that those chosen will speak and communicate with Master Nicolas Martin to agree on how to arrange the roles of this mystery planned to be acted in the city

This theatrical connection might seem to lend support to the idea that Henry Fresneau was similarly employed, even if his polyphonic music is very different. Martin's monophonic collection's simple, clear-cut, melodies suggest folk tunes much more than the lively patter, the choppy, dissected, restricted melodic shape, and the tortuous phrasing of Fresneau's polyphony (see Pl. 7).

Martin is a very common name throughout Europe; it seems unlikely therefore that Nicolas was related to Claude Martin of Couches-les-Mines, who printed nine chansons and a practical treatise at Paris between 1549 and 1557,[96] or to the Nicolai Martin,[97] rector of a school at Bartenstein in East Prussia, who later dedicated a Latin epigram to the lutenist Mathäus Waissel, in a collection of preludes and dances published in Frankfurt in 1591.

(xxiii) Richard Crassot

Richard Crassot, who was probably born in Nantes, was employed as choirmaster at Troyes between 1556 and March 1560, at Orléans in 1572, and at Tours in 1581.[98] After fleeing from Troyes without notice, leaving behind debts, he may have spent some time in Switzerland before emerging in Lyons, where his homophonic four-voice settings of

---

[94] V. Angley, *Histoire du diocèse de Maurienne* (Turin, n.d.), 290.

[95] F. Truchet, 'Le Mystère de la passion à Saint Jean', in *Congrès des sociétés savantes de la Savoie*, 13 (1872), 259–452.

[96] F. Lesure and G. Thibault, 'Bibliographie des éditions musicales publiées par N. du Chemin', *Annales musicologiques*, 1 (1953), 269–373.

[97] Brown, *Instrumental Music*, 373.

[98] F. Lesure, 'Some Minor French Composers of the 16th Century', in J. La Rue *et al.* (eds.), *Aspects of Medieval and Renaissance Music: A Birthday Offering for Gustave Reese* (New York, 1966; repr. 1978), 538–44 at 540.

the new Genevan psalter[99] were published by Thomas de Straton in 1564 and reprinted in the following year by Jean Huguetan. He was still living in Lyons in October 1566, signing a four-year lease there to rent three rooms in the house of a collar-maker.[100]

(xxiv) *Giovanni Antonio de Mayo*

Little is known of the Neapolitan Giovanni Antonio de Mayo, whose first book of four-voice madrigals was issued in 1567 by Antoine Cercia. Nothing in this book helps his identification, since there is no dedication and the texts are conventional. Of the twenty-two poems set, eight are by Petrarch and one each by Bembo, Ariosto, and Sannazaro. The name Maio or Majo was common in Naples, but Giovanni Antonio's music (see Music Example 6), although generally homophonic, is neutral in style and does not display the Neapolitan manner of the *villanesche* of Giovanni Tommaseo di Maio (Majo), who flourished a generation earlier.[101] In 1570 the town council in Geneva refused to grant Jehan Antoine di Mayo permission to print certain 'Chansons spirituelles qu'il a mises en ritme' because the music 'had many faults'. Like the choice of Antoine Cercia as printer for his madrigals, this Genevan application suggests that the composer was a Protestant, which was rare for a Neapolitan. Laurent Guillo[102] cites a personal privilege granted in 1570 for six years by the French king Charles IX to 'Jehan Anthoine de Mayo, musicien neapolitan demourant en nostre ville de Lyon' to publish 'several little books of chansons in Latin, French, and Italian and others that he would compose in the future, lest other printers should, after all the time spent composing or all the expense incurred recovering those he had already written, deprive him of remuneration for such expense'.

(xxv) *Claude Goudimel*

The composer of the four-voice settings of Louis des Masures's *Vingt-six cantiques*[103] is not acknowledged in Jean de Tournes's edition of 1564, but it may have been Claude Goudimel, who was in Metz with the poet at that time.

Goudimel left Metz for Lyons in 1569. Proof of his presence rests on two letters written to Paul Melissus dated 30 November 1570 and 23

[99] Douen, *Clément Marot*, i. 113; ii. 44 and no. 136; Guillo, 'Recherches', ii, nos. 72 and 76.
[100] Lyons, Archives départmentales du Rhône, Notaire Tixier, 3E 8031.
[101] A. Einstein, *The Italian Madrigal*, 3 vols. (Princeton, 1949), i. 355; iii. 78–9.
[102] Guillo, 'Recherches', ii, Documents 41 and 42.
[103] Goudimel, *Œuvres complètes*, xiv. 85–102.

August 1572,[104] as well as several near contemporary accounts[105] of his death in the St Bartholomew's Day Massacre there on 27 August 1572. During this period he published an ode in the *Opuscules poétiques* by the Genevan poet Pierre Enoch and revised a selection of chansons by Arcadelt, who had died at Paris four years earlier, substituting devout texts in the Protestant manner. These *chansons spirituelles* were published by the younger Jean de Tournes in 1572 and reprinted in 1586. The last work composed by Goudimel himself appeared at the end of Corneille de Blockland's treatise, the *Instruction de musique*, issued by De Tournes in the following year.[106] In 1574 Goudimel was linked with Lassus as the 'two most excellent musicians of the time' in two chanson publications, the first of which is prefaced by an epitaph for Goudimel in the form of a sonnet, which was subsequently set to music for six voices in Jean Servin's *Premier livre de chansons nouvelles* (Lyons, 1578, fo. 23ᵛ).

(xxvi) *Regolo Vecoli*

In 1577 Clément Baudin published the *Primo libro de madrigali a cinque voci* by Regolo Vecoli, 'musician from the famous signoria of Lucca', dedicated to his 'most respected patron, Lorenzo, son of Giovanni Buonvisi, gentleman from Lucca'. According to Luigi Nerici, Regolo, son of Vincenzo Vecoli, was absent from the staff of the Palatine church in Lucca between 1561 and 1581, living in Lyons and exercising his skill (*bravura*) as a cornettist and composer.[107]

In the mid-sixteenth century Lucca, like Ferrara, was a sanctuary for Protestants. It is possible that Vecoli was tempted to go to Lyons at the very time when its city council was dominated by Protestants. At all events, he left some time before 1586, when he published his second book of five-voice madrigals with Le Roy and Ballard in Paris, indicating in the preface that he had been compelled to leave by the 'misfortunes which presently afflict Lyons'.[108] The religious conflict clearly had a significant effect upon composers at this time, as can be seen from similar remarks made in a dedication signed by Jean de Castro at Lyons in 1580.[109]

---

[104] P. Melissus, *Schediasmatum Reliquiae* (n.p., 1575), fos. 82ʳ–4ʳ.

[105] See *Mémoires de l'estat de France sous Charles IX* (Middelburg, 1578), 369–70; E. Trillat, *Claude Goudimel, le Psautier huguenot et la Saint-Barthélémy lyonnaise* (Paris, 1948).

[106] Goudimel, *Œuvres complètes*, xiii. 267.

[107] L. Nerici, *Storia della musica in Lucca* (Lucca, 1879), 193 and 271.

[108] F. Lesure and G. Thibault, *Bibliographie des éditions d'Adrian Le Roy et Robert Ballard* (Paris, 1955), 47.

[109] Guillo, ii, Document 49.

(xxvii) *Corneille de Blockland*

Corneille de Blockland (Brockland, alias Montfort) epitomized Renaissance versatility in that he acquired a reputation as a doctor, astrologer, mathematician, and musician, and even tried his hand at writing Latin verses. Born in Montfoort near Utrecht around 1543 he was active in Saint-Amour and Lons-le-Saunier (both near Lyons, in the Franche-Comté) between 1571 and 1586. A number of books on various subjects published at Lyons at this time describe him as 'Medicum Batavum', 'Doctoris medici Stichtigenae', and 'Gentilhomme Stichtois'—*het Sticht* signifying the Bishopric of Utrecht.[110]

Blockland's first musical publication was a simple didactic treatise entitled *Instruction de musique*, written at Saint-Amour in 1571 and published at Lyons in 1573. A second edition was issued in 1581, a third in 1587—with a revised dedication to his pupil Louis de La Baume, Baron of Saint-Amour, signed at Lons-le-Saunier in 1586—and a fourth (also from Geneva) in 1617. In his third chapter Blockland mentions a Latin treatise 'touchant l'entière cognoissance de la Musique' which he had dedicated to Guillaume de Popet, Abbé de Baume. The *Instruction* provides little evidence of Blockland's own musical abilities, since it is largely an eclectic synthesis of other writers, particularly Glareanus, Bourgeois, and Guilliaud, quoting liberally from the latter and reproducing some of his tables and examples. However, it does present some new tables, printed with rounded notes resembling those cut by Granjon, as well as numerous musical illustrations, quoting from the repertoire of the preceding generation, with one motet ('Qui consolabatur me' by Clemens non Papa), one Provençal song (the anonymous 'Qui vo ouy una chanson'), two Italian madrigals, and thirty-one French chansons; only one chanson (Phinot's 'Plorez mes yeux') comes from Lyons, while ten appeared in the second edition of Attaingnant's ninth book (four by Certon, two by Maille, and one each by Maillard, Sohier, Le Hugier, and Mornable), and seven others (four by Arcadelt, two by Lassus, and one by Janequin) from Le Roy and Ballard's more recent publications.

The only compositions by Blockland which have survived are found in the superius part-book of *Le II Livre du Jardin de Musique*,[111] a collection of secular chansons and 'voix de ville' printed by De Tournes in 1579. The book is dedicated to Gabrielle de Dinteville (née Stainville), Baronne de Bohan, Dame de Creissia, but includes

---

[110] F. Dobbins, 'Blockland, C. de', *Die Musik in Geschichte und Gegenwart*, xv (Kassel, 1973), 856–7.

[111] C. de Montfort, *Jardin de Musique*, facs., ed. L. Guillo and M. Chomarat (Lyons, 1983).

occasional pieces addressed to other members of the Burgundian nobility, such as Louis de La Baume, Mme Urbaine Victoire, and Mme de Bellegarde (probably Anne de Bellegarde, the 'demoyselle Savoisienne' whose grace and beauty were celebrated in a poem by Guillaume de la Taissonnière published in Lyons in 1574; she was perhaps related to the King Charles IX's gentleman-in-ordinary, Roger de Bellegarde, to whom Goudimel dedicated a collection of psalms in 1568). One of the texts—'Pour satisfaire à la branche promise' (p. 39)—is Des Périers's *Dizain sur Pâques fleuries*, but there are also four complete settings of sonnets by Ronsard, two short stanzas from Du Bellay's *Jeux*, and other poems by Charles Fontaine, Antoine Macault, and Clément Marot. The collection is prefaced by a sonnet and a *dizain* addressed to the composer by a fellow doctor, astrologer, and mathematician, Guillaume de la Taissonnière, who also wrote the text for an *Epithalame* (p. 32) celebrating the marriage of Louis de La Baume and Catherine de Bruges. After Blockland's dedicatory epistle, the book presents a Latin poem in praise of music by Claude Morel of Vallefin, a lawyer and 'Recteur des Escoles de Saint-Amour'.

Blockland himself signed two Latin poems in honour of the Florentine mathematician and theologian Francesco Giuntini, who published many books in Lyons between 1567 and 1585.[112] According to Antoine du Verdier's *Bibliothèque* (p. 238), Blockland also wrote several ephemerides, one entitled *Placart pour connoître le point et aube du jour* (Lyons, B. Rigaud, n. d.), issued under his own name, but most using the pseudonym' Imbert de Billy'; those of 1578, 1582, 1587, and 1588, published by Rigaud in Lyons, are known, as indeed are two (possibly counterfeit) dated 1602 and 1611, published in Paris. In these Billy is described as 'natif de Charlieu en Lyonnais' and 'tailleur d'habits du Sieur de Perez', the latter being the same Louis de La Baume to whom the *Instruction* is dedicated. That Billy was in fact Blockland in disguise seems likely in view of the extravagant praises found in Billy's *Almanach* for 1578 and that for 1582; in the latter's address to the councillors and bourgeois of Lons-le-Saunier, the author writes that he is merely the mouthpiece of his preceptor—'Le Docteur de Montfort'—who had recently settled in the town. Blockland is described as of noble birth, raised in the Catholic religion, and 'instructed at good and famous universities, and a graduate of a famous college'. A concern to please and impress the town councillors and to receive ecclesiastical approval suggests that Blockland may have been suspected and persecuted as a Protestant. The 1578 and 1582 almanachs include an

---

[112] F. Giuntini, *Speculum astrologiae universam mathematicam scientam* (Lyons, 1581).

portrait[113] of Montfort at the age of 38, followed with Greek and Latin eulogies by another doctor, Jean Willemin, and by the school rector Claude Morel. Two more prefatory poems in Latin and French in another almanach for 1582 signed by Morel himself[114] lament the memory of Montfort, 'brilliant in the ethereal arts, as in the salutary art of Apollo and famous as a doctor in Burgundy', while an address to the reader mentions 'the one who hides under the mantle of Billy'. Whether or not Morel was trying here to protect Blockland by pretending that he was dead, he certainly wrote more verses for similar almanachs attributed to Billy in 1585, 1586, and 1587. Blockland's signing the third edition of his *Instruction* at Lons-le-Saunier suggests that he was still alive and active in a neighbouring town in August 1586.

(xxviii) *Jean Servin and Paschal de L'Estocart*

In 1578 Charles Pesnot of Lyons published three books of chansons for four to eight voices by Jean Servin, who lived in Geneva between 1572 and 1597. The first was dedicated to Guy-Paul de Coligny, Count of Laval, the second to Henri de La Tour, Viscount of Turenne, and the third to 'Monsieur de la Place, gentilhomme françois', none of whom were known to have had any special connection with Lyons. In the following year Pesnot issued a collection of Servin's settings of Latin psalms, written over thirteen years earlier by the Scotsman, George Buchanan.[115] Servin also composed three-voice versions of the 1562 Psalter, using the Genevan texts and melodies, for a collection published at Orléans in 1565; but the only biographical data which has so far come to light[116] links him with Montargis and Geneva, and there is no concrete evidence that he ever resided in Lyons.

Paschal de L'Estocart's settings of the 1562 Psalter, of Antoine de Chandieu's *Octonaires*, and of Guy du Faur de Pibrac's *Quatrains*, as well as a collection of *Sacrae Cantiones*, were published in Lyons by Barthélemy Vincent in 1582–3, although they were actually printed in Geneva by Jean de Laon with the same typography as Servin's later collections. Archival documents recently uncovered by Laurent Guillo[117] indicate that a 'Pascal Estoquart' escaped being condemned to death after a long legal process instituted by the family of a port official

---

[113] The portrait is reproduced in F. Dobbins, 'Blockland', *Die Musik in Geschichte und Gegenwart*, xv, Tafel 29.

[114] *Diaire ou Journal pour l'an 1582* (Lyons, B. Rigaud, n.d.).

[115] G. Buchanan, *Psalmi* (Edinburgh, 1566).

[116] See Droz, 'Simon Goulart'.

[117] Guillo, 'Recherches', i. 115.

whom he was accused of having killed in 1560, and that a 'noble Pasquard de l'Estoquart, sieur de Tilly près de Saint Quentin en Picardie' married Claudine Bernardine Guigue in Lyons in February 1565. However, this person might not be the learned musician from Noyon who, according to the dedications and prefactory pieces in his musical publications, frequented a circle of Huguenot refugees, including Antoine de Chandieu, Jean de Sponde, Théodore de Bèze, Simon Goulart, and Robert de La Marck in Geneva and Basle, where he matriculated at the university in 1581 when he was 42 years old.[118] The dedicatory epistle prefacing his *Octonaires* suggests that L'Estocart had previously spent some time in Italy and had not been involved with music for many years. In April 1582 he was in Nancy, receiving payment for dedicating his settings of Pibrac's *Quatrains* to Duke Charles III of Lorraine, and in 1584 he was registered as a member of the Abbot of Valmont's chapel in Normandy when his motet 'Ecce quam bonum' won the silver harp prize at the St Cecilia's Day competition in Evreux.[119]

(xxix) *Jean de Maletty and Gilles Maillard*

While there is archival evidence showing that the Provençal composer Jean de Maletty rented a house in the rue de la Boucherie Saint-Pol in 1583,[120] his only surviving music—two books of four-voice settings of sonnets and chansons by Ronsard and Desportes (1578), a four-voice song in Provençal dialect (RISM 1583[8], no. 2) published in Paris, and seven Huguenot psalms for five and six voices (RISM 1597[6], nos. 1–7) printed in Heidelbeurg—appeared elsewhere.[121]

Antoine du Verdier, who lived in Lyons, asserted that Gilles Maillard, a native of Thérouanne in Picardy, composed a collection of four-, five-, and six-part chansons, entitled *La Musique*, printed by Jean de Tournes in 1581, and he lists a number of other works ready for publication, including several four-part settings of *Sonnets Spirituels* by Jacques de Billy, of *Chansons Spirituelles* by Pierre d'Epinac, Archbishop of Lyons, as well as several Latin pieces, including an introit, a Magnificat, a Benedictus, a *Te Deum*, some psalms for four voices, and some vespers

---

[118] Wackernagel, *Die Matrikel der Universität Basel*, ii. 301.

[119] E. Droz, 'Jean de Sponde et Paschal de l'Estocart', *Bibliothèque d'Humanisme et Renaissance*, 13 (1951), 312–26; see also J. Chailley and M. Honegger, Introduction to Monuments de la Musique Française au temps de la Renaissance, 11 (1958), i–xiii.

[120] F. Lesure, 'Jehan de Maletty à Lyon', *Revue de musicologie*, 35 (1953), 78–9.

[121] Lesure and Thibault, *Bibliographie des éditions d'A. le Roy & R. Ballard*, 150–1 and 218; F. Dobbins, 'Maletty, Jean', *New Grove Dictionary*, xi. 572.

for four, five and six voices.[122] He also confirmed that the musician was still resident in Lyons in 1584. Gilles may have been related to Jean Maillard, a prolific composer active in Paris in the preceding generation.[123]

(xxx) *Jean de Castro*

It is likely that Jean de Castro, a prolific composer from Liège, active in Antwerp in the early 1570s, visited Lyons between 1575, when he dedicated a book of three-voice chansons to 'Justinien Pense Lionnoy's, and 1580, when he addressed a second book of three-voice chansons, madrigals, and motets to 'councillor [François] de la Porte', lamenting recent events which had compelled him to leave the Low Countries. However, these collections were both published in Paris and reprinted in Antwerp.[124]

Castro's connections with Lyons date back to March 1571, when Jean Pollet of Lille copied three books of his four- and five-part chansons[125] for Justinien Pense, who was then representing his family's textile business in Antwerp.[126] The lavish vellum manuscript contains an extraordinarily confidential collection of settings of poems documenting the young music-lover's quarrel with his mother, Margarite Pournas, over Pense's association with Jane Orlandi.

After the customary platitudes about the Ancients' respect for music and the patron's singular love for 'theoretical, practical, and instrumental music', Castro's dedication to Pense expresses more intimate 'affection' than is usual. The first song, embracing four stanzas of six decasyllabic lines, is addressed by Pense to François Platel, another textile merchant from Lyons. The second, a sonnet expressing the author's nostalgia for Lyons and his beloved despite the pretty girls of Antwerp, was probably also written by Pense himself. The third, entitled 'Margarite Pournas à son filz', presents a sequence of twelve awkward six-line alexandrine strophes, expressing the mother's disappointment with her son's choice of fiancée and pleading with him to obey her wishes in abandoning any thought of marriage. The fourth,

---

[122] Du Verdier, *Bibliothèque*, 1225.

[123] F. Lesure, 'Maillard, Jean', *Die Musik in Geschichte und Gegenwart*, viii. 1519–22.

[124] Lesure and Reibault, *Bibliographie des éditions d'A. le Roy et R. Ballard*, nos. 184 and 238; revised editions were printed by Phalèse and Bellère in 1582.

[125] Superius and Bassus parts are in Paris, Bibliothèque nationale, MS f. 25536 and MS n. acq. fr. 1818. I am grateful to Dr Jeanice Brooks for locating the Superius part.

[126] See R. Gascon, 'Lyon, marché de l'industrie des Pays-Bas au XVIᵉ siècle et les activités commerciales de la maison Panse (1481–1580)', *Cahiers d'histoire* (Universities of Clermont, Lyon, and Grenoble), (1962), 492–536.

entitled 'Justinien Pense à sa mère', replies in similar form with much enjambment, regretting his behaviour and meekly agreeing his mother's demands to forget the fair 'Orlandine'. Margarite then concludes with another twelve stanzas declaring her satisfaction with her son's eventual compliance.

The second book begins with settings of three seven-line strophes written by Pense for his 'preceptor' Milles de Norry, mathematician, poet, and lutenist, who, after abjuring Protestantism, worked as a schoolmaster in Lyons between 1567 and 1574.[127] Norry (or Castro himself) may have written the two eight-line strophes beginning 'Bien sçay que tu n'as par d'or ny d'argent besoing, which explain Pense's interest in poetry, singing, and instrumental music rather than in amassing worldly wealth, and it is thus not surprising that the Antwerp branch of the family business soon failed. Pense himself wrote the three stanzas addressed to 'Jean Jacques de Ferraris' from Mantua, as well as 'Ce Dieu lascif', another multi-stanza piece thanking God for delivery from the devastating effects of lust, and perhaps the Italian sonnet 'Giamai nel mar', which includes his name.

The third book, containing five-part chansons, also abounds in personal texts by Pense for his friends and family, with *sextines* for his sisters Leonora and Marie, the latter's husband Palemon Cacherano, 'senator of Turin' and counsellor to the Duke of Savoy, and Balthazar Pecoul Lyonnois, and *Quintines* for his cousin César Pense and for Jacques Bornicard, another young textile-merchant from Lyons.

Although Pollet's manuscript was undoubtedly tailored to the personal requirements of a typical representative of the Lyonese *nouveaux riches* seeking nobility as a patron of music and letters, Castro's music, with its polyphonic style and through-composed form, remains firmly rooted in the northern tradition of Antwerp. Even the unusually extended multi-stanza structures and madrigalian figures (abounding especially in 'eye-music'), which reflect Italian models, can hardly be considered concessions to the poetry and music of Lyons, since by this time the fashion had reached the Low Countries.

(xxxi) *Michel Coyssard*

The Jesuit poet-musician Michel Coyssard (1547–1623) clearly spent a number of years teaching in the Jesuit colleges at Vienne and, from 1579, Lyons (formerly the Collège de la Trinité) before he died in the town on 10, June 1623. He was one of the first of the new Catholic

---

[127] J. Brooks, 'Jean de Castro and Music Patronage in Sixteenth-Century Lyon' (forthcoming).

educators to provide verse translations of popular hymns and canticles, no doubt influenced by the success of the Huguenot psalm-settings. The four-voice music for his *Paraphrases des hymnes et cantiques spirituelz*, published in Lyons by Jean Pillehotte (RISM 1592[7]), was probably written by an anonymous composer rather than by Coyssard himself. New settings included in later editions published in Antwerp and other towns were ascribed to Virgil le Blanc, but it is not clear whether Le Blanc composed the older ones as well.[128] A dedication in one edition published in Antwerp in 1600 explains that the music was composed at the request and expense of Louis d'Orléans, a Ligue supporter who fled to Antwerp in 1594.

It is thus unlikely that Coyssard himself wrote or arranged any of the music, which resembles the simple homophony of earlier Huguenot psalm-settings. In the preface to another edition of hymns published by Louis Muguet in Lyons in 1619, Coyssard explains that he originally wished to include, for the new canticles, music like 'that printed in Rome in 1573' (presumably a reference to the *laudi spirituali* composed by Giovanni Animuccia and others for the Oratory of Filippo Neri), but that after being unable to find suitable notes he had postponed publishing the music. He suggests that meanwhile 'people could use the tunes published earlier in this town and later in Antwerp, or they could adapt other serious and devout ones'.[129] Seven other editions of his hymns were printed in Paris by P. Ballard between 1623 and 1655.

A defence of Coyssard's popularizing, propagandist work is presented in the *Traicté du profit que toute personne tire de chanter en la doctrine chrestienne & ailleurs les hymnes & chansons spirituelles en vulgaire*, published in Lyons by Jean Pillehotte in 1608.

---

[128] For example, *Les hymnes sacrez et odes spirituelles, Airs composez par Virgil le Blanc sur quelques paraphrases des Hymnes de R. P. Michel Coyssard* (Antwerp, 1606); see Guillo, 'Recherches', i. 179–85.

[129] See Guillo, 'Recherches', i. 184.

6

The Music of Lyons

(i) *Motets*

THE fragmentary state of the manuscript recently discovered in the municipal library of Lyons (see above, p. 137) and the international repertoire of the other manuscripts that were arguably copied in the area invalidates detailed assessment of the polyphonic masses and motets that survive in those sources, even if some of their music might have been heard in the city during the first quarter of the sixteenth century. Despite the official proscription of polyphony in the cathedral it is certain that the visiting chapels of the Philippe le Beau, of Louis XII, Margaret of Austria, and Francis I furnished numerous opportunities for at least some of the citizens to hear the sacred music of Agricola, Brumel, Compère, Févin, Ghiselin, Josquin, Le Petit, Mouton, and others.

During the second quarter of the century the increased output resulting from the publishing activities of Gueynard, Du Ry, and Moderne following the arrival of Francesco de Layolle provides a clearer picture, particularly of the music associated with the Florentine community and their chapel in the Dominican church of Notre-Dame de Confort, where Layolle was organist. Caution must still be exercised when considering collections such as the motets of Layolle found in the British Library Tenor part-book, since many, if not all, of these pieces may have emanated from Florence, Rome, Venice, or other Italian states. The commercial opportunities caused by the hiatus in the activity of the printer Antico (*c.* 1522–36), the troubles of republican Florence (1527–30), and the uncertainty following the sack of Rome in 1527 were eagerly seized by the enterprising publishers of Lyons, who had the technical skills and, with Layolle's help, the access to musical material, as well as the distributional outlets provided by the fairs to satisfy a wide European market, stretching from Spain and Portugal to Germany and the Low Countries, Switzerland, and Italy.

The twelve motets contained in the British Library Tenor are:

1. O domine Jesu Christe
2. O clara virgo Christi
3. Passio tua domine, *2.p.* Venite sitientes

4. In illo tempore extollens vocem, *2.p.* Beatus venter qui te portavit
5. Jubilate deo omnis terra
6. Averte domine afflictionem servo tuo *2.p.* Ego dixi semper dominus
7. Confiteantur tibi populi omnes, *2.p.* Consumetur
8. O admirable comertium (a 5)
9. Celorum candor splenduit
10. O bone Jesu
11. Ave virgo sanctissima (a 5)
12. Stabat mater dolorosa (a 5), *2.p.* Eya mater, *3.p.* Virgo virginum

These incipits suffice to show that the collection is very similar in nature to the other anthologies of motets by Josquin, Mouton, Carpentras, Richafort, Willaert, and the Festa brothers printed by Petrucci or Antico in Venice a few years earlier (RISM 1519[1-3], 1520[2], 1521[4-5]), offering a variety of Marian antiphons, psalms, and other texts, with no clear liturgical sequence or function.

The musical style, more fully revealed in the last two five-voice pieces by Layolle, which survive in later sources,[1] is also typical of the post-Josquin era, with consistent imitative (fugal) or canonic writing prevailing. 'Ave virgo sanctissima' presents a series of short conventional chant-derived motives, similar to those of the 'L'homme armé' theme, in canon at the unison between the two tenor parts, preceding each with a series of imitative entries in the other voices, which are based on the same motives or which decorate them with melismatic counterpoint. The much longer 'Stabat mater' is divided into three separate sections, presenting an ostinato cantus firmus of five *longae* (*la sol fa re mi*) in the second tenor part, while the other voices weave imitative counterpoints above and below. Layolle's techniques, as well as his melodic motives, were thus already reminiscent of the masses and motets of Josquin and the previous generation.

The next surviving motets by Layolle appear at the end of the mass Propers[2] printed by Gueynard in 1528, and, like the three motets included at the end of the mass Ordinaries printed by Moderne in 1532, may have some connection with the preceding masses. At all events, the first two pieces—a centonized Marian antiphon, 'Salve Virgo salutaris', and a hymn 'Media vita in morte'—share with the preceding Proper settings the design of presenting a plainchant part (here the tenor) in equal notes, while the other three voices add derived imitative entries or independent counterpoints in varied rhythm. Both are set for four

---

[1] D'Accone (ed.), Music of the Florentine Renaissance, 5, nos. 6 and 36.
[2] Ibid., nos. 1, 19, and 30; see also Sutherland (ed.), *The Lyons Contrapunctus*, ii. 87–96.

low voices. The final 'Ave Maria' is arranged for three equal voices as a three-in-one canon at the unison.

The motets appended to the 1532 Ordinaries include 'Stephanus autem', which has the same mode, clefs, and melodic basis as the preceding 'Missa Stephane gloriose' by Pierre Moulu, 'Libera me de morte eterna', which has the same mode, clefs, and melodic ideas as Layolle's 'Missa Adieu mes amours' (although it is composed with an extra voice derived in canon from the Superius), and the Marian antiphon 'Beata dei genitrix', which shares the mode and clefs, if not the melodic motives, of Richafort's 'Missa Veni sponsa Christi'. David Crawford[3] suggests that the second motet, like the mass upon which it is modelled, may have been composed to commemorate the death of Louise of Savoy, whom Layolle could have met when she resided in Lyons as regent during her son's captivity between 1525 and 1526.

Layolle no doubt played a key role in the gathering and editing of the eight anthologies containing two hundred and thirty motets printed by Moderne between 1532 and 1542. While Attaingnant printed one motet collection in 1528 and another in 1529, he did not turn seriously to the genre until 1534–35, when he published no fewer than thirteen books, thus compensating for Moderne, who printed no motets between 1532 and 1538. Moderne himself was clearly filling a vacuum left by the Italian publishers, who issued no sacred music between 1527 and 1538. No German, Spanish, Swiss, or Netherlandish religious works were printed until after 1537; thus for some time Moderne's only rival outlets were the scriptoria of Alamire, Parvus, and other copyists.

Moderne's first book contains thirty-three motets for four voices by Courtois (2), Gombert (3), Layolle (3), L'Héritier (2), Lupus (4), Piéton (2), Richafort (4), De Silva, Sermisy, Verdelot, Willaert, and others. With Layolle as the sole Italian representative, the collection includes the leading contemporary Franco-Flemish composers, many of whom were actually living and working in Italy. While Layolle could have received his material through the mail, it is possible that some of his major contributors such as Arcadelt, Gombert, L'Héritier, Piéton, and Verdelot, whose exact whereabouts in the early 1530s is unknown, may have delivered their pieces in person. This first book is very much a reflection of its time and place, revealing a repertorial relationship with the manuscript and published collections associated with the Medici popes, Leo X (1513–21) and Clement VII (1523–34), with republican Florence (1527–30) or, to a lesser extent, with the courts of King

[3] D. Crawford, 'Reflections on Some Masses from the Press of Moderne', *Musical Quarterly*, 63 (1972), 82–91.

Francis I and the Emperor Charles V. The pieces are mostly new, although a few are found in older sources, including Lupus' setting of the psalm 'In convertendo' (copied in Bologna, Civico Museo Bibliografico Musicale, MSS Q 19 and Q 20), Richafort's 'Peccata mea' (copied in the Vatican MS Palatini Latini 1976–9) and 'Quem dicunt homines' (in Padua, Biblioteca Capitolare, MS A 17), L'Héritier's psalm 'Qui confidunt' (in Bologna MS Q 20 and Chicago, Newberry Library, Case MS Vm 1578. M91), Willaert's prayer 'Pater noster' (also in the Newberry MS, copied in Florence around 1528, as well as in the Vatican MSS 1976–9), and Verdelot's setting of the antiphon for his name-saint Philip, 'Tanto tempore' (printed in Rome around 1526). The contributions of De Silva, Penet, both of whom served Pope Leo X, and of Richafort could be older; indeed the latter's 'Quem dicunt homines', which was imitated in masses by Divitis, Lupus, and Mouton, may have been composed for the meeting of King Francis I and Pope Leo X at Bologna back in 1516.

A number of the texts were associated with marriage, notably 'Beati omnes' (Ps. 127), set twice, by Piéton and Lupus, and the two centonizations from the Song of Solomon, 'Unica est columba mea' and 'Veni in hortum meum'—both anonymous here, although the latter was attributed to Hesdin when reprinted by Attaingnant two years later.[4] Another motet, actually ascribed here to Hesdin, adds to the first six words of the familiar 'Ave Maria' prayer a rhymed trope ending with the words 'Nunc rosa juncta liliis Munda nos a filio Et tuo junge Filio'; this may refer to the wedding of Francis I and Charles V's sister Eleanor, arranged, along with the release of the hostage sons of Francis, by the Treaty of Madrid in 1530. The 'redeemed princes' were also mentioned in 'Letare et exaltare', an anonymous motet remarkable for its virtuosic melismas and word-painting.

Some of the other motets in Moderne's first book may also refer obliquely to the princes' Spanish captivity, through familiar psalm texts lamenting the Babylonian captivity, like Andreas de Silva's centonization 'Letare nova Sion',[5] expressing gratitude for freedom, Sermisy's 'Nisi quia dominus' (Ps. 123), mentioning 'escape from the broken snare', and Lupus' 'In convertendo' (Ps. 125), although the inclusion of the latter in a manuscript copied around 1518 would suggest selection based on general rather than particular relevance. The same may be true of Gombert's 'Super flumina Babilonis' (Ps. 136), whose question

---

[4] A. Smijers and A. T. Merritt (eds.), *Treize livres de motets parus chez Pierre Attaingnant en 1534 et 1535* (Monaco, 1934–63), 4, no. 25.

[5] Andreas de Silva, *Opera omnia*, ed. W. Kirsch (Corpus Mensurabilis Musicae, 49; American Institute of Musicology, 1970), i, no. 10.

'How shall we sing the Lord's song in a strange land?' might equally apply to his personal feelings about serving his master, Charles V, in Spain rather than his native Netherlands.[6]

L'Héritier's 'Qui confidunt in domino' (Ps. 124) may represent a plea for peace during the siege of Florence by Charles V's army in 1530. Connections with Florence, which might be expected from Layolle and his immigrant republican friends in Lyons, can be seen in the inclusion of two motets by Verdelot: one, 'Gabriel archangelus' (from Luke 1: 11–15) prophesies the birth of John the Baptist, patron saint of Florence and, incidentally, of the cathedral of Lyons. The same prophecy was expressed in 'Descendit angelus domini' (a centonization from Saint-Luke's gospel, 1: 13), set by Hilaire Penet, and in 'Inter natos mulierum' (from John 1: 6 and Matt. 11: 11), set by Layolle, who also included the penitential Psalm 50, 'Miserere mei', beloved of Savonarola. However, hints of republicanism that might be inferred from this setting contrast with the inclusion of works by composers in the service of the Medici popes. The prevailing spirit of the collection is one of reconciliation, symbolized by the Ladies' Peace arranged by the French queen mother, Louise of Savoy, and the Emperor's aunt, Margaret of Austria, in 1529, which led, the following year, to the release of the princes and Treaty of Madrid, sealed by the marriage of Francis I and Eleanor of Austria.

While the political or occasional character of some of this repertoire is obvious, much of it remains appropriate to liturgical or private devotional use. There is no evident liturgical planning, such as is found in Attaingnant's subsequent motet series. However, Moderne's collection begins with De Silva's Christmas responsory, 'O regem celi', loosely based on the Gregorian chant, and ends with Piéton's long 'O admirable commercium', setting the five antiphons for the office of the Circumcision with reference, like Josquin's setting, to the Ambrosian chant. The anonymous Easter responsory 'Virtute magna', (later ascribed by Attaingnant to Lasson) also strictly follows the liturgical text, as do the responsories for Corpus Christi (Lupus's 'Panis quem ego dabo', no. 18), Sts Peter and Paul (Richafort's 'Quem dicunt homines', no. 19), and Christmas (De Silva's 'O regem cell', no. 1): all are set with reprise in the aBcB form, as is the secular motet for the released princes. Domin's 'Virgo prudentissima' (no. 20) and Gombert's 'Aspice domine' (no. 26) are related to Magnificat antiphons, but changes in text and re-ordering might have made liturgical performance unlikely.

[6] C. Crozet's M.Mus. thesis, 'Moderne's *Motetti del Fiore*' (London, 1989) includes transcriptions of all the first book's motets not already available in modern edition.

The predilection for setting complete psalms in no less than eight motets (nos. 7, 8, 13, 14, 21, 24, 25, and 27) is characteristic of the age and may imply performance during private gatherings in Lyons and elsewhere.

A similar pattern is followed in Moderne's second book of motets for five voices (RISM 1532[9]; Pogue, nos. 6–7), with four pieces by Richafort, three each by Willaert, L'Héritier, and Gombert, two each by Courtois, Jacquet, and Verdelot, and one each by Lupus, La Fage, and Moulu. No less than thirteen of book's twenty-four pieces were copied around 1531 by Antonio Moro in a manuscript possibly owned by Roberto di Antonio Pucci, a Florentine diplomat working in Rome.[7] The Florentine connection is confirmed by the inclusion of 'Recordare domine' (no. 13), Verdelot's prayer for delivery from the plague, which, like Willaert's 'Ecce dominus veniet' (no. 8), and 'Si bona suscepimus' (no. 18), appeared in the Newberry manuscript copied in Florence a few years earlier. Lupus' 'In te domine speravi' (no. 14) and Richafort's 'Hierusalem luge' (no. 22) might also be connected with Savonarola and hence the Florentine republic. Pierre Moulu's 'Vulnerasti cor meum' (no. 17) may have been composed in 1518 for the wedding of Lorenzo de' Medici, Duke of Urbino and Madeleine de la Tour d'Auvergne.[8] But, like L'Héritier's 'Nigra sum' (no. 24), which also has a text from the Song of Solomon, and Gombert's 'Beati omnes' (no. 16), it could have been reselected as appropriate for a more recent wedding, perhaps that of Francis and Eleanor.

None of the pieces is clearly topical, and many may be associated with the liturgy. Curiously, there are no less than three settings of the same Marian antiphon, 'Alma redemptoris mater' (nos. 1, 11, and 20), by De Silva, Jacquet, and L'Héritier—all expatriates working in Italy, and all using the plainchant melody very obviously. There are three other Marian antiphons—Richafort's 'Salve regina' (no. 7), Willaert's 'Ave Maria ancilla' (no. 23), and L'Héritier's 'Nigra sum' (no. 24), four responsories (10, 13, 18, and 22), and five psalms (6, 9, 14, 16, and 21). While no less than seventeen of the twenty-four motets are in two separate sections and two (nos. 7 and 9) are in three, only one uses the aBcB responsory structure that occurred six times in the first book. Curiously, a decline in the use of aBcB structure between the first and

---

[7] See E. Lowinsky, 'A Newly Discovered Sixteenth-Century Motet Manuscript at the Biblioteca Vallicelliana in Rome', *Journal of the American Musicological Society*, 3 (1950), 173–232, reprinted in E. Lowinsky, *Music in the Culture of the Renaissance and Other Essays*, ed. B. J. Blackburn, 2 vols. (Chicago, 1989), ii. 433–82. For a summary of James Haar's thesis that the manuscript was owned by Pucci, see ibid. 482.

[8] See *The Medici codex of 1518*, ed. E. Lowinsky (Monuments of Renaissance Music, 3–5; Chicago, 1968), no. 44.

the second books corresponds to an increase in the number of two-
and three-section works. The modes and clefs are the common ones
and show no overall sequential planning. Two motets, Willaert's 'Ecce
dominus' and Verdelot's 'Recordare', are canonic (the former being
unusual in introducing the *comes* in the Superius at the interval of a
seventh above the *dux* in the Quintus). Two others, Moulu's 'Vulnerasti
cor meum' and Willaert's 'Ave Maria ancilla', employ a cantus firmus in
long notes with a different text. One motet, Richafort's 'Misereatur mei'
(no. 19), exploits an ostinato figure, but the remaining pieces all use
through imitation.

Moderne's second book of motets for four voices, also published in
1532, is similar in content, containing several psalms (nos. 7, 14, 16, 21,
23, and 25) and antiphons (nos. 9, 10, 20, and 22 addressed to the
Virgin, nos. 5 and 18 to St Cecilia). It includes many responsories (nos.
2–6, 12–13, and 17) as well as a psalm (no. 7; L'Héritier's 'In te Domine
speravi', ascribed here to Verdelot) with the reprise structure aBcB,
generally associated with the responsory. Three motets (nos. 1, 3, and
8) are related to the burial service and may have been written for some
recent funeral, perhaps that of the French queen mother, Louise of
Savoy. The psalm 'Beati omnes' (no. 14), set by Benedictus, could have
been composed for the wedding of Francis and Eleanor, like the two
settings of 'Quam pulchra es', a centonization from the Song of
Solomon, by Johannes Lupi (no. 8) and Nicolas Gombert (no. 20), or
'Filiae Jherusalem' (no. 24) by Arcadelt. Two motets by Gombert (nos.
12 and 17), partly using the same text, relate to the feast of St John the
Baptist, celebrated with pomp in both Florence and Lyons. Layolle's
settings of the penitential psalms beloved of Savonarola (nos. 8 and 25)
may also indicate a Florentine, and perhaps specifically republican,
connection. But, again, none of the motets is obviously political or
topical.

Unlike the second book for five voices, this four-voice collection
contains few pieces that had appeared in earlier sources. It is clearly
more modern and includes the first published works of Arcadelt,
Manchicourt, Dambert, and Paignier, as well as the first attributed work
of Benedictus (Appenzeller) and Gosse. All the motets employ through
imitation and the common modes, although Manchicourt's 'Peccantem
me' is exceptional with its homophonic opening.

Moderne does not appear to have printed any further motet
anthologies during the next six years. However, recent research by
Laurent Guillo[9] has uncovered Moderne's undated edition of Piéton's

[9] Guillo, 'Les Motets de Layolle; the psalms are transcribed in Clark, 'The Penitential Psalms of Loyset Piéton'.

seven penitential psalms, whose typography and singular format (four octavo oblong part-books) would seem to indicate an early date. This is confirmed by its purchase at Lyons in 1535 recorded in the Columbus catalogue. The distribution of Piéton's works in Florentine or Roman manuscripts of the early 1530s and in Moderne's first motet-books suggests that the composer may have visited Lyons, probably at the instigation of Layolle, for the printing of his music.

The publication in Lyons of so many penitential psalms (including several in Moderne's motet anthologies and three sets recorded in the Columbus catalogue) may indicate a response to local requirements, perhaps at the Florentine church of Notre-Dame de Confort, or even more specifically an expression of Savonarolan or republican ideas amongst the émigré Florentine community centred around the Strozzi, Alamanni, and their friends. Piéton's settings of the lesser doxology, his use of the psalm-tones, and his addition of the final antiphon 'Ne reminiscaris Domine' implies the possibility of liturgical use, although their length would seem to make this impractical.

Piéton's four-voice music is generally similar in style to that of the leading Franco-Flemish contemporaries, paraphrasing the psalm-tones and mostly proceeding with through-imitation; 'Miserere mei' (Ps. 50) is exceptional in repeating an ostinato phrase fourteen times in the Superius, perhaps as a homage to Josquin's five-voice setting, whose Tenor has another inverted ostinato phrase beginning on successive descending degrees.

Moderne resumed publishing motet anthologies in 1538, with his third book for five and six voices. More than any of its predecessors this collection was a reflection of the political events of its time. At the instigation of Queen Eleanor and Pope Paul III, a peace conference to end military hostilities between Francis I and Charles V was arranged at Nice in 1538. Although the negotiations, carried out indirectly through the mediation of the Pope, were abandoned after three weeks on 20 June, the protagonists met on 14 July at Aigues-Mortes, a port in the Camargue, agreeing a truce and a territorial division of Savoy and Piedmont. The three magnates were accompanied by some of their musicians, whose testimony was represented shortly afterwards in the new publications of Lyons.

Thus Moderne's third book opens with Johannes Lupi's 'Vidi speciosam sicut columbam',[10] whose text, based on the Song of Solomon (5: 12, 2: 1), although known liturgically as two separate

---

[10] This and the seven other motets by Lupi printed in Moderne's motet collections of 1538–9 are included in Johannes Lupi, *Opera Omnia* II, ed. B. J. Blackburn (Corpus Mensurabilis Musicae, 84; American Institute of Musicology, 1980–6), i. nos. 5, 7, 12, 13; ii, nos. 4, 8, 12, 15.

antiphons, includes references to the dove and the joining of roses and lilies, appropriate to the hopes for peace between the Habsburgs and Valois, already symbolized in the marriage of Eleanor and Francis. Eleanor's yearning for peace between her husband and brother is even more clearly expressed in the words 'Propter frates meos et proximos meos loquebar pacem de te' (For my brothers' and companions' sakes I will now say 'Peace be within thee') from the second part of the second motet, 'Rogate que ad pacem' (Ps. 121: 6–9)—also known as a gradual and verse in masses to pray for peace. It was set here by Johannes Courtois, who, like Lupi, was associated with Cambrai. Lupi's 'Gregem tuum, pastor eterne' (no. 4), with a text based on the Collect for St Clement and other popes, including the new words 'Tu pacis es pincerna, fac nos tecum pace frui' (You are the cupbearer of peace, Let us enjoy peace with you), and 'Pontificum sublime decus' (no. 14) may have been addressed to the mediating Pope Paul. Lupi's 'Gaude proles speciosa' (no. 11) includes the refrain 'Salva nos et conserva a procella sempiterna' (Save and protect us from the eternal tempest), which may also be an expression of hopes for an end to the conflict rather than a landlubber's plea for safety on the galley of Charles V. Two of the three motets by Layolle himself, 'Congregate sunt gentes' (no. 15) and the final 'Da pacem domine in diebus nostris' (no. 26), use the same Gregorian cantus firmus, expressing the wish for 'peace in our time'.

Not all the pieces in this book were new. A few—such as Gombert's 'O beata Maria', Willaert's 'Regina celi letare', Verdelot's 'In te domine speravi' and 'Sancta Maria virgo virginum', Arcadelt's 'Congregati sunt', and Eckel's 'Cantabo domino'—had appeared in earlier sources; so had Costanzo Festa's 'Hierusalem luge', although with a different text, the present one perhaps relating to Pope Paul's desire for Francis and Charles to unite in a crusade against the Turks. Benedictus (Appenzeller) probably composed his low-voiced lament for Erasmus[11] shortly after the latter's death in July 1536.

While this third book was still dominated by the same established composers from Cambrai, Florence, Rome, and Venice, two Germans— Leonhard Paminger and Matthias Eckel—make their appearance, along with Guillaume le Heurteur, whose second motet 'O sanctum virum', although akin to the Magnificat antiphon for Vespers on the feast of St Martin, Bishop and Confessor, may have particular reference to Martin Fournier, the young Archbishop of Tours, where in 1545 the composer was choirmaster at St Martin's Cathedral. The music of the third book is broadly similar to that in Moderne's second book for five voices of

[11] See A. Dunning, 'Een tombeau musical voor Erasmus', *Mens en melodie*, 34 (1969), 368–70.

1532, with six pieces using a cantus firmus, two of them in canon, and the other eighteen imitation. Seventeen pieces are divided into two *partes*, with four (nos. 5, 11, 14, and 21) showing the responsory or refrain structure aBcB. Thirteen are set in the transposed Dorian mode, four in transposed Ionian, three in Dorian, two in Aeolian, one in Mixolydian, and one in Phrygian.

Moderne's third book of motets for four voices (1539) offers fewer occasional pieces and more that are liturgically appropriate. Thus it includes many short motets—thirty-seven in all, only half of which were divided into two *partes*, as opposed to the twenty-four with fifteen in two *partes* in the second book for four voices. Layolle sets the tone with his short opening prayers 'Pater noster' (62 breves) and 'Ave Maria' (40 breves), while one piece, Foucher's 'Egredientem de templo' is strictly liturgical, setting only the alternating sections of the Easter antiphon 'Vidi aquam.' There are significantly fewer psalms (Jaquet's 'Levavi oculos meos' being the only example) but more antiphons, including no less than four for St Cecilia's day (Manchicourt's and Carette's 'Cantantibus organis', Hugier's and Carette's 'Cecilia virgo'), as well as the usual high number (six) of Marian pieces. The increase in the proportion of motets in responsory aBcB form (ten examples) is also notable. The only clearly political motet is 'Felix es Regno Francisce', an encomium addressed to Francis I set by Benedictus (Appenzeller), who was at this time working within the Imperial orbit in Brussels, as choirmaster to Mary of Hungary, regent of the Netherlands.

> Foelix es Regno Francisce et Francia foelix
>   Et te res foelix publica rege suo.
> Imperium nobis vexillum lilia olivum
>   Nomine quod summus dicere christicola
> Atque caput nunquam dubitasti offerre periclis
>   sunt que foelicem te monimenta probant.
> [*2.p.*] Rex Francisce tuus Franciscus te cupit esse
>   foelicem adventu consiliisque tuis
> O fortunatos tua quos presentia tante
>   Sortis participes efficit esse tue.
> Optamus memores Europa, Asia, Africa totus
>   Crbis Francisci pareat Imperiis.

> Fortunate are you, Francis, in your kingdom, and France is fortunate
>   and the nation is fortunate in you its king.
> [Having] power to command us, [bearing our] banner [of] lilies, anointed,
>   because you are called by the title Most Christian
> and you have never hesitated to expose your life to danger.
>   There are testimonies that prove your good fortune.

King Francis, your Francis [Frenchman] wishes you to be
   fortunate in your arrival and in your counsels.
O happy those whom your presence gives
   a share in your great good fortune.
Remembering this, we wish that Europe, Asia, Africa, the whole
   world may obey the rule of Francis.

Certain other liturgically related motets, such as Villiers's 'Benedicat nos
Imperialis maiestas' and 'Ecce vere Israelita',[12] F. de Lys's 'Vir inclitus
Vincentius', and Foucher's 'In dedicatione templi', may have alternative
occasional significance.

   This book takes only just over half its pieces from the usual
established composers (four from Layolle, three from Piéton, three
from Jacquet— one of them unattributed—two from Gombert, two from
L'Héritier, two from Conseil, and one each from Arcadelt, Benedictus,
Lupus, Manchicourt, and Willaert). Few of these pieces are known in
earlier sources. Several of the new composers, such as Carette, C. Dalbi,
N. Foucher, H. Fresneau, Hugier, F. de Lys, and P. de Villiers, may be
local figures; but others, for example Hotinet Bara, Jo. du Billon, and
Mornable, are known to have been associated with other places. Two
motets ('O sacrum convivium' and 'Videte oculis vestris') are
unascribed, although the first of these was attributed to Jacquet of Mantua
in a publication of Girolamo Scotto at Venice in the same year.[13]

   The older, established composers continue to dominate in Moderne's
fourth book of motets for five and six voices (1539), which was perhaps
the last edited by Layolle, who included four motets of his own.
Gombert contributed six pieces, Jacquet, L'Héritier, and Manchicourt
two each, Arcadelt and Lupi one each. With the possible exception of
Foucher, Gosse, and Du Moulin (was this the 'Du Mollin' mentioned in
Rabelais's *Quart Livre*?), the newcomers all seem to have been French
or Flemish composers working in Italy, such as Billon, Buus, Gardane,
and Maître Jhan. Two of the motets reappear in Moderne's fifth book
with different ascription, the anonymous 'Inviolata integra et casta es
Maria' (no. 19) being later attributed to Garsius, and Gombert's 'In illo
tempore dixit Iesus' (no. 22) to Jacquet: this uncertainty may indicate a
change of editor. At least four pieces (nos. 5, 12, 18, and 23) survive in
older sources, while several others may also be of earlier origin. All the
texts appear to be liturgical, mostly antiphons, and several use passages
from the psalms. Half are divided into two separate sections, but only
two use the responsory structure aBcB. As with Moderne's earlier motet

[12] Transcribed in Pogue, *Jacques Moderne*, 382–7.
[13] *Jacheti musici . . . motecta quinque vocum* (Venice, 1539); *Opera omnia*, P. Jackson and G.
Nugent (Corpus Mensurabilis Musicae, 54; American Institute of Musicology), 4 (1982), no. 23.

collections, there seems to be no particular ordering of pieces by feast, mode, or clef. Again, the pieces are nearly all imitative in texture, although Layolle's are inclined to be less consistently so and use more homophonic passages. L'Héritier's 'Ave verum corpus' has one part in canon, while Arcadelt's 'O pulcherrima mulierum' has a cantus firmus in its second tenor.

Although published in the same year, Moderne's fourth book for four voices includes no motets by Layolle and, like the third book for four voices, is generally more modern in content, with a significantly higher proportion of homophony, especially in the pieces by Coste, Du Boys, and Morel. This may indicate that Layolle was no longer acting as editor. If elsewhere through-imitation still predominates, no pieces use canon or cantus firmus. Half of the thirty pieces are divided into two *partes*, but only four show the aBcB responsory structure. The older generation is thinly represented with single motets by Lupus, Lupi, Benedictus, and Sermisy, while there are three pieces by the Spaniards, Morales and Narváez, who accompanied Charles V to the peace conferences at Nice and Aigues-Mortes in 1538.

Three motets were ascribed to Ernoul Caussin, choirmaster at the new church of the Madonna della Steccata in Parma, although one of these, 'Adversum me susurrabant', was reprinted two years later in Venice by Girolamo Scotto with attribution to Gombert;[14] the other two were both secular motets addressed to individuals, 'Gaude foelixque Papia' and the final 'Nomine si vastus', an encomium on the military prowess of Alfonso d' Avalos, Marchese del Vasto (1502–46),[15] who was sent by Charles V and Francis I to dissuade Venice from making separate peace with the Turks in 1538 and who was leader of the army which relieved the Turkish siege of Nice in 1542. Two motets were ascribed to 'Robert Naich'; presumably this was Hubert Naich from Liège, who dedicated a collection of madrigals entitled *Exercitium seraficum*, published by Antonio Blado in Rome around 1540, to Bindo Altoviti; another member of the same Florentine patrician family had received the dedication of the Lyons *Contrapunctus* in 1528. The first of these motets, the antiphon 'Ave regina caelorum', is unusual in being set with a signature of two flats, indicating a twice-transposed Dorian mode (C minor). The second motet, the Cecilian antiphon 'Cantantibus

---

[14] *Nicolai Gomberti Musici imperatorii motectorum . . . liber secundus* (Venice, 1541): *Opera omnia*, ed. J. Schmidt-Görg (Corpus Mensurabilis Musicae, 6; American Institute of Musicology), 6 (1964), 36–44.

[15] Avalos, the author of the verse for some famous madrigals, including Arcadelt's 'Il bianco e dolce cigno' and Rore's 'Ancor che col partire', also received the dedication of Gombert's first book of motets printed by Scotto in Venice in 1539.

organis', was later attributed to Gombert, in an anthology published by Susato in Antwerp.[16] Uncertainty of attribution is also seen in the antiphon 'Rex autem David', ascribed here to Lupus, but earlier to Gascongne (RISM 1521[5] and 1535[3]) and La Fage (1521[6]).

Some of the names in the fourth book—Jacob Hanenze, Jehan du Boys, Mortera, and Jo. Preian—were unique to this collection, while Laurens Lalleman and Hugo de la Chapelle appear only in this and in Moderne's next book of motets. Others, such as N. Benoist, G. Coste, and P. de La Farge, appear in several publications in Lyons but none elsewhere, which suggests that they may be of local origin. One motet was ascribed to Morel—presumably Clément Morel, later choirmaster at the cathedral in Nevers and no less than four to the Autun choirmaster, Pierre Colin, who was to become a leading contributor to Moderne's later publications.

Apart from the two secular motets by Caussin, all the pieces in the fourth book appear to be liturgically based; as usual, there is a preponderance of antiphons, with a number of psalms (nos. 6, 7, 13, 17, 20, 22, 26, and 27) and responsories (1, 5, 8, 10, 11, 12, 15, 20, and 21).

The fifth book of motets for five and six voices, which appeared in 1542, after Layolle's death, contains a similar selection of mainly liturgical pieces. The older generation is sparsely represented, with one motet ('Audi filia et vide') attributed to Gombert, one to Benedictus, and three ('Repleatur os meum', 'Murus tuo', and 'In illo tempore dixit Iesus') to Jacquet, all three having already been printed by Gardane in Venice with more specific ascriptions to Jachet Berchem. The first of these motets by Jacquet had already appeared in Moderne's fourth book, with attribution to Gombert. Another piece, the sequence 'Inviolata integra et casta', attributed here to Ge. Garsius or Jarsius, had also been published in Moderne's fourth book, as anonymous. 'Peto domine', one of two pieces ascribed here to Ernoul Caussin, had even been included in the motets by Gombert published the previous year in Venice by Scotto. Such unreliable attribution in Moderne's last motet anthologies would seem to provide further evidence of a change of editor. The new editor might have been P. de Villiers, who provided the last two motets and who had contributed a new mass to the 1540 edition of the *Liber decem Missarum*, as well as numerous chansons in the *Parangon* series published by Moderne between 1538 and 1543. The concluding six-voice motet 'Sancte Stephane', by Villiers, the only clearly non-liturgical piece in the collection, is associated with Augsburg.[17]

Morales's six-voice 'Jubilate deo' must have been salvaged from the

---

[16] RISM 1555[11], fo. 5[v]; ed. in Gombert, *Opera omnia*, 10, 50–7.
[17] The first part is transcribed in Pogue, *Jacques Moderne*, 393–401.

1538 peace conference, as is clear from the text, expanding upon the opening line of Psalm 99:

Jubilate deo omnis terra
cantate omnes jubilate et psallite.
Quoniam suadente Paulo
Charolus et Franciscus, principes terrae
convenerunt in unum
et pax de caelo descendit.
    O foelix etas O foelix Paule
O vos foelices principes
qui Christiano populo
pacem tradidistis.
Vivat Paulus, vivat Charolus, vivat Franciscus:
vivant simul et pacem nobis donent in eternum.

Cry with joy unto God, all the earth,
sing ye all, cry with joy, and make melody.
For at Paul's urging
Charles and Francis, the princes of the earth,
have met together,
and peace hath come down from heaven.
    O happy age, O happy Paul,
O ye happy princes,
who to a Christian people
have delivered peace.
Long live Paul, long live Charles, long live Francis,
may they live and also give us peace for ever.

As in the previous book, Moderne includes here a second motet by Morales ('Spem in alium') and one by Narváez ('O salutaris hostia'); these might have been acquired from the Spaniards at Nice or Aigues-Mortes.

Pierre Colin, who was introduced in the last two books, received the honour of having a whole book, containing eight masses, eight motets, and eight Magnificats, published by Moderne in 1542—an honour which in Lyons had only been previously accorded to Piéton's penitential psalms, Layolle's *Canzoni*, and Janequin's chansons, and which was to be repeated only in the cases of Morales's masses and Magnificats and Rampollini's *Canzoni*. Most of Colin's motets[18] are antiphons or reponsories for various feasts. One, 'O Leodegar', sets the text of a Benedictus antiphon for the feast of St Leodegarius, who had been bishop of Autun in the seventh century. This suggests that Colin was already associated with Autun, where, according to the title-page and preface of a collection of French psalms printed in Paris by N. du

---

[18] See Lengefeld, 'The Motets of Pierre Colin'.

Chemin[19] in 1550, he was choirmaster in the cathedral church dedicated to St Lazarus. The fact that Colin also set Marot's translations of the seven penitential psalms[20] may echo the vogue for penitential psalms in Lyons, seen earlier in the Latin settings of Piéton and Layolle.

Moderne's next motet publication was another mixed collection of three masses, four motets, and two Magnificats, entitled *Harmonidos Ariston tricolon ogdoameron in quo habentur Liturgiae vel Missae tres celeribus ac volubilis numeris*, (RISM 1547[2]; repr. 1548[1]) this time by vaious composers. While Colin contributed two of the three masses and both the Magnificats, the motets were composed by Clemens non Papa, Philibert Jambe de Fer, and P. de La Farge, who had made his début in Moderne's fourth book for four voices in 1539. The four-voice motet, the Lenten responsory 'Pater peccavi' set by the famous Clemens non Papa, begins in a unusually homophonic manner, but the five- and six-voice motets by P. de la Farge, both liturgical pieces, are set in a conventional imitative manner. The most curious motet is Jambe de Fer's 'Salve salutaris victima', which ends with the lines 'Regem nostrum H. Tu conserva, salve defende guberna Amen' intoned in alternating melismatic counterpoint and sustained chords (see Music Example 4):

Salve salutaris victima
Salve oblata pro nobis in cruce hostia.
Fortitudo fragilium
Tu nobis fer auxilium
O bone Jesu dulcissime,
O Jesu clementissime.
Regem nostrum H[enricum]
Tu conserva salva defende guberna. Amen.

Hail the saving victim
Hail the sacrifice suffered for us on the cross.
The strength of the weak
Bring thou help to us
O good, sweetest Jesus
O most merciful Jesus
Our King H[enry]
Keep, save, defend, and govern. Amen.

These lines suggest that the piece might be a coronation anthem composed for the new king, Henry II, who succeeded Francis I after the

---

[19] P. Colin, *Les Cinquante Pseaulmes de David traduictz par Clement Marot . . . mis en musique par M. Pierre Colin, Maistre des enfans de l'Église d'Autun, à quatre parties en quatre volumes en chant non vulgaire: mais plus convenables aux instruments que les aultres par cy devant imprimez* (Paris, 1550).

[20] Also published in Paris by Du Chemin, with a dedication to Philippe de Marcilly indicating that Colin was still living in Autun.

latter's death on 31 March 1547. Henry's arrival at Lyons in September 1548 was greeted with great musical pomp and ceremony, although Jambe de Fer was not registered as a musical organizer, as he was for the entry of Charles IX in 1564. If Jambe de Fer's king 'H' was indeed Henri de Valois—and not Henry Tudor (who died on 28 January 1547)—the date of 1546, cited by Robert Eitner for the copy once in the Königsberg (now Kaliningrad) State Library and followed by Pogue, must be erroneous.[21]

Few motets were published by Moderne's successors. The Beringen brothers printed two collections by Dominique Phinot, who was employed in the service of the Duke of Urbino between 1545 and 1555, and one by Simon Joly, containing four- and five-voice settings of twenty-one Latin paraphrases of Psalm 50, dedicated to François de Tournon, who made his ceremonial entry into Lyons as Archbishop in September 1552.

Phinot's first book (1547) contains thirty motets for five voices, although nos. 24 and 25 were presented as two *partes* of the same piece when the whole collection was reprinted at Venice by Antoine Gardane in 1552, after Beringen's five-year royal privilege had expired. Neither edition shows any textual or liturgical arrangement, although Gardane regroups the pieces in a more consistently modal order. Most of the texts are antiphons, sung at Magnificat or Benediction (six taken from the Gospel according to St John); there are also several responsories, two complete psalms, and a few biblical fragments without any known liturgical significance. Although similar to that found in Moderne's motet-books, the selection probably reveals more about the requirements of the chapel in Urbino or the predilections of the Genoan merchant dedicatee, Lucca de Grimaldo, than the liturgical practice of any church in Lyons.

Phinot's style is consistently imitative, with smooth melody and harmony, exploiting a restricted expressive range, similar to that of Willaert and most of his Franco-Flemish contemporaries. One motet, 'Te gloriosus apostolorum chorus' (no. 10), has an ostinato phrase in the fifth voice, 'Omnes sancti orate pro nobis', repeated four times. Only one other motet, 'Regina coeli' (no. 11), is closely based on the traditional plainchant melody (presented in long notes in the second tenor), as are the five settings of this text by Willaert, Piéton, De la Farge, Fouchier, and Villiers published by Moderne. Two responsories—'Tua est potentia' (no. 6) and 'Auribus percipe Domine'

[21] R. Eitner, *Bibliographie der Musik-Sammelwerke* (Berlin, 1899), 96; Pogue, *Jacques Moderne*, 194.

(no. 20)—use the reprise form aBcB, while two antiphons, 'O quam gloriosam' (no. 14) and 'Gabriel angelus' (no. 16) have the final section repeated, as in contemporary chansons.

Phinot's second book (1548) includes ten motets for six voices, two for seven, and five for eight voices, divided into two matching four-voice choirs. Again there seems to be no liturgical or musical ordering; the set begins with a complete psalm (divided into two sections) and closes with the first eight verses of the fifth chapter of the Lamentations of Jeremiah (in four sections). Again there are several texts from St John's gospel, as well as two from the Song of Songs, and a few medieval ones. Three texts (nos. 2, 4, and 6) are known to have been used as responsories, the first and last of these following the reprise structure aBcB. Others are known as antiphons (no. 9, 'Stella ista', at Vespers for Epiphany Sunday, no. 13, 'O sacrum convivium', at Magnificat for Corpus Christi, and no. 14, 'Tanto tempore', at Vespers and Lauds for the Feast of SS Philip and James). No. 8, 'Exaudi Domine', a centonization of psalms 60 and 70, has a canonic fifth voice; but all the other six- and seven-part pieces are conventionally imitative. Most remarkable are the last five antiphonal pieces, with their magnificent homophonic writing, offering early examples of a genre which was to flourish in Willaert's Venice and elsewhere in northern Italy, but which could hardly have been practical for the limited resources of Lyons.

The last Latin motets to appear in Lyons were those of Barthélemy Beaulaigue,[22] purportedly a fifteen-year old choirboy at the cathedral of Marseilles, printed by Robert Granjon in 1559. The collection includes five motets for five voices, two for six, one for seven, and two for eight, all imitative in texture, although three (nos. 3, 7, and 11) incorporate a Gregorian cantus firmus in the tenor part, while the last, the second five-voice setting of 'Vidi turbam magnum', has a canon by inversion between the two upper voices. Like earlier collections of motets published in Lyons, there is no clear liturgical, modal, or vocal ordering. The long first piece, 'Surgite omnes gentes', is inscribed to the Cardinal of Lorraine, Charles de Guise, 'passing through Marseilles en route for Rome' (where he was to become the patron of Arcadelt, who dedicated to him a collection of three masses printed in Paris in 1557). The third motet, 'Aperi oculos meos', incorporates the Gregorian antiphon for peace, *Da pacem Domine in diebus nostris*, presented four times in the tenor beginning on a' or d'. 'Hodie Maria Virgo' (no. 11) is similar, presenting the seven-note *Ave Maria* phrase five times in

[22] Edited in A. Auda, *Barthélemy Beaulaigue, poète et musicien prodige* (Brussels, 1958), 97–239.

the second tenor of this seven-voice piece. 'Salvatore omnium subacta morte' (no. 8) is addressed to St Victor, and 'Videns Dominus flentes sorores Lazari' (no. 13) to St Lazarus, who were both patron saints of Marseilles. Unlike those of Phinot, Beaulaigue's eight-part motets are not antiphonal, although composed for four pairs of voices using the same clefs. The collection closes with a French *épigramme* dedicated to Diane de Poitiers, Duchess of Valentinois, mistress of the French King Henry II. Like Colin's, this publication seems to represent a repertoire associated with another provincial town.

(ii) *Masses*

While it is difficult to link the repertoire of manuscripts Copenhagen 1848 and Uppsala 76a directly to local practice, a better case can be made for the fragments in Lyons, Bibliothèque de la Ville, MS 6632, which include three anonymous four-voice masses composed in a non-imitative late fifteenth-century style, the third having a cantus firmus in the Tenor. The Lyons fragments begin with the two lower voices of a three-part Introit 'Puer natus est nobis'. Then, after a two-voice version of 'Lugentibus in purgatorio' (with a third voice added in a later hand) and some textless pieces, there are five plainsong invitatories with their antiphons, in different tones, for Easter, St Stephen's Day, and Christmas. Such obviously liturgical pieces might be related to local observance, although no direct evidence of this has yet be offered.

The first polyphonic publication which can clearly be associated with local practice, if not exclusively intended for it, was the *Contrapunctus* collection of mass Propers, published in large choir-book format by Gueynard in 1528. The book contains a cycle of thirteen masses taken from the Temporale and Sanctorale, celebrating the most important feasts from Christmas and to All Saints, beginning with the processional antiphon *Asperges me*, sung throughout the year, and ending with the Easter antiphon *Vidi aquam*. Most of the masses include polyphonic settings for the Introit, Responsory verse (the Gradual was called 'Responsorium' in Dominican usage), Alleluia, and its verse, Offertory, and Communion, alternating with plainchant found in the Gradual. Each movement begins with plainchant printed in square, non-mensural, black notation, usually in the tenor, occasionally in the bass, and marked CHORUS when it is not accompanied by the three polyphonic voices. At the end of the surviving copies are some pages with blank staves, which may have been intended for manuscript additions in accordance with local practice. The copy now in the

Biblioteca Nazionale in Florence includes here a four-voice setting of Gaudeamus omnes', the Introit for the feast of the Assumption, signed in the hand of the owner of the book, Joannes Baptista de Landini, canon and cantor of Monteloro near Florence.[23]

Although the printer's dedicatory epistle suggests that the music was 'selected from first-rate masters' old and new, the recurrent elements and stylistic consistency of contrapuntal writing and cadential patterns suggest a single composer, the most likely candidate being Francesco de Layolle, whose name actually appears above the three motets appended at the end of the book. David Sutherland[24] suggests that the *Contrapunctus* may reflect Layolle's teaching programme for establishing a new polyphonic chapel in Notre-Dame de Confort, and he interprets remarks in the book's second dedication about progressing to works where the 'greatest musicians can offer their own models and imitations' as implying the intention to publish 'parody' or 'imitation' masses based on polyphonic models. He also wonders whether the anonymity of the *Contrapunctus* reflects its modest nature as a mere contrapuntal gloss, whose authorship a composer might not consider worthy of credit, and which might indeed be related to an improvisatory tradition described by Tinctoris and later theorists and reflected in several early sixteenth-century manuscript sources, including one from Florence containing Propers by Francesco Corteccia[25] set in the *contrappunto alla mente* or *falsobordone* manner. He further considers the *Contrapunctus* as occupying a stylistic position between the free polyphonic elaboration of Heinrich Isaac's *Choralis constantinus* of c.1510 and Corteccia's non-imitative and possibly improvisatory settings of c.1540.

The continuous motion of the plainchant cantus firmus, notated mostly as even semibreves in black non-mensural notation, obviously limits the accompanying polyphony: imitative entries, often based on newly composed motives, are freely used, while dovetailed syncopated cadences are devised to assist flow or to underline structural articulation. But despite their lack of scholarly techniques or expressive underscoring, the settings are distinguished by their melodic skill and harmonic variety.

Whatever Layolle's exact role in the *Contrapunctus*, he was crucially involved in the book of mass Ordinaries printed in similar large choirbook format by Moderne in 1532. The printer's dedication to Charles

---

[23] This Introit and the printed music are included in Sutherland, *The Lyons Contrapunctus*.
[24] Ibid. i, pp. xii–xiii.
[25] D. Sutherland, 'A Second Corteccia Manuscript in the Archives of Santa Maria del Fiore, Florence', *Journal of the American Musicological Society*, 25 (1972), 79–85.

d'Estaing not only applauds the canon's zealous support for harmonized music in church ceremonies in the face of the traditionalist opposition, but singles out for special mention 'the conspicuous correction[s] of the distinguished musician Francesco de Layolle' (et demum oculatam D. Francisci de Layolle insignis Musici castigationem).[26] Considering this acknowledgement together with his prominent role as a contributor, it seems likely that the Florentine composer also played a leading role in the collecting and editing of all Moderne's sacred music publication until 1540.

The *Liber decem missarum* opens with Pierre Moulu's 'Missa Stephane gloriose', an old mass which had already appeared in manuscript sources copied at least a decade earlier. Moulu's technique is imitative, using a little more melisma and verbal repetition than is usual in French masses of the time. All five movements begin in similar fashion with the same motif (*sol fa mi fa sol . . . re*), which serves throughout as an ostinato, transposed, augmented, or rhythmically modified; it is sometimes associated with a countersubject (*ut mi fa sol*), based perhaps on the St Stephen's Day antiphon *Stephanus autem*.

The second mass, 'Adieu mes amours', composed by Layolle himself, is, like other masses by Obrecht and Andreas de Silva, based on the chanson tune, which survives in different four-voice settings by Josquin and Mouton. Layolle uses the chanson's opening five-note motif *re fa mi re la* as an ostinato in the tenor, where it appears eighty–eight times in succession (beginning each time on G, albeit rhythmically varied), before being extended to include the whole melody in the third Agnus, which adds a canonic fifth voice.

Richafort's 'Missa Veni sponsa Christi', the longest mass of the set, paraphrases the four motives of the Gregorian antiphon in succession, ending with a canonic six-voice Agnus III, the third entry being in cancrizans. Mouton's 'Missa Quem dicunt homines' is loosely based on a motet composed by Richafort, possibly for the meeting of François I and Pope Leo X at Bologna in 1516. Moderne prints no Agnus, but suggests that the words be fitted to the Kyrie music.

After this series of works by established figures, Moderne includes as his fifth mass 'Ces fascheulx sotz' by the otherwise unknown Guillaume Prévost. This is loosely based on the chanson which survives in an anonymous three-voice version published by Attaingnant in 1529. Prévost begins his Kyrie, Credo, Sanctus, and Agnus with a head-motif, a double point of imitation akin to the opening superius and mid-point

---

[26] This dedication, along with that of the *Contrapunctus*, is reproduced in Pogue, *Jacques Moderne*, 71.

tenor motives from the anonymous chanson. Six years later Moderne was to publish a two-voice parody of this chanson by Antoine Gardane, who contributed the sixth Mass to the 1532 collection, 'Si bona suscepimus'; this was probably a parody of a contemporary motet (although not that of Sermisy or Verdelot).

The seventh mass, ascribed to Lupus, is entitled 'Ferrarie Dux Hercules'. Its inspiration was clearly Josquin's mass, based on the solmization syllables corresponding to the vowels in the name Hercules Duke of Ferrara, *re ut re ut re fa mi re* (i.e. D–C–D–C–D–F–E–D). However, Lupus' cantus firmus is G–F–D–F–D–E–D–F–E–D,, which, to correspond to its title, would require a mutation from the soft to the natural hexachord at the start to explain the solmization syllables *re ut re ut* and would still have two extra notes (*re mi*) in the middle. It has been suggested[27] that Lupus may have written this mass for the marriage of the heir to the duchy of Ferrara, the younger Ercole d'Este, to Renée, daughter of King Louis XII of France, in 1528 and that the additional notes represent *erit*, curiously signifying that 'Hercules *will be* Duke of Ferrara', as was the case two years after the work's publication. Another commentator[28] doubts the reliability of the title, suggesting that it might have been added by Moderne or Layolle because of the resemblance to Josquin's mass. The survival of a five-voice mass with the title 'Carolus Imperator Romanorum Quintus', probably composed for the coronation of Charles V as Holy Roman Emperor in 1530, suggests that Lupus had a penchant for masses based on *soggetti cavati*.

The next mass, 'La Bataille', attributed to Janequin, is closely modelled on his famous chanson celebrating Francis I's victory at Marignano in 1515. This mass is typical of later 'parody' masses in that it begins each of the five main sections with 'head-motif' reference to all four voices of the model, with only slight rhythmic changes, and quotes successively from one or more voices. To describe it as closer to contrafactum than parody[29] is something of an exaggeration, when it contains as much new material as many other mid-century masses. While Reese's contention[30] that it concentrates on material from the first part of the chanson is generally true, there is substantial reference to the descriptive second section in the Gloria (particularly the Qui

[27] A. Thurlings, 'Die *Soggetti cavati dalle vocali* in Huldigungskompositionen und die Herculesmesse des Lupus', *Bericht über den zweiten Kongress der Internationalen Musikgesellschaft* (Leipzig, 1907), 183–94.

[28] B. Blackburn, 'Lupus', *New Grove Dictionary of Music*, xi. 338; see also Blackburn, 'The Lupus Problem', 108–22.

[29] H. M. Brown, 'Janequin', *New Grove Dictionary of Music*, ix. 492.

[30] G. Reese, *Music in the Renaissance* (London, 1954), 340.

tollis), even if the rhythmic repetition is slightly more restrained than the hubbub of the model. The expansion of the Osanna to six voices is more unusual than the inclusion of a fifth voice in the third Agnus. This mass remained popular throughout the century and was imitated by a number of later composers. It seems to have been performed during Carnival week at St Mark's in Venice as late as 1564, despite having been singled out for criticism at the Council of Trent in August 1562.[31]

In the index of the first edition the mass entitled 'Jouissance' is ascribed to 'Jo. Sarton', but above the music in the revised edition of 1540 is the ascription 'Jo. Certon'. Neither name is found in any other contemporary musical source and it is possible that there was some confusion here with the Parisian master Pierre Certon, although Moderne published several of the latter's chansons, correctly attributed, between 1538 and 1543. The mass is a parody upon Claudin de Sermisy's famous four-voice chanson printed by Attaingnant in Paris in 1528 and many times thereafter. The borrowing technique is very similar to that of the preceding 'Battle' mass. The Kyrie opens with the first two lines of the chanson with little modification, before passing a new imitative phrase between the four parts and closing with the music from the end of the chanson's third and fifth lines. The Christe begins with a rhythmically augmented version of the chanson's fourth line, before introducing another new imitative point. The second Kyrie starts with the chanson's bass with modified upper parts and, after presenting some new material, reverts to the melismatic ending found at the end of the chanson's third and fifth lines. The Gloria begins with paired imitation based on the chanson's opening superius and bass parts, the Credo and Sanctus having an augmented version, while the first three bars of the first Agnus are exactly like those of the Kyrie. The third Agnus adds a fifth voice, with a new point resembling that of the three-voice Benedictus, combined with the chanson's opening bass figure. The second Agnus, like the similarly two-voiced Crucifixus, Et resurrexit, and Pleni sunt, introduces much new material, as do other sub-sections, scored normally for four voices.

The final mass in the 1532 edition is Layolle's 'O salutaris hostia'[32] which, judging from the similarity of many passages throughout the work, appears to be a parody of an earlier motet (although not of the settings of La Rue, Mouton, or Narváez). With the Benedictus set for just two voices, the Pleni and Agnus II for three, and the final Agnus III for five, the work follows a pattern commonly found in many contemporary four-part masses.

[31] B. Blackburn, *Music for Treviso Cathedral* (London, 1987), 25 n. 31 and 28.
[32] *Music of the Florentine Renaissance*, ed. D'Accone, 6, 21–40.

The revised edition of the *Liber decem missarum* appends two more masses. The first, ascribed to P. de Villiers, is entitled 'De Beata Virgine' in the index but 'Trinitas in unitate' above the music. The 'Trinity unified' refers to the fact that all three voices derive in canon from the single notated part, but may have had additional significance for Villiers's literary friends who worked in the Collège de la Trinité. An unusual feature is the joining of the Christe to the framing Kyries, perhaps another symbolic gesture of trinitarian unity. The opening figure of the Kyrie and Credo (*mi fa mi re mi la*) may be derived from the plainchant Christe IX or Credo I, just as the Gloria, Sanctus, and Osanna begin with a figure akin to the Gregorian Kyrie IX (*re . . . fa sol la*). The Gloria has an unusually high proportion of repeated notes, especially at the phrase 'Domine fili unigenite Jesu Christe', which is declaimed as thirteen Cs or Gs in succession. The form of the opening figure in Agnus II (*re fa mi re la*) is reminiscent of the 'Adieu mes amours' theme found in Layolle's mass from the same book. The whole mass is transcribed in Music Example 5.

The second mass appended in 1540, Layolle's 'Ces fascheux sotz,' is loosely modelled upon an anonymous three-voice chanson published in Paris in 1529. The superius and tenor of Kyrie I are based on the chanson's opening melody, extended by modified melismas and accompanied by a new counter-subject in the altus and bassus. The Christe's opening point is taken from the chanson's second line, continuing with the altus and bass from the chanson's third line. Kyrie II, like the chanson's fourth line, repeats the opening superius and tenor, adding a counter-subject from the model's altus, with a free continuation. The Gloria begins with the opening superius figure, adding new counterpoint and extension, while the second-line figure is prominent in the Qui tollis and Cum sancto sections. The Credo opens like the Kyrie, another reminder of the head-motif technique which underlies the new fashion for parody. The Sanctus offers new variants on the first and third lines of the chanson's superius, but the Osanna is based on the bassus and altus parts. The two-voice Pleni and three-voice Benedictus revert to the opening superius figure. Like Mouton's 'Quem dicunt homines', no Agnus is printed, implying reuse of the Kyrie music.

Moderne's publication in 1542 of eight masses, eight motets, and eight Magnificats by Pierre Colin, like the similar large choir-book of ten masses, was dedicated to Charles d'Estaing. The first two four-voice masses, 'Ave gloriosa' and 'Beatus vir', appear to be parodies. Both employ the same (D) mode and clef-combination (G2 C2 C3 C4), although the Agnus II of the first mass adds a fifth voice. The following two four-part masses, in the transposed first mode, are also parodies:

'Tant plus de bien' is related to a chanson by Philippe Lapperdey copied in a contemporary manuscript from Bruges,[33] and 'Regnum mundi' to an anonymous motet printed by Attaingnant in Paris (RISM [1528][2]). The next two, 'Emendemus in melius'[34] and 'Christus resurgens' (in the A and F modes), are parodies of motets by Richafort. 'Peccata mea', for five voices, is modelled on Pierre Certon's motet, while the final mass, for six voices, 'Beata es maria', also appears to be a parody. All eight masses employ a similar imitative technique, while there is a single example of canon by inversion in the Agnus II of 'Tant plus de bien'. The eight Magnificats all set the even-numbered verses and are based on the conventional plainsong tones.

The eight masses by Morales, reprinted by Moderne in 1545 and 1546 from Dorico's Roman edition of the previous year, can have had little connection with Lyons, even if three of the motet models, Gombert's 'Aspice domine', Moulu's 'Vulnerasti cor meum', and Verdelot's 'Si bona suscepimus', had all been published Moderne in 1532.

Pierre Colin reappears in 1547, contributing the first two masses to Moderne's *Harmonidos Ariston*. 'Veni sponsa Christi' paraphrases the Marian antiphon, while 'Angleus Domini' is probably another parody. The third mass in the collection is Antoine Gardane's 'Vivre ne puis', based on Sermisy's four-voice chanson. In contrast to the eleven-bar Kyrie I and II, the Agnus II is an extended six-voice piece with the two extra voices derived in canon, one by inversion.

In 1554 Moderne pirated a second book of masses by Morales from Dorico's 1544 Roman edition, dedicated to his employer Pope Paul III. Between 1545 and his death in 1553 Morales worked in Spain, first in Toledo, then Málaga, where there was no tradition or establishment for printing sacred polyphony. Moderne could have received the composer's sanction for publication, although the second book appeared shortly after his death. However, even the eight four-voice Magnificats by Morales which Moderne printed in 1550 were probably taken from earlier sources, in particular from Scotto's Venetian edition of 1542.

Although similar to those of Morales in their grand folio-sized choir-book format, Moderne's editions of Pierre Colin's sacred music are quite new and original. The last of these editions, entitled *Liturgicon musicarum* (1556), contains ten four-voice and two five-voice masses; its prefatory dedication to the deacon and canons of St Lazarus cathedral in Autun, dated October 1554, explains the composer's concern for textual continuity and clarity, as well as for the avoidance of

---

[33] Lengefeld, 'The Motets of Pierre Colin', 41–3.
[34] The Gloria is transcribed in Pogue, *Jacques Moderne*, 365–9.

anything 'harsh or forced'. This attitude, characteristic of the Reformation and of the subsequent Counter-Reformation (enshrined in the contemporary meetings of the Church Council in Trent), is reflected in the fact that no less than three of these new masses were based on Colin's own simple settings of Marot's French translations of psalms and prayers, which had been published by Nicolas du Chemin in Paris in 1550, without, however, using the official Genevan melodies. Thus the textures of 'Père de nous'[35] (the Lord's Prayer), 'Estans assis' (Ps. 137), and 'Qui au conseil' (Ps. 1) are clearer than those of the masses based on Latin motets, including Colin's own 'Deus in nomine tuo' and 'Super flumina Babylonis' (Ps. 137 again), as well as Jean Conseil's 'Adiuva me domine' (published in Paris in RISM 1535³). To judge from the similarity of material at the openings of the main sections and from subsequent analogies, the other six masses also appear to be parodies.

If the thirty-five ordinaries introduced by Moderne between 1532 and 1556 can in any sense be said to represent the mass in Lyons, we can draw some general conclusions. First, they share the French preference for clarity of texture and brevity—the most extreme examples being shown in the seven-breve Kyries from Colin's two masses based on metrical psalms. While imitative writing predominates, homorhythmic passages occur more frequently in the more textually intensive Gloria and Credo. Duo- and trio-writing, with more melismas, is usually found in the subsections of the Sanctus (Pleni and Benedictus), occasionally in those of the Credo (Crucifixus and Et resurrexit) and also in the second Agnus when there are three, rather than the usual two subdivisions. Conversely, the texture is frequently increased by one or two voices in the final Agnus, sometimes by means of canonic writing. Binary rhythm prevails, with rare passages in triple metre, while coloration and ligatures are increasingly rare. Latin accentuation is sometimes careless and word-painting almost non-existent. Finally, the relentless advance of parody technique is marked to the point where the masses by Gardane and Colin all adopt and standardize it in the manner later described by Pontio and Cerone.[36]

(iii) Noëls

The first French publication to include polyphonic music may have been the *Nouelz nouvaulx de ce present an 1512, dont en y a*

---

[35] The Gloria is transcribed in ibid. 370–4.

[36] See L. Lockwood, 'On "Parody" as Term and Concept in 16th-Century Music', in Jan La Rue *et al.* (eds.), *Aspects of Medieval and Renaissance Music: A Birthday Offering to Gustave Reese* (New York, 1966, 2nd edn. 1978), 560–75.

plusieurs notez a deux parties dont l'une n'est que le plain chant,
Composez par Maistre François Briand, maistre des escolles de Sainct-
Benoist en la cité du Mans (n.p., n.d.). Henri Chardon,[37] who published
an edition in 1904, supposed that the original was printed in Lyons,
perhaps by Claude Nourry. It has been impossible to confirm this, since
the sole surviving copy, reported to have been in the Bibliothèque
communale of Bourg-en-Bresse, has disappeared. According to
Chardon, the schoolmaster from Le Mans presented twenty strophic
noëls sung before or after four mystery plays (one including a farce),
performed by children on the four Sundays of Advent. Four noëls
include music notated for two voices of alto and tenor range, beginning
with dactylic motifs treated in imitation; but the many errors found in
the edition, whether emanating from the original printer or perhaps a
copyist (since Chardon suggests that music was often added by hand in
such books), make the music difficult to perform. The first piece is
designated to be sung to a Marian hymn, while most of the others
suggest popular melodies. The third piece proposes either 'Ses faulx
jaloux' or 'la note de la teneur qui s'ensuyt'; this turns out to be a duet
version of the same melody, which also survives as the tenth piece in
the monophonic chansonnier, Paris MS fr. 12744. Briand's twelfth noël,
'Tous les regretz qu'oncques furent au monde', suggests no timbre but
provides music similar in outline to a four-part setting by Antoine
Brumel of a courtly quatrain with the same first line. Several of the
given timbres are cited in other sources; one noël, 'Plaisante fleur, rose
tant adorée', has the rubric 'Sur une chanson du Vau de Vire', while
another is a dialogue between the shepherd Robin and his unnamed
shepherdess, introducing the last mystery, a Nativity play for Christmas
Eve.[38]

   The numerous surviving sources imply that the noël, a carol with
simple vernacular (or even patois) text on Christian subjects generally
connected with the Christmas or Easter feasts, enjoyed a great vogue in
the sixteenth century.[39] A manuscript collection owned by Charles VIII
and Louis XII in the late fifteenth century[40] suggests that noëls were
sung in courtly circles; but the modesty of most published examples
indicates a wide and popular distribution. Some noëls were issued as
broadsides: such is the case for the *Noel fait en maniere de dyalogue*
qui se peult chanter sur le mettre 'En l'ombre d'ung (buissonet)' . . .

[37] F. Briand, *Nouelz nouvaulx de ce present an 1512*, ed. H. Chardon (Paris and Le Mans, 1904).
See also id., *Quatre histoires par personnaiges*, ed. H. Chardon (Paris and Le Mans, 1906).
[38] Dobbins, 'The Chanson', i. 205–7.
[39] See A. F. Block, *The Early French Parody Noël* (Ann Arbor, 1983).
[40] Paris, Bibliothèque nationale, MS fr. 2368.

(n.p., *c*.1515),[41] which prints a monophonic melody above the first stanza. However, most noël collections do not include music, but rather propose suitable tunes; most of these tunes are of popular origin, although a few are known in polyphonic settings. The procedure is illustrated by the collections of Beaulieu and Aneau described earlier.

Examples of noëls both with and without music appeared throughout the sixteenth century in Lyons, as they did less frequently in Angers, Neuchâtel, Le Mans, Rouen, Antwerp, and other provincial cities. The first, dated 1504 and attributed by Vaganay[42] to the publishers Pierre Mareschal and Barnabé Chaussard, is entitled *Les nouelz faictz a l'onneur de Jhesuchrist et sont ordonnez com[m]ent on les doit chanter*. It contains many of the same strophic texts that are found in contemporary Parisian sources. The Columbus catalogue lists several collections purchased in Montpellier and Turin but published in Lyons by Olivier Arnoullet and Claude Nourry.[43] The latter's *Noelz nouveaulx sur tous les aultres composez allegoriquement selon le temps qui court Sur aucunes gayes chansons. Avec le noel des eglises et villaiges du Lyonnois non jamais que a present imprimez* includes four pieces without music:

Noel nouveau sur le chant de *Fringuez sur l'herbette Murchez sur le jonc*, ou sur *S'il est à ma porte Il aura m'amours*. Ou sur *Je suis trop jeunette Pour avoir mari Liron Liron viste*

Noel nouveau sur le chant *L'autre jour jouer m'alloie Au joly boys pour reverdir*

Noel sur *Il faut que feste die Adieu car je m'en voys*

Noel en langaige Lyonnois rural sur *Monseigneur de savoye que dieu vous fasse honour*

'Je suis trop jeunette' is found as the refrain to a *virelai* with a first stanza beginning 'S'il est à ma poste' in a monophonic chansonnier.[44] Both verse and refrain are used in a three-voice setting by Gascongne;[45] a four-voice chanson by Hesdin (1529², no. 27)[46] sets only the verse, while a *branle* printed by Attaingnant (1530⁷, no. 37), also entitled 'S'il est à ma poste', uses the tune common to the three other versions, as do two later parodies by Gombert and Castro.[47]

[41] Listed in Picot, *Catalogue des livres composant la bibliothèque . . . de Rothschild*, iv. 324–5.

[42] H. Vaganay, *Recueils de noëls imprimés à Lyon au XVIᵉ siècle* (Autun, 1935).

[43] J. Babelon, *La Bibliothèque francaise de Fernand Colomb* (Paris, 1913), nos. 155 and 156.

[44] Paris, Bibl. nat., MS fr. 12744, fo. 17; ed. Paris and Gevaert, *Chansons du XVᵉ siècle*, 25.

[45] P. Attaingnant, *31 chansons musicales à troys parties* (Paris, 1535), fo. 11ᵛ; repr. A. Gardane (Venice, 1541¹³), 58.

[46] P. Attaingnant, *Trente et une chansons musicales à quatre parties* (Paris, 1529²), fo. 14ᵛ; ed. H. Expert in Maîtres Musiciens de la Renaissance Française, 5 (Paris, 1897), no. 27.

[47] Gombert à 5, 1550¹³, fo. 3ᵛ; Gombert à 3, 1552¹⁰, fo. 21ʳ; Castro à 4, 1574⁴, fo. 10ʳ.

The timbre of the second noël is again related to a four-voice piece in Attaingnant's *31 chansons* (1529[2], no. 2),[48] although the text set by Conseil has a different continuation, as do subsequent parodies by Appenzeller (1542, fo. 18[v]), Certon (1550[7], p. 12) and Du Buisson (1578[15], fo. 4). An anthology of chanson verse printed by Nourry in the 1530s presents a text closer to that of the polyphonic versions;[49] the topos goes back to sources as old as 'La geste de Blancheflour et Florence', which begins 'L'autrier m'en aloi jouant'.[50]

Pogue[51] attributes to Moderne the publication of four unsigned books of noëls bought for Columbus at Lyons in 1535. Their contents and *timbres* are listed by Jean Babelon, who also describes one collection, *La fleur des Noelz nouvellement notés en choses faictes imprimez en l'honeur de la nativité*... (n.p.n.d.), which includes printed music.[52]

The first melody, for the Advent hymn *Conditor alme siderum*, exceptionally uses black lozenge notation. This piece opens several other noël collections, such as that of Lucas le Moigne, printed in Paris in 1520 (which also includes nos. 2 and 6); it also provided a model for many *chansons spirituelles* and polyphonic settings, including the motet 'Puer natus est' by Coste, published in Moderne's fifth book (1542), using the plainchant as a cantus firmus in the first section and modifying it in the second section, which has the French words 'Noe, noe, voici le temps que Dieu fust né.'

The second piece, 'A la venue de Noel', like the first and third, is also found in older sources, such as the manuscript which once belonged to Charles VIII and Louis XII and a collection thought to have been published in Lyons by Mareschal and Chaussard.[53] The same tune is listed in Moderne's contemporary *S'ensuivent plusieurs basses dances* (Pogue, no. 132) and is mentioned as being played on *buccines* in Rabelais's *Cinquième livre* (ch. 32b).

The third piece, 'Puer nobis nascitur', has a melody akin to that used in the superius of a three-voice setting copied twice in the Lyons manuscript, Copenhagen 1848 (pp. 402 and 409), once with ascription to Haquinet. Its first four strophes reappear with the direction 'for

[48] Ed. H. Expert, Maîtres Musiciens, 5, no. 2.

[49] C. Nourry (publ.), *S'ensuyvent plusieurs belles chansons nouvelles*... *avec aulcunes de Cl. Marot* (Lyons, n.d.), no. 4.

[50] C. Oulmont (ed.), *Les Débats du Clerc et du Chevalier dans la littérature poétique* (Paris, 1911), 167.

[51] Pogue, *Jacques Moderne*, nos. 106–7 and 127–8.

[52] Babelon, *La Bibliothèque française de Fernard Colomb*, nos. 152–4; see also J. Babelon, 'La Fleur de Noëls', *Revue des livres anciens*, 1 (1914), 369–404.

[53] See Block, *Early French Parody Noel*, ii. 14–17.

Sunday at mass' in the *Noelz vieux et nouveaux*, published by Jean de Tournes in Lyons in 1557. The same first three noëls also open a later collection published in Lyons by Benoist Rigaud.[54]

The fourth piece, 'Noel pour l'amour de Marie', gives the tune as well as the rubric 'Sur *Trahison Dieu le mauldie*', a timbre also indicated in the Lyonese collections of Mareschal, Arnoullet, and Rigaud. 'Meigna, meigna, bin devons noel chanta' (no. 6) has a text in Savoyard dialect and mentions the town of Belley, which lies some fifty miles east of Lyons; the text recurs in other collections published in Lyons with the *timbre* 'Noel, noel iterando Noel', while the music is akin to the cantus firmus of Haquinet's four-voice 'Noe, noe, iterumque noe', which, like the third noël, was copied in Copenhagen manuscript 1848.

'Reveillez vous, cueurs endormis' (no. 7) reappears in the *Noelz nouveaulx* published in Lyons by Olivier Arnoullet with the *timbre* 'Vivray je tousjours en soulcy', a chanson set for four voices by Sermisy in 1528 with a melody similar to that given by Moderne. 'Laissez paistre vos bestes' (no. 8), which uses Lyonese dialect, is also found in noël collections published by Arnoullet, De Tournes, and Rigaud, as well as later ones, and survives in oral tradition to the present century with a melody similar to that cited by Moderne.[55]

The tune for 'Chantons Noel par grant desir' (no. 9) resembles that of 'De mon triste desplaisir', set by Richafort in 1529[3]; this tune is itself akin to that of Henry VIII's 'Pastime with good company'[56] and is cited as a timbre for another noël of similar structure beginning 'David, Jacob, Ezechias', as well as for a *chanson spirituelle* by Eustorg de Beaulieu. The last melody printed by Moderne for 'Noel chantons que chascun se resveille' (no. 10) is similar to the tenor of the chanson 'Qui la dira la peine de mon cueur', set for three and five voices by Willaert (1536 and 1572[2]) and for eight voices by Verdelot (1572[2]).[57] The remaining eleven noëls suggest appropriate timbres. 'Au boys de dueil' (no. 12) was included in several contemporary verse anthologies described as 'la mère des chansons', while a variant text beginning 'Au joly bois' was set for four voices by Sermisy (1529[2]) and for two and five voices by Certon (1538 and 1570). The tune for 'Ce n'est pas trop que d'avoir ung amy' (no. 17) is found in a four-voice setting by

[54] B. Rigaud (publ.), *La Grand Bible des Noelz tant vieux que nouveaux Composez de plusieurs Autheurs tant du présent que du passé* . . . (Lyons, n.d.).

[55] See J. de Smidt, *Les Noëls et la tradition populaire* (Amsterdam, 1932), 140–6.

[56] Richafort's setting is included in Brown, *Theatrical Chansons*, no. 16; Henry's is in J Stevens (ed.), *Music of the Court of Henry VIII*, Musica Britannica, 18 (London, 1969), nos. 7 and 7a.

[57] Block, *Early French Parody Noël*, ii, no. 46; Willaert's five-voice and Verdelot's eight-voice settings are included in C. Jacobs (ed.), *Le Roy & Ballard's 1572 Mellange de Chansons* (Pittsburgh, Pa., 1982), 36–8 and 581–5.

Vermont (also in 1529[2]), while that for 'Est-il conclud' (no. 18) survives in the form of pavanes for lute (Brown 1551[2]) or instrumental ensemble (Brown 1557[3]).[58]

While Moderne's collection shows the noël's variety of melodic sources representing different traditions—oral and written, monophonic and polyphonic, sacred and secular—Barthélemy Aneau's *Chant Natal* (1539), like the contemporary *Noelz* of Jehan Chaperon,[59] reveals a more sophisticated approach, drawing mainly on courtly poems by Marot, Francis, I, and others, which had been set polyphonically during the previous decade. On the other hand, Nicolas Martin's *Noelz & Chansons* appear to be independent of the familiar repertory, either popular or courtly. Martin's preface to his printer, Macé Bonhomme, stresses the novelty of his pieces, excusing the wanton nature of the 'twenty shepherd songs', but suggesting that even gentlemen enjoy motets and chansons in patois. The noëls show a predilection for simple folk-like melodies in major modes, with clear-cut if occasionally alternating rhythm and various repetitive strophic structures with or without refrain, similar to contemporary psalms and *voix de ville*. Martin's French chansons favour simple diatonic melody with little modulation, but they are more akin to those of older, polyphonic collections in their rhythm and cadence formulae.[60]

In 1557 Jean de Tournes published his *Noelz vieux et nouveaux en l'honneur de la nativité [de] Jesus Christ et de sa tresdigne mere*, with thirteen Latin, ten French or patois, and two macaronic texts, most of which had already appeared in older manuscript or printed collections. Only two pieces indicate *timbres*, but most include rubrics for performance during masses and Offices between Advent and Epiphany. The preface suggests that whereas in older times 'Christmas hymns and canticles in both Latin and French were composed to the tunes of existing church hymns, more recently many rhymsters have written noëls to the texts of lustful songs, adding humorous words far removed from the holy mysteries and more likely to inspire derision than devotion'.

La Grand Bible des Noelz tant vieux que nouveaux composez de plusieurs autheurs tant du present que de passé, printed in Lyons by Benoît Rigaud in the 1580s, borrows its title and much of its contents from a similar undated collection published a little earlier by Nicolas Bonfons in Paris, including much of the older repertoire, with no music.

[58] See Block, ii, nos. 45, 20, and 42.

[59] J. Chaperon, *S'ensuyt plusieurs noelz nouveaulx* (Paris, 1538); repr. E. Picot (Paris, 1879).

[60] The preface, musical incipits, and four complete pieces are illustrated and transcribed in Dobbins, 'The Chanson at Lyons', i. 210–14.

If the large number of noëls printed in Lyons suggests that the genre enjoyed a vogue for many years, this vogue hardly matched that for amorous chansons, many of which were also printed without music.

(iv) *Chansons*

There can be little justification for claiming the existence of an independent and characteristic 'chanson lyonnaise' at any time in the sixteenth century. There were too few distinguished musicians living in the town long enough to establish a distinctive local tradition, and there was no sustained patronage on the scale that promoted secular song in the great courts of France, Italy, and the Low Countries. The most concentrated period of production—the second third of the century—corresponded to, but did not match, the city's golden age in literature.

The situation during the first three decades is obscured by lack of local sources. With the frequent presence in the town of Louis XII and Francis I during the Italian campaigns, as well as the occasional visits of the Burgundian heirs, the courtly repertoire was probably much the same as that represented in the few surviving French manuscript chansonniers,[61] as well as in the Venetian publications of Petrucci, *Odhecaton, Canti B,* and *Canti C* (RISM 1501, 1502[2], 1504[3]), and Antico (1520[6], 1521[6-7], and 1536[1]), and the earliest Parisian collections of Attaingnant (1528[3]–1535[6]).[62] In view of the size and influence of the Florentine community, which included members of the Medici, Rinuccini, and Strozzi families, it is possible that some of the pieces found in Italian manuscripts of the early sixteenth century were also heard in Lyons.[63] The manuscripts that were arguably copied in Lyons (see above, ch. 4) certainly reveal a wide and eclectic range of popular and courtly verse set for three or four voices by various composers, spanning the three generations from Dufay to Sermisy. A predilection for popular tunes, often with ribald texts, is apparent in this repertoire, as in some of the chansons subsequently published by Moderne, as well as in local collections of noëls with contrafactum texts and anthologies of chanson poetry without music.

---

[61] Monophonic sources include Paris, Bibliothèque nationale, MS fr. 9346 and 12744; three-part settings of popular verse and melodies predominate in Paris, MS fr. 2245; British Library, MSS Add. 35087 and Harley 5242; Cambridge, Magdalene College, Pepys Library, MS 1760; four-part settings of formal courtly verse in Paris, MS fr. 1597 and in Brussels, Bibliothèque royale, MSS 228 and 11239. For further information, see *Census-Catalogue of Manuscript Sources of Polyphonic Music 1400–1550,* 5 vols. (American Institute of Musicology, 1979–88).

[62] The music is discussed in H. M. Brown, 'The Genesis of a Style: The Parisian Chanson, 1500–1530', in James Haar (ed.), *Chanson and Madrigal, 1480–1530* (Cambridge, Mass., 1964), 1–50.

[63] See above, Ch. 4, nn. 2–4.

It is probable that the chansons printed in Venice by Antico between 1520 and 1536 were paralleled in Lyonese publications during the same period. One of the five now lost Lyonese chanson collections acquired by Ferdinand Columbus in Lyons in 1535—'Chansons de la coronne libre premier' (no. 13757)—contained twenty-three pieces, ending with 'Sus l'herbe brunete', purportedly by Layolle; an anonymous three-voice setting of this text in the *Chansons à troys* published by Antico and Luc'Antonio Giunta in Venice in 1520 (RISM 1520[6], no. 37) could be the same piece. However, the other three books of polyphonic chansons which Columbus purchased at Lyons (nos. 13748 (identical to no. 9199), 13758, and 13943) appear to be more akin to Attaingnant's early publications.

Another item listed in the Columbina catalogues as 'Chanson in language provensal cum cantu d'organo'—beginning with 'Maudit sia tant de (ratun)'—must refer to the monophonic collection adopted for one of the celebrations of the *Basochiens* of Aix-en-Provence. This book contains five pieces, each having the same design: a two-line refrain, with nonsense syllables, recurring between each of the many ensuing stanzas and repeated at the end.[64] The simplicity of the texts (typified in the last piece, a plea on behalf of the poor worker) and melodies suggests a closer proximity to popular origin than do the monophonic or polyphonic chansons in manuscripts or prints connected with aristocratic circles. It is thus no surprise that the refrain of the first piece appears with a French text, 'Mauldit soit le petit chien', in numerous other sources. As well as passing references in at least three contemporary farces,[65] the tune is proposed as a *timbre* for *chansons spirituelles* by Marguerite de Navarre[66] and Eustorg de Beaulieu.[67] An anonymous three-voice chanson, beginning 'Je m'en allé veoir m'amye', from a contemporary Florentine manuscript[68] opens with a melody closely akin to that used for the stanza of the Provençal version and concludes with the same refrain tune. It is also fleetingly quoted in the superius (bars 46–7) of H. Fresneau's *fricassée* from the third book of the *Parangon des Chansons*.[69]

The most significant corpus of secular polyphonic songs published in Lyons was Moderne's *Parangon des Chansons*, which appeared between 1538 and 1543. Du Verdier's *Bibliothèque* (1585), notes that

---

[64] The five pieces are transcribed in Dobbins, 'The Chanson at Lyons', fo. 204[v].

[65] See Brown, *Music in the French Secular Theater*, 238.

[66] 'Maudit soit le cruel chien'; see *Les Marguerites*, ed. F. Frank, 4 vols. (Paris, 1873), iii. 129–31.

[67] 'Mauldict soit le faulx chrestien'; see E. de Beaulieu, *Chrestienne Resjouyssance*, no. 85.

[68] Florence, Biblioteca Nazionale Centrale, MS Magl. XIX, 117, no. 5; ed. H. M. Brown, *Theatrical Chansons of the Fifteenth and Early Sixteenth Centuries* (Cambridge, Mass., 1963), no. 37.

[69] Transcribed in Dobbins 'The Chanson', ii, no. 32.

the series comprised eighteen books; but his figure may refer to the totality of Moderne's secular polyphony, including the reprints of the first four books, the two books of the *Difficile des Chansons*, or the two books of *canzoni* by Layolle and the Petrarchan settings of Rampollini. At all events, only eleven books are known to have survived, and there is no other evidence that Moderne revived the *Parangon* series after 1544.

A detailed study of literary and musical concordances[70] shows the majority of pieces to be courtly *épigrammes*, mostly *quatrains* or *huitains*, and the minority contractions of older *formes fixes*, single stanzas of strophic poems, or rustic chansons with refrain. The most extended text is 'Estant assis', Marot's paraphrase of Ps. 137, set in three sections by the Calvinist composer Abel. While Marot (with twenty texts), Francis I (with ten), and Mellin de Saint-Gelais (with six) continue to dominate the repertoire, there are a number of pieces by local poets, including Pernette du Guillet (four), Eustorg de Beaulieu (three), Bonaventure des Périers, Charles de Sainte-Marthe, and Maurice Scève, as well as half a dozen pieces in Italian set by Layolle and P. de Villiers. The characteristic rhythmic patterns and structures associated with the typical decasyllabic verses and the treble-dominated textures are generally akin to those found in contemporary Parisian chanson publications. Recent analysis of chansons by provincial composers[71] suggests that the work of Coste, Fresneau, and P. de Villiers tends to be more extended by textual repetition and motivic interplay, more varied and complex in texture (perhaps under the influence of the Low Countries' composers), more assymetrical in phrasing, but more respectful of poetic caesurae than that of Parisian contemporaries such as Sermisy, Certon, and Sandrin. This may reflect greater concern in the Italianate city's neo-Platonist and Petrarchist circles for setting texts of literary quality.

There is no later representative corpus of chansons by such a variety of composers, including local talent. The first book of Moderne's *Difficile des Chansons* series is entirely devoted to pieces by Janequin which had already been printed by Attaingnant (the latter's eighth book of chansons includes thirteen of Moderne's twenty-two). The second book presents a novel repertoire consisting almost entirely of narrative

---

[70] Dobbins, 'Jacques Moderne's *Parangon des Chansons*'; see also Dobbins, 'Doulce mémoire'.

[71] L. Miller, 'The Chansons of French Provincial Composers 1530–1550; A Study of Stylistic Trends' (Ph.D. diss., Standford University, 1978); see also Miller (ed.), *Thirty-six Chansons by French Provincial Composers (1529–1550)* (Recent Researches in the Music of the Renaissance, 38; Madison, Wisc., 1981). The French provincial repertoire is also discussed in L. Bernstein, 'The "Parisian Chanson": Problems of Style and Terminology', *Journal of the American Musicological Society*, 31 (1978), 193–240.

pieces, including three erotic anecdotes involving monks and three involving the conventional rustics, Robin, Katin, and Perrichon, set in the light syllabic manner. Half of the total twenty-six pieces are ascribed to Henry Fresneau, including two relating the misadventures of members of monastic orders in Lyons, as well as two, 'Ung laboureur sa journée commansoit assez matin' and 'Thenot estoit en son clos rejouy', which were later attributed to Sanserre in Attaingant's seventeenth book (RISM 1545[10-11]).[72] This might indicate that Fresneau came from Sancerre near Bourges, although the Parisian publisher seemed most uncertain about Fresneau's authorship, ascribing the same chanson to him and to Guyon in successive books 1545[12-13] and 1546[12-13], while attributing another of his pieces ('Le jeu m'ennuye') to Janequin in 1547[10]. Attaingnant's seventeenth book of chansons also includes 'Ung jour Katin venant d'estre batue', attributed to Janequin, although Moderne had ascribed it to Du Metz.

Other curiosities in Moderne's second 'Difficult' book include the extended opening 'Battle in Spanish', set in eight sections by the elder Mateo Flecha and the closing psalm paraphrase by Marot, 'Du fons de ma pensée', set in three sections by Gentian. Some of the composers, such as Leo la Saigne and P. de la Farge—known only from Moderne's motet books—may have been local figures.

While there is no direct evidence that Dominique Phinot held any official appointment in Lyons, the dedications to prominent citizens and the texts of the two books of his chansons printed by the Beringen press certainly suggest an extended visit during 1547–8. The modernity of most of the verse, which would have been available in Lyons much more readily than in Italy, and the wording of the first book's dedication suggest that some, if not all, of the songs had been recently composed for Nicolas Bave and his friend César Gros:

> Vaquant ces jours non à l'oisiveté,
> Mais au loisir, que Musique demande
> En ces chansons me suis exercité
> Pour en après les mettre en la commande
> De ta vertu ...

> Spending these days, not in indolence
> But in the leisure demanded by Music,
> I have been busy on these chansons
> So that I could then place them at your virtue's command ...

Local flavour is underlined by the choice of no less than six poems by Charles Fontaine, a teacher at the Collège de la Trinité during the

---

[72] A Seay (ed.), *Pierre Attaingnant: Dixseptiesme livre* (Colorado Springs, Colo., 1979), nos. 5 and 13.

1540s, and three by Maurice Scève, not to mention Clément Marot's tribute to Lyons ('On dira ce qui l'on vouldra Du Lyon') and an anonymous poem ('Maugré Saturne') celebrating the traditional planting of a May tree by the printers of the city. The literary quality of both books is confirmed by the inclusion of seven poems by Clément Marot, five by Mellin de Saint-Gelais, three by Étienne Forcadel, three by Pietro Bembo (in the translations of Jean Martin), two by Michel d'Amboise, and two by Jacques Peletier. Yet in the first book Phinot, or his patrons, shows a marked predilection for amusing, anti-clerical, erotic anecdotes such as 'Une Nonain de l'Abbesse reprise', '"Laissez cela" disoit une nonette', 'Un gros Prieur son petit filz baisoit', 'Dame Margot à son amy Brandoville', 'Une fillete à son vicaire alla', and 'Frerot un jour aux Cordeliers alla', set in the syllabic manner of Janequin and Passereau. The courtly *épigrammes* (mostly *huitains* and *dizains*) are similar in style to those of Sandrin and Certon, with ballade structure (AABC) and a suave homophonic texture. However, many of the quatrains are unusual in having the opposite structure (ABB), resulting from repeating the last couplet rather than the last line. Phinot's first collection was also the first in France to specifically designate sequential stanzas with the term 'Responce', which Susato had introduced in Antwerp in 1543 (nos. 3–4, 8–9, 17–18, 19–20, 22–3). While the four-in-one canons using inversion and retrograde at the end of each collection have a long pedigree, the eight-in-four and twelve-in-one canons which precede them are more unusual. Also novel are Phinot's antiphonal eight-voice chansons 'Vivons m'amye' (I, no. 37) 'Qu'est-ce qu'Amour' (II, no. 2), and 'Par un trait d'or' (II, no. 26).

Another innovative aspect of these chansons is their use of musical metaphor or simile, now sometimes called 'madrigalism' after its use by Rore and others in Italy during the 1540s. Phinot's examples include poignant E flat chords in 'Plorez mes yeux' (I, no. 2) and 'Mort et amour' (I, no. 21), rich animated melismas on *vie entière* in 'En chascun lieu' (II, no. 24), the rests following *souspire* in 'Quand je te voy' (I, no. 19), and the multiple suspensive dissonances for *meschamment* in 'Je l'ay perdu' (II, no. 7). Also madrigalian is his setting of Jean Martin's translation of 'Quando io pens'al martire', which recalls Arcadelt's famous setting not only in its opening figure but in its subtle contrast of rhythm and phrasing, responding to the six- and ten-syllable alternation which imitates Pietro Bembo's original seven- and eleven-syllable lines.

The Beringen press followed the publication of Phinot's sixty-six chansons in 1548 with a third book containing thirty-five similar pieces set for four voices by Didier Lupi Second. Again Lupi's connections with the writers Guillaume Guéroult, Barthélemy Aneau, and Jean du Peyrat, as well as the appearance of four musical publications between 1547 and 1559, certainly suggest an extended sojourn in Lyons. Although Lupi's book includes no canons or eight-voice pieces, its texts and musical structures are very akin to Phinot's. Charles Fontaine and Clément Marot are again favoured, providing four and five texts respectively, while Étienne Forcadel provides one. As in Phinot's first book, there are a number of amusing anecdotes treated in lively syllabic counterpoint, even if Lupi prefers tales of wife-beating and connubial dispute to the sexual misadventures of nuns and monks: 'Un compagnon s'amye menassa', 'Quelquefois je veis une femme', 'D'un gros baston', Une dame pour mieulx venir',[73] Un mary sa femme batant', and 'Un vieillart amoureux'. Such texts, typical of the priests Janequin and Passereau, contrast with the puritanical earnestness of the prefaces to Lupi's psalms and spiritual songs. However, most of the pieces are courtly *huitains* or *dizains* of similar construction, with the second couplet using the same music as the first and the last couplet repeated. The few quatrains (nos. 14, 15, 33, 34) and *cinquains* (nos. 21, 22, 24, and 25) share with Phinot's settings the unusual ABB form, repeating the final couplet rather than the final line. But unlike Phinot's, his sequential poems ('Par ton deffault/Par mon deffault' and 'Que gaigne-je/Sans aucun fruict') are not specifically indicated as 'Responces'. Lupi's collection also differs in following a modal arrangement. A few pieces, such as 'Chantres un jour' and 'Souvent je veux baiser Catin' (see Pl. 4), make unusually virtuosic demands through velocity and diminution. While both Phinot and Lupi match Sandrin and Janequin in courtly and anecdotal styles, neither attempts the new strophic *voix de ville*, which were appearing in Parisian publications of this time.

The dedication of Lupi's chansons to a group of Luccan businessmen living in Lyons[74] acknowledges their friendship and patronage and promises 'something in a higher style' to come. This may refer to his *chansons spirituelles* or to his settings of thirty psalms translated by Gilles d'Aurigny, printed by Beringen in 1548 and 1550 respectively.[75] The dedication of these psalms to the Lyonese banker Nicolas Baillivi explains that Lupi, at the request of some of his friends, had spent the previous year composing secular songs 'unworthy of a Christian man'. This new Calvinist tone echoes that of Loys Bourgeois's dedication to André Chenevard preceding his fifty psalms translated by Clément Marot and published by Beringen in 1547.

The next polyphonic chansons to appear in Lyons were the *Chansons*

---

[73] Dobbins (ed.), *Oxford Book of Chansons*, no. 38.
[74] Guillo, 'Recherches', ii, no. 22 and document 10.
[75] Ibid., ii, nos. 23 and 26 and documents 7 and 13.

nouvelles composées par Barthelemy Beaulaigue, excellent Musicien. Et par luy mises en Musique à quatre parties, published by Robert Granjon in 1559 (or, according to the tenor part-book, 1558). The collection's dedication to Henry II's mistress, Diane de Poitiers, which describes the composer as a 15-year-old choirboy in the cathedral of Marseilles, is followed by a woodcut portrait of the young prodigy.[76] Neither dedication nor portrait are dated, but three of the chansons are addressed to the 'Seigneur prieur de Capue', one of them specifying 'on his arrival from Malta'. François Lesure[77] has identified the Prior of Capua as Leone Strozzi, a naval commander based at Marseilles from 1549 to 1551. This would suggest either that Beaulaigue was between five and seven years old at the time of composition, or that Granjon printed the music years after the composer had written it, presenting an old portrait, or even that the whole publication, and that of the subsequent motets, was a hoax. The word 'composed' on the printed title-page suggests that the young chorister also wrote the poems, all of which are conventional extended courtly epigrams with regular decasyllabic lines, in the style of Mellin de Saint-Gelais, favoured in the 1540s. They are set for four voices in the predominantly homophonic manner typical of similar extended epigrams set by Villiers, Sandrin, Certon, and other chanson composers of the 1540s, using the same AABCC structures. Like many of Villiers's chansons, no less than seven of Beaulaigue's thirteen begin with the rhythm breve, two semibreves, minim; four begin with the more common narrative formula, semibreve, two minims, semibreve, and one with its diminutive equivalent, minim, two semiminims minim. One chanson (no. 10) begins in triple metre (₵3) and seven others have brief internal phrases in triple metre.

Granjon's other chanson publications, also printed in similar small octavo part-books, were two anthologies entitled 'Trophies of Music', containing a variety of four-voice chansons 'selected from the flower of composition by the most famous and excellent musicians ancient and modern' (RISM 1559[14-15]). Old pieces by Maillard, Cadéac, Villiers, Godard, Goudeau, Certon, Sermisy, Lupus, Jacquet, Sandrin, Boyvin, and Gombert rub shoulders with newer pieces by Arcadelt, Gentian, Jambe de Fer, and Roussel. Several of Granjon's attributions conflict with those of earlier and later Parisian publications. Thus he ascribes

---

[76] The portrait is reproduced with added background on the cover of Auda, *Barthélemy Beaulaigue*.

[77] Lesure, 'Beaulaigue, Barthélemy', *Die Musik in Geschichte und Gegenwart*, 1 (Kassel, 1949). See also H.-A. Durand's review of Auda, *Barthélemy Beaulaigue* in *Provence historique*, 8 (1958), 176–8.

'Puisque vivre en servitude' to Arcadelt and 'Qui souhaittez avoir tout le plaisir' to Gentian: both these chansons had been printed ten years earlier by Attaingnant with ascription to Sandrin. Similarly, he attributes to Gentian 'Voyez le tort d'amour', which both Attaingnant (in 1535) and Moderne (in 1541) had ascribed to Sandrin. However, his attribution of 'Vous qui voulez avoir contentement' to Gentian was followed by Du Chemin in 1567, if not by Le Roy and Ballard, who in 1561 ascribe the piece to De Bussy. And his ascription to 'Viliers' of 'Venus avoit son filz Amour perdu' conflicts with Attaingnant's to Delafont (1545^{12-13}). Three unattributed pieces in Granjon's second book are ascribed in Parisian publications to Gentian, Guyon, and Maillard.

Although this uncertainty suggests that Granjon did not have direct access to a great stock of new material, some of his repertoire was unique. Thus he introduces Maillard's 'Un grand désir' and 'Ceste belle petite bouche', Certon's 'De son cueur et du mien', as well as Arcadelt's 'De mil' ennuiz', 'Si faux danger', and 'O le grand bien'. But while he or his music-editor could have brought or received this material from Paris, he probably found at least three pieces locally: Jambe de Fer's setting of the translation by Claude le Maistre of Ps. 42, 'Comme le cerf longuement pourchassé', Lupi Second's setting of Jean du Peyrat's poem for Clémence de Bourges, 'O que je vis en estrange martire', and 'Qui veut avoir liesse' set by François Roussel.

During the ensuing decade, no more secular chansons appeared in Lyons, except for a collection of unspecified four- and five-voice pieces by Simon Gorlier or the 'Chansons and Vaudevilles' by Alamanno Layolle, reportedly published by Simon Gorlier in 1561. However, Hubert-Philippe de Villiers's funeral air for the Protestant champion Louis de Condé may have been published there in 1569 (see above, ch. 4, pp. 186–8).

If the 1560s were dominated by the publication of Huguenot psalms and canticles, the Protestant spirit also affected the chansons published in Lyons during the 1570s. Thus the 'excellent' four-part songs by Arcadelt, selected and edited by Goudimel for Jean de Tournes in 1572, present forty-four amorous pieces originally issued between 1538 and 1565 with new 'spiritualized' contrafactum texts added. Although this edition has disappeared, a later one issued by Jean de Tournes II in 1586 (purportedly in Lyons but probably in Geneva) has survived.[78]

Two similar selections presenting the 'Flower of the songs of the two most excellent composers of our time ... Lassus and ... Goudimel',

---

[78] Guillo, 'Recherches', ii, nos. 84 and 95.

purportedly printed by Jean Bavent in 1574, purify only the four more sensuous texts (I, nos. 3, 7, 8, and 21—Lassus' 'Fleur de quinze ans', 'Petite folle', 'Vray Dieu disoit une fillette', and 'Je ne veux rien qu'un baiser'). The first book offers twenty-three four-part songs by Lassus, originally published between 1555 and 1564, adding only two pieces by the late lamented Goudimel, both of them appearing for the first time.[79] The second book for five voices similarly offers twenty-one pieces by Lassus, first printed between 1560 and 1571, with seven pieces by Goudimel, all of them new except for one which had appeared in a monumental Parisian collection two years earlier.[80] It is possible that Goudimel composed some of these new pieces during his stay in Lyons (1569–72), but nothing in the texts confirms it, while the lightly contrapuntal musical style and through-composed structures are typical of the composer's earlier chansons.

Goudimel's 'last four-part chanson', a setting of Antoine de la Roche Chandieu's lament on the death of his daughter, 'Par le désert de mes peines', was printed by Jean de Tournes in 1573, at the end of a musical treatise by Corneille de Blockland. Blockland may have acted as editor for Jean Bavent's publication of the *Fleur des chansons* by Lassus and Goudimel, before bringing out his own *Jardin de Musique, semé d'excellentes & harmonieuses chansons & voix de ville* ('Garden of Music sown with excellent and harmonious chansons and vaudevilles') with Jean de Tournes in 1579. Only the second book, containing thirty-six pieces of various kinds, survives.[81] It opens with a sonnet in alexandrines addressed to the book's dedicatee, Gabrielle de Dinteville, set to a jaunty melody in through-composed form. The next piece, 'Musiciens qui chantez à plaisir', is a decasyllabic *dixain* treated in the characteristic manner of the mid-century *épigramme*, with reprises of both opening and closing couplets, similar to an earlier setting by Guyon (in RISM 1550[9]). This AABCC structure recurs in many of the pieces. Others are even more repetitive, for example the simple tune accompanying the short irregular lines of the third song, 'Vous aimans qui joïr pretendez' (no. 3). This piece probably requires extra stanzas, in accordance with the title-page's designation *voix de ville*, although none are included in the sole surviving (Superius) part-book.

Some of the texts are very old: no. 9, 'Elle m'aime, je le sçay bien' (seven lines with a *rentrement*) comes from a *rondeau*, and no. 30, 'Qu'en as affaire', is a complete *rondeau quatrain* with two *rentrements*; both were published in the *Jardin de Plaisance* in 1502, as

---

[79] See Goudimel, *Œuvres complètes*, xiv, nos. 36 and 39.
[80] Ibid., nos. 1, 7, 10, 33, 37, 50, and 51.
[81] For the fac. edn., see Ch. 5, n. 111.

was no. 22, 'Faute d'argent', which uses the same text and tune as did Josquin, who died in 1521. Others are more recent, such as Charles Fontaine's 'Resjouy toy, o populaire' (no. 23), originally published in 1543, but here inscribed as a celebration for the New Year in 1577. Among the occasional pieces is an epithalamium (no. 24) written by Guillaume de La Taissonnière for the nuptials of Baron Louis de La Baume and Catherine de Bruges, celebrated in Saint-Amour in June 1574, and a little *voix de ville* (no. 32) addressed to M[adame] de Bellegarde, who was probably the subject of the *Passions amoureuses, chantées à la beauté and bonne grace de Anne de Bellegarde*, published, according to Antoine du Verdier, in Lyons by Pierre Roussin in 1574. Blockland's activity offers an example of a versatile Renaissance polymath, serving various members of the local aristocracy and publishing both his astrological and musical works in the southern metropolis.

Other northern musicians active in or around Lyons around this time include Jean de Castro, who wrote chansons, madrigals, and motets for Lyonnais patrons between 1570 and 1580, and Gilles Maillard, who is reported to have published sacred and secular chansons with Jean de Tournes in the early 1580s. Despite reference to Lyons on the title-pages of some editions, it is probable that the *Octonaires, Quatrains* and motets by Paschal de l'Estocart from Saint-Quentin in Picardy were all printed in Geneva in 1582–3, as were the curiously chromatic chansons and *chansons spirituelles* (1578–9) of Jean Servin, who lived in the Swiss city at the time. But with Jean de Maletty of Saint-Maximin in Provence joining Blockland, Castro, Maillard, and possibly L'Estocart, there was certainly a flourishing group of chanson composers in Lyons between 1575 and 1585, writing in the same styles that prevailed elsewhere in France and Switzerland.

(v) *Italian Madrigals*

Two books of Italian *Canzoni* set by Francesco de Layolle for four and five voices respectively were printed by Moderne, probably as a tribute to the composer, shortly after his death.[82] A few *canzoni* by Layolle were copied in Florentine manuscript anthologies dating from the 1520s and 1530s, including 'Questo mostrarsi lieta', a frottolistic setting for three voices of a *ballata* by Lorenzo Strozzi, found alongside similar pieces by his colleagues Bartolomeo degli Organi and Bernardo Pisano, which were probably composed in Florence during the second decade

---

[82] All are included in D'Accone, *Music of the Florentine Renaissance*, 3–4.

of the century. Other settings by Layolle of younger poets such as Filippo Strozzi, Luigi Alamanni, and Ludovico Martelli were included in madrigal collections published in Venice as the work of Verdelot, Arcadelt, Maistre Jhan, Corteccia, and even Rore. A letter sent from Lionardo Strozzi in Lyons to his brother Ruberto in Rome in 1534 indicates that Layolle and his immigrant friends and patrons sang *canzoni* by Arcadelt, Verdelot, and others recently received from Florence.[83] Although not published until around 1540, Layolle's *canzoni* must for the most part have been composed in Lyons during the 1520s and 30s, thus constituting and important contribution to the new (essentially Florentine) madrigal school.

Layolle's 'fifty' four-part pieces include seven settings of Petrarch, the first piece, 'Tasso la dolce vista', being a seven-line cento from seven different poems, the third a *ballata* strophe, the tenth and twenty-eighth complete single-strophe *ballate*, the twentieth a *sestina* strophe, the thirty-sixth a sonnet's first quatrain and the thirty-eighth a sonnet's final sestet. This predilection for setting *ballate* and poetic fragments was characteristic of Verdelot, Arcadelt, and the first generation of madrigalists. Layolle also sets the lament 'Qual sara mai' from Poliziano's *Orfeo*, *ballate* and *canzone* stanzas by the Florentine poet Lodovico Martelli, a *canzone* stanza by Pietro Bembo, another by his friend Luigi Alamanni, as well as complete madrigals by the Florentine poets Biagio Buonaccorsi and Niccolò di Giovanni Martelli. Filippo Strozzi's madrigal 'Gite sospir dolenti' may have been composed during the republican leader's exile in Lyons in the late 1520s, while his *canzone* stanza 'Rompi de l'empio', reportedly written during his final imprisonment under Duke Cosimo de' Medici in 1537, may be the 'canzona'[84] sent from Venice to Palla Strozzi in Lyons to be set by Layolle in April 1539.

The ascription of no less than eight of Layolle's four-voice madrigals 'Lassar il velo', 'I' ho nel cor', 'Il vago e dolce sguardo', 'Occhi miei lassi', 'Gite, sospiri dolenti', 'Amor la tua virtute', 'Dolce parole morte', and 'Dal bel suave raggio' to Arcadelt in various Venetian publications between 1538 and 1541 is symptomatic of their similarity of compositional style. Both composers favour short chanson-like settings (between twenty-five and seventy breves), with clear homorhythmic declamation and rare imitative snatches, little or no word-painting, simple vocal parts of limited range, and brief codas based on inverted pedal-points. Also akin to the French chanson is the tendency, found in

---

[83] Agee, 'Ruberto Strozzi and the Early Madrigal', 1–17.
[84] Agee, 'Filippo Strozzi and the Early Madrigal', 236–7.

fifteen of the fifty *canzoni*, to repeat last lines. But repetition of openings is found only in Alamanni's 'Lasso la bella fera', while internal reprise is rare and restricted mainly to matching *piedi* in *ballate* (such as Petrarch's 'Perche quel che mi trasse' and 'Lassar il velo' and the anonymous 'S'alla mia immensa voglia') and *ottava* stanzas ('Seguimi lasso'). Although repetition of internal lines is also found in the madrigals 'Donn' io non son' and 'Se, chi vostro bel viso', as well as the *canzone* stanzas 'Il vago e dolce sguardo' and 'Dolce parole morte', through-composition clearly predominates, even in 'Anima bella', which sets the two quatrains of Petrarch's sonnet followed by a reprise of the first line with new music. 'Mentre' el ciel chiaro' is exceptional in its blank verse and in its inclusion of a *secunda pars* of similar structure, listed as a separate piece in the table.

These madrigals are arranged in sequences according to mode and clef. The rare appearance of the treble clef, in 'Amor che tutto vedi' and 'Nessun visse giamai', and the predilection for low clef combinations in nos. 25–42, most notably 'Vagha di passo in passo' and 'Occhi mirando in voi', both of which use exclusively F clefs, underlines the predominance of male-voice ensembles; this is confirmed in the references to performance in the contemporary correspondence of the Strozzi family. The collection closes with an unattributed canzona 'on the death of Francesco de Layolle'.

The colophon in the Superius part-book of the *Venticinque Canzoni a cinque voci di Francesco de Layolle* confirms the date of Moderne's publication as 1540. Five-voice madrigals are rare in sources before this time; only two of Layolle's found their way into Venetian publications, 'Aprimi, Amor', included anonymously in Rore's second book (Gardane 1544[17]) and 'Che sono io senza lei', ascribed to Corteccia in *Le dotte et excellente compositioni de i madrigali a cinque voci* (Scotto 1540[18] and Gardane 1541[17]).

These twenty-three madrigals (two French chansons are included) again show Layolle's literary discernment, with nine texts by Petrarch (mostly fragments from sonnets, *canzone*, and a *ballata*), one by Boccaccio (a *ballata* fragment), one by Lorenzo Strozzi, and one by Luigi Alamanni. While most of the pieces again are through-composed, the only complete sonnet—Petrarch's 'O passi sparsi'—uses the same music for the second quatrain; this and a few other pieces (nos. 9, 16, 20, 22, 23, and 24) also include a short terminal reprise. The five-voice madrigals and chansons use more imitative counterpoint than the four-part pieces and dovetail the entries for each poetic line. Again, the whole collection is arranged modally, beginning with pieces in transposed Dorian on G and progressing via F, C, and A to G

Mixolydian, with a predominance of male-voice clefs (C1–F4; only nos. 15–17 use the treble clef).

Like his 'canzoni', some of Layolle's thirteen French pieces—for example 'J'ay mis mon cueur' and 'En douleur et tristesse' (*25 Canzoni*, nos. 9 and 11)—and both three- and four-voice versions of 'La fille qui n'a point d'amy' (1538[18], no. 18 and 1538[15], no. 13), using texts and melodies from the old monophonic chansonniers, were probably old pieces. However, in the fourth book of the *Parangon des Chansons* (1538[18]), the three *bicinia* are new and up to date; one chanson, 'Les Bourguignons', sets a text relating to the siege of Péronne in 1536, while two others, 'Doulce mémoire' and 'Vaincre n'a peu', add a counter-subject to a superius from recent four-voice chansons. Layolle's remaining four-voice pieces are in the typical 'Parisian' manner, although one, 'Ce me semblent choses perdues', sets a quatrain from an old *rondel* printed in the *Jardin de Plaisance*.

Layolle's music epitomises the marriage of Italian and French cultures, old and new, opening the gateway of transalpine influence into France, reflected in the increasing madrigalian tendencies found in the chansons of Phinot and Roussel, as well as in the later madrigals of Matteo Rampollini, Giovanni Antonio di Mayo, Regolo Vecoli, and Jean de Castro.

Moderne published an undated collection containing seven complete *canzoni* by Petrarch set to music by Matteo Rampollini[85] with a dedication to Duke Cosimo II of Florence. Rampollini follows the precedent of Jachet Berchem in setting whole cycles of extended poems by Petrarch and that of Willaert and Rore in using black (*note nere*) notation with a C signature for the prevailing four-part settings. The last strophe or two in each poem is actually set for five or six voices in the old *misura commune* with ₵ signatures. Each poem uses the same clefs and mode, and occasionally certain melodic, rhythmic, or harmonic patterns recur (notably in the sixth *canzone*, 'Poi che per mio destino'). However, there is great variety in texture (with ensembles ranging from three to six voices employing both imitative and homophonic passages), in metre (with skilful use of syncopation and alternation of duple and triple metre), and in structure (each through-composed strophe reflecting poetic form and expression).

While it is not known if Rampollini came to Lyons for the publication of his *Canzoni*, the next collection of madrigals printed in Lyons (in

---

[85] D'Accone, *Matteo Rampollini: II primo libro de la musica*, in Music of the Florentine Renaissance, 7; see also F. D'Accone, 'Matteo Rampollini and his Petrarchan Canzone Cycles', *Musica disciplina*, 27 (1973), 65–106.

1567) was supervised by its composer, the Neapolitan Giovanni Antonio di Mayo, who was still living in the town in 1570.

Mayo's madrigals resemble Rampollini's in using both white (₵) and black notation (C) and in favouring extended poems by Petrarch, notably the *sestine* 'Giovanne donna' and 'Non ha tant animal', each set in six sections, the *ballata* 'Quel foco ch' io pensai', set in three sections (*ripresa* and two *stanze*), as well as the sonnets 'Amor, fortuna', (see music Example 6) 'Quel foco', and 'Passer mai', each set in two sections. They also present Sannazaro's *canzone* 'Sovra una verde e dilletosa riva', set in six sections. However, like Layolle, Mayo also includes incomplete poems, as for example the first eight lines of Petrarch's sonnets 'Morte m'a morto', 'Gli occhi de ch' io parlai', and 'Quand' io veggio', the first seven-line strophe of 'Voi mi poneste in foco' from Bembo's *Asolani* and the single eight-line strophe 'Gravi pen' in amor' from Ariosto's *Orlando furioso*. These use the largely homophonic parlando manner of mid-century *madrigali ariosi* of Barre, Rore, and early Lassus. Their predilection for syncopated rhythms and chords on the flattened seventh degree in major-mode pieces may have derived from the *villanella* or *villanesca alla napolitana* repertoire published a little earlier in Venice by Giovan Tomaso di Mayo and others. At the same time these features, along with the declamatory narrative rhythms, are found in association with classic literary texts in contemporary settings of Ronsard's odes and sonnets by French provincial composers such as Pierre Clereau and Guillaume Boni.

Regolo Vecoli dedicated his first book of five-voice madrigals, published in Lyons in 1577, to Lorenzo Buonvisi, the Luccan patron who received similar honours from Vincenzo Bastini (First book of madrigals for five and six voices, Venice, 1567), Ippolito Baccusi (Third book of six-voice madrigals, Venice, 1579), Nicolo Dorati (First book of madrigals for six voices, Venice, 1579), and Paolo Isnardi (Third book for five voices, Venice, 1581). Vecoli's dedication describes his pieces as 'my first musical compositions written with much labour and study'. In his *Storia della musica in Lucca* (pp. 53–5), Luigi Nerici claims that Vecoli was absent from his native Lucca between 1561 and 1581, exercising his skill as a cornettist and living in Lyons. If this was the case, it can safely be assumed that Regolo actually wrote these pieces in the French city. However, they are very similar to the five-voice madrigals by other members of his family, such as Francesco Vecoli, whose first book was published in Venice in 1575 (his setting of Bartolomeo Gottifredi's *ottava* 'Danzava con maniere sopr'umane' was included in Regolo's collection) and Pietro Vecoli, whose first book was printed in 1581 in Turin, where he served as a musician to Duke Charles Emmanuel of Savoy; these all suggest a Luccan manner, modelled on the four books of the sackbut-player Nicolo Dorati published in Venice between 1549 and 1567. The majority of Regolo's texts are sonnets by Petrarch, Varchi, and others, set in two sections, but there are also two *sestina* stanzas by Petrarch and a few *ottave* by Ariosto and later poets. Regolo's second book of five-voice madrigals was published in 1586 in Paris, where, according to his dedication to the Luccan lady Caterina Burlamacchi, he sought refuge from the 'misfortunes which presently afflict Lyons', and where he perhaps joined his kinsman Pietro Vecoli, whose six-voice madrigals were printed in 1587. Regolo's setting of 'Amor fortuna' is presented in Music Example 7.

The three-voice chansons, madrigals, and motets dedicated to prominent citizens of Lyons in 1575 and 1580 by Jean de Castro may also have been composed when he was living in Lyons, after fleeing the troubles of the Low Countries. However, these pieces were printed in Paris and show no significant divergence from those he had already published in Antwerp and Louvain, except perhaps for the greater literary distinction of the later collection's chansons (all but one by Ronsard) and madrigals (all by Petrarch).

(vi) *Huguenot Psalms*

In Geneva Jean Calvin encouraged Clément Marot and later Théodore de Bèze to translate the psalms into French verse, charging his musicians to write or adapt melodies for congregational singing. Recognizing music as a gift from God, Calvin acknowledged the power of song in his preface to *La Forme des Prières et Chants Ecclesiastiques* (Geneva, 1542):

We know from experience that singing has great power and strength to move and enflame men's hearts, to invoke and praise God with a more vehement and ardent zeal. Remember that the singing should not be light or flighty, but should have weight and majesty, as Saint Augustine said, and so there is a big difference between the music made by men for their enjoyment at table and at home and the psalms which are sung in Church in the presence of God and his angels.

These aims were realized by setting strophic verse syllabically in regular semibreves and minims, with simple, conjunct melodies devoid of word-painting or melismas.

Whether or not the melodies used for the fifty translations of Marot published in Geneva in 1543 were written or arranged by Guillaume Franc, who was employed by the town council to teach the children to sing the psalms in the temple between 1541 and 1545, it seems that his successor Loys Bourgeois was not entirely happy about them. For in the preface to the *Pseaumes octante trois*, published by J. Crespin in Geneva in 1551, Bourgeois not only claimed to have composed the melodies for the thirty-four new translations of de Bèze but to have rewritten or 'improved' thirty-six others. This led to his condemnation and imprisonment by the Council, before Calvin himself intervened on the composer's behalf, explaining that the changes were caused by 'the error of the printers of Lyons' and agreeing that the old melodies be restored.[86] Calvin's claim suggests that the music type-setting was done in Lyons, although the music-type (probably acquired from Pierre Haultin II) is not known outside Switzerland.

Bourgeois' choice of Lyons for the publication of his four-voice psalm-settings is symptomatic of the town's increasing interest in Protestantism, championed by the German Beringen brothers. Moderne had already included two extended four-voice settings by Abel and Gentian of individual psalms translated by Marot in his chanson collections of 1539 and 1544, although Attaingnant in Paris was the first to publish whole sets of Marot's verse translations in polyphonic settings with Certon's collection of thirty-one, including the new Genevan melodies, and Mornable's twenty-three freer pieces—both printed in 1546. However, over the next two decades Lyons became the more important publishing centre for psalms, particularly four-voice settings, which, unlike the monophonic melodies, were not sanctioned in Calvin's Geneva.

The success of the harmonizations of Marot and de Bèze in attracting simple people to the Protestant cause in Lyons enraged Claude de Rubys, who observed: 'the voices of men and women singing melodiously together and blending in musical harmony . . . is a bait that Satan has always used as a means of deceiving and attracting to him women and ignorant people.'[87]

The title-page of the *Pseaulmes cinquante de David . . . traduictz en vers françois par Clément Marot* (Beringen, 1547) specifies that Bourgeois had set them in 'four parts in equal counterpoint matching the words' (i.e. syllabic homophony), while the dedication to André Chenevard indicates that 'such music is usually appropriate for all instruments' and mentions another set composed a 'little more freely'.[88]

[86] See Pidoux, *Le Psautier huguenot*, ii. 52.
[87] Rubys, *Histoire véritable de la ville de Lyon*, 390.
[88] Bernet Kempers, *37 Psalmen . . . van Loys Bourgeois*.

This no doubt refers to *Le Premier livre des Pseaulmes de David contenant XXIIII pseaulmes composé par Loys Bourgeois en diversité de Musique: à sçavoir familière, ou vaudeville: aultres plus musicales: et aultres à voix pareilles, bien couvenables aux instrumentz* (Beringen, 1547).[89] While the first collection of fifty psalms consistently uses the official tenor melodies printed separately by the Beringen press in 1548 and 1549, but already familiar through their earlier publication in Geneva, the second set of twenty-four includes only three of the approved melodies unchanged, in homophonic settings, with thirteen others paraphrased. The eight 'more musical' examples abandon the orthodox tunes altogether in favour of freely derived imitative entries in motet style. With these two collections Bourgeois established the patterns that were to be followed in the settings of Janequin, Colin, Goudimel, Certon, and Arcadelt published in Paris during the next twelve years. In 1554 Godefroy Beringen printed Bourgeois's *Pseaulmes LXXXIII de David*, an expanded edition of his simple four-voice settings, incorporating the thirty-four new translations by de Bèze, with his own approved melodies.

Meanwhile the Beringen brothers introduced a collection of thirty psalms translated by Gilles d'Aurigny, set for four voices by Didier Lupi Second. Lupi's tenor is treated as a cantus firmus and is thus generally simpler than the other parts, which sometimes include brief imitative entries (see Music Example 8).

The fashion for psalms is continued in Simon Joly's four- and five-voice settings of the twenty-one Latin verses paraphrasing Ps. 50, published by the Beringen brothers in 1552, and in the new French translations of the psalms by Jean Poitevin, Claude le Maistre, and Maurice Scève that were added to the fifty of Clément Marot, the whole collection being 'set to music' by Philibert Jambe de Fer and published in 1555 by Michel du Bois.[90] The melodies for Marot's psalms are the official ones which had already been printed by Jean Crespin in Geneva in 1551; the new ones, devised by Philibert,[91] are mostly similar in their metrical rhythm and melody. All are noted in the alto (C3) or tenor (C4) clef, except for the last sixteen of the twenty-two 'octonaires' of Psalm 119, which, like some earlier psalms (nos. 7–10, 13–18, and 22), use the soprano (C1) or (like nos. 11–12 and 19–21), the treble (G2) clef. The difference in clefs, like the rhythmic and melodic character of some of these pieces, particularly the use of syncopations, rests, and anacrustic repeated notes characteristic of middle entries, and the

---

[89] Ed. P. A. Gaillard in Monuments de la musique suisse, 3 (Basle, 1960).

[90] See Guillo, 'Recherches', i. 75–81; ii, no. 30.

[91] See Pidoux, *Le Psautier huguenot*, i. 159–98; ii. 84–8.

unusual specification of subsemitonal G and F sharps (in nos. 8, 10, 16, 20, 22) suggest that some of these melodies were actually superius parts taken from polyphonic versions. Four-part settings of the *Octonaires* by Jambe de Fer were in fact listed in Antoine du Verdier's *Bibliothèque* (Lyons, 1585) as being published in Lyons by Thomas de Straton in 1561.

Philibert's four-voice setting of one of the psalms, 'Comme le cerf longuement pourchassé' (no. 42, translated by Le Maistre), was included in Granjon's chanson anthology entitled *Premier Trophée de Musique* (Lyons, 1559, p. 32). Granjon's tenor part is missing, but a reconstruction[92] shows that Du Bois's 1555 tenor matches the other parts perfectly. This largely homophonic setting fits comfortably into the chanson collection, having the common structure associated with many contemporary decasyllabic *huitains*, with the second couplet reusing the music of the first and with the last line repeated.

In 1559 Michel du Bois printed a collection of forty-one psalms translated by Théodore de Bèze, set for two, three, four, or five voices by Jambe de Fer, with a dedication to Georg Obrech, a banker from Strasburg resident in Lyons between 1544 and 1567. The title-page describes the psalms as being 'harmonized in variable Music' (i.e. for different vocal ensembles) 'with the common tune inviolably observed'.[93] In fact, only thirty-four of these psalms use the official melodies which had been published in Geneva in 1551; the other seven, along with some prayers by Marot, were newly composed, presumably by Philibert. The thirty-four settings of de Bèze reappear with slight modification in Jambe de Fer's complete hundred and fifty psalms for four or five voices printed by Antoine Cercia and Pierre de Mia in 1564 and reprinted by the latter with the composer's corrections in the same year.[94] This collection, addressed to King Charles IX, for whose ceremonial entry into Lyons Philibert had organized the music, includes four-voice settings of two dedicatory pieces, 'Qui d'un sainct Roy voudra ouyr et voir' and the sonnet 'Qui est-ce qui pourra redorer vostre France', based on the king's device, 'Pietate et justitia'. Most of these psalms are homophonic settings, with the Genevan tunes unchanged in the tenor part.[95] In similar style are the appended Commandments, Prayers, and Canticles, including the first settings of

---

[92] See Dobbins, 'The Chanson at Lyons', ii, no 79.
[93] See Guillo, 'Recherches', ii, no. 37; Pidoux *Le Psautier huguenot*, ii. 114–15; Gaillard, 'Die Psalmodie de XLI Pseaumes royaux', 111.
[94] Guillo, 'Recherches', ii, nos. 73 and 74; Pidoux, *Le Psautier huguenot*, ii. 143–5.
[95] Fifteen are scored in N. Labelle, *Les Differents Styles de la musique religieuse en France: Le psaume de 1539 à 1572* (Henryville, 1981), ii. 111–36.

Bonaventure des Périers's 'Cantique de Moyse' and 'Dizain de la Loy et de la Foy'.

Typical of Protestant concern for middle-class edification and education is the fact that Jambe de Fer followed Loys Bourgeois's *Droict Chemin* (Geneva, 1550) in publishing a simple French treatise on music for amateurs, *Épitome Musical des tons, sons et accordz, es voix humaines, Fleustes d'Alleman, Fleustes à neuf trous, Violes, et Violons. Item Un petit devis des accordz de Musique, par forme de dialogue interrogatoire et responsif entre deux interlocuteurs P. & I* (Musical Epitome on the tones, sounds, and harmony of human voices, flutes, recorders, viols, and violins. Also a little discussion on the harmonies of music, in the form of a dialogue with questions and answers between two speakers, P and I.).[96] The book was printed in 1556 by Michel du Bois, with a dedication to Jean Darud, a Protestant trader in cloth and spices who, like the composer, came originally from the Franche-Comté. Jean may be the 'I' who at the end discourses with 'P' (Philibert) on music and harmony.

The first part of the treatise deals in a conventional manner with the gamut, clefs, hexachords, mutation (modulation), rhythmic values, ligatures, proportions, and tactus (beating time), following earlier theorists such as Ornithoparchus, Heyden, Frosch, Le Gendre, Guilliaud, Martin, and Bourgeois, all of whom are acknowledged. The more original second part describes the ranges, fingering, and playing-techniques of the flute, recorder, treble, tenor, and bass viol, and violin, including illustrations with fingering charts. The last section, dealing with harmony, prohibits consecutive fifths and octaves, recommends a mixture of perfect and imperfect chords, but it postpones a discussion on *accords faux* (discords), although its examples include cadences with 4−3 and 7−6 suspensions.

Michel Ferrier's three-voice settings of Marot's psalms, with the Canticle of Simeon and the Ten Commandments, were printed in Lyons by Robert Granjon in 1559 and reprinted in Paris by Nicolas du Chemin in 1568. In both cases only the tenor part survives; while this preserves the official Genevan melodies, its spacing suggests paraphrased, polyphonic treatment. According to both title-pages, Ferrier, like Marot himself, originated from Cahors; but there is no evidence that he ever lived or worked in Lyons.

The complete Huguenot psalter, along with the ten Commandments and the Canticle of Simeon (Nunc dimittis), set for four voices by Richard Crassot was published in Lyons by Thomas de Straton in 1564

---

[96] Lesure, 'L'*Épitome Musical* de Philibert Jambe de Fer (1556)', which includes a fac. edn.

and reprinted by Jean Huguetan in the following year.[97] Unlike other polyphonic psalms printed in Lyons (or Paris), Crassot's are presented in choir-book rather than part-book format, with the official melody indicated by a marginal trefoil or hand, so that it could be sung alone if necessary. As the preface explains, this melody is retained unchanged, albeit usually in the superius rather than the conventional tenor, with the three accompanying voices added in simple homophony with few rests or suspensions.

If the music of Paschal de L'Estocart and Jean Servin was in fact printed in Geneva, no further psalms appeared in Lyons after 1566, when two of Goudimel's four-voice settings with contrafactum texts were introduced in Louis des Masures's biblical drama *La Musique de David*, along with the Genevan melodies for the Commandments of God and the Canticle of Simeon.

(vii) Chansons spirituelles *and* Cantiques

Contrafactum texts were characteristic of the *chanson spirituelle*, which, along with the metrical psalm, became the principal musical form of the new reformed sects, although examples were occasionally written or performed by Catholics. At first the term was applied to collections of chanson texts which substitute 'purified' sacred, moral, or polemical words, retaining a familiar opening gambit and an identical prosodic structure from a secular model. These pieces frequently give indications that they should be sung to a pre-existent tune which originally had an amorous ditty. The use of contrafactum texts and timbres was already popular in the noël by the early sixteenth century. The same principle is applied in Eustorg de Beaulieu's *chansons spirituelles* published without music under the title *Chrestienne Resjouyssance* in 1546. New texts based on well-known secular models and tunes were also written by Marguerite de Navarre and published in 1547 by Jean de Tournes in the *Marguerites de la Marguerite des Princesses* (1547).

Guillaume Guéroult's *Premier livre de chansons spirituelles*, published by the Beringen brothers in 1548, breaks new ground by introducing new music, specially composed by Didier Lupi Second in four-part homophony with melodic tenor parts, similar in style to that used in his metrical psalms.[98] In fact, the first five of the twenty-one

---

[97] See L. Guillo, 'Les Psaumes de Richard Crassot', in *Le Mot dit: Chroniques rassemblées par les amis des bibliothèques municipales de Lyon* (Lyons, 1986), 36–41. Fifteen of Crassot's psalms are included in Labelle, *Les Differents Styles*, ii. 137–62.

[98] The whole collection is scored and studied in Honegger, 'Les Chansons spirituelles de Didier Lupi Second'.

pieces in Lupi's book *are* psalms, translated by Guéroult; the sixth is a strophic setting of the lamentations of Jeremiah, the seventh a Te Deum translation, the eighth and ninth two versions of the Apocryphal tale of Susanna and the elders. The second of these, 'Susanne un jour', acquired exceptional popularity and was emulated in at least thirty-seven later polyphonic settings by Mithou, Certon, Rore, Roussel, Lassus, Castro, Le Jeune, Servin, Byrd, and many others.[99] Some pieces in this collection suggest parody, if not contrafactum, notably the opening psalm, which quotes from Sermisy's setting of Marot's chanson 'Tant que vivray', and nos. 16–18—'Doulce mémoire', 'Contentement', and 'Contentes vous'—which are all based on familiar four-voice courtly chansons. Later editions by Thomas de Straton (1561) and Benoît Rigaud (1568)[100] include new pieces set by Arcadelt, Certon, Janequin, and Jambe de Fer, as well as 'Hélas mon Dieu', attributed to Maillard, as in some Parisian collections (1549[18], 1549[28], 1569[10]), although originally published (in 1545[8-9]) with ascription to Janequin. The two Susanna laments ('Susanne un jour' and 'Dames qui au plaisant son'), reappeared with other *chansons spirituelles* by Guéroult and Joachim du Bellay in *La Lyre chrestienne avec la Monomachie de David*, published by Simon Gorlier in Lyons in 1560 with music by Antoine de Hauville.

The twenty-six *Cantiques chantés au Seigneur* by Louis des Masures were set to music in four parts probably by Claude Goudimel,[101] who was a close friend of the poet, living near him in Metz in 1564 when Jean de Tournes published the collection in Lyons. The title-page suggests that readers who do not understand music can sing some of these canticles to the common psalm-tunes, which are accordingly indicated in eleven of the ensuing texts. The homophonic four-part settings are similar in style to the simpler psalms of Jambe de Fer and Goudimel himself, with the melody in the tenor part, to which the subsequent strophes are appended.

Lyons played an important role in the composition and diffusion of the *chanson spirituelle* during the 1540s, through the efforts of Guillaume Guéroult, Didier Lupi, and others.[102] Interest soon extended to Venice, where a five-voice collection by Jacques Buus was published,[103] then to Antwerp and Louvain, where the settings of Hubert Waelrant and Jean Caulery appeared during the 1550s. Finally, in La

---

[99] See Levy, 'Susanne un jour'.

[100] Guillo, 'Recherches', i. 87–8; ii, nos. 52 and 82.

[101] See Goudimel, *Œuvres complètes*, xiv. 85–102.

[102] See Guillo, 'Recherches', i. 117–22.

[103] J. Buus, *Libro primo delle canzoni francese* (Venice, 1550).

Rochelle and Geneva, during the 1570s and 1580s, Jean Pasquier and Simon Goulart produced numerous contrafactum texts for the chansons of Lassus and for the sonnets of Ronsard set by Guillaume Boni and Antoine de Bertrand; Goulart probably also wrote many of the new spiritual texts included in the three books of chansons set by Jean Servin. In similar vein were the *Octonaires de la vanité et inconstance du monde* by the Calvinist preacher Antoine de Chandieu, set to music by Paschal de l'Estocart; these were printed by Jean II de Laon in Geneva, although some editions bear a title-page claiming publication in Lyons, no doubt a ploy to increase circulation. The same ploy was probably used by Jean II de Tournes in 1586 for a re-edition of chansons by Arcadelt with substitute texts edited by Goudimel, and perhaps for the two *Fleur de Chansons* books of Lassus ascribed to the otherwise unknown publisher Jean Bavent of Lyons in 1574, but almost certainly printed by De Tournes in Geneva. Perhaps the last new *chanson spirituelle* to appear in Lyons was Goudimel's 'Par le désert', included in Blockland's *Instruction* in 1573.

The fact that such books of *chansons spirituelles* were purchased mainly by Protestants and censured by Catholic authorities is confirmed by a report in Jean Crespin's *Histoire des Martyrs* (Geneva, 1619, fo. 245^v), which claims that on 9 January 1554 Matthieu Dymonet, citizen of Lyons, was interrogated by the royal lieutenant and his officials simply because his books included a 'petit livre de chansons spirituelles en musique'. This may refer to the *Cinq Chansons spirituelles composées par cinq Escoliers detenus prisonniers à Lyon en l'an 1553*, whose tunes might have been written by Guillaume de la Mœulle.[104]

After the Counter-Reformation, Catholics responded to the Calvinists' earlier popular success with the publication in 1592 of sixteen of the favourite hymns and canticles recently translated into French verse by the Jesuit Michel Coyssard (1547–1623), set to music for one voice with three optional homophonic lower parts, similar in style to the psalms of Richard Crassot. An enlarged edition of these hymns, published by Joachim Trognese in Antwerp in 1600, includes eight of the sixteen harmonizations amongst the 'Airs composez par Virgile Le Blanc', although this attribution may be unreliable. In another edition, published by Jean Pillehotte in Lyons in 1608, Coyssard mentions that his hymns were often sung to the accompaniment of the spinet and other musical instruments. This edition also includes a 'Treatise on the benefit that everyone can gain from singing hymns and *chansons*

---

[104] Published by Simon du Bosc and Guillaume Guéroult in Geneva in 1554; see Pidoux, *Le Psautier huguenot*, ii. 74–6. Also see above, Ch. 5 (*xiii*).

spirituelles in his native language', explaining the propagandist and mnemonic value of vernacular versification and musical setting for indoctrinating children, which the Protestants had already exploited. In yet another edition of the hymns (Lyons, L. Muguet, 1619) Coyssard explains that he would like to have added music to his canticles as 'in the book [of *laude spirituali*] published in Rome in 1573', but that since he could not find any suitable 'notes' (i.e. type) he had postponed the task, leaving the reader meanwhile to use 'Airs already published in this town and in Antwerp or adapt other grave and devotional ones...'. Several secular tunes were suggested as timbres for further *Odes et chansons spirituelles qu'on chante à Sainte Ursule corrigées par le R. P. M. Coyssard*, published by Muguet in 1623.[105]

The contrafactum principle, used so successfully by Simon Goulart in Geneva in the 1580s, was also adopted by the Jesuits, in a collection containing a hundred four- or five-voice airs, chansons, noëls, and *balletti* by Pierre Bonnet, Pierre Cerveau, Pierre Guédron, Guillaume Chastillon de la Tour, and Giovanni Giacomo Gastoldi, with unattributed spiritual French texts, published by Louis Muguet in 1615 under the title *Amphion sacré*.[106]

Thus the last music to be printed in Lyons for more than a hundred years was no more than a reprint of music composed earlier in Paris, Caen, or Mantua, a sad epilogue to an illustrious century of activity.

(viii) *Dramatic Music*

During the first half of the sixteenth century the plays presented in Lyons by the *Basochiens* and other groups used the current repertoire of popular song in the traditional manner. While Barthélemy Aneau's early morality and mystery plays, performed in the grammar school where he taught, also show the use of art-song and noëls with modified texts, his second Christmas drama, published in 1559, offers new, four-part music composed by Claude Goudimel, Didier Lupi, and perhaps [Étienne] du Tertre.[107] A precedent for publishing music within a drama is found in Joachim Coignac's Protestant tragedy, *La Desconfiture de Goliath*, printed by Adam and Jean Riverez in Geneva in 1551; this not only has suggestions for *timbres* from contemporary psalms and canticles but inserts, at the end, a new melody, notated in the tenor clef in simple *voix de ville* style, with thirteen five-line strophes appended.

---

[105] Guillo, 'Recherches', i. 179–87; ii, no. 97.
[106] Ibid. ii, no. 100. RISM 1615[7].
[107] See above, Ch. 2 (*ii*).

More continuous music in one, two, three, and four parts is found in biblical dramas by Louis des Masures, published in Geneva in 1566. In the same year a similar play appeared anonymously in Lyons, from the press of Jean Saugrin, entitled *La Musique de David* and subtitled *La Rejection des Juifs et la Reception des Gentils*. It has six characters, five of them (Abraham, Moses, David, Jesus, and the Gentile) singing singly or in groups. The dialogue, presented in verse, is liberally interspersed with nine musical pieces. Abraham's opening speech, in decasyllabic sonnet form, gives way to a heptasyllabic couplet sung to two melismatic phrases in F major of tenor range. Moses then enters, singing a heptasyllabic quatrain, 'Leve le cœur, ouvre l'aureille', which is in fact Clément Marot's translation of God's Commandments, with the same syllabic C major melody first used by Loys Bourgeois in a four-part setting in 1547 and later incorporated into the Genevan psalter. Moses and Abraham continue in spoken dialogue of decasyllabic lines with alternating rhyme before joining in a hexasyllabic couplet notated for two tenors (C3 and C4 clefs). David enters next, praising his predecessors' harmony and voices with nine octosyllabic lines; he then sings his own decasyllabic quatrain with four simple phrases of tenor range (C3 clef) in F major. After further dialogue in verse, the three characters sing the four-part harmonization of Marot's Psalm 115, 'Non point à nous', published by Goudimel two years earlier. The text does not explain who should perform the superius part which is notated in the C1 clef; but this clef is used for the ensuing octosyllabic quatrain sung by Jesus, who is welcomed by David as completing the choir:

> Nostre chapelle est maintenant fournie
> Pour bien chanter la celeste musique.

This ensemble is confirmed in the ensuing dialogue, with Jesus claiming that he can sing the *dessus* (superius part) without falsetto, while Faith (represented by Abraham), takes the *basse contre* (bass) and Law (Moses and David) the *taille* (tenor). Jesus then repeats 'Leve le cœur', which is still notated in the alto (C3 clef). After further dialogue, the four voices again join to sing the 'mottet', 'La loy de grace et de concorde', which is in fact a contrafactum of Ps. 59, using Goudimel's harmonization of 1564, with the Genevan melody in the tenor. A Jew then appears, praising this 'fine song' and engaging in extended dialogue with the four main protagonists, before they again join to perform 'Or laisse Créateur'—Marot's translation of the Nunc dimittis—in Goudimel's 1564 setting, with the official Genevan tune in the tenor. This wins the admiration of a Gentile, who then sings the tenor part alone. David concludes the piece with the moral that 'the Scriptures are in perfect accord, just like the four concordant parts in music'.

While no composer is named in this play, or in the three by Louis des Masures printed in Geneva in 1566, it is likely that the music was all composed or arranged by Claude Goudimel, who lived near Des Masures in Metz in the 1560s, before moving to Lyons; at all events, his harmonizations were used in three of the four ensembles.

Although the funeral air for Louis de Condé by Hubert-Philippe de Villiers published in 1569 is presented in the form of dramatic dialogue (see above, pp. 166–8), no further music dramas from Lyons survive. However, an idea of the kind of music provided for later plays there may be gleaned from Loys Papon's *Pastorale*, presented in Montbrison to celebrate a Catholic victory in 1587: this included a band of shawms, choirboy actors, and a four-part dance and a victory air, all of which are notated in the surviving manuscript (British Library, Harley 4325).

(ix) *Instrumental Music*

Testimony to the popularity of instrumental music in the city is provided by the intense activity of the instrument-makers and of the players employed by the municipality. It is characteristic of the patterns of employment and publication in the sixteenth century that a number of composers who were active as instrumentalists, such as Eustorg de Beaulieu, Francesco de Layolle, Charles Cordeilles, Guillaume de La Mœulle, and Regolo Vecoli, published no instrumental music. The music that was printed, like the production of the instrument-makers and the treatises of Bonaventure des Périers and Philibert Jambe de Fer, reflects the wealthy amateur market for indoor music, particularly for lute, guitar, cittern, spinet, flute, recorder, and viol.

While a number of books of instrumental music—particularly those of Simon Gorlier for flute, spinet, guitar (or gittern), and cittern—have been lost, one collection of music for instrumental ensemble and four for lute have survived. The first of these, an undated publication by Jacques Moderne entitled *Musicque de Joye*, is described on its title-page as 'suitable for voices, spinets, violins, and flutes, with selected basses danses, pavanes, galliards, and branles, from which the measures and cadences of music and all dances may be learned'. Its 'various accomplished and excellent' composers include Adrian Willaert, together with his Venetian colleagues Giulio Segni, Girolamo Parabosco, and Girolamo Cavazzoni, who provide twenty of the collection's twenty-two ricercars; eighteen of these had appeared, along with two by

Nicolas Benoist and Girolamo Parabosco, in *Musica nova accom-modata per cantar et sonar sopra organi et altri strumenti*, in Venice in 1540.[108] Two additions to the Lyons edition include another ricercar by Willaert and one by G. Coste, who may have been a local figure. These two pieces differ from the other imitative ricercars, the first in using predominantly short equal note-values akin to the chanson or later instrumental canzona, the second in being monothematically based on a single lively rhythmic motive. Moderne also, curiously, reprints one ricercar twice (on folios C3 and D1), attributing it first to Segni, as in the Italian publication, and then to Willaert.

The Lyons collection adds twenty-eight dances, arranged in a some-what haphazard order, beginning with five pairs of *Bassedance* plus *Tordion* (three of them related to four-part chansons by Roquelay, Sandrin, and Sermisy), followed by four Pavanes. The first pavane, entitled 'La Bataille', inspired by Janequin's successful chanson, was included in Claude Gervaise's third book of *Danceries* published by Attaingnant in 1557, while the third re-harmonizes the melody of Janequin's 'Il estoit une fillette'. Next are two unrelated *Gailardes* and twelve *Branles*, six of them specified as 'Burgundian', three as 'single' and three as 'gay'· (the variants are described in Arbeau's treatise, *Orchésographie*, published in Langres in 1589). Although it is easy to imagine how these simple homophonic settings with tunes in the upper part might have been played by Cordeilles, La Mœulle, and their fellow waits, there is nothing in this selection of particular local significance. Seven of the dances are also found amongst the fifty printed in Attaingnant's 'second' book of *Danceries* in 1547,[109] while others may have been included in his first book, which has not survived. Thus Moderne's collection is a curious combination of learned contrapuntal ricercars by Italian organists and popular chordal dances by anonymous French waits, notated by 'learned musicians' such as Claude Gervaise, who wrote or edited four books of dance-band music for Attaingnant between 1550 and 1555.

While Paris also led the way in introducing lute-tablatures printed cheaply by single impression, with Attaingnant's publications of 1529–31 and those of Michel Fezandat and Adrian le Roy of the 1550s, printers in Italy, Spain, and Germany (using different tablature systems) as well as in the Low Countries (following the French system) responded to an apparently unquenchable thirst for lute-music between these dates. Moderne in Lyons filled the gap in the French market, with

---

[108] See Slim (ed.), *Musica Nova*.
[109] Ed. Meyland, nos. 2, 7–9, 17, 25, 37.

three books that remain closer in format, content, and tablature system to the second generation of Italian production, which began with the printing of works by Francesco Canova da Milano in Milan and Venice in 1536 and continued with a spate of works by his compatriots Abondante, Barberiis, Domenico Bianchini, and others in the 1540s. Moderne's three books are thus small oblong volumes, containing a succession of ricercars (or, synonymously, 'fantasias'), transcriptions of chansons (and occasionally madrigals or motets), and dances, intabulated in the Italian numerical system.

Moderne's first lute-book was the *Tablature de lutz en diverses formes de Fantasie, Bassedances, Chansons, Pavanes, Pseaulmes, Gaillardes*, 'composed by different musicians and intabulated for lute by Mr Francesco Bianchini from Venice', with a dedication to François Gouffier, who was appointed Bishop of Béziers shortly before his death in 1548. Francesco may be related to Domenico Bianchini alias 'Rossetto', Venetian lutenist and mosaicist, who published a similar lute-book[110] with Antonio Gardane in 1546. But while Francesco's closing pavanes and galliards have Italian titles, many of his other pieces suggest French—and perhaps even Lyonese—origin. His collection begins with a single extended 'Fantasia' similar in style and structure to the ricercars of Francesco da Milano and Domenico Bianchini. Following ten bars of scalic improvisation, a basic tetrachord motive (A–G–E–F–G–A–F–E) is presented imitatively in a form very similar to that of the eighth ricercar in the *Musicque de Joye* (ascribed to Julius de Modena, i.e. Giulio Segni). After several imitative entries between the four parts, this motif is modified (A–E–G–F–E), inverted (A–B–D–C–B–G–A) and abbreviated (A–B–C–A, A–G–F–E) in different rhythms, the piece ending with a repeated final section and a short plagal coda.

The Fantasia is followed by arrangements of five four-part chansons, the first, 'Quant tu vouldras', ascribed to Isaac L'Héritier (a name found in only two other sources, both chansons published by Moderne in 1541 and 1543), and the second, Est il regret', to the otherwise unknown G. Bichenet. A third chanson offers a more ornamented version of Crecquillon's 'Si j'ay l'amour', which was not published in Antwerp until 1552, but which may have been included with other pieces by this composer in the lost eleventh book of the *Parangon des Chansons* in 1543 or 1544. While imitative entries in brisk rhythm are unaltered, divisions replace long notes and pre-cadential patterns,

---

[110] D. Bianchini, *Intabolatura de lauto di Dominico Bianchini ditto Rossetto di ricercari, motetti, madrigali, canzon francese, napolitane et balli libro primo* (Venice, 1546); fac., ed. A. Mann (Neuss, 1977).

particularly in the upper part. Maillard's 'Ung grand desir', included in a later collection of chansons published in Lyons by Granjon (RISM 1559[14]) also incorporates some decorative division of the tenor and bass parts, as does Entaygues's 'Dame sante'. The last chanson, 'Vous semblet il' by G. de la Mœulle, the Genevan instrumentalist active in Lyons in the 1540s, is more imitative and less ornamented (see Music Example 9).

Despite their Latin titles, the next three pieces are arrangements of psalms translated into French by Clément Marot and set for four voices by Pierre Certon and Antoine de Mornable in collections published in Paris in 1546. Thus Bianchini's 'In domino confido' offers an ornamented version of the melody found in Mornable's 'Veu que de tout en Dieu mon cœur s'appuye', while 'Domini est terra' similarly arranges Mornable's 'La terre au Seigneur appartient' and 'Benedic anima mea' recasts the four parts of Certon's 'Sus, sus, mon âme'.

The collection ends with six dances. The first, the *Bassedance* 'Quant j'ay congneu', has a highly decorated melody with some similarity in outline to the one used in Pierre Sandrin's 1538 setting of the poem by King Francis I, although it lacks Sandrin's harmony and metrical changes. The second, *Bassedance* 'La Mestresse', has a similar twelve-bar melody, with rudimentary harmony, including parallel fifths and octaves. After these old-fashioned French dances come four modern Italian ones, two pavanes and two galliardes. The *Pavane* 'La Millanese' is constructed upon the *Romanesca* bass, although most 'Milanese pavans' use the slightly different *Passamezzo antico* sequence. The *Pavane* 'La Favorita' also employs a set chord-sequence, but does not correspond to the melodies or basses found in later dances with the same title. The final *Galliards*, entitled 'El peschadore' and 'El mulinero', are not related to the preceding pavanes or to each other.

Moderne's second lutebook, *Tablature de Lutz en diverses sortes comme Chansons, Pavanes, Gaillardes et La Bataille*[111] 'all composed by Jean Paulo Paladin from Milan', begins with four arrangements of well-known chansons by Jacotin, Arcadelt, and Sermisy, faithfully transcribing the models' four original voices, adding only a little division at the cadences. Next come two fantasias, which begin imitatively but proceed freely with interlocking scales and sequences, quite lacking in Bianchini's motivic developments. The ensuing two *Pavanes* have the usual tripartite structure, with each eight- or sixteen-bar section repeated with variation (AA'BB'CC'); a third *Pavane*, with an

---

[111] J. P. Paladin, *Œuvres*, ed. M. Renault and J.-M. Vaccaro (Corpus des Luthistes Français; Paris, 1986).

ABA structure, is identical with the 'Pavana ditta la Malcontenta' ascribed to another Milanese lutenist, Pietro Paolo Borrono, in a lute-book published in Milan by Giovanni Casteliono in 1536. The following *Gaillarde* provides a triple-metre version of the first *Pavane*, giving way to a sequel entitled 'La Reprise', which actually follows the bass and harmony of the third pavane. Another *Gaillarde* and *Reprise*, beginning in the minor mode and closing in the major, appears unrelated to any earlier pavane. The collection closes with an arrangement of Janequin's 'La Bataille' which had been ascribed to Francesco da Milano in Marcolini's Venetian edition of his works in 1536.

A manuscript inscription on the parchment cover of the single surviving copy of Paladino's book gives its date as 1549. But the only clearly dated lute-book published by Moderne was the *Intabulatura Valentini Bacfarc Transilvani coronensis. Liber primus*,[112] issued under a local three-year privilege in January 1553, with a dedication to François de Tournon, Archbishop of Lyons. The Hungarian lutenist Bálint Bakfark travelled to Lyons from Augsburg in quest of a printer for his music. Since he did not remain long in the town, his collection can hardly be said to be of local significance, although he may have taken some of his musical models from Lyonese publications. Beginning with four *Recercate*, which are all extended imitative polythematic pieces in the *Musica Nova* manner, each in a different mode, he continues with arrangements of vocal polyphony, including four-, five-, and six-part motets by Gombert, Jacquet of Mantua, Piéton, and Richafort, all taken, no doubt, from Moderne's *Motetti del Fiore* (1532^{9-10}), as well as six chansons by Crecquillon, Janequin, and Rogier, and six madrigals by Arcadelt and Verdelot. Bakfark's intabulations are remarkably faithful to their models, despite the difficulty of reproducing all the essential entries in Piéton's six-part 'Benedicta es coelorum'. A little more ornament is added to Rogier's 'D'amours me plains', Arcadelt's Quand io pens'al martire', and Verdelot's six-part 'Ultimi mei sospiri', but most of his transcriptions remain very strict and unadorned.

Paladino, who stayed on in Lyons, earning a good living through foreign trade at the fairs, may have been dissatisfied with Moderne as a publisher. At all events, in 1553 he turned instead to the obscure printer Giovanni Pullon de Trino to bring out a new lute-book; this was reissued in 1560 by Simon Gorlier, with a new initial gathering, presenting a fresh title-page, a brief illustration of Italian lute-tablature and a table of contents, all written in French. Gorlier's remaining ten gatherings (A–H4) merely reproduce Pullon's Italian tablature and

---

[112] V. Bakfark, *Opera omnia*, i, ed. I. Homolya and D. Benkő (Budapest, 1976).

titles, offering the usual succession of fantasias, madrigals, chansons, motets, and dances.[113]

Paladino's six new fantasias are more extended and developed than his two earlier examples, but their texture remains lighter and more flexible than Bakfark's dense and continuous counterpoint. While his themes are shorter than Francesco da Milano's, they are presented and developed with greater variety and virtuosity. The second fantasia was reprinted with few changes and without acknowledgement in Morlaye's second lute-book in Paris in 1558. The sixth piece, described as 'Fantasia senza canto' because it does not use the top string (*chanterelle*), is of impressive sombre intensity. The relationship of the fantasia (or, synonymously, the ricercar) to the imitative motet or madrigal is seen in four subsequent pieces, where a transcription is followed by a much freer reworking of the same model entitled 'Fantasia upon the said Madrigal'. Thus his lightly ornamented intabulation of an anonymous four-voice setting of Ariosto's 'Alcun' non po saper' is followed by a longer fantasia largely based on the madrigal's opening four-note motive of two rising thirds. While his arrangement of Arcadelt's 'Quand'io penso al martir' gradually introduces increasing amounts of diminution, the ensuing fantasia is less ornate, reducing the model to a few motives, like the opening seven notes of the Tenor, which are worked much more intensively.

Paladino's transcription of 'Ave sanctissima', unlike Albert de Rippe's, does not inflate Sermisy's light three-part texture; but the ensuing fantasia, extending over 280 measures, is the longest piece in this book, expanding upon several motives from the motet's 125 measures. On the other hand, the fantasia following the transcription of Jacotin's 'Proba me domine' is considerably shorter than the model (214 measures). While Paladino's intabulation of Janequin's 'Or vien ca vien' is more ornate than Bakfark's or de Rippe's, his transcriptions of Certon's 'M'amye un jour' and Sandrin's 'Si j'ay du bien', both adding different coloration for each of the four appearances of the main section in the AA'BAA' structures, do not match the instrumental virtuosity of Le Roy's two exuberant glosses published in Paris in 1559.

A comparison of Paladino's extended 'Pavana chiamata la Milanesa' with Francesco Bianchini's brief 'Pavane La Millanese' shows great advances in instrumental and compositional technique. Paladin's slightly different bass and chord sequence corresponds to Morlaye's 'Pavane la Milanoise' (1558) or to what was also known as the *Passamezzo antico*,

---

[113] J. P. Paladin, *Premier livre de tablature de luth* (Lyon, 1560); fac. edn., Geneva, 1983; modern edn., in Paladin, *Œuvres*.

presented here with three variations, each marked 'Altro modo'. The ensuing *Gagliarda*, based on the same ostinato, also has three variations with increasing diminution, followed by an unrelated major mode 'Represa'. The second *Gagliarda*, designated 'Gaillarde Italienne' in the new table of contents, has three strains of ten or twelve bars, each repeated with divisions. Next comes a pavane and galliard pair named 'la Paladina' after the composer; each dance has two twelve-bar strains with ornamented doubles, while at the end is a *Represa* with a repeated sixteen-bar strain, unrelated in melody or harmony to the preceding galliard. The final *Gagliarda*, described as 'Gaillarde nouvelle' in the table, has two twenty-one bar strains repeated in 'Altro modo' (meaning with variation), followed without break by a *Represa*.

Although none of Gorlier's other instrumental publications survive from his years in Lyons, we have his arrangements for guitar of two- and three-voice motets and chansons by Josquin, Jacotin, Certon, Sermisy, Sandrin, and Janequin, printed by Fezandat and Granjon in Paris in 1551, with a dedication to his 'friend, Françoys Pournas from Lyons'.[114]

Antoine du Verdier's *Bibliothèque* (Lyons, 1585) signals a collection for spinet containing fantasias, motets, chansons, madrigals, and dances published by Gorlier in 1560, as well as Guillaume de Brayssingar's book containing ricercars and variations printed by Moderne in 1536. But no sources of keyboard music from Lyons survive, even if some music composed in the town may have been included in Aleman Layolle's manuscript score,[115] copied during his later Florentine years. This possibility is reinforced by the fact that this score contains three pieces—Rore's 'Ancor che col partire', Berchem's 'Qual anima ignorante' and Janequin's 'La Bataille'—which had been arranged for lute by Paladino, two of them published by Gorlier, who also issued Layolle's *Chansons et Vaudevilles* in 1561.

The absence of any instrumental music published in Lyons after 1560 parallels the situation throughout France and reflects the vagaries of the press rather than the religious wars or market forces.

[114] See Brown, *Instrumental Music*, 1551$_1$.
[115] D'Accone, 'The Intavolatura di M. Alamanno Aiolli'.

Epilogue

THE general picture of music composed, published and practised in Lyons does not perfectly match that of other important European cities or courts, like Mantua, Ferrara, and Bruges, which have been the subject of recent studies. One obvious reason for this is the absence of a resident princely patron or choral foundation permanently imposing political or practical requirements. The frequent and extended visits of the French royal court in pursuit of the Italian wars and the ensuing military and diplomatic encounters are only intermittently reflected in the music copied and published during the first half of the century. Some of Moderne's motet publications in particular include political themes, most notably the joy at the release of the royal hostages in 1530, the dynastic marriage of Francis I and Eleanor of Habsburg in the same year and the hopes for peace following the meetings between Francis, the Emperor Charles V and Pope Paul IV at Nice and Aigues-Mortes in 1538. But others show republican aspirations which might echo the feelings of the many exiled Florentines who supported the musical chapel in the Dominican church of Notre-Dame de Confort, where Moderne's editor Francesco Layolle was organist. Others still suggest wider concerns, no doubt showing the eclectic nature of Moderne's repertoire and his business interests as a publisher in satisfying a wide European market through the international fairs of Lyons.

The plainsong-dominated tradition in the cathedral and its satellite parish churches denied any regular local demand for complex Latin polyphony, although the music composed and edited by Layolle for Gueynard and Moderne may indicate the independence of the Florentine community's church. There is further archival evidence to support this and to suggest the presence of professional organists and singers in the churches of Saint-Nizier and Saint-Paul, as well as in those of the Augustinian, Franciscan, and other monastic orders. At all events, after the flurry of activity represented by the masses and motets of Gueynard, Moderne, and Beringen, publishers abandon Latin liturgical music in favour of vernacular psalms, whose simple four-voice settings suggest domestic rather than professional performance. The damage to music books and organs during the Protestant uprising of 1562 was less significant than the decline in the strategic importance of Lyons to the Valois after the final renunciation of their Italian claims with the treaty signed at Cateau-Cambrésis in 1559.

While some later publications, particularly those of Granjon, were no doubt directed at the international market, others had a more localized orientation. Thus Beringen's books of motets, chansons, and psalms by Phinot, Joly, Didier Lupi, and Loys Bourgeois, like the treatise by Jambe de Fer, were addressed to individual local patrons, as were Moderne's later books of lute pieces by Bakfark and Bianchini. So too were the treatise and chansons of Blockland and Castro, as well as the madrigals and *canzonelle* of Regolo Vecoli and Fiorino. While Moderne's dedicatees were prominent prelates (the Bishop of Beziers and the Archbishop of Lyons) and Blockland's members of the local aristocracy, Beringen's included Italian, French, or German bankers or traders resident in Lyons. The patrons of Vecoli and Fiorino were members of the Luccan patrician family of Buonvisi, some of whom lived and traded in Lyons, while Jean de Castro, who resided temporarily in Lyons, enjoyed the patronage of Justinien Pense, a spice merchant whom he had served earlier in Antwerp. The pattern of patronage here clearly shows a move away from broad distribution of music originally composed for royal or ducal establishments to one of limited publication aimed at and supported by wealthier members of the bourgeoisie.

Chansons and madrigals had long enjoyed a broad appeal to the bourgeoisie as well as to the aristocracy. But while Mayo and Vecoli continue to set the fashionable verse of Petrarch and their imitators, the particularly personal nature of many of the texts set by Blockland, Castro, and Fiorino represents a new departure, although the musical style is not accordingly changed. One exception to this is the funeral air composed in *voix de ville* manner by H. P. de Villiers for the Protestant prince Louis de Condé. Blockland also followed this style in some of the pieces in his 1573 collection, but the style was naturally the product of the fashion for monophonic and simple homophonic psalms, canticles, and spiritual songs, emanating from Geneva but firmly established in Lyons by Bourgois, Didier Lupi, Jambe de Fer, and others. Here there was clearly a domestic demand for such simple pieces amongst the local Protestant community, as documented in the town's chronicles and archival records. However, the printers again were not slow to exploit a wider demand throughout France by means of the trade-fairs. The same musical style pervades the notated music dramas of Aneau and Des Masures, even if the former's earlier plays with music were originally intended for the local grammar school.

In fact this simple homophonic syllabic manner of setting stanzaic sacred texts of various metres is the only discernible style for which Lyons might claim precedence. And this precedence could be challenged by the claims of prototypes found in Lutheran hymns by Johann Walter and others. However, the matching of simple melodies from the noël and other popular repertoire to the simple homorhythmic style already found in certain Italian frottole and villotte in setting the new metrical translations of psalms by Marot, Bèze, and other Lyonese poets certainly enjoyed a great success in the Calvinist community, reflected in the many collections of psalms, canticles, and *chansons spirituelles* published from the 1540s to the 1560s. There is no consistency of style to be found in the secular chansons or madrigals published in Lyons that could form the basis of a claim for a local manner, although the prevailing concern for texts of literary quality by local poets, as well as the enduring tradition of Petrarch, might be a reflection of the city's literary pre-eminence. A greater respect for syntactic propriety in the chansons of Coste and P. de Villiers than that found in most Parisian contemporaries may also betray local poetic concerns.

Most chansons published in Lyons alternate between the concise syllabic and lightly melismatic textures of the French court composers and the more involved counterpoint of those in the Habsburg orbit. The scurrilous anecdotes set by Fresneau and Didier Lupi are more apt to follow Janequin's animated textures and simple harmony, while Phinot's amorous epigrams show a predilection for gentle word-painting by means of harmony, as found in some contemporary Italian madrigals by Arcadelt and Rore. Phinot and Lupi also show an unusual inclination to repeat final couplets rather than punch lines in setting quatrains. Layolle's fondness for setting *ballate* and poetic fragments was shared by Verdelot and Arcadelt, while the fact that so many of his madrigals were reprinted under Arcadelt's name underlines their musical similarities to the contemporary Florentine and Roman styles. Whereas Rampollini's Petrarch settings follow Berchem in choosing complete *canzoni* and Mayo's favour the parlando manner of the *madrigali ariosi* of Barre and Rore, Vecoli's five-part pieces suggest a sonorous manner initiated perhaps by Nicolo Dorati, another wind-instrumentalist from Lucca.

General stylistic characteristics are difficult to relate directly to the Lyonese environment rather than individual composers' idiosyncrasies or repertorial trends. Even the successive vogue for monophonic noëls, homophonic psalms, and spiritual contrafacta are not totally unique to Lyons. Indeed, the very cosmopolitan nature of the market town no doubt encouraged its receptivity to foreign initiatives and contributed to its blend of ideas.

The chronicles include descriptions of musical entertainments provided for some of the royal *entrées*, as well as for other lesser but more frequent public and private celebrations. The civic accounts often provide more detail, indicating that the city employed trumpets, fifes and drums on a regular basis for signalling and proclamations, while requiring cornetts, shawms, rebecs or violins, lutes, and organs for banquets and receptions. The civic accounts not only describe some of the commissions and payments but show that a very large number of people registered their employment as musicians, particularly as instrumentalists. Even though many played a second instrument, some found insufficient work or remuneration, claiming rate reductions or plying a second trade as instrument-makers, carpenters, painters, vinager-makers, pastry cooks, etc. One notable exception, Giovanni Paolo Paladino, a lutenist from Milan, owned a large house and vineyard, acquired no doubt from his profits as a merchant in the international fairs rather than as the composer of at least two books of lute music published in Lyons.

While most of the lutenists registered in the archives (including Mezangeau, no doubt the lutenist-composer employed at the court of Louis XIII, but not his colleague Ennemond Gaultier 'de Lyon' who served Marie de'Medici) may have been capable of playing from tablatures, the majority of instrumentalists probably learned their trade aurally through the traditional apprenticeships, even if free trade rather than guild organization prevailed in Lyons. However, the publication of rather crudely harmonized chansons attributed by Moderne to the shawm-player Charles Cordeilles and the more polished chansons and psalms ascribed to Guillaume de la Mœulle, who seems to have earned his living in Lyons as an instrumentalist, suggests that at least some of the registered players were musically literate. This was certainly true also of the madrigal composer Regolo Vecoli, who, following his fellow cornettist Luca di Partigliano, left Lucca to 'exercise his craft' as a cornettist in Lyons.

The prominence of Italians, and to a lesser extent of Germans, amongst the instrumentalists is reflected also in the many recorded instrument-makers. These include the most famous names of the time—notably the flute- and recorder-maker Claude Raffin (or Rafi), praised by Clément Marot and Baïf, as well as the *luthier* Gaspard Duiffoproucart (Tieffenbrucker), whose portrait engraved by Pierre Woeiriot in 1565 (Pl. 3) shows him surrounded by some of the lutes, guitars, viols, and harps which made him rich and famous, some of which still survive in museums and private collections. The archives show that while most professionally registered instrumentalists played outdoor instruments, notably drums, trumpets, cornetts, shawms, violins, rebecs, or organs, the makers and traders were more concerned with the amateur market for lutes, guitars, citterns, viols, violons, flutes, spinets, and clavichords, the very same indoor instruments for which Moderne intended his lute-books and *Musicque de Joye*. If Gorlier's last tablatures for guitar, cittern, flute, and spinet cannot directly confirm the continuing demand, the preoccupation of Jambe de Fer's treatise with the flute, recorder, and viol certainly can.

The surviving music for these instruments does not differ significantly from that found in other contemporary publications. Indeed, much of Moderne's collection for instrumental ensemble appears to have been pirated from earlier Venetian and Parisian editions, while the lute-books of Bakfark, Bianchini, and Paladino reflect a repertoire, organization, and technique similar to contemporary Italian tablatures, even if some of the arrangements were based on polyphonic models, composed or published locally. (See Music Example 9.) While archival records confirm the rebuilding of organs after the damage sustained during the Protestant uprising, as well as the continued employment of organists (including Francesco Layolle) in the Dominican and Franciscan churches, no keyboard music from Lyons survives.

Paradoxically, prevailing international peace did not enhance the city's prosperity, which notably declined during the second half of the century as privileges were withdrawn and internecine religious conflict increased. Having been a relatively safe haven where republicans and reformers could exchange and propagate music, is well as literary, political, and philosophical ideas, the city became little more than an outpost for the French distribution of Calvinist or Counter-Reformation propaganda. The lively and significant renaissance in music, as in literature, which had been supported by the cosmopolitan city's rich mixture of civic independence and private enterprise, could not be sustained, and the cultural prominence of Lyons rapidly declined in the seventeenth century.

APPENDIX I

Musicians Mentioned in the Archives of Lyons

Except where otherwise specified, the sources in the following tables are a collection of unnumbered leaves copied by the late archivist Georges Tricou, currently in the possession of François Lesure. While these notes do not give precise details, they sometimes indicate the notary responsible for drawing up the original documents. The minutes of the notaries are deposited in the district record office (Archives départementales du Rhône) and in some cases the exact sources have been identified. Other information comes from documents registering taxes and communal charges or civic payments preserved in the municipal archives of Lyons. Summary catalogues of these, drawn up by F. Rolle, M. C. Guigue, G. Guigue, and J. Vaesen (*Inventaire sommaire des archives communales antérieures à 1790*), were published in Paris between 1865 and 1962. These cover the period from the formal establishment of the commune in the early fourteenth century to 1790, with the first three volumes including the Renaissance period. The first series of entries (prefaced by the letters AA) concern privileges, franchises, and political correspondence. The second series (BB) covers civic administration between 1416 and 1790, including consular deliberations, acts, and appointments, registers of levies and exemptions for civic construction and repair, and nominations and elections of aldermen. The third series (CC) and the one most valuable for information on musicians, as on other professional groups, contains taxes and accounts, including lists of local tax-payers (*nommées*), recording occupations and assessments of property. A similar catalogue, compiled by F. Rolle and A. Steyert (*Inventaire sommaire des archives hospitalières antérieures à 1790. Ville de Lyon. La Charité ou Aumône Générale*), published in five volumes in Lyons between 1874 and 1908, provides an inventory with extracts from the records of the city's main charitable institution. These are classified as foundation acts, privileges, and decisions (A), property acquisitions and gifts (B), ecclesiastical matters (C), inventories (D), administration (E), registers of admission and discharge (F), including teaching arrangements for orphans (G), and correspondence (H).

Other documentation can be found in the 'Inventaire Chappe', a manuscript catalogue in twenty-two volumes, containing non-inventoried items from municipal records at the Archives municipales, with an accompanying alphabetical list of subjects, available in the regional room of the Bibliothèque municipale.

The archives, especially the ecclesiastical records, suffered considerable losses during the Protestant uprising of 1562–3 and during the Revolutionary period, the siege of Lyons in 1793 proving particularly devastating. The history and organization of the city and district administrative, judicial, charitable, and notarial records is described in L. Niepce, *Les Archives de Lyon, municipales, départementales, judiciares, hospitalières et notariales* (Lyons, 1875).

Additional information found in the tables below is given in secondary sources identified by the following sigla:

Baffert   J. M. Baffert, 'Les Orgues de Lyon', *Cahiers et mémoires de l'orgue*, 11 (1974), 1–85

Baudrier   J. Baudrier, *Bibliographie lyonnaise*, 12 vols. (Lyons, 1895–1921)

Byrne   M. Byrne, 'Instruments by Claude Rafi in the Collection of Manfreda Settale', *Galpin Society Journal*, 18 (1965), 126–7

Cohen   A. Cohen, 'Henry, Jehan', *New Grove Dictionary*, viii (London, 1980), 486

Coutagne   H. Coutagne, 'Gaspard Duiffoproucart et les luthiers lyonnais du XVIᵉ siècle', *Mémoires de l'Académie des Sciences, Belles-lettres et Arts de Lyon*, 3 (1893), 418–81

Dobbins   F. Dobbins, 'The Chanson at Lyons in the Sixteenth Century' (D.Phil. diss. Oxford, 1971)

Dufour   A. Dufour and F. Rabut, *Les Musiciens, la musique et les instruments de musique en Savoie du XIIᵉ au XIXᵉ siècle* (Chambéry, 1878; repr. Geneva, 1972)

Dufourcq   N. Dufourcq, *Documents inédits relatifs à l'orgue français* (Paris, 1934–5)

Gascon   R. Gascon, *Grand commerce et vie urbaine au XVIᵉ siècle: Lyon et ses marchands* (Paris, 1971)

Guigue¹   M. Guigue, G. Guigue, and J. Vaesen, *Inventaire sommaire des archives communales antérieures à 1790*, iii (Paris, 1887)

Guigue²   G. Guigue, *La Magnificence...relations et documents contemporains* (Lyons, 1927)

Guillo¹   L. Guillo, 'Recherches sur les éditions musicales lyonnaises de la Renaissance' (Doctoral thesis, École Pratique des Hautes Études, IVᵉ Section, Paris, 1986)

Guillo²   'Giovanni Paolo Paladino à Lyon', *Revue de musicologie*, 73 (1987), 249–53

Lesure¹   F. Lesure, 'La Guitare en France au XVIᵉ siècle', *Musica disciplina*, 4 (1950), 187–95

Lesure²   F. Lesure, 'La Facture instrumental à Paris au seizième siècle', *Galpin Society Journal*, 7 (1954), 11–34 (= Lesure, *Musique et musiciens français du XVIᵉ siècle* (Geneva, 1976), 63–109

Mahillon   V. Mahillon, *Catalogue descriptif et analytique du Musée instrumental du Conservatoire...de Bruxelles*, 5 vols. (Ghent, 1880–1922)

Nerici   L. Nerici, *Storia della musica in Lucca* (Lucca, 1879)

Ricaud   J. Ricaud. *Discours du massacre de ceux de la religion réformée fait à Lyon* (Lyons, 1574; repr. 1848)

Rolle   F. Rolle, *Inventaire sommaire des archives communales antérieures à 1790*, ii (Paris, 1875)

Rolle 1   F. Rolle, *Inventaire sommaire des archives communales antérieures à 1790*, i (Paris, 1865)

Steyert   A. Steyert, *Inventaire sommaire des archives hospitalières antérieures à 1790*, 5 vols. (Lyons, 1874–1908)

Tricou[1]   Unnumbered manuscript notes in the possession of F. Lesure

Tricou[2]   G. Tricou, 'Philibert Jambe de Fer', *Revue musicale*, 3 (1903), 511–13

Tricou[3]   G. Tricou, *Documents sur la musique à Lyon au xvie siècle* (Lyons, 1899)

Tricou[4]   G. Tricou, 'Les Musiciens lyonnais et le Roy des Violons', *Revue musicale de Lyon*, 1 (1903–94), 148–50

Tricou[5]   G. Tricou, 'Duiffoproucart et Lejeune, luthiers', *Revue musicale de Lyon*, 1 (1903–4), 89–91

Tricou[6]   G. Tricou, 'Claude Rafi, "fleustier" lyonnais,' *Revue musicale de Lyon*, 1 (1903–4), 13 and 25

Tricou, J.   J. Tricou, *Armorial et répertoire lyonnais*, 7 vols. (Paris, 1955)

Vallas   L. Vallas, *Un Siècle de musique et théâtre à Lyon* (Lyons, 1932)

MUSICIANS (unspecified)
(designated *musicien* in Tricou[1] unless otherwise indicated)

AGNIEL (AIGNEL), Philippe (19 July 1538)
     Rhône, Not. Chaliard 3E 336, fo. 33^r

AMAT, Poncet (30 Oct. 1508)
     Rhône, Not. Delagrange 3E 4203. See also Appendix III(i)

BENOIT, Jehan, dit d'Ecosse (1507–48)
     See Appendix III(b) D'ECOSSE

BLASI, André de (1578)
     musicien véronais; Tricou[1]

BOCHARD, Ollivier (before 1573)
     en son vivant musicien; Tricou[1]

BOURG, Jehan (1586)

BOURGEOIS, Loys (1553–7)
     Me. musicien. See Ch. 5 (*xiv*)

CARLET, César (1582)
     Me. musicien; Tricou[1]

DARBALOYS (1587)

DARDINELLY, Jean (1576–97)

DARDON, Barthélemy (1579)
     Rhône, Not. Accayre; Tricou[1]. See App. III(k) and IV(g), DARDON, François

DUPRE, Jehan (1579)
     See App. III(i) DUPREY

     FROYSSAR, Antoine (1566–95)
          See App. III(c) FROYSSARD

GACHOUX, Helye (1561)
  Guillo², Doc. 33
GAULTERET, Gabriel (1588–97)
JAMBE DE FER[T], Philibert (1553–64)
  1553 Rhône, Not. Chaliard. Tricou², 511; 1561 Guillo², Doc. 33; 1564 CC
  1112, fo. 35ʳ. See Ch. 5 (xvi)
MAILLARD, Gilles (1575–87)
  Me. musicien Rhône, Not. Dumont; Tricou¹. See Ch. 5 (xxix)
MALETTY, Jehan de (1583)
  Me. musicien. See Ch. 5 (xxix)
MELLILAMA, Jean (1575)
ROUSSELLO, Françoys (1561)
  Me. musicien; Guillo², Doc. 33. See Ch. 5 (xx)
SANZY, Jehan (1595)
SOURCIN, Gabriel (1575–97)
  See App. III(*c*)
TIXIER [TESSIER?], Guillaume (1575)
  CC 176; Rolle, 235
VALLA, Laurent (1582)
VINCENNES, François de (d. 1561)

APPENDIX II

Singers

(except where otherwise indicated, designated *chantre* in Tricou[1])

BOUCHER, Estienne (7 Sept. 1559)
Sous m[aistr]e des enfants, Actes capitulaires de Saint-Paul, 16, p. 308
BRUN, François (1516)
Sous Me. de choeur à Saint Jean
COMMARMOND, Jean (n.d.)
Manécantant
CORAILLE, Jean (1583)
Manécantant de Saint Jean
CREMEAULX, Antoine de (n.d.)
DRONIN, Tristan (1540–82)
See below, II(*d*) and (*k*)
FASSON, Antoine (n.d.)
Manécantant
FAURE, Claude (n.d.)
Manécantant
GROS, Claude (n.d.)
Manécantant de Saint Nizier
MAGNIN, Grégoire (1522)
*Sous maistre du cueur Saint Nizier pour une grant messe du Sainct
Esprit . . . pour prier Dieu pour le Roy, pour la paix et que Dieu luy doint
bon conseil*, CC 693; Guigue[1], 115
MARREZZIEU (n.d.)
Manécantant de Saint Nizier
MELLIER, Jehan (1548–60)
1548–51 *Chanoyne, procureur général de l'église collégiale de Sainct Nizier*,
CC 981, 983, 986; 1556–60 *Chantre et procureur général . . .* (1556–7), CC
1043, 1053, 1064, 1078; Guigue[1], 221, 223, 226, 248, 251, and 257
MONTBERTET, Pierre (n.d.)
MYOLAND, Antoine (1589)
Manécantant de Saint Jean
NIZORET, Antoine (1515)
PARIS, Méry (1556–8)
Manécantant en l'église collégiale de Sainct Nizier (1556–7), CC 1043;
Guigue[1], 243. *Presbtre et chanoine de l'église collégiale de Sainct Nizier*
(1557–8), CC 1053; Guigue[1], 248
PARRAC, de (1584)

Chantre de Saint Jean
PERRIN, Pierre (1558–9)
Presbtre manécantant des six clergons de la livraison en l'église de Sainct Nizier (1558–9), CC 1064; Guigue[1], 252
REGNAULD, Jean-Baptiste (*c.*1495)
Cantor
RICHARD, Antoine (1576)
Chantre de Fourvière
ROUILLET [ROILLET], Nicolas (1541–3)
1541–2 *Chantre, procureur et recepveur...pour...chapître de l'église collégiale de Sainct Nizier*, CC 948; Guigue[1] 203; 1542–3, CC 954; Guigue[1] 205
VIAL, Claude (1573)
Chantre. See below, III(*b*) BELLON

APPENDIX III

Instrumentalists

(a) LUTENISTS
(designated *joueur de luth* (*lut, lutz, luc, leu, or leuz*))

BARETE, Jean (1503)
26 March 1503 (played at civic banquet in honour of visiting 'Archduke'), CC 556, no. 2, fo. 11[v]; Guigue[3], 71

EDENTOS, Guillaume (15/1)
Tricou[1]. Perhaps related to Charles, Jacques, and Richard Edinthon or Edington, lutenists of Scottish origin active at the court of Henry II

FERRAND, Petit Jean (1499–1504)
1499 *joueur de luth et pâtissier*, CC 230; Rolle, 210

HOSTE, Gaspard (1489–92)
1492 *Gaspard joeuz de leuz*, CC 105; Rolle, 112; 1493 *Allemand*, CC 4 (*Nommées*-parish of Saint-Paul); Rolle, 8; 1499, CC 230, fo. 51[v]; Rolle, 210 (facsimile in Dobbins, 122)

LA MOTTE, Robert de (1597)
Tricou[1]

LUC, Symon du (1530–75)
Tricou[1]. See also below, SIMON

LUXEMBOURG, Loys de (1492–1524)
1492 *faiseur de moles de quartes*, CC 105; Rolle, 112; 1493, CC 4; Rolle, 8; 1499, CC 230; Rolle, 210; 1524 *arpeur*, CC 261; Rolle, 224

MEZANGEAU (1597)
Tricou[1]

PALADIN, Jehan Paule (1547–65)
9 Dec. 1553 (purchase of house with land and vineyard), Rhône 3E 5384 bis, fos. 95[v]–102; 4 Sept. 1565 (crown attorney's decision against claims by various Florentine, Milanese, German, and other merchants on the estate of the late *joueur d'instrument millanois ... marchand frequentant les foires de Lyon*), Rhône BP 447, fos. 193[v]–5[r]; Guillo[2]

SIMON, Maître (1568–73)
1571, CC 150; Rolle, 152; Coutagne, 461. (Possibly identical with LUC above or to D'AYME in App. III(*k*); see also SIMON in App. IV(*a*))

VARIN, Guillaume (1540)
Cytharedus (this may refer to guitar, cittern, or even harp); Tricou[1]

VEGGIO, Francesco (1560)
Tricou[1]

(b) REBEC-PLAYERS
(designated *joueur de rebec* except where otherwise indicated)

BOULANGER, Jean (1545)
Rebecquet, CC 40; Rolle, 61

D'ECOSSE, Jehan (1507–48)
1518 (listed with Jehan de Saint-Lasne and Mohlet in application for guild organization, opposed by the *tabourins et menestriers de la ville*), CC 652; Tricou[4]. A 'Jehan Grand dit d'Ecosse' was employed as bagpiper at the French court in 1515; see above, App. II, BENOIT

GUILLEMIN, [GUILLAUME] (1503)
16 Mar. 1503 (played in a band at a civic banquet in honour of 'Archduke')

MARANDIER, joieur de rabet (1493–1503)
1493, CC 7; Rolle, 10; 1499 *joueur de robec*, CC 107; Rolle, 115; 1503, CC 167; Rolle, 169

MOHLET *le rebecquet* (1518)
1518, CC 652; Tricou[4]

SAINT-LASNE, Jean de (1530–5)
1517 *le rebecquet dict 'Petit Jehan le Rebecquet' de La Baume en Viennoise*, CC 25; Rolle, 46; 1518, CC 652; Tricou[4]; 1519 Jean de Santa Lana, Rhône Not. J. Cropper 385, fo. 150[r]; Tricou[4]; 1523 *Petit Jehan de Sainct-Lance, rebecquet*, CC 259; Rolle, 223; 1524 *Petit Jehan de Sant-Lant rebecquet*, CC 711; Guigue[1], 119; 1530–5, CC 140; Rolle, 143

(c) VIOLINISTS
(designated *violon* except where otherwise indicated)

BADOUILLE (BADOY), Rambert (1582–1616)
Me. illumineur, peintre et joueur d'instruments; Tricou, J., ii. 153

BENIGNO (1571)
CC 147; Rolle, 149

DESBARGUES, Martial 1574–80
1574 (*Marçial de Bargues* paid for illuminating town council minutes), CC 1239; Guigue[1], 326; *enlumineur et joueur de violin*; Vallas, 7

FROYSSART, Antoine (1566–83)
1583 (civic banquet for Henry III), CC 1481; Guigue[1], 367; Tricou[4] describes him as *natif de Turin, Vyolon du roy valet de chambre de M'sr. le Prince de Genevers et de M'sr. le Duc de Nemours*, indicating that he arrived at Lyons in 1566 and that his children's names are found in the baptismal records of 1595

GODEFFROY, Barthélemy (1571–85)
Tricou[1]. See App. III(*k*) GOTTEFROIDE

LABRI, Jean (1573–4)
CC 1219; Guigue[1], 275. See below, LA VIS and LA VYTE

LAVIGNE, Thomas (1576–1600)
Piémontais, me joueur de violon; Tricou[1]

La Vis, Jean (1571–2)
  CC 152; Rolle, 155
La Vyte, Jean de (1586)
  CC 46; Rolle, 68. See App. III(*k*) Lavy
Perrache, Antoine (1589–97)
  Natif de Montecallieu; Tricou[1]
Sourcin, Gabriel (1575–97)
  Basse de violon; Tricou[1]

(*d*) VIOLIST
(designated *violeur*)

Dronin, Tristan (1540–82)
  1557 *violeur*; Coutagne 435; also listed as *chantre, musicien*, and *joueur d'instruments*. See also App. III(*k*) Dronin

(*e*) FLUTE-PLAYERS
(each designation specified; *fleustier*, like *luthier*, is taken to indicate a maker rather than a player)

Fabre, Toussaint (1530)
  joueur de flûte; Tricou[1]
Fantin, Pierre (1 Oct. 1548)
  fiffre (Henry II's *entrée*), CC 987, no. 2
La Noue, Mathelin (Mathurin) de (1523–38)
  (1530) *flosteur*; Coutagne, 462; 1536 *flustier*, CC 274; Rolle, 233. See also App. III(*k*) and IV(*d*)
Ludovic (1521)
  le fleusteur; Tricou[1]
Pillon, Jacques
  1499 *joueur de fluste*, CC 107; Rolle, 115. See also App. IV(*d*)
Raffin, Michaud (1506–24)
  1512 *fleusteur*, CC 115; Rolle, 123; (father of Claude Raffin), Tricou[5]. See App. IV(*d*) Rapin

(*f*) SHAWM- AND CORNETT-PLAYERS
(designated *joueur d'haultboys* unless otherwise indicated)

Baraillon, Anthoine (1533)
  1533 *de Fourest et autres ses compaignons tant dudit pays que de ceste ville de Lyon que de Villefranche et Trévol, en nombre seize, tous trompetes et aulxboys* (Commission for the entry of Queen Eleanor and the dauphin), CC 273; Rolle, 230
Cordeilles, Charles (1548)
  18 Sept. 1548 (engaged to play in a band of nine *cournetz et haultboys*

during Henry II's *entrée*, BB 67, fo. 253ʳ; Guigue², 181; 2 Oct. 1548 (payment for same), CC 981, no. 1, fo. 109ʳ; Guigue², 318. See Chs. 3 (i) and 5 (xv)

GENTIL, Luc *Joueur de cornet* (1545–52)

1545, CC 40; Rolle, 61; 1552, CC 284; Rolle, 238; 1560 *Marchant, citoyen de Lyon*, Rhône, Not. Popon, Donations, 22; Coutagne, 462. (Charles Fontaine's *Ruisseaux* (Lyons, 1555, p. 67) includes an *épigramme* dedicated to 'Luc Gentil et à son Fils, menestriers de Paris et musiciens du Roy'; Baudrier ii. 366; iv. 267. See also App. IV(*e*) and (*g*)

PARTIGLIANO, Luca di (1542–3)

1542 ... *prima de essere ascritto fra i sonatori della Signoria di Lucca esercitava l'arte sua in Lione*; 1543 ... *ad presens Lugduni habitator sonator cornetti*; Nerici, 203

PELLAT, Antoine (1544–5)

1544 *Menusier, joueur d'aulbois*, CC 282; Rolle, 237; 1545, CC 41, fo. 31ʳ; Rolle, 61

PYROUET (PERRYET), Charles

18 Sept. 1548 (engaged to play in band with CORDEILLES for Henry II's *entrée*) BB 67, fo. 253ʳ; Guigue², 181; 2 Oct. 1548 (paid for same) CC 981, no. 1, fo. 109ʳ; Guigue², 318

VALLETTE, Pierre (1554–9)

1554 *Meneur d'aultboys*; Tricou[1]

VECOLI, Regolo di Vincenzo (1561–81)

Sonator di cornetta, musico lucchese abitante a Lione; Nerici, 53–5. See Ch. 5 (xxvi)

(g) TRUMPETERS

(designated *joueur de trompete* unless otherwise indicated)

BARAILLON (BARILLON), Anthoine (1533)

See above, App. III(*f*)

BERGIER, Jehan (1534–40)

1534–9 (Council payments for opening and closing the city gates and signalling same from Fourvière), CC 859, 885, 899, 911; Guigue¹, 168, 183–6; 1535–40 (payment by the rectors of the Aulmosne generalle to proclaim a lottery for charity), Archives hospitalières E 5

BERNARD (BONNARD), Claude (1575–9)

(Council payments as *trompette ordinaire de la ville*) CC 1243, 1245, 1255, 1264, 1275; Rolle 328–9, 333 337, 341

BOYDARD (BRIDARD), Françoys (1548)

1 Oct. 1548 (paid along with P. BRET, COUGNET, MARQUET, and VALFO for playing aboard the galleys on the Saône for Henry II's *entrée*), CC 981, no. 3; Guigue², 318

BRET, Jehan (1548)

13 Sept. 1548 (commissioned to play for Henry II's *entrée* along with André and Michel Noyret, Françoys Gourdet, Christofle Genet, and Nycolas Fuzy,

joueurs de trompettes, mandez, expressement venuz du lieu de Chambéry ou ils sont demeurans . . .'), BB 67, fo. 251^v; Guigue^2, 181; 27 Sept. 1548 (paid 20 sous per day with them), CC 981, no. 9; Guigue^2, 316. Bret's activities in Chambéry are confirmed in Dufour, 121

BRET, Pierre (1545–6)

1545–6 (paid to sound morning and evening signal for opening and closing the city gates), CC 968; Guigue^1, 216; 1548 (sent to Montbrison to find 12 trumpets for Henry II's *entrée*), CC 981, no. 10; Guigue^2, 315; 1555 (paid with the town crier to issue proclamations of policy for the Aulmosne generalle), Archives hospitalières 3 E164; Steyert iii.396

BUSSIERE, Barmond (1564)

June 1564 (Paid 12 livres as livery allowance for Charles IX's *entrée*) CC 1112; Guigue^2, 275

CHENU (CHENA), Claude (1527–31)

1527–8 *le guet* (civic duties), CC 759; Guigue^1, 130; 1529–30, CC 779; Guigue^1, 140; 1529–31 (livery allowance as *trompette de la ville*), BB 49; Rolle 1, 23. (He is probably identical with Claude CHEVAL and with Claude CHENU who was registered on 13 Nov. 1539 as 'farmer for one year', CC 940; Guigue^1, 200

CHEVAL (CHAVAL), Claude (1527–37)

In 1527 the *Consulat* rented a house for him (CC 760); in 1529 it paid him as watchman on Fourvière *et faire des cris avec sa dicte trompete* (CC 779–81) and for serving the town in the execution and banishment of those accused of pillage during the rebellion (CC 789, fo. 22^r); in 1530 it replaced his uniform and broken trumpet (CC 796). In 1537 he was succeeded as *trompette ordinaire* by Bastien Lucas (BB 428); Guigue^1, 131, 140–1, 148; Rolle 1, 308

COUGNET, Guillaume (1548)

1 Oct. 1548 (paid for playing on a galley during Henry II's *entrée*), CC 981, no. 3; Guigue^2, 318

CRESTIEN, Jehan (1594)

1593 (name included in a list of butchers), CC 1439; Guigue^1, 396; 1594 (payment for guard duty), CC 1445; Guigue^1, 399

DU PRE (DUPREY, DUPRA), Jehan (1452–1510)

Appointed in 1452 as watchman to sound the alarm from the tower on the Fourvière Hill (BB 6; Rolle 1, 3), he continued in this post through 1472 (CC 451; Guigue^1, 39), 1479 (CC 485; Guigue^1, 49), and 1493 (CC 502; Guigue^1, 52; CC 525–6; Guigue^1 58); by 1493 he owned two houses, a garden, and vineyard and was taxed as a man of property (CC 15; Rolle, 27); in 1503 he was still *guetteur du clocher de Fourvière* (CC 111; Rolle, 149), retaining the position (CC 558–9, 562, 566, 578, 584; Guigue^1 72–81) until he was eventually replaced by Simon Potat in 1510 (CC 605; Guigue^1 88)

GLATARD, Gabriel (1590)

Joined Jean Glatard as escort to the Archbishop of Lyons on a journey into Burgundy, CC 1401; Guigue^1, 385

GLATARD, Jean (1582–94)

Annual payments as civic trumpeter and guard, CC 1304, 1313, 1323, 1334, 1341, 1343, 1367, 1378, 1391, 1401, 1403, 1416, 1439, 1444; Guigue[1], 354, 357, 361, 364–5, 367, 375, 378, 382, 385–6, 389, 396, 399; succeeded by J. CRESTIEN; see above

LUCAS, Bastien (1537–40)

1537 (appointed by King Francis I to succeed C. CHEVAL (above) as *trompette ordinaire*), BB 428; Rolle 1, 308; between 1538 and 1540 he served with BERGIER or PINAULT at Fourvière, signalling the opening and closing of the city gates, CC 898, 911, 926; Guigue[1] 183–95

MARQUET, Bonaventure (1548)

1 Oct. 1548 (paid for Henry II's *entrée*), CC 981, no. 3; Guigue[2], 318

MORANGE, Julien (1526–7)

Civic duties, CC 746; Guigue[1], 146

PAJARD, SIMON (1517)

dit Treze Mestiers, trompette, commis à faire l'esveil tous les lundis en commemoration des trespassés, CC 633; Guigue[1], 96. See below, POJOUD and SIMOND

PINAULT, Arnault (1539–40)

Pinault and LUCAS were given livery for the *entrée* of the Cardinal of Ferrara, CC 926; Guigue[1], 195

POJOUD, Simon (1529)

de son vivant brigandier et trompette, CC 137; Rolle, 140

POTAT, Simon *Trompillon* (1511–12)

Succeeded J. DUPREY as watchman on Fourvière, CC 605; Guigue[1], 88

REGNAUD, Antoine (1577–81)

Civic duties shared with Bonard, CC 1264, 1275, 1284, 1293; Guigue[1], 337, 341, 347, 350

SIMOND *la Trompette* (1517–18)

Paid for 'crying' at all the crossroads to seek volunteer labourers to repair the Hospital Saint-Laurent des Vignes, CC 656; Guigue[1], 104. See above, PAJARD or POTAT?

TENARD, Claude (1531–3)

Like P. BRET, paid to signal proclamations for the rectors of the alms houses, Archives hospitalières E 138; Steyert iii. 382

VALFO, Jehan (1548)

1 Oct. 1548 (paid 10 livres tournois for playing in a band with BOYDARD, CONGNET, and MARQUET in the galleys on the Saône during Henry II's entrée), CC 981, no. 3; Guigue[2], 318

(*b*) DRUMMERS

(designated *Joueur de taborin, taborineur*, or *tamborin*)

ALISANT, Jehan (1569–70)

Civic duties, CC 1166; Guigue[1], 295

ALIX, Benoit d' (1557)

Coutagne, 435

BELLON, Benoît (1548)

1 Oct. 1548 (Bellon and four 'companions' were paid 45 sous for playing in the galleys on the Saône, the day before the King's departure, when the Cardinal of Ferrara's boat caught fire. The 'companions' may have been André Thevillon, Benoist de Lachault, Claude Vial, and Laurens Babotte who, along with the fife-players, Cousturier and Fournier—all brought in from the neighbouring Fourestz area—were paid 12 crowns for playing in Henry II's entry procession), CC 981, no. 5; Guigue², 318

BENOÎT, Jehan (1548)

25 Feb. 1548 (played with other *fiffres, tabourins, hautbois et violons* for a civic banquet in honour of the Swiss ambassadors), CC 977, no. 25, fo. 4ʳ

BLANC, Jean (n.d.)

CC 217; Rolle, 195

BONSENE, Barthélemy (1529)

Tambourineur et espinglier, CC 137, fo. 129ʳ; Rolle, 140

BULICHON, Louis (1587–8)

Shared civic duties with MORELLET, CC 1367; Guigue¹, 375

CARTELLET [CARTERET], Claude (1569–87)

Shared civic duties with ALISANT, ISSARD, LA MARQUISE/MARCUSE, and SAINCT MARTIN *pour sonner du tambour tous les soirs et matins... et pour assembler la garde*, CC 1166, 1167, 1272, 1304; Guigue¹, 295–6, 340, 354

CHARDON, Gabriel (1528–72)

1528, CC 37; Rolle, 56; 1529, CC 137, fo. 69ʳ; 1530–5, CC 140, fo. 25ᵛ; 1537, CC 188; 1538, CC 142, fo. 71ᵛ; 1571–2, CC 150, CC 1197; Coutagne, 462. See App. III(*k*)

CHARDON, Pierre *dit Miroleret* (1544)

CC 284; Rolle, 238

CRONYER, Jean (1548)

1 Oct. 1548 (paid for Henry II's *entrée*), CC 987, no. 2; Guigue², 318

FAGOT, Antoine (1529)

CC 137, fo. 22ᵛ; Rolle, 139

GAGERE, Claude (1581)

batteur de tambour, CC 157; Rolle, 162

GAPT, Pierre (1569–70)

Civic drumming duties, CC 1167; Guigue¹, 296

GENEVY, Benoît (1545)

Peintre et taborin, CC 282; Rolle, 237

CORDILLARD (GARDILLAR), Claude (1557)

Coutagne, 435

GOUJELLIN, Claude *dit le More* (1548)

25 Feb. 1548 (banquet for the Swiss ambassadors), CC 977, no. 25, fo. 4ʳ

ISSARD (YSSARD), Claude (1583–6)

Paid for civic duties and for assembling the guard each morning and evening at Fourvière or Saint-Nizier, CC 1304, 1334, 1341, 1343; Guigue¹, 354, 364–5, 367

LAGNY, Antoine de (1529)

CC 137; Rolle, 140

LA MARRE, Robin de (1503)

Taxed as a bowstring-maker, he claimed exemption, 'having no trade other than being *tabourin*', CC 112: Rolle, 121. See App. III(*k*) LA MARRE, Claude de

LA MARQUISE, Jacques de (1570)

Civic duties, CC 1167; Guigue[1], 296. Probably identical with Jacques Marcuse, paid for the same duties in 1569, CC 1166; Guigue[1], 297

LA MONNOYE, Guillaume de (1548)

25 Feb. 1548 (engaged with LE CHAT and others to play for the Swiss ambassadors' banquet), CC 977, no. 25, fo. 4[r]

LE CHAT, Benoît (1548)

25 Feb. 1548 (engaged to play at a civic banquet for the Swiss ambassadors), CC 977, no. 25, fo. 4[r]

LA SENAZ, Jehan de (1502)

26 March 1502 (engaged with the lutenist BARETE and the organist PONCET to play at a civic banquet for the 'Archduke'), CC 556, no. 2 fo. 11[v]

LA VIZ, Antoine de (1537–44)

1537–8, CC 900; Guigue[1], 164; 1544, CC 284; Rolle, 238

MARTIN, Girard (1535–40)

Archives hospitalières E 5; Steyert, iii. 13

MARTIN, Pierre (1578)

Civic duties shared with CARTELLET, CC 1272; Guigue[1], 340

MORELLET, Louis (1587–8)

Shared civic duties with BULICHON, CC 1367; Guigue[1], 375

PIRONET, Claude (1529)

CC 137, fo. 169; Rolle, 139

QUILLE, Jean *dit Mochet* (1507–24)

Me. juré de l'art de tabourin; Tricou[4]

SAINCT MARTIN, Etienne de (1569–86)

Civic duties, CC 1166, 1304, 1323, 1334, 1343; Guigue[1], 295, 354, 361, 364–5

SAINCT VALLIER, Monsieur de (1529–31)

'... qui residait la plupart du temps à Lyon ... exemption des droits d'entrée du vin pour ce qu'il est personnage pour faire beaucoup de plaisirs à la ville en matière de blez ou autrement...', BB 49; Rolle 1, 23. Claude Bellièvre dedicates an epitaph in verse to 'folz Sainct Vallier, taborin... grand yvroigne'; Pairs, Bibliothèque nationale, MS fr. 13127, fo. 163[r]

TRAFFAU, Jehan (1569–70)

Shared civic duties with CARTELLET, GAPT, and LA MARQUISE, CC 1167; Guigue[1], 267

TREBILLON, Pierre (1529)

Tambourin et maçon, CC 137, fo. 23; Rolle, 139

(i) ORGANISTS
(designated *Organiste* or *Joueur des orgues*)

AMAL, Poncet (1517)
Died in poverty en route for Methelin, CC 132; Rolle, 134. See AMAT and PONCET

AMAT, Poncet (1508)
30 Oct. 1508, Rhône, Not. Delagrange 3 E 4203, fo. 283^r. See AVRAT and PONCET

AVRAT, Poncet (1515)
CC 122; Rolle, 129. See AMAL and PONCET

AMEIL (ARNEIL), Pierre (1515)
CC 126; Rolle, 131

AVIGNON, Louis d'(1515–24)
1515, CC 22; Rolle, 41; June 1524, CC 263; Rolle, 225; Tricou[3], 34. Oct. 1524 (decease recorded), CC 267; Rolle, 227; 1533 (decease confirmed), CC 287; Rolle, 240

BONTEMPS, Nicolas (1523)
EE 4, 198d, fo. 116^r. See App. IV(c)

BOULIER (BOULYE), Gaspard (1571–2)
1571, CC 151–2; Rolle, 154–5; 1572, CC 275; Rolle, 234

BRUSSELLES, Jehan de (1571–85)
1571, CC 147; Rolle, 149. See also Tricou[3], 34

COLINET (1498)
EE 4 198d, fo. 114^r; Tricou[3], 32

CORNE, Gaspard (1535)
EE 4 198d, fo. 117^r; Tricou[3], 32

DELAROAR [= LAYOLLE?], François (1529)
CC 137; Tricou[3], 34

DULOYE, Mathieu (1597)
Natif de Lyon; Tricou[3], 33

DUPREY, Jehan (1595)
Rhône, Not. Bégule, 3 E 258, fo. 172^r; *Marchand confiseur, Me. compositeur et organiste* (contract with the Consul of the Florentine community to maintain and play the organ at Notre-Dame de Confort on Sundays and feast-days for 15 months, with the bellows being operated by Louis Coste); Tricou[3], 33

FERAULT (FERAUD), Guyon (1538–45)
1538, CC 142, fo. 54^r; Rolle, 141; 1545, CC 40, 283; Rolle, 61, 238

FLEURS, Mathieu de (1559–62)
Although described as organist at Notre-Dame de Confort, he received alms of 10 sous per week during these years, Archives hospitalières E 10, 492; Steyert ii. 39

JACQUES, (Maistre) (1552)
CC bis 122d, fo. 304^r; CC bis 130d, fo. 328^r; Tricou[3], 34. See below, VOLET

KORN (CORNE), Gaspard (May 1535)
   EE IV 198d, fo. 117^r; Tricou^3, 32
LAYOLLE, Aleman (1551–76)
   24 Sept. 1552 *Organiste à Lyon*, Rhône 3 E 3942, fo. 140^v; Dec. 1571 *Feu Aleman Layolle, bourgeois de Florence*; Tricou^3, 29–30; 13 Mar. 1576 (will in favour of daughter), Rhône B 38, Insinuations, fo. 225^r. See also App. III(*k*) and Ch. 5 (xxi)
LAYOLLE, Françoys de (1523–38)
   June 1523, EE IV 198, fo. 116^r; 23 Sept. 1523 *Me. Françoys organiste*, CC 713, fo. 9^r; CC 259, fo. 37^v; CC 711, fo. 14^r; 1524 *Françoys organiste*, CC 263, fo. 53^v; CC 267; Rolle, 227; 1525–6 *Françoys de Layol, organiste*, CC 271, fos. 28^v and 30^v (facsimile in Dobbins, 127); 1528–9 *maistre Françoys, organiste à Notre Dame de Confort*, CC 38, fo. 10^r; *organiste (habitant en la maison Poculot, rue Saint Jean)*, CC 137; Rolle, 58, 140; 1538 *Françoys de Layolle organiste*, CC 206; Tricou^3, 1–9
LEFEBVRE, Jehan and Antoine (1592–3)
   Maistres organistes (father and son), Rhône Notaire Buirin; Tricou^1. According to Dufourcq (392–3) Antoine was later active in Toulouse (1596–1612) and Bordeaux (1619). See App. IV(*f*)
MANNUCCIQUA, Piero (1548)
   Organista della natione Fiorentina in Nostra Dama. Composed music for the *intermedi* presented between the acts of Bibbiena's *La Calandia* for Henry II's *Entrée*; Guigue^2, 105
PIERRE (1561)
   EE IV 198d, fo. 18; Tricou^3, 35. This *Me. Pierre* may be MANNUCCIQUA, listed above
PINOT, Guillaume (1579)
   Tricou^3, 35
PONCET, Amal, [Amat, Avrat] (1503–16)
   26 March 1503, civic banquet for the 'Archduke', CC 556, fo. 11^v. In 1505 he married Odette Mallet, and in 1508 sued her father for non-payment of her dowry, Rhône, Not. Delagrange 3 E 4203, fo. 283^r. Between 1512 and 1516 he lived in the Fourvière quarter, as did the organist listed above as AMEIL or ARNEIL, CC 122; Rolle, 120
VELA, Loys de (26 Mar. 1556)
   Organiste de St *Paul*; Tricou^2, 35 According to Dufourcq (173) a Loys Devella was organist at Aix (1585–9), Riez (1589–99), Avignon (1602), and Nîmes (1603)
VOLET, Jacques (1557)
   Rhône, FF 9 Donations; Tricou^3, 35; Establies . . . du côté du Rhône, EE IV, 198, fo. 119^r; Coutagne, 435
YDEUX (IDEULX), Philibert (1570–3)
   Organiste du couvent de Notre Dame de Confort, Rhône, 3H 40, no. 3; Tricou^2, 35

(*j*) HARPSICHORDISTS

CLEMENT, Jean (1569–98)
Musicien, joueur d'espinette; Tricou[1]

(*k*) UNSPECIFIED INSTRUMENTALISTS
(designated joueur *d'instruments* except where otherwise indicated)

AYME, Simon d' (1583)
CC 1341 (banquet for Henry III); Guigue[1], 367

BERAULT, Jean (1548)
25 Feb. 1548 (with Benoit, Goujellin, La Monnoye, and Le Chat he was one of the *fiffres* or *tabourins* who joined the *hautbois* or *violons* Gabriel, Girard, and La Mœulle to play at a civic banquet arranged for four visiting Swiss ambassadors returning from court after attending the baptism of Henry II's daughter Claude. Sixty people, including the governor Saint André and other local dignitaries, enjoyed a lavish entertainment costing the city 2,500 livres, CC 977, no. 25, fo. 4[r]; Guigue[1], 215

BERTAUD, Jean (1515–17)
vinaigrier et menestrier, CC 33; Rolle, 53

BERTAULT, Jean (1503)
meunier (tax waived *pour ce qu'il n'a mestier que de joueur d'instrument*), CC 112; Rolle, 121. See above, BERTAUD

BESSON, Jean (1570)
Tricou[1]

BLANC, Jacques (1598)
Baudrier, i. 321.

BURGNESY, Julio-Curtio (1585–8)
Tricou[1]. See below, CURSIO and App. IV(*a*)

CARDETTES, Charles (1560)
4 July 1560 (witness to the marriage of Antoine Mollard—see below, MOLLARD), Rhône, FF Not. Decublize; Tricou[1]

CHARDON, Benoist (1559–62)
Archives Hospitalières E10; Steyert ii. 492

CHARDON (CERDON) Gabriel (1536–72)
1536–7, CC 888; Guigue[1], 179; 1571, CC 150; Rolle, 152; 1555–70 *Natif de St Paul-en-Jarrez*, Rhône, Notaires Dorlin and De la Forest; Coutagne, 462. According to the *Mémoires de l'estat de France sous Charles IX* Middelburg, 1578, p. 370), Chardon was mutilated and killed as a Protestant in the St Bartholomew's Day Massacre

CURSIO, Julio (1583)
CC 1341 (banquet for Henry III); Guigue[1], 367

DARDON, François (1582–98)
1582 *Natif de Turin*, Rhône, Not. Foillet; Tricou[1]. See App. IV(*g*)

DELAUDUY, Jchan (1574–84)
1574 Rhône, Not. De la Forest; Tricou[1]

DESBARGUES, Mayet (1575)
  Vallas. See App. III(*c*)
DRONIN, Tristan (1569)
  1 May 1569, CC 1174; Guigue[1], 149. See below, TRISTAN
DUZAIX, Jehan (1548)
  25 Feb. 1548, CC 977, no. 25, fo. 4[r]
FRANCISQUE, M[aîtr]e (1581)
  CC 157; Rolle, 162. See App. IV(*f*), DES OLIVIERS?
GABRIEL, Robert (1548)
  25 Feb. 1548 (played shawm or violin at a banquet for visiting Swiss ambassadors), CC 977, no. 25, fo. 4[r]
GERGEAU, Sébastien (1586)
  CC 46; Rolle, 68
GIRARD, Jacques (1548)
  25 Feb. 1548 (played shawm or violin at banquet for Swiss ambassadors), CC 977, no. 25, fo. 3[r]
GOTTEFROIDE, Barthélemy (1583)
  Banquet for Henry III, CC 1341; Guigue[1], 367
GUILLOT (1545–54)
  1545, CC 144, fo. 12[r]; Rolle, 147; 1554, CC 283; Rolle, 238
HENRY, Jehan (1581)
  CC 156; Rolle, 161. For Jean Henry in Paris, see Cohen
JOLY, Nicolas (1574)
  Coutagne, 463. See App. IV(*a*), JULY
LA MARRE, Claude de (1545)
  CC 41, fo. 30[v]. See App. II(*b*), LA MARRE
LAMBERT, Jean (1515–45)
  1515–38 *dict de Troyes*, CC 24; Rolle, 45; 1545, CC 40; Rolle, 61
LA MOLE, Guillaume (1545–8)
  1545, CC 40; Rolle, 61; 25 Feb. 1548 (banquet for Swiss ambassadors), CC 977, no. 25, fo. 4[r]. See above, Ch. 5 (xiii)
LA NOUE, Mathelin (1538)
  ménétrier, CC 142; Rolle, 144. See also App. III(*e*) and IV(*d*)
LAVY, Jean de (1581–86)
  1581, CC 157; Rolle, 162. See also App. III(*c*), LABRI, LA VIS, LA VYTE and III(*b*), LA VIZ
LAYOLLE, Aleman (1551–76)
  13 March 1576, Rhône B. 38, fo. 225; Tricou[3], 29. See above, Ch. 5 (xxi) and App. III(*i*)
LUSSAULT, Philibert (1571)
  CC 150; Rolle, 153
MANET, Jean (1552–4)
  1552; Tricou[1]
MARTIN, Étienne (1542)
  27 Feb. 1542; Baudrier, i. 441
MARTIN, Jacques (1556)

10 Jan. 1556, CC 57; Rolle, 82

MELLILAMA, Jean (1575)

    Tricou[1]

MOLLARD, Anthoine (1560)

    4 July 1560, Rhône, FF, Not. Decublize, Donations, 22, fo. 2^r

RAFFEL, Antoine (1560)

    4 July 1560 (witness at the wedding of Antoine Mollard), Rhône FF, Not. Decublize, Donations, 22, fo. 2^r

TRISTAN, Maître (1568)

    CC 146; Rolle, 149. See also App. III(*d*)

VARIN, Louis (1531)

    3 March 1531 (marriage contract); Baudrier i. 65

VIGNE, Thomas (1583)

    Banquet for Henry III, CC 1341; Guigue[1], 367

VOLET, Jacques (1557)

    EE IV 198, fo. 119^r

APPENDIX IV

Instrument-Makers

(*a*) LUTES, GUITARS, VIOLS, AND VIOLINS

AUGUSTINI, Simon (1567–87)
> *dit du Lutz, venètien, Marchand de luths et instruments de musique*; Tricou, J., i. 153.

BURGNESY, Julio-Cursio (1571–97)
> 20 July 1583 *Marchand d'instruments de musique . . . cede vingt . . . lutz mis en banque publique à son fils, Antoine, marchand à Lyon*; 1587 . . . *vend une caisse de cordes de lutz de 249 paquets à 50 sols le paquet*; Tricou[5], 91. See also App. III(*k*)

DUIFFOPROUCART, Gaspard (1553–71)
> Born in 1514 in Tieffenbruck in Bavaria, he settled in Lyons in 1553, with a shop in the rue de Flandres, and was granted French nationality by Charles IX in 1559. In August 1570 eight of his lutes were confiscated in payment of levies on the rents from houses and inheritances of Protestants in Lyons (Rhône, Not. Nicholas Dorlin, 20 Sept. 1570, fo. 185). References to him in the archives are frequent (e.g. CC 141, 158, 167, 177, 180; Inventaire Chappe IV, p. 362, no. 31; Rhône, Ser. B cour et jurisdiction 1557–9; Not. Laurent la Grange, Minutes, p. 23 (1 Aug. 1554), p. 26 (19 Nov. 1555); Sénéchaussée, Décrets, rentes 630 (1574–5), p. 28; Coutagne, 421–81; Tricou[5] 89–90. A viol signed by him is found in the Donaldson Collection at the Royal College of Music, London and another in the Brussels Conservatoire; Byrne, 126; Mahillon

DUIFFOPROUCART, Jehan (1585)
> Son of Gaspard; Coutagne, 480–1

FLAC (Flach), Philippe (1567–72)
> *Faiseur de luths, allemand.* Twice also listed as *faiseur de guiternes.* CC 146–7, 149–50, 153–4, 275; Rolle, 149, 152, 157–8, 234; Coutagne, 460

GRAIFF, Mango (1584)
> 12 Oct. 1584 *Me. faiseur de luths, allemand.* Graiff and 'Duyffoproghard' claimed that a public sale of their lutes organized by Burgnesy failed because his prices were too high; Tricou[5], 90

HELMER, Jean (1571–91)
> *Faiseur de guiternes,* listed with FLAC in same tax records; Coutagne, 460

HOUMOLLET, Jean (1589)
> Tricou[1]

HUTMEYER (1596)

Rhône, Not. Foillet; Tricou[1]

JULI (JOLY), Nicolas (1572–97)

1572 *Faiseur de luths*, CC 275; Rolle, 234; 1575 *Marchand d'instruments*, CC 277; Rolle, 236; *vendeur et joueur d'instruments*; Coutagne, 463

LE CAMUS, Pierre (1573–5)

1573 *Faiseur de luths, étranger, rue Pomme Rouge*, 1575 CC 276; Rolle, 235; CC 277; Rolle, 236; Coutagne, 461

LE JEUNE, Benoist (1557)

Faiseur de luths, faiseur de guiternes; Tricou[5], 89–90. He was tried by the Senechaussée court for faking Duiffoproucart's mark on his instruments; Lesure[1]

RENEDY, Georges (1535)

Luthier EE 21 Tricou[1]

SIMON, Me faiseur de luths (1568–80)

1571 CC 150 Rolle, 152; 1571–3 CC 147, Rolle, 153–55, 275–277 Coutagne, 461; 1580 imported lutes from Padua for Parisian dealer Claude Denis, Lesure[2], 34.

TURQUEY, Jacques (1594)

M(aîtr)e faiseur de viollons Tricou[1]

VEIGLE, Jean (1576)

Faiseur de lutz, natif d'Epostolein [en] Allemagne Tricou[1]

VILLE, Jean (1578)

Faiseur de lucs Tricou[1]

VINATTE, André (1568–72)

Faiseur de violles...poitevin. Laboureur. EE 25 Coutagne, 459–460. Like G. Chardon, Vinatte was a victim of the St Bartholomew's Day massacre: Ricaud.

(b) STRING MANUFACTURERS AND DEALERS
(Designated *Fabbricant de cordes à boyau[d]*)

BELLET (BILLET), Philibert (1580–84)

Tricou[1]

BURGNESY, Julio-Curtio (1571–97)

(see App. III(*k*) and IV(*g*))

DESCLEFS (DES CLEFS), Gaspart (1580–6)

After inheriting Bellet's business, he died in 1586; Tricou[1]

MASSER, Pierre (1599)

Tricou[1]

ORLANDIN (ORLANDINI) (1569)

Marchand de cordes de luth; imported strings from Mantua and Milan, CC 169; Rolle, 170

ROLE, Jean (1580–8)

Tricou[1]

TERRASSON (1569)

Marchand de cordes de luth, CC 169; Rolle, 170

(c) SPINETS AND CLAVICHORDS

BONTEMPS, Nicolas (1516)
Faiseur de manicordions, CC 3. See App. III(*i*)

DE LEVRES (DE L'ŒUVRE), Honoré (1523–45)
June 1523 *Faiseur d'espinettes*, owner of a house near Moderne's in rue Raisin, CC 260; Rolle, 223; June 1526, EE 20; Coutagne, 459; 1529, CC 39; Rolle, 60; CC 136; Rolle, 137; 1538–40, CC 138, 143; Coutagne, 459; 1545, CC 41, 144, 281; Rolle, 62, 147, 237

DE LEVRES Pierre de (–1551)
4 Dec. 1551 *hoirs feu Pierre* (possible scribal error for Honoré) *de Levres, faiseur d'espinettes*, CC 44; Rolle, 66

(d) FLUTES

CLAUDE (1528–9)
1528 *fleustier* (listed separately from RAFFIN), CC 38; Rolle, 57; 1529, noted as deceased, CC 137, fo. 61^r; Rolle, 140

LA NOT, Mathurin de (1529)
fleustier, CC 137; Rolle, 140 (cf. LA NOUE)

LA NOUE, Mathurin (Mathelin) de (1523–55)
1536 *flustier*, CC 274; Rolle, 233. Coutagne (p. 462) cites other documents describing him as *faiseur d'instruments* (1523), *fleustier* (1529), *flosteur* (1530), and *menestrier* (1538), noting his death in 1555; this conflicts with evidence from the Archives nationales suggesting that he died in 1542. See App. III(*e*)

PIERRE (1528–9)
fleustier, residing with CLAUDE (see above), CC 38; Rolle, 57

PILLON, Jacques (1503)
Faiseur de flustes (his son Jacques is also listed as a furrier), CC 237; Rolle, 213. See App. III(*e*)

RAFI (RAFFIN), Claude (1523–53)
Fleustier; Tricou[6] identifies Claude as the son of Michaud Rapin and brother of Pierre, citing documents CC 38, 40, 137, 250, 271, and 711. A flute by C. Rafi survives in the Brussels Conservatoire collection (Mahillon, ii, no. 1066) and others are mentioned in Byrne

RAFFIN, Pierre (1523–9)
1523, CC 259; Rolle, 223; 1529, CC 38; Rolle, 57

RAPIN (RAPHIN), Michaud (1512–29)
1523 *Faiseur de fleustes*, CC 259; Rolle, 223; 1529, CC 22; Rolle, 41. Father of Claude Rafi; Tricou[5]. See App. III(E), RAPHIN

(e) TRUMPETS AND CORNETTS

BALLIF, Claude (1557)
Trompettier; faiseur de trompettes; Tricou[1]

FLACHIERES, Pierre (1556–8)
  Faiseur de cornets; Tricou[1]
GENTIL, Luc (1551)
  Faiseur d'instruments, CC 44; Rolle, 66. See also App. III(*f*) and IV(*g*)
LA VANELLE, Simon de (1529–45)
  1529 *graveur*, CC 281; Rolle, 237; 1530 *Faiseur de trompettes*, CC 796; Guiguu[1] 148; 1545 *Trompetier*, CC 41, fo. 6[v]; Rolle, 62. Another archival reference cited by Baudrier (i. 65) indicates that he died before 1561

(*f*) ORGANS

DES OLIVIERS, Francisque (1531–70)
  3 Mar. 1570 *Composeur d'orgues, natif de Lyon*. Replaced organ at Notre Dame de Confort, Rhône 3H 40, pièce no. 3. Dufourcq (p. 68) notes 'François des Oliviers, composeur d'orgues, demeurant à Troyes' contracting to build an organ for the Sainte-Chapel in Dijon in 1560, after working earlier in Beauvais (1531), Amiens (1543), Tours (1550), and Troyes (1555)
KORN (CORNE), Gaspard (1523–35)
  1535 *Faiseur d'orgues, allemand*, EE 21; Tricou[1]
LEFEBVRE, Jehan and Antoine (1593)
  Père et fils maistres organistes. Paid by Luccan patricians for replacing the organ at the Franciscan church destroyed during the Protestant uprising of 1562. BB 129, fo. 155[v]; Tricou[2], 261
SEURAT, Nicolas (1576)
  Paid 4 livres tournois for restoring organ in the general hospital, Archives hospitalières E 608

(*g*) UNSPECIFIED MANUFACTURERS AND DEALERS
(designated *faiseur d'instruments de musique*)

AUGUSTINI, Simon (1587)
  See App. IV(*a*)
BAONO (BANO) (1572)
  Tricou, J., ii. 54
BONTEMPS, Nicolas (Mar. 1507)
  Coutagne, 459
BURGNESY, Julio-Cursio (1571–97)
  See App. IV(*a*)
DARDON, François (1582–98)
  Rhône, Not. Copprer; Tricou[1]. See App. I and III(*k*)
FAURE (FAVRE), Toussaint (–1555)
  1555 (will deposited), Rhône B FF, Donations 9, fo. 2. *Marchant, faiseur d'instruments de musique*; Coutagne, 461
FURET, François (1582–4)
  Married Jacqueline Lasalle, orphan, Archives hospitalières E 188; Coutagne, 463

GENTIL, Luc (1551)
   Marchand & faiseur d'instruments, rue St. Sebastien, CC 44; Coutagne, 461.
   See App. III(*f*)
GONELLE, Jehan (1583)
   27 Mar. 1583 Rhône, Not. Foillet, p. 31; Tricou[1]
LA NOUE, Mathurin (Mathelin) de (1523)
   June 1523 EE Establies; Coutagne, 462. In Mar. 1542 Mathurin de la Noue,
   'maistre faiseur d'instrumens demeurant en la ville de Lyon' took on an
   apprentice in Paris; by September 1542, when a contract with a Parisian
   wood-turner to supply a set of German flutes to a Parisian dealer was signed,
   he is described as 'deffunct'; on 11 August 1544 an inventory of his estate
   included sets of flutes, *grosses fleustes*, recorders, fifes, *chalumeaulx servans
   à musette*, bagpipes, and shawms; Lesure[2], 19–22
LE VACHET, Claude (1572)
   Son of Rogier Le Vachet; Tricou[1]
LE VACHET, Rogier (1572)
   Tricou[1]
VINGLE, Jehan (1583)
   27 Mar. 1583, Rhône, Not. Foillet; Tricou[1]

APPENDIX V

Music Printed in Lyons

(This list excludes liturgical chant-books and reprints but includes monophonic songs and psalms. Unless otherwise specified all the books are for four voices. Entries in square brackets indicate books which according to the title-pages were published in Lyons but which were probably printed in Geneva.)

c.1525	(Du Ry)	*Motetti*; British Library K. 8. b. 7 (5)	Guillo no. 1
c.1526–30	(Blanchard)	*Chansons nouvelles en lengaige provensal* (à 1)	Guillo no. 8
1528	Gueynard	*Contrapunctus*	ed. D. Sutherland
1532	Moderne	*Liber decem missarum*	Pogue no. 3
	Moderne	*Motteti del Fiore* I–II, II à 5	Pogue nos. 4–8
c.1532	Moderne	Piéton, *Davidici Poenitentiales Psalmi*	RISM P 2344
(c.1535)	(Moderne)	*Fleur des Noelz . . . notés* (à 1)	Pogue no. 107
1538	Moderne	*Parangon des Chansons* I–IV	Pogue nos. 10–14
	Moderne	*Motteti del Fiore* III à 5	Pogue nos. 15–16
1539	Moderne	*Motteti del Fiore* III–IV, IV à 5	Pogue nos. 17–19
	Moderne	*Parangon des Chansons* IV à 2–3, V	Pogue nos. 20–1
1540	Moderne	*Liber decem missarum* (rev. edn.)	Pogue no. 22
	Moderne	*Parangon des Chansons* VI–VII	Pogue nos. 26, 29
	Moderne	*Parangon des Chansons* II (rev. edn.)	Pogue no. 28
	Moderne	Guerson, *Regules musicales*	Pogue no. 25
	Moderne	Layolle, *25 Canzoni* à 5	ed. F. D'Accone
(c.1540)	Moderne	Layolle, *50 Canzoni*	ed. F. D'Accone
	Moderne	*Difficile des Chansons* I	Pogue no. 27
1541	Moderne	*Parangon des Chansons* VIII–IX	Pogue nos. 30–1

1542	Moderne	Colin, *Octo missarum* à 4–6	Pogue nos. 33, 119
	Moderne	*Motteti del Fiore* III à 5–6, V à 5–7	Pogue nos. 34–35
1543	Moderne	*Motteti del Fiore* V à 5–7	Pogue no. 36
	Moderne	*Parangon des Chansons*, III (rev. edn.), X–XI	Pogue nos. 37–9
1544	Moderne	*Difficile des Chansons* II	Pogue no. 40
(*c*.1544)	Moderne	*Musicque de Joye*	Pogue no. 41
1545–6	Moderne	Morales, *Missarum Liber* I à 4–6	Pogue nos. 47–8
1547–8	Moderne	*Harmonidos Ariston*	Pogue nos. 49–50, 52
(*c*.1547)	Moderne	Bianchini, *Tabulature de Lutz*	Pogue no. 51
1547	Beringen	Bourgeois, *Pseaulmes 50 à 4*	*Pidoux 47/1*
	Beringen	Bourgeois, *Premier livre des Pseaulmes*	Pidoux 47/11
1547–8	Beringen	Phinot, *Liber Mutetarum* I–II	ed. J. Hofler
1548	Beringen	Phinot, *Chansons* I–II	ed. R. Jacob
	Beringen	D. Lupi, *Chansons* III	Guillo no. 22
	Beringen	D. Lupi, *Chansons spirituelles*	Pidoux 48/111
1548–9	Beringen	Marot, *Pseaulmes 50* (à 1)	Pidoux 48/II, 49/1
c.1549	Moderne	Paladino, *Tabulature de Lutz*	ed. M. Renault
1550	Beringen	D. Lupi, *Psalmes 30*	Pidoux 49/III
1550–2	Moderne	*Morales, Magnificat*	Pogue nos. 54, 56
1551–2	Moderne	Morales, *Missarum Liber* II	Pogue nos. 55, 57
1552	Beringen	S. Joly, *Psalmi quinquagesimi*	Guillo no. 27
1553	Moderne	Bakfark, *Intabulatura* I	ed. I. Homolya
1554	Beringen	Bourgeois, *Pseaulmes LXXXIII*	Pidoux 54/II
1555	Bonhomme	N. Martin, *Noelz and Chansons*	Guillo no. 31
1555	Du Bois	Jambe de Fer, *150 Pseaulmes* (à 1)	Pidoux 55/VIII
1555	Du Bois	Jambe de Fer, *epitome musical*	ed. F. Lesure
1556	Moderne	Colin, *Liturgicon musicarum*	Pogue nos. 60–1
(*c*.1557)	Moderne	Rampollini, *Musica* I	ed. F. D'Accone

1558–9	Granjon	Beaulaigue, *Chansons*	ed. A. Auda
1559	Granjon	Beaulaigue, *Mottetz*	ed. A. Auda
	Granjon	*Premier Trophée de Musique*	RISM 1559[14]
	Granjon	*Second Trophée de Musique*	RISM 1559[15]
	Granjon	M. Ferrier, *49 psalmes* à 3	Pidoux 49/IV
	Du Bois	Jambe de Fer, *Psalmodie* à 4–5	Pidoux 59/V
	Beringen	*Genethliac* [de B. Aneau]	Guillo no. 36
1560	Beringen	Davantes, *Pseaumes* (à 1)	Pidoux 60/I
	Gorlier	Paladino, *Tablature de Luth* I	ed. M. Renault
	Gorlier	Hauville, *La Lyre Chrestienne*	Baudrier ii. 47–8
1561	(Saugrin)	*Complainte faitte à Dieu* (à 1)	Guillo no. 49
	Straton	(D. Lupi *et al.*), *Chansons spirituelles* à 4	Pidoux 61/V
	(De Tournes)	*Les (90) Psalmes de David* (à 1)	Guillo no. 51
1562–4	Vincent *et al.*	*Pseaumes* (à 1) (16 edns.)	Guillo 52–6, 60–70
1564		De Mia *et al.*	Pidoux 64/III–IV
		Jambe de Fer, *CL Pseaumes* (à 4–5)	
	Straton	Crassot, *Pseaumes* à 4	Pidoux 64/V
	De Tournes	*26 Cantiques . . . par Louis des Masures*	Pidoux 64/IX
1565	Huguetan	Grassot, *Pseaumes* à 4	Guillo no. 76
1566	Saugrin	[Goudimel], *Musique de David*	Guillo no. 78
1567	Cercia	G. A. di Mayo, *Madrigali* à 4	RISM M 1487
1568	Rigaud	D. Lupi *et al.*, *Chansons spirituelles*	RISM 1568[9]
1569	(Unidentified)	H. P. de Villiers, *Aer funebre* (à 1–3)	Guillo no. 83 bis
1573	De Tournes I	Blockland, *Instruction fort facile*	Guillo no. 85
1574	Bavent	Lassus/Goudimel, *Fleur des chansons* I–II	RISM 1574[1–2]
1577	Baudin	R. Vecoli, *Madrigali* I à 5	RISM 1577[10]
	(G. Fiorino)	G. Fiorino, *Canzonelle*	Guillo no. 90
[1578	Pesnot	Servin, *Chansons* I–III à 4–8	RISM 2838–40]

[1579	Pesnot	Servin, *Psalmi a Buchanano* à 4–8	RISM S 2841]
1579	De Tournes II	Blockland, *Jardin de musique* II	RISM B 4522
1581	De Tournes II	Blockland, *Instruction de Musique*	RISM B–VI, 155
[1583	B. Vincent	L'Estocart, *126 Quatrains de Pibrac* à 3–6	RISM L2074]
[	B. Vincent	L'Estocart, *Octonaires* I–II à 2–6	ed. H. Expert]
[	B. Vincent	L'Estoncart, *150 Pseaumes* à 4–8	Pidoux 83/I]
[1586–7	De Tournes II	Arcadelt, *Excellence des chansons*	Guillo no. 95]
1592	Pillehotte	Coyssard, *Paraphrase des hymnes*	RISM 1592⁶

APPENDIX VI

Resident and Visiting Patrons of Music

Altovita, Bernardo Banker
Patrician of the Florentine community. Dedicatee of the *Contrapunctus* (1528). Ch. 4 (ii)

Arnolfin, Joseph (Gioseffo Arnolfini)
(One of the Luccan merchants and bankers acknowledged in the dedication of Didier Lupi's chansons (1548). Ch. 5 (xviii)

Baillivi, Nicolas
Lyonese banker. Dedicatee of Didier Lupi's *Psalmes* (1550). Ch. 5 (xviii)

Barthelemy, Anthoine and Jean-Baptiste
Silk merchants from Lucca. Dedicatees of D. Lupi's chansons (1548). Ch. 5 (xviii)

Bave, Nicolas
Dedicatee of D. Phinot's first book of chansons (1548). Ch. 5 (xvii)

Bonvalot, François
Archbishop of Besançon. Dedicatee of Phinot's second book of motets (1548). Ch. 4 (iv)

Bourbon, Charles de
Archbishop of Lyons. Ordered music for a banquet to entertain Philippe le Beau in 1503. Ch. 3 (i)

Buonvisi, Lorenzo
Luccan patrician. Dedicatee of R. Vecoli's madrigals (1577). Ch. 4 (xiii); Plate 12

Buonvisi, Lucretia
Wife of Girolamo Buonvisi, Luccan merchant. Dedicatee of G. Fiorino's *Canzonelle* (1577). Ch. 4 (xiii)

Capponi, Laurent (Lorenzo)
Commissioned masque for his marriage to Hélayne Guadagni in 1554. Ch. 4 (i)

Carniccion, Vincent (Vincenzo Carniccioni)
Luccan merchant. One of the dedicatees of D. Lupi's chansons (1548). Ch. 5 (xviii)

Cinamy (Cenami), Joseph
Member of Luccan merchant family involved in spice, cotton, and wool trade at Lyons. One of the dedicatees of D. Lupi's chansons (1548). Ch. 5 (xviii)

Champier, Symphorien
   Patron of Fourvière Academy and Trinity College. Ch. 2 (i)

Chenevard, André
   Dedicatee of both psalm collections by Loys Bourgeois (1547). Ch. 6 (vi)

Darud, Jean
   Spice- and cloth-merchant from the Franche-Comté resident in Lyons between 1533 and 1572. Dedicatee of Jambe de Fer's *Épitome* (1556). Ch. 6 (vi)

Diane de Poitiers
   Duchesse du Valentinois, mistress of Henry II. Dedicatee of Beaulaigue's chansons and motets (1558–9). Ch. 6 (iv)

Dinteville, Gabrielle
   Baronne de Bohan, Dame de Creissia, Burgundian lady. Dedicatee of Blockland's *Jardin* (1579). Ch. 5 (xxvii)

Du Peyrat, Jean
   Royal lieutenant-general. Patron to E. de Beaulieu. Ch. 2 (vii). His son Jean II supported F. Roussel. Ch. 5 (xx)

Epinac, Piere d'
   Archbishop of Lyons. Patron and author of *Chansons spirituelles* set by Gilles Maillard mentioned by A. du Verdier (1585). Ch. 5 (xxix)

Estaing, Charles d'
   Apostolic notary and canon of Lyons cathedral. Dedicatee of Moderne's *Liber decem missarum* (1532; repr. 1540) and *Liber octo missarum ... Quae omnia Petrus Colinius ... composuit*. Ch. 4 (iii) and Ch. 5 (xi)

Este, Ippolito d'
   Archbishop of Lyons. Commissioned *intermedi* by Mannuciqua for *La Calandria* in 1548. Ch. 3 (i)

Gondi, Hélène et Marie-Catherine de Pierrevive
   Daughter and wife of the Florentine diplomat Antoine de Gondi, patrons of Beaulieu. Ch. 2 (vii)

Gouffier, François
   Bishop of Béziers. Dedicatee of F. Bianchini's lute-book. Ch. 6 (ix)

Grimaldo, Lucca de (Luca de Grimaldi)
   Genoan merchant. Dedicatee of Phinot's first book of motets (1547). Ch. 5 (xvii)

Grolier, Jean
   Viscount of Aguisy, financier and statesman. Patron of Gafori in Milan (1511–18). Ch. 2 (i)

Gros, César (Cesare Groso)
   Alderman of Lyons, silk trader and banker originally from Piedmont. Dedicatee of Phinot's second book of chansons (1548). Ch. 5 (xvii)

Gruyere, Comte de

Dedicatee of Guéroult's *Chansons spirituelles* set by D. Lupi (1548). Ch. 5 (xviii)

Guadagne, Thomas de (Tomasso Guadagni)
Banker, Florentine patrician, benefactor of Notre-Dame de Confort and probably of F. Layolle (1523–39). Ch. 5 (iv)

Guadagne, Guillaume de
Son of Thomas, seneschal of Lyons, patron of F. Roussel (1568). Ch. 5 (xx)

La Baume, Louis Poupet de
Comte de Saint Amour, Baron de Corgenon, Seigneur de Peres. Dedicatee of Blockland's *Instruction* (1573: repr. 1581 and 1587). Ch. 5 (xxvii)

La Porte (François de)
Conseiller in Lyons. Dedicatee of Castro's *Second livre de chansons* published in Paris in 1580. Ch. 5 (xxx)

Michel, Jerosme (Girolamo, Micheli)
Textile merchant and banker from Lucca. One of the dedicatees of D. Lupi's chansons (1548). Ch. 5 (xviii)

Obrech, Georges
Banker from Strasburg, financier to Francis I, *conseiller* during the period of Protestant control; dedicatee of Jambe de Fer's *Psalmodie* (1559) and mentioned in the dedication of the *Épitome Musical* (1556). Ch 5 (xviii)

Orsuccio, Alaman
One of the dedicatees of D. Lupi's chansons (1548). Ch. 5 (xviii)

Popet, Guillaume
Abbé de Baume. Mentioned in Blockland's *Instruction* (1573, 1581, and 1587) as dedicatee of a (lost) Latin treatise on music by Blockland

Pense, Justinien
Textile merchant. Dedicatee of Castro's chansons copied by Pollet in Antwerp in 1571 and of another collection published in Paris in 1575. Ch. 5 (xxx)

Pournas, François
Seigneur de la Pimente, Lyonese landowner. Dedicatee of Gorlier's guitar collection published in Paris. Ch. 6 (ix)

Strozzi, Leone
Prior of Capua, naval commander in Marseilles, patron of B. Beaulaigue. Ch. 6 (iv)

Strozzi, Lionardo
Banker, member of the Florentine patrician family, patron of F. Layolle. Ch. 6 (v)

Tournon, François de
Cardinal, poet, statesman and master of the Chapel Royal. He was officially installed as Archbishop of Lyons in September 1552. In the same year he

received the dedication of Simon Joly's *Psalmi Quinquagesimi*, and in 1553 of Bakfark's lute-book. Ch. 3 (iv), Ch. 6 (ix)

Trivulce, Pompone (Pomponio, Trivulzio)
  Governor of Lyons. Patron of Eustorg de Beaulieu (1532–7). Ch. 2 (vii)

As reported in Ch. 3 and with some details in App. III, the Consulat (city council) commissioned music for the ceremonial entries of Queen Eleanor and the dauphin (1533), Henry II and Queen Catherine (1548), Charles IX (1564), Henry III (1574), Henry IV (1595), and Henry IV with Marie de' Medici (1600), for the installation of Archbishops François de Rohan (1506), Ippolito d'Este (1540), and François de Tournon (1552), for the release of the royal hostages (1530), for the visit of the Swiss ambassadors (1547 and 1548), for the arrival of the royal lieutenant Jean Tignat (1551), for the celebration of the peace of Cateau-Cambrésis (1559), and for the victory at Jarnac (1569).

Music Examples

1. Gabriel Coste, 'Vien soulas'
2. F. de Lys, 'En lieu du bien'
3. P. de Villiers, 'Je n'oseroys'
4. Philibert Jambe de Fer, 'Salve salutaris victima'
5. P. de Villiers, 'Missa Trinitas in unitate'
6. Giovanni Antonio di Mayo, 'Amor, fortuna'
7. Regolo Vecoli, 'Amor fortuna'
8. Didier Lupi Second, 'Prens garde à moy'
9. Francesco Bianchini, 'Vous semblet il'

Ex. 1. Gabriel Coste, 'Vien soulas' (text by Bonaventure des Périers). *Le Parangon des Chansons* VII (Moderne, 1540[7]), fo. 25

318

Ex. 2. F. de Lys, 'En lieu du bien' (text by Pernette du Guillet). *Le Parangon des Chansons* VI (Moderne, 1540[16]), fo. 10

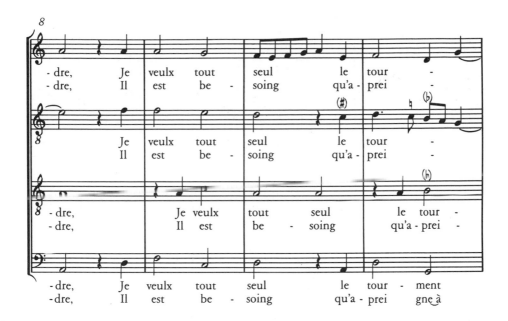

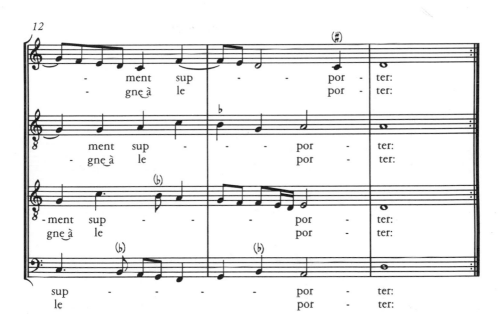

Ex. 3. P. de Villiers, 'Je n'oseroys' (text by Pernette du Guillet). *Le Parangon des Chansons* VI (Moderne, 1540[16]), fo. 6

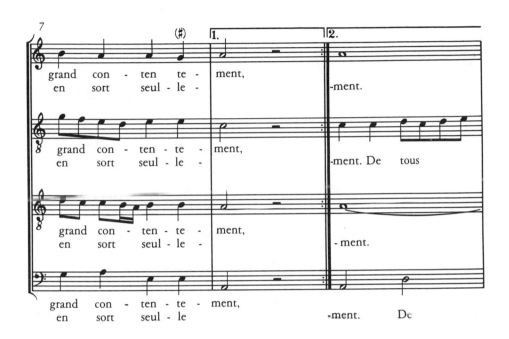

326

Ex. 4. Philibert Jambe de Fer, 'Salve salutaris victima' for Henry II. *Harmonidos Ariston* (Moderne, 1547²), fos. 33ᵛ–35

Ex. 5. P. de Villiers, 'Missa Trinitas in unitate'. *Liber decem missarum* (Moderne, 1540[1]), fos. 101[v]–104

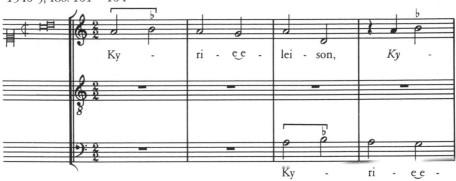

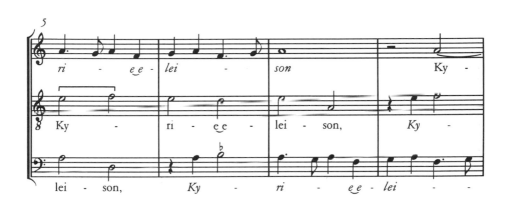

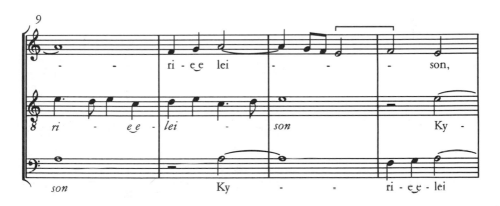

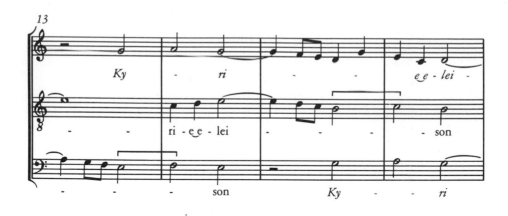

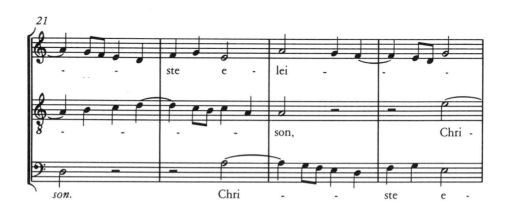

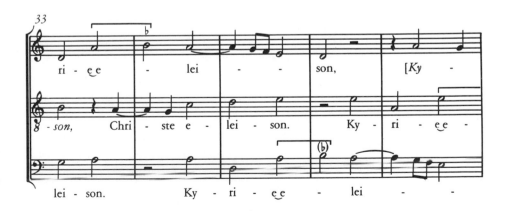

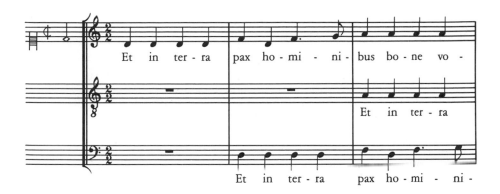

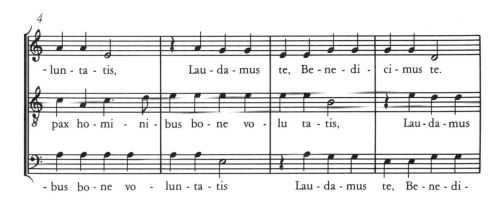

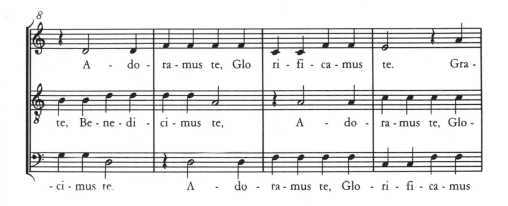

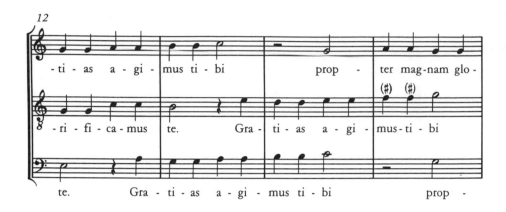

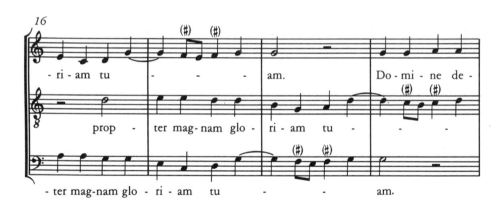

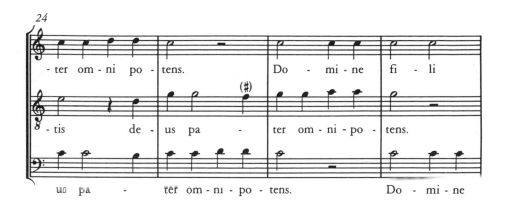

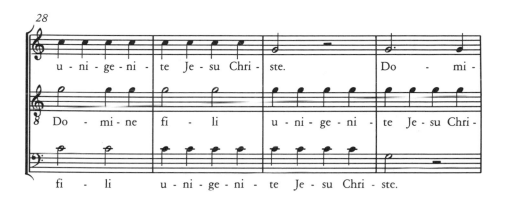

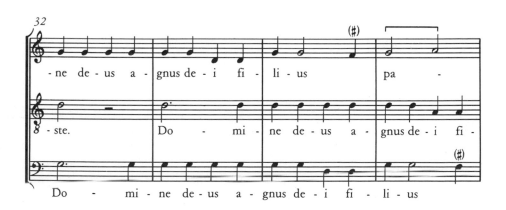

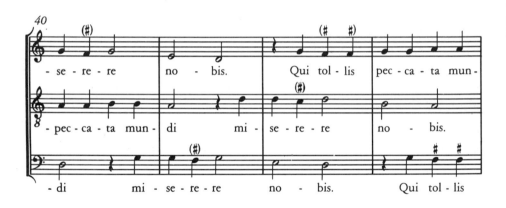

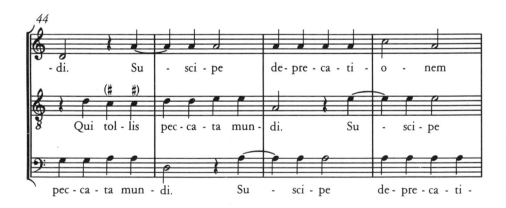

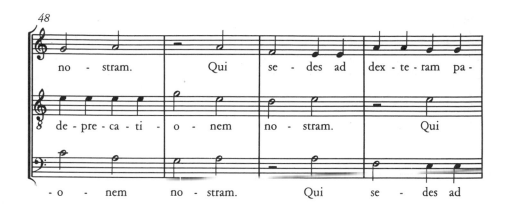

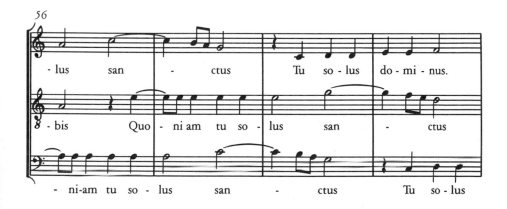

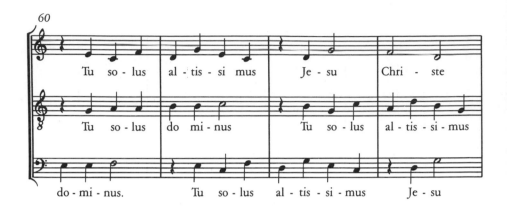

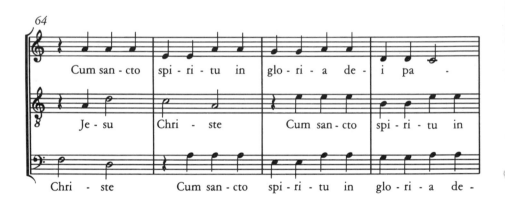

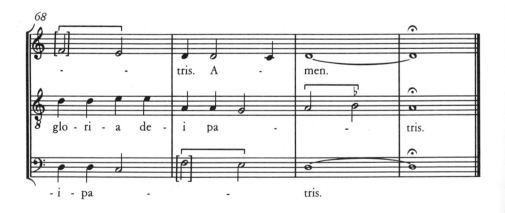

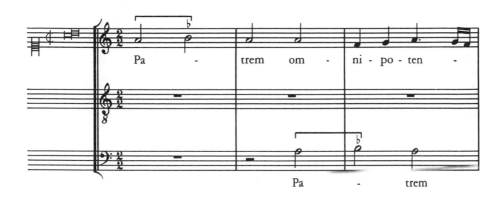

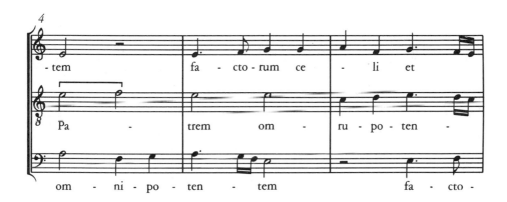

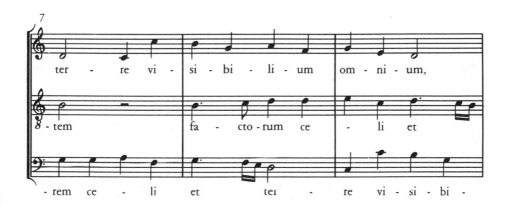

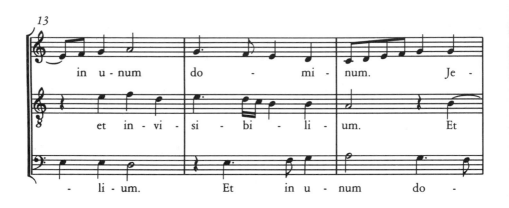

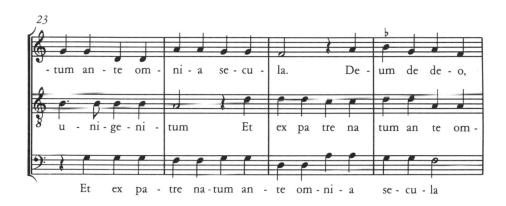

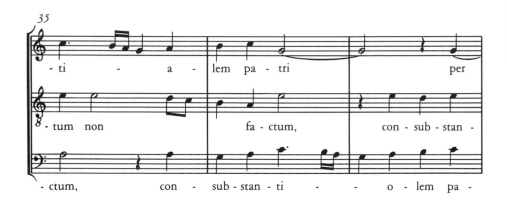

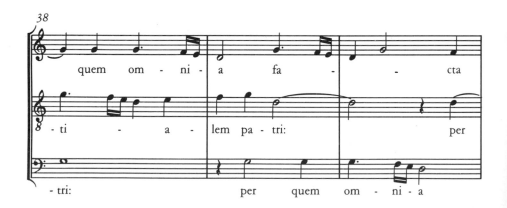

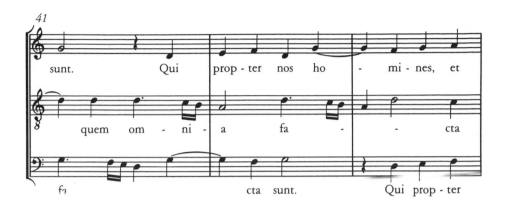

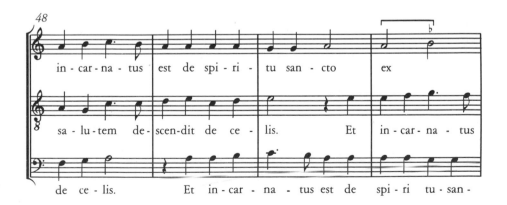

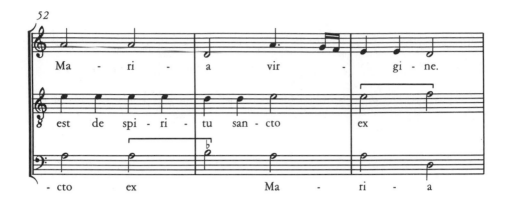

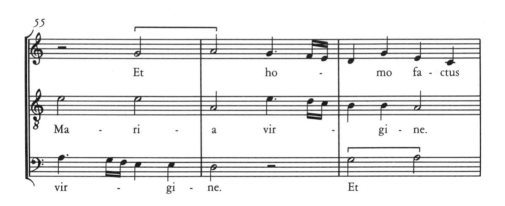

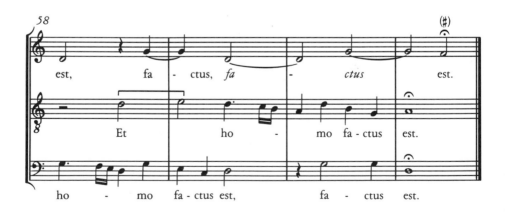

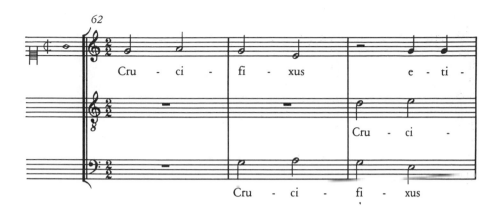

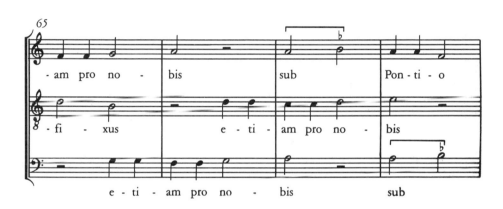

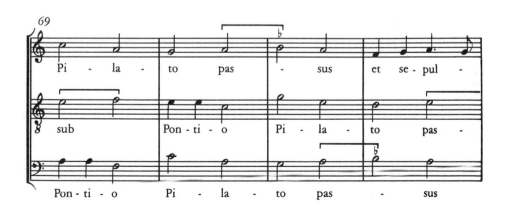

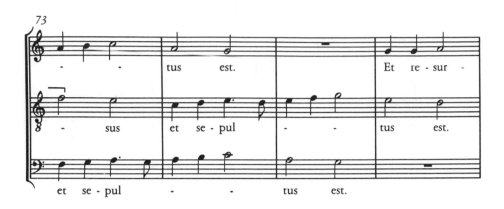

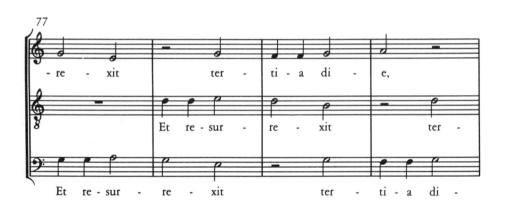

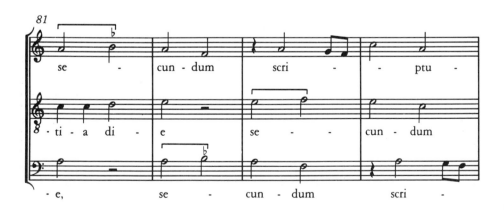

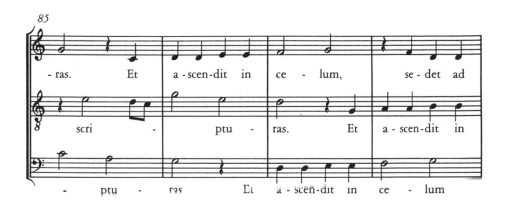

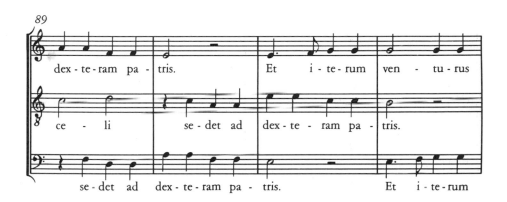

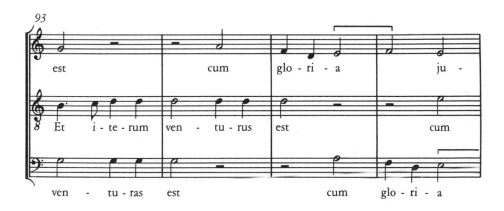

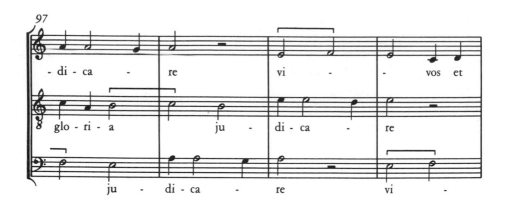

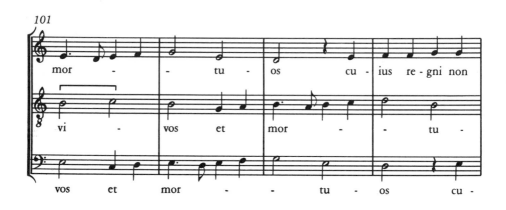

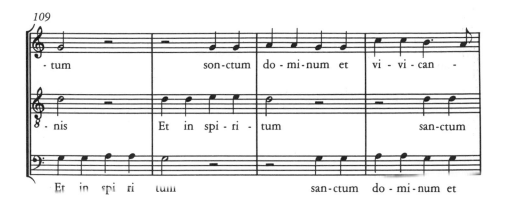

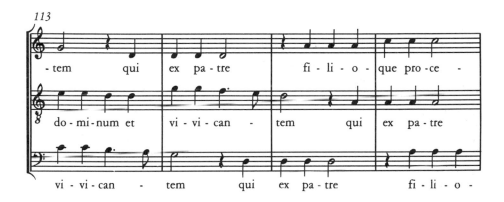

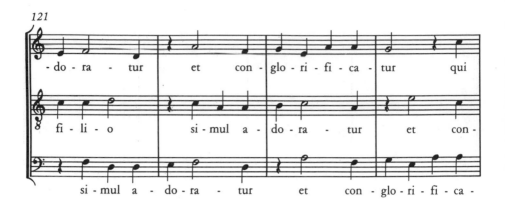

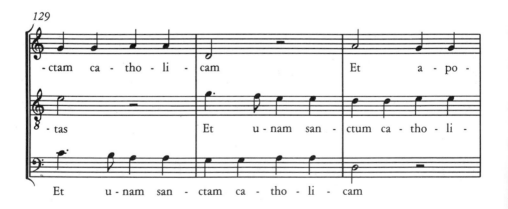

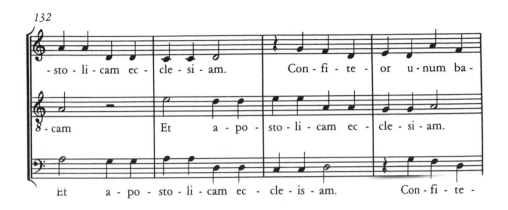

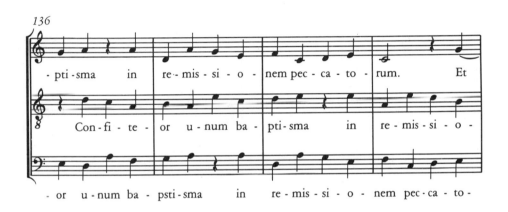

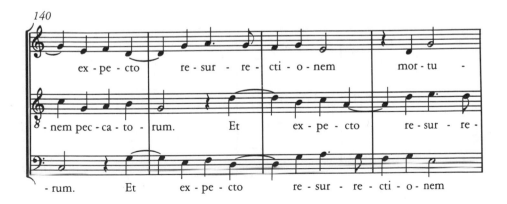

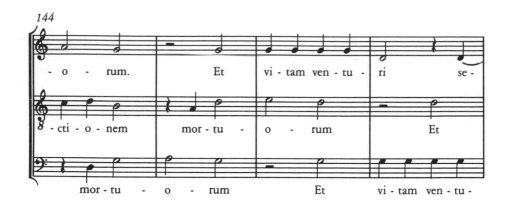

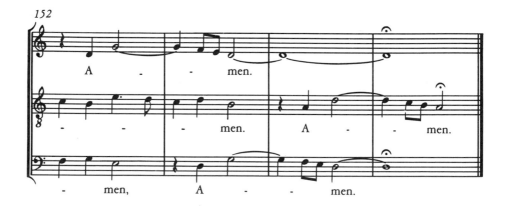

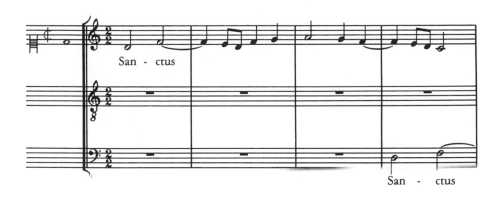

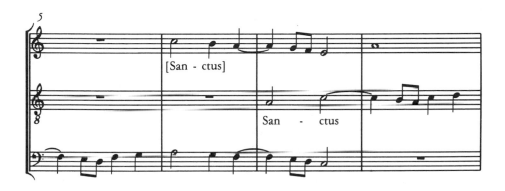

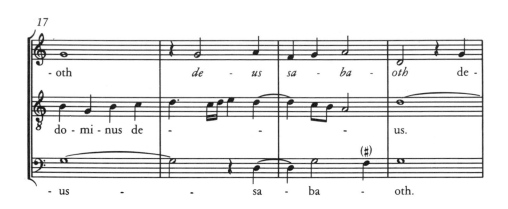

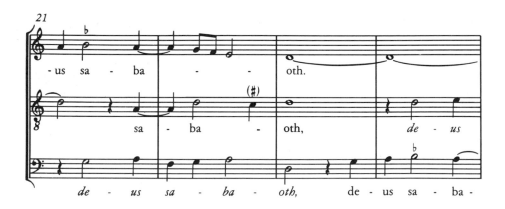

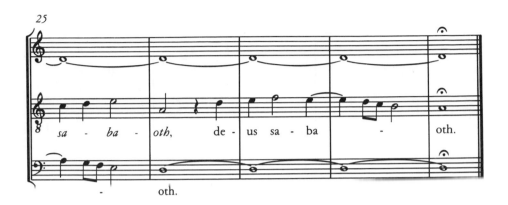

sa - ba - oth, de - us sa - ba - oth.

- oth.

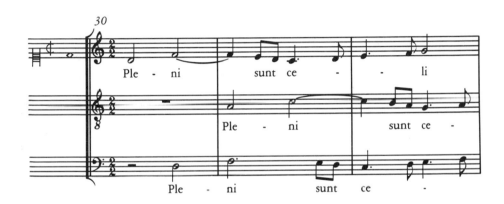

Ple - ni sunt ce - li

Ple - ni sunt ce -

Ple - ni sunt ce -

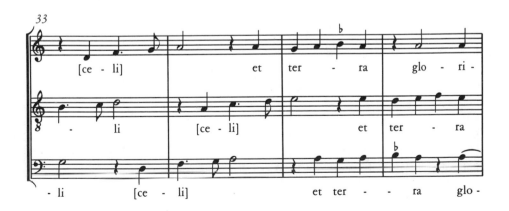

[ce - li] et ter - ra glo - ri -

- li [ce - li] et ter - ra

- li [ce - li] et ter - ra glo -

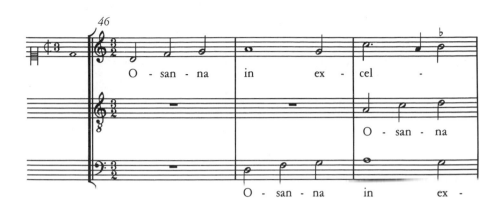

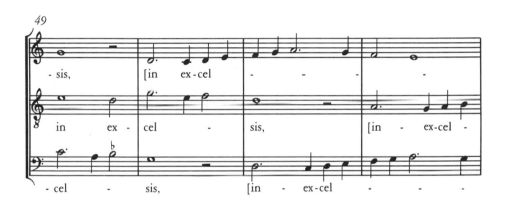

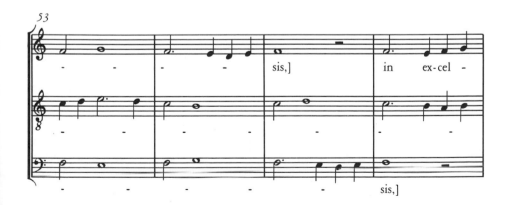

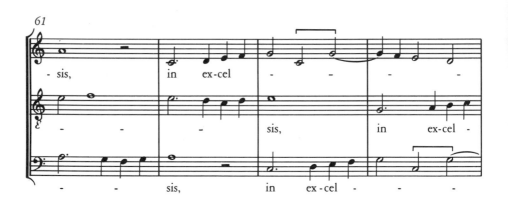

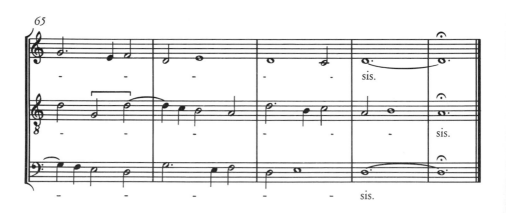

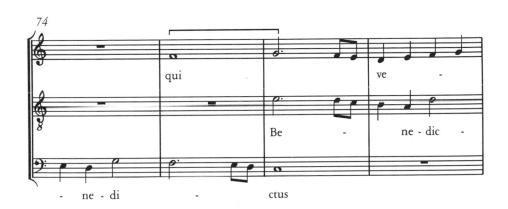

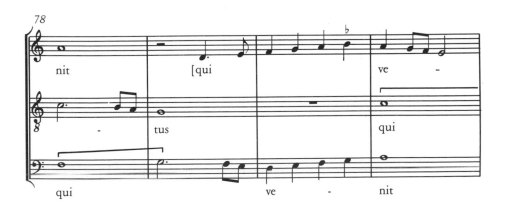

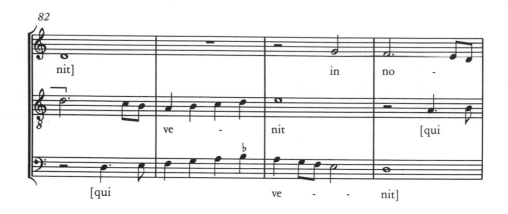

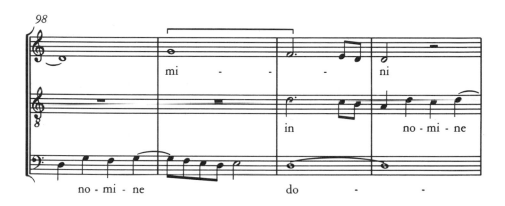

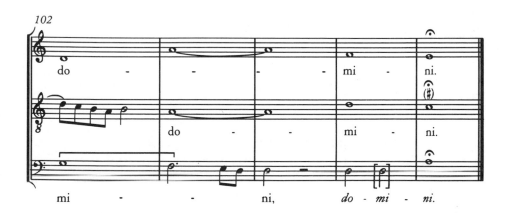

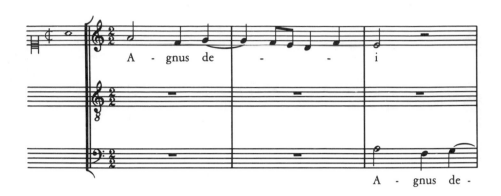

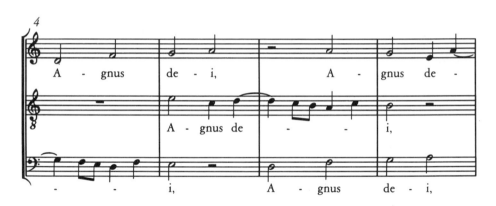

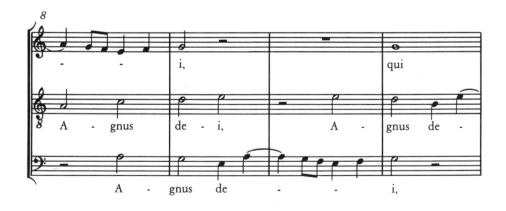

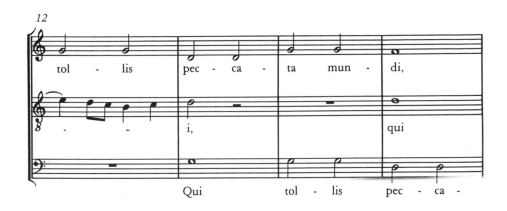

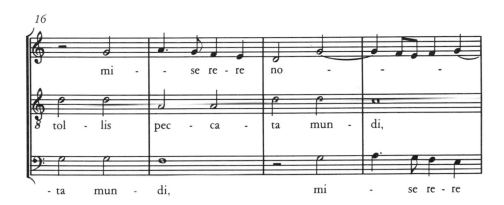

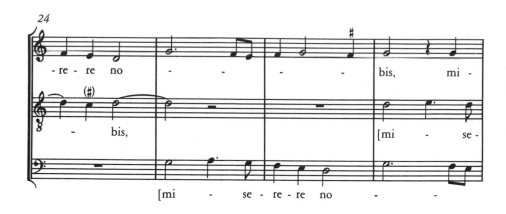

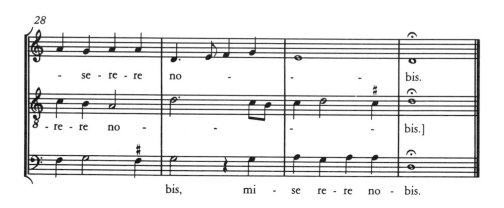

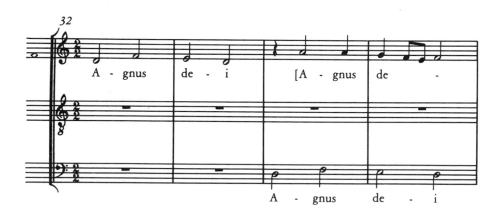

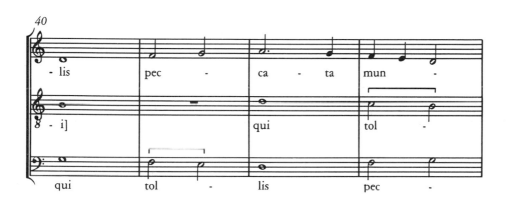

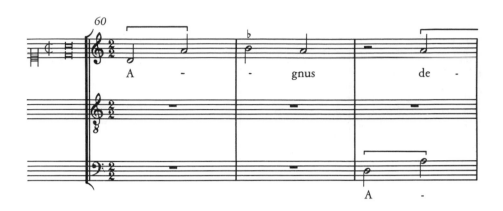

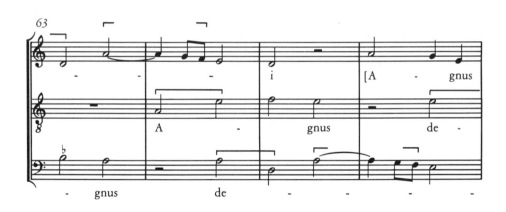

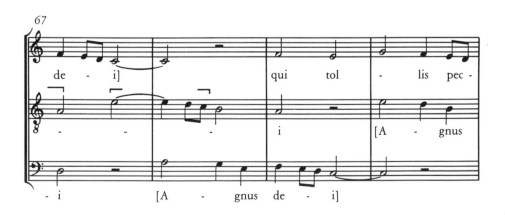

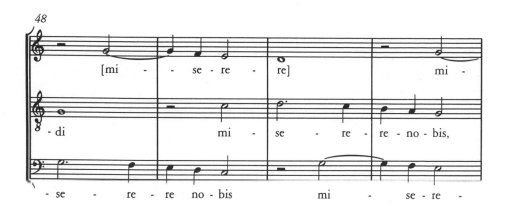

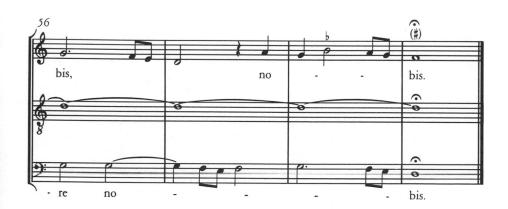

374

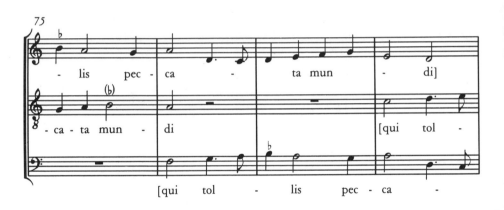

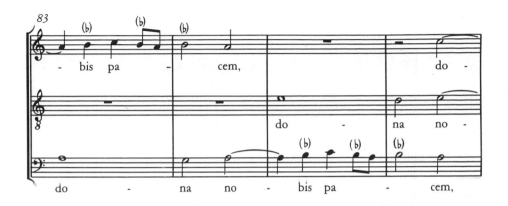

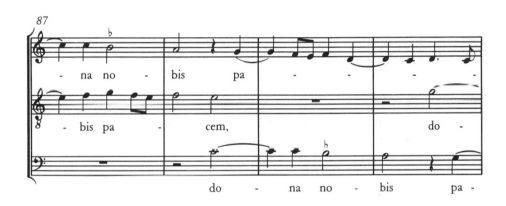

376

Ex. 6. Giovanni Antonio di Mayo, 'Amor, fortuna' (text by Petrarch). *Primo libro di madrigali* (Cercia, 1567), pp. 2–3

Ex. 7. Regolo Vecoli, 'Amor fortuna' (text by Petrarch). *Primo libro de madrigali a 5* (Baudin, 1577), pp. 8–9

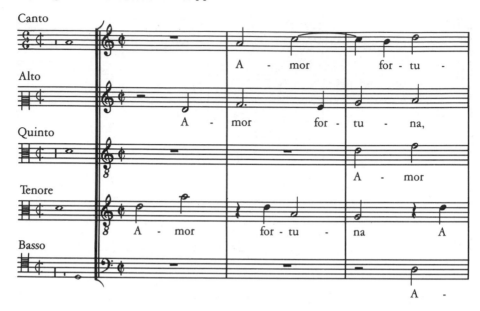

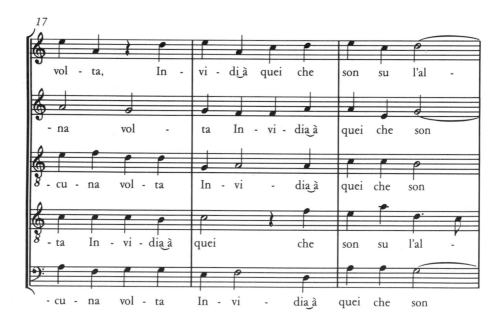

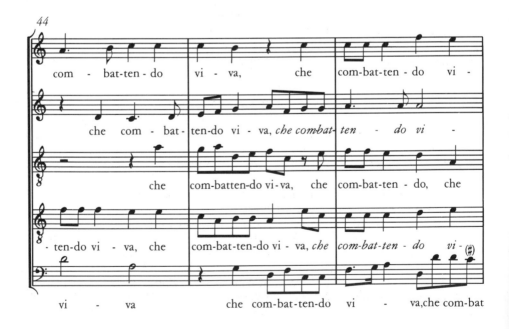

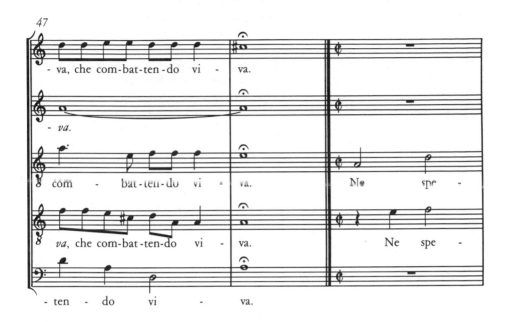

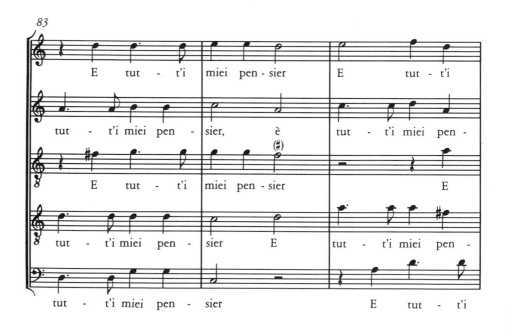

Ex. 8. Didier Lupi Second, 'Prens garde á moy' (Gilles d'Aurigny's translation of Ps. 16, *Conserva me Domine*). *Psalmes* (Beringen 1549), pp. 4–5

2. J'ay confessé à Dieu ma forfaicture,
   Disant, Seigneur, ta creature suis
   Qui aulcun bien sans toy faire ne puis,
   Tout vient de toy, et du mien tu n'as cure.

3. De te servir (Seigneur) j'ay prins grande peine,
   Faisant prouffit à tes esleuz et sainctz
   Voire à tous ceulx qui au monde sont pleins
   De ferme foy et de bonté certaine.

4. Quand le pur sang des bestes pour victime
   On t'a offert, compte n'en as tenu
   Et de ma part je me suis abstenu
   De parler d'eux, sans plus en faire estime.

5. Le Seigneur est maintenant le partage
   Rançon, calice, et le pris du Chrestien
   Car il nous a rendu le propre bien
   (Qu'avons perdu) au celeste heritage.

6. Ma portion m'a esté assignée
   En lieu plaisant, quand mon lot fut jecté,
   La contrée est pleine d'amenité,
   En plus beau lieu n'eust peu.

7. Parquoy je ren grace au Dieu de clemence
   Qui m'a donné si vif entendement,
   Qu'en pleine nuict mes forces promptement
   Ay corrigé selon ma conscience.

8. Comme un vray but à mon salut utile
   J'ay eu tousjours le Seigneur à mes yeulx,
   En moy je sents, et me suys en tous lieux,
   Me costoyant de peur que ne vacile.

9. Voila pourquoy joye s'est presentée
   Devant mon coeur, et que, tant à propos,
   Ma chair prendre au sepulchre repos
   Lors qu'ell' sera pour ton nom tourmentée.

10. Car je suis seur qu'en l'infernal demeure,
    Ne souffriras mon ame aulcunement,
    Ne que celuy qu'aymes tant fermement,
    Soit corrompu, ou corrompu demeure.

11. Mais bien plustost me monsteras la voye
    Qui meine à toy le fidele Chrestien:
    Afin d'avoir (en contemplant ton bien)
    Gloire en ta dextre, et eternelle joye.

Ex. 9. Francesco Bianchini, intabulation of Guillaume de La Mœulle's 'Vous semblet il'. *Tabulature de lutz* (Moderne, 1547[27]), pp. 16–17

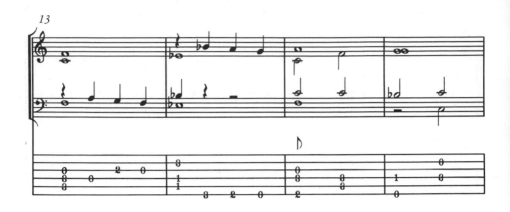

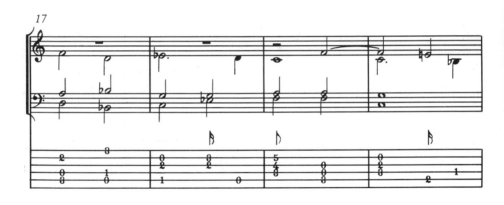

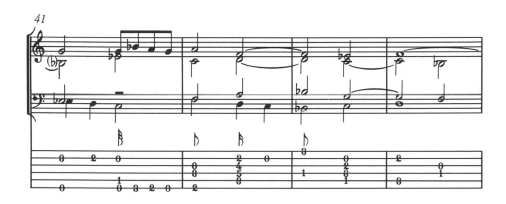

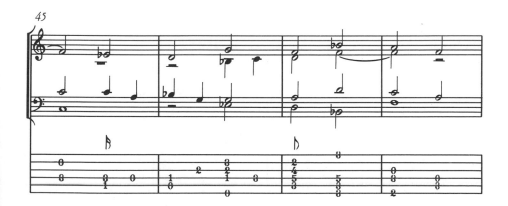

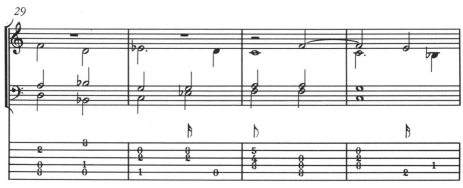

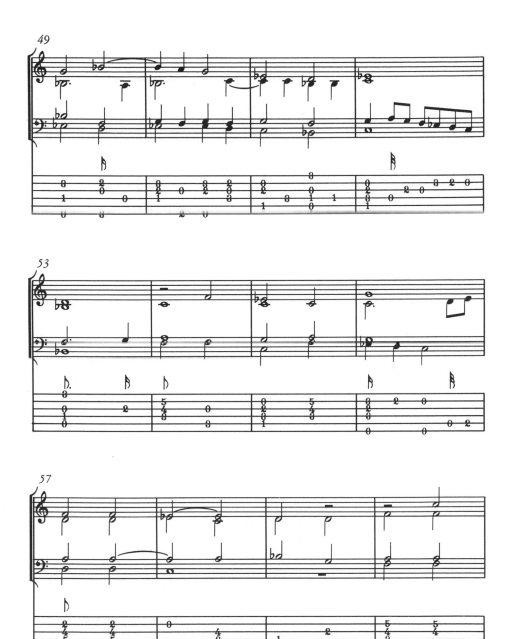

Bibliography

The Bibliography is limited to sources cited more than once.

AGEE, R., 'Filippo Strozzi and the Early Madrigal', *Journal of the American Musicological Society*, 38 (1985), 227–37.

—— 'Ruberto Strozzi and the Early Madrigal', *Journal of the American Musicological Society*, 36 (1983), 1–17.

ALLUT, P., *Étude biographique et bibliographique sur Symphorien Champier* (Lyons, 1859).

AMIET, R., *Inventaire général des livres liturgiques de Lyon* (Paris, 1979).

ATTAINGNANT, P., *Danseries à 4 parties: Second livre (1547)*, ed. R. Meylan (Paris, 1968).

AUDA, A., Barthélemy Beaulaigue, Poète et musicien prodige (Brussels, 1958).

BAUDRIER, J., *Bibliographie lyonnaise*, 12 vols. (Lyons, 1895–1921).

BEAULIEU, E. de, *Chrestienne Resjouyssance* (n.p., 1546).

—— *Les Divers Rapportz* (Lyons, 1537); ed. M. A. Pegg (Geneva, 1964).

BERNET KEMPERS, K. P., *37 Psalmen in vierstemmige bewerking van Loys Bourgeois uit 1547* (Delft, 1937).

BLOCK, A. F., *The Early French Parody Noël*, 2 vols. (Ann Arbor, Mich., 1983).

BOURDEILLE, P. de, *Œuvres complètes*, ed. L. Lalanne, 11 vols. (Paris, 1864–82).

BOURGEOIS, L., *Le Premier Livre des psaumes*, ed. P. A. Gaillard (Monuments de la musique suisse, 3; Basle, 1960).

—— *Responce à la seconde Apologie de Simon Gorlier* (Lyons, 1554).

BRÉSARD, M., *Les Foires de Lyon aux XVe et XVIe siècles* (Paris, 1914).

BROWN, H. M., *Instrumental Music Printed before 1600: A Bibliography* (Cambridge, Mass., 1965).

—— *Music in the French Secular Theater, 1400–1550* (Cambridge, Mass., 1963).

—— *Theatrical Chansons of the Fifteenth and Early Sixteenth Centuries* (Cambridge, Mass., 1963).

CARTIER, A., *Bibliographie des éditions des de Tournes* (Paris, 1937).

CHAMPIER, S., *Cy commence ung petit livre de l'antiquité, origine et noblesse . . . de Lyon: Ensemble de la rebeine et conjuration ou rebellion du populaire . . . contre les conseilliers de la cité et notables marchands, à cause des bledz* (Lyons, 1529–30; repr. Lyons, 1884).

—— *Liber de quadruplici vita* (Lyons, 1507).

—— *La Nef des princes* (Lyons, 1502).

CHRISTIE, R. C., *Etienne Dolet, the Martyr of the Renaissance* (London, 1880).

CLARK, R., 'The Penitential Psalms of Loyset Piéton' (M.Mus. thesis, London, 1986).

COLONIA, P. de, *Histoire littéraire de Lyon*, 2 vols. (Lyons, 1730).

COYECQUE, E., *Recueil d'actes notariés relatifs à l'histoire de Paris*, 2 vols. (Paris, 1905–23).

CRESPIN, J. (ed.), *Recueil de plusieurs personnes qui ont constamment enduré la mort pour le nom de nostre Seigneur* (Geneva, 1555; 2nd edn., 1556); revised as *Histoire des martyrs* (Geneva, 1597; repr. 1619).

D'ACCONE, F., 'The *Intavolatura di M. Alamanno Aiolli*', *Musica disciplina*, 20 (1966), 151–74.

DES PÉRIERS, B., *Œuvres*, ed. A. du Moulin (Lyons, 1544).

—— *Œuvres françoises*, ed. L. Lacour, 2 vols. (Paris, 1856).

DOBBINS, F., 'The Chanson at Lyons in the Sixteenth Century' (D.Phil. diss., Oxford, 1971).

—— *Doulce mémoire*: A Study of the Parody Chanson', *Proceedings of the Royal Musical Association*, 96 (1969), 85–101.

—— 'Jacques Moderne's *Parangon des Chansons*: A Bibliography of Music and Poetry at Lyon 1538–1543', *Royal Musical Association Research Chronicle*, 12 (1974), 1–90.

DOUEN, O., *Clément Marot et le psautier huguenot*, 2 vols. (Paris, 1878).

DRAUDIUS, G., *Bibliotheca exotica* (Frankfurt, 1625).

DROZ, E., 'Simon Goulart, éditeur de musique', *Bibliothèque d'Humanisme et Renaissance*, 14 (1952), 266–76.

DUFOURCQ, N., *Documents inédits rélatifs à l'orgue français*, 2 vols. (Paris, 1934–5).

DU GUILLET, P., *Rymes de gentile et vertueuse dame, D. Pernette du Guillet Lyonnoise* (Lyons, 1545); ed. V. E. Graham (Geneva, 1968).

DU VERDIER, A., *Bibliothèque* (Lyons, 1585), ed. R. de Juvigny in *Les Bibliothèques Françoises* . . . , iii (Paris, 1772).

GACHARD, L. P., *Collection des voyages des souverains du Pays-Bas* (Brussels, 1876).

GAILLARD, P. A., *Loys Bourgeois* (Lausanne, 1948).

—— 'Die *Psalmodie de XLI Pseaumes royaux*', *Jahrbuch für Liturgik und Hymnologie*, 2 (Kassel, 1956), 111–12.

GOUDIMEL, C., *Œuvres complètes*, xiii–xiv, ed. P. Pidoux and M. Egan (Boston, 1974, 1982).

GUÉRARD, J., *La Chronique lyonnaise de Jean Guérard, 1536–1562*, ed. J. Tricou (Lyons, 1929).

GUIGUE, G., *La Magnificence . . . relations et documents contemporains* (Lyons, 1927).

GUILLO, L., 'Les Motets de Layolle et les Psaumes de Piéton: Deux nouvelles éditions lyonnaises du seizième siècle', *Fontes artis musicae*, 32 (1984), 186–91.

—— 'Recherches sur les éditions musicales lyonnaises de la Renaissance' (doctoral thesis, École pratique des Hautes Études IVe section, 1986).

Revised as *Les Éditions musicales de la Renaissance lyonnaise (1525–1615)* (Paris, 1991), using same reference numbers.

HARVITT, H., *Eustorg de Beaulieu, a Disciple of Marot* (Lancaster, Pa., 1918).

HEARTZ, D., 'A New Attaingnant Book and the Beginnings of French Music Printing', *Journal of the American Musicological Society*, 14 (1961), 9–23.

——*Pierre Attaingnant, Royal Printer of Music* (Berkeley and Los Angeles, 1969).

HONEGGER, M., 'Les Chansons spirituelles de Didier Lupi et les débuts de la musique protestante en France' (doctoral thesis, Paris, 1970).

LABELLE, N., *Les différents styles de la musique religieuse en France: Le psaume de 1539 à 1572* (Henryville, 1981).

LEMAIRE DE BELGES, J., *La Concorde des deux langaiges* (Paris, 1513) (fac., ed. M. Françon, Cambridge, Mass., 1964).

——*Les Epistres de L'amant Verd* (Lyons, 1511) (fac., ed. M. Françon, Cambridge, Mass., 1964).

——*Œuvres*, ed. J. Stecher, 4 vols. (Louvain, 1882–91).

LENGEFELD, W. C., 'The Motets of Pierre Colin (fl. 1538–1565)' (Ph.D. diss., University of Iowa, 1969).

LESURE, F., 'L'*Épitome musical* de Ph. Jambe de Fer (1550)', *Annales musicologiques*, 6 (1963), 341–86.

——and Morcourt, R. de, 'G. P. Paladino et son "Premier Livre" de Luth (1560)', *Revue de musicologie*, 42 (1958), 170–83.

——and Thibault, G., *Bibliographie des éditions d'A. le Roy et R. Ballard* (Paris, 1955).

LEVY, K. J., '*Susanne un jour*: The History of a 16th-Century Chanson', *Annales musicologiques*, 1 (1953), 375–408.

Lyons Contrapunctus, The, ed. D. A. Sutherland (Recent Researches in the Music of the Renaissance, 31–2; Madison, 1976).

MARTIN, N., *Noelz et Chansons nouvellement composez tant en vulgaire Françoys que Savoysien dict Patoys* (Lyons, 1555, repr. 1556); ed. J. Orsier (Paris, 1879); ed. C. Gardet (Annecy, 1942, repr. 1973).

MINOR, A., and Mitchell, B., *A Renaissance Entertainment* (Columbus, Mo., 1969).

Musica Nova, Venice, 1540, ed. H. C. Slim (Monuments of Renaissance Music, 1; Chicago and London, 1964).

Music of the Florentine Renaissance, ed. F. D'Accone (Corpus Mensurabilis Musicae, 32; American Institute of Musicology, 1966–73).

ORSIER, J., 'Un poète-musicien au xvie siècle, N. Martin, ses noëls et ses chansons', *Revue de la Renaissance*, 9 (1908), 181–203 (repr. Paris, 1916).

Oxford Book of French Chansons, ed. F. Dobbins (Oxford, 1987).

PACIFICI, V., *Ippolito II d'Este* (Tivoli, 1920).

PALADINO, G. P., *Premier livre de tablature de luth* (1560); fac. edn., Geneva, 1983; mod. edn. M. Renault and J. M. Vaccaro, Corpus des luthistes français (Paris, 1986).

PARADIN, G., *Mémoires de l'histoire de la ville de Lyon* (Lyons, 1573).

PARIS, G., and Gevaert, A., *Chansons du XVe siècle* (Paris, 1875).

PHINOT, D., *Opera omnia*, ed. J. Hofler and R. Jacob (Corpus Mensurabilis Musicae, 59; American Institute of Musicology, 1972–82).

PICOT, E., *Catalogue des livres composant la bibliothèque de feu M. le Baron James de Rothschild*, 5 vols. (Paris, 1884–1920).

—— *Les Français italianisants au XVIe siècle*, 2 vols. (Paris, 1906–7).

PIDOUX, P., *Le Psautier huguenot du XVIe siècle*, 2 vols. (Basle, 1962).

Pierre Attaingnant: Dixseptiesme livre, ed. A. Seay (Colorado Springs, Colo., 1979).

PIRRO, A., *Les Clavecinistes* (Paris, 1924).

POGUE, S. F., *Jacques Moderne: Lyons Music Printer of the Sixteenth Century* (Geneva, 1969).

Remonstrances et Memoires pour les Compagnons Imprimeurs de Paris et Lyon: Opposans. Contre les Libraires, Maistres Imprimeurs desdits lieux (n.p., c.1572).

ROLLE, F., Guigue, M. C., Guigue, G., and Vaesen, J. (eds.), *Inventaire sommaire des archives communales de Lyon*, 5 vols. (Paris and Lyons, 1875–1962).

RUBYS, C. DE, *Histoire véritable de la ville de Lyon* (Lyons, 1604).

SAINTE-MARTHE, C. de, *La Poésie Françoise* (Lyons, 1540).

SANDRIN, P., *Opera omnia*, ed. A. Seay (Corpus Mensurabilis Musicae, 47; American Institute of Musicology, 1968).

SAULNIER, V. L., 'Dominique Phinot et Didier Lupi, musiciens de Clément Marot et des Marotiques', *Revue de musicologie*, 43 (1959), 61–80.

—— 'Maurice Scève et la musique', in *Musique et poésie au XVIe siècle*, ed. J. Jacquot (Paris, 1954), 89–103.

SERMISY, C. DE, *Opera omnia*, ed. G. Allaire and I. Cazeaux (Corpus Mensurabilis Musicae 52; American Institute of Musicology, 1974–).

TRICOU, G., *Documents sur la musique à Lyon au XVIe siècle* (Lyons, 1899).

—— 'Les Musiciens Lyonnais et le Roy des Violons', *Revue Musicale de Lyon*, 1 (1903–4), 148–50.

—— 'Philibert Jambe de Fer', *Revue musicale*, 3 (1903), 511–13, repr. in *Revue musicale de Lyon*, 5 (1907–8), 793–6.

TYARD, P. de, *Erreurs amoureuses* (Lyons, 1554); ed. J. A. McClelland (Geneva, 1967).

—— *Solitaire Second* (Lyons, 1555), ed. C. M. Yandell (Geneva, 1980).

VAN DER STRAETEN, E., *La Musique aux Pays-Bas*, 8 vols. (Brussels, 1867–88; repr. New York, 1969).

VIAL, E., 'La Légende de l'Académie de Fourvière'. *Bibliothèque d'Humanisme et Renaissance*, 8 (1946), 253–66.

WACKERNAGEL, W. G., *Die Matrikel der Universität Basel*, 2 vols. (Basle, 1956).

Index

Names occurring only once in the Appendices are not included here